Essential Statistics for the Social and Behavioral Sciences

A Conceptual Approach

Essential Statistics for the Social and Behavioral Sciences
A Conceptual Approach

Anthony Walsh

Boise State University
Boise, Idaho

Jane C. Ollenburger

California State Polytechnic University
Pomona, California

Prentice
Hall

Upper Saddle River, New Jersey 07458

Library of Congress Cataloging-in-Publication Data

Walsh, Anthony, 1941–
    Essential statistics for the social and behavioral sciences : a conceptual approach /
Anthony Walsh & Jane C. Ollenburger.
        p. cm.
    Includes bibliographical references (p.) and index.
    ISBN 0-13-019339-9
    1. Social sciences—Statistical methods.   I. Ollenburger, Jane C.   II. Title.
HA29 .W33573 2000
300′.7′27—dc21   00-061174

VP, Editorial Director: Laura Pearson
AVP Publisher: Nancy Roberts
Editorial Assistant: Lee Peterson
Production Liaison: Fran Russello
Project Manager: Kelly Ricci, The PRD Group
Prepress and Manufacturing Buyer: Mary Ann Gloriande
Cover Art Director: Jayne Conte
Cover Designer: Bruce Kenselaar
Director of Marketing: Beth Gillett Mejia

This book was set in 9.5/10.5 Baskerville by The PRD Group
and was printed and bound by Courier Stoughton.
The cover was printed by Phoenix Color Corp.

Printed in the United States of America

Reprinted with corrections May, 2001.

10 9 8 7 6 5 4 3 2

ISBN 0-13-019339-9

Prentice-Hall International (UK) Limited, *London*
Prentice-Hall of Australia Pty. Limited, *Sydney*
Prentice-Hall Canada Inc., *Toronto*
Prentice-Hall Hispanoamericana, S.A., *Mexico*
Prentice-Hall of India Private Limited, *New Delhi*
Prentice-Hall of Japan, Inc., *Tokyo*
Pearson Education Asia Pte. Ltd., *Singapore*
Editora Prentice-Hall do Brasil, Ltda., *Rio de Janeiro*

CONTENTS

Chapter 9   Nonparametric Measures of Association   167

Chapter 10   Elaboration of Tabular Data   191

Chapter 11   Bivariate Correlation and Regression   213

Chapter 12   Multivariate Correlation and Regression   237

PREFACE

This text is the result of a combined total of 30 years of teaching statistics and research methods to both graduate and undergraduate students. Teaching statistics to students in the social and behavioral sciences at any level is a challenge. Each of us has tried numerous approaches over the years using a variety of statistics texts from relatively simple "cookbooks" to the more rigorous and complex texts. Students learn fairly easily from the former, but uniformly come away with no conceptual understanding of statistics. Rigorous texts are more meaningful to the better prepared students, but leave many students perplexed and frustrated. We have tried to strike a balance here between ease of learning the material and the student's obtaining a satisfactory grasp of the role of statistics in the human sciences. We propose to do this in a number of ways, beginning with providing straightforward and consistent formulas, step-by-step instructions, and thorough interpretations.

COMPUTING NUMBERS

One of the important things we have learned from our teaching is that many students come to our classes with a minimal background in mathematics. Some are math phobic and dread the idea of a class requiring them to fiddle with numbers. The only assumption we make about the mathematical backgrounds of students is that they have an elementary grasp of algebra. The calculation of each statistic is introduced with a very simple example, and students are given step-by-step instructions to reach its solution. We also provide sufficient problems at the end of each chapter so students can readily improve their calculational competence. Solutions are given for odd-numbered problems in order to provide immediate feedback and improve calculating abilities.

WHAT DOES IT MEAN?

It doesn't mean much to arrive at the correct solution (a computer can do that) if we do not know what the solution means or what to do with it. To facilitate understanding, we include a line-by-line discussion of computer printouts for the majority of statistics. These printouts are based on actual data, and thus convey the feel of real-world research problems. We interpret the findings in the printouts in the simplest language possible while still endeavoring to include the necessary formal terminology of statistics. The combination of simple prose and formal terminology will help you become statistically literate, which is necessary to become proficient in reading and understanding the professional literature. Because so many excellent statistical packages are available for use, we do not rely on any one package.

The practice applications at the end of each chapter facilitate understanding. These applications pose a social science problem and use each of the statistical techniques taught in the chapter to provide answers. If you follow the applications from start to finish, you will greatly improve both your computational and interpretation skills. These exercises further develop an appreciation for the relevance of statistics in the social science.

THE SCOPE OF THE TEXT

Statistics texts usually conform to one of two types. The first emphasizes statistical techniques that are rarely used nowadays and introduce many techniques that are beyond the understanding of undergraduates. Few of these texts give adequate treatment to multivariate techniques, such as multiple ordinary least squares regression or the increasingly popular logistic regression. Students come away from such texts with an impression that social scientists are only interested in univariate and bivariate analysis, when in fact this is rarely the case. A basic understanding of multivariate techniques is an absolute must.

The second type of text is encyclopedic in its coverage, and includes statistics that most practicing researchers rarely, if ever, employ. While we have attempted to include only the most relevant techniques, we do include some statistical techniques not typically found in an elementary text. Because tests of significance are highly sensitive to sample size, we stress that a measure of association should always accompany such tests. Thus, we emphasize computing phi-squared and the odds ratio with the chi-square test, and eta squared with the t and F tests. Measures of association help us to decide whether the established relationship is a meaningful, substantive one.

To provide continuity throughout the text, we take examples from one of the data sets explored here and use it throughout so that we can continually refer back to earlier chapters. For instance, one of the many ways we take advantage of continuity is to show that a relationship assumed to be true in a bivariate analysis may not turn out to be the case in a multivariate analysis.

We would like to thank the reviewers, Audie Blevins of University of Wyoming, Debra S. Kelley of Longwood College, and Gwen Wittenbaum of Michigan State University.

Anthony Walsh
Boise State University—Boise, Idaho

Jane C. Ollenburger
California State Polytechnic University—Pomona, California

Chapter 1

INTRODUCTION TO STATISTICAL ANALYSIS

WHY STUDY STATISTICS?

As civilizations become more complex and technical, it becomes increasingly necessary for the thinking of the average person to become more complex and technical. The Industrial Revolution was the beginning of the end of a long period in history in which people could feel comfortable at home in their culture with only strong backs and the authority of received opinion to sustain them. Eventually it became imperative for citizens to understand, interpret, and analyze the written words of their culture. People who did not have the opportunity or the ability to adjust to this new requirement for full cultural participation were, by and large, condemned to lives of poverty and ignorance. Illiterates came to be assigned society's least meaningful roles. H. G. Wells, writing in the nineteenth century, stated that "statistical thinking will one day be as necessary for efficient citizenship as the ability to read or write." We believe that day has arrived.

We hear today about computer literacy and dire talk about the consequences of being left behind in the race to acquire it. The computer is a tool, however, a repository of the techniques that enable us more quickly and thoroughly to understand, interpret, and analyze data about phenomena. Its function is analogous to that of the library, a tool and a repository of the written word. To use the library, one must first learn the symbols of the written word that convey knowledge to us. If one cannot read, the library is not a tool; it is just another building. If one does not understand the symbols generated by the computer, it too is not a tool, it is just another electronic gadget. It is our belief that an understanding of statistics will be as important to the educated person of the future as reading was to our great grandparents—and for much the same reason.

Many people have an aversion to statistics, and students may have a tendency to mask their fears by denigrating it. It is a lot easier to think of some sharp and witty reasons to avoid our fears than to confront and master them. British Prime Minister Benjamin Disraeli's famous dictum that "there are three kinds of lies: lies, damned lies, and statistics," and W. H. Auden's admonition to his fellow poets, "Thou shalt not with statisticians sit, or commit a social science," are attempts to dignify ignorance. We do not deny that people lie with statistics. But this is precisely why one should understand their possibilities and limitations. People often mistrust what they do not understand.

THINKING STATISTICALLY

Statistics are numbers that allow us to analyze, evaluate, and summarize large quantities of data. Think about what a single statistic, your GPA, can tell about you. Each semester's GPA will allow analysis of your progress over time, evaluation of your overall scholastic ability, and summarization of your intellectual performance over many different subjects, teachers, and semesters. You may object that a single number cannot possibly serve to evaluate a person's intellectual abilities: GPA indicates what you *have* *done,* not what you *can do.* True enough, there is always room for additional information to help those who evaluate intellectual ability. However, that information will be in numeric form also, and may include IQ scores, SAT scores, hours spent studying, and so on. Taken as a whole, these numbers may provide an accurate picture of an individual's intellectual performance when compared to the average person's performance. Thus, any analysis, evaluation, or summary must be based on numerous observations.

Although statistics is not just another math class, one of the first things you will do is perform some simple calculations. Knowing how to come up with the right numbers is an essential part of statistics, but it is only the beginning. Few, if any, of the people who so annoyed Disraeli or Auden got the math wrong. Quite honestly, computing statistics is the easiest part of a statistics class. The difficult part is interpreting what those calculations mean. Statistics are numbers representing some form of reality, such as everything that makes your GPA what it is. When those numbers are subjected to computational procedures and an answer produced, that number or numbers must be translated back into the reality the raw numbers were supposed to represent. If you get the calculations right but misinterpret what they mean, the exercise is useless.

The following list provides some statistical findings of the type we run into almost every day as consumers of information, both inside and outside the university. After reading these findings, see if you can think of ways in which the conclusions based on them could be in error. All of these examples actually appeared in the literature.

1. It appears that gender is a substantial cause of TV watching. We found that women watch significantly more TV than men (up to 50 percent more).
2. Researchers from the First Fundamentalist Church University have found a highly significant relationship between a preference for rock music and unwed motherhood. The researchers suggest that rock music be banned from the home as detrimental to the morals of young people.
3. Racism still pervades our criminal justice system. Findings indicate that, on the average, black defendants receive significantly more severe sentences than white defendants.
4. Fifty percent more teachers in the 1996 sample said that U.S. educational standards were declining than said so in the 1995 sample. It is a sad fact that U.S. education standards continue to fall behind those of other industrial nations.

Did you find any flaws in these so-called research findings? The first three statements are examples of what social scientists call *misspecified models.* Misspecification is the omission of crucial explanatory variables from the model. No doubt women may have watched more TV than men in the 1960s when this study was conducted, but not because they were women, but because women were less likely to be employed outside the home than men, and thus may have had more time to watch TV. Similarly, we would not argue with a finding that reports a strong link between a preference for rock music and unwed motherhood. However, both preferences for rock music and unwed motherhood are also strongly associated with age. So age can be said to influence both musical preference and unwed motherhood. Nor would we particularly disagree with a finding that blacks are punished more severely than whites by the criminal justice system. But before we start talking about racism we would certainly like to know if the possibility that blacks in the sample may have committed more serious crimes and possessed more serious criminal records than whites in the sample had been taken into account.

Notice that we have no argument with any of the simple statements of the findings. They are what they are. The problems arise when faulty interpretations are made and based on incomplete information. We avoid this type of problem by including other theoretically relevant variables in the model: employment status in the first case, age in the second, and crime seriousness and prior record in the third.

The problem with finding number 4 is the way it is presented. As presented it tells us nothing. What were the answer categories? Perhaps 10% said they were declining, 50% said they were not declining, and 40% actually said they were improving. What were the sample sizes? Perhaps the 1996 sample was considerably increased over the 1995 sample, and this alone accounted for the additional 50%. If we don't know the answers to these questions, the statement is meaningless.

To interpret statistics properly, you must know the origin of the data and how statistics are computed. If the person or group presenting the findings has an agenda, such as the need to prove how bad our schools are, that we live in a racist society, or how sinful rock music is, their findings may be suspect. We also need to know how the statistics underlying reported findings are computed and whether or not they were appropriate for the task to which they were applied.

Statistics is the language of science. It is a mathematical language that enables us to draw logical conclusions within known boundaries of error from a set of data. Data (singular, datum) are simply a set of numerical scores relating to the phenomenon under investigation. Statistics enables us to reduce thousands of separate pieces of numerical information to a few easily understood summary statements. For instance, the primary database that we will be working with throughout this book consists of 637 males convicted of felony crimes. Fifty-one separate pieces of information associated with the criminal and his case were collected on each of the 637 cases, for a total of 32,487 pieces of data. Once we have organized them by the techniques of statistics, these data enable us to make a multitude of statements about crime and punishment.

DESCRIPTIVE AND INFERENTIAL STATISTICS

DESCRIPTIVE STATISTICS

A major function of all statistics is to describe the phenomenon under investigation. By convention, statisticians have reserved the label **descriptive statistics** for information that can be organized and presented in simple and direct ways. We are all familiar with such basic descriptive statistics as baseball batting averages, the annual rainfall in an area, the number of Japanese cars on American roads, and divorce rates. Percentages, ratios, proportions, frequencies, charts, tables, and graphs are used to organize, summarize, and describe these data. Descriptive statistics are limited to the data at hand and do not involve any inferences or generalizations beyond them.

INFERENTIAL STATISTICS

Inferential statistics are statistical techniques that enable us to make inferences or generalizations about a large group on the basis of data taken from a subset of that group, called a **sample.** When we have sample data we are not really interested in the sample per se; we are interested in the population from which the sample came. If we have data on an entire population (i.e., a complete tabulation of some characteristics of interest from all elements in a population), we have a census.

Census refers to not only the enumeration of the populace that the government undertakes every decade but also any comprehensive tabulation of many different kinds of populations. The term *population* does not necessarily mean a body of people, although it almost always does in social science. **Population** refers to all cases about which a researcher wishes to make inferences. If we want to make general statements about U.S. citizens, the entire population of the United States is the population. If we are interested in the religious practices of Mormons, all Mormons are the population. If we are interested in the recreational activities of members of the New York City Police Department, the NYPD is the population.

For virtually all statistical research in the behavioral sciences, the intention is to use information derived from a representative sample in order to make statements about the population from which the sample was drawn. Even the census bureau started taking samples in 1998 in order to maximize efficiency. Technically, we say that we use sample **statistics** to estimate population **parameters.** Both a statistic and a parameter are numbers, the former being a proxy for the latter. We all make decisions based on samples even if we are not aware that we are doing so. Many students go to two or three different sections of an introductory course to sample the teaching style and class requirements of different professors. On the basis of the sample, the student decides in which section he or she will enroll. The student *infers* from the sampling of classes what the remainder of the classes will probably be like in terms of subject matter, requirements, and level of difficulty. Likewise, it is hardly necessary to eat the whole cow before deciding that the meat is tough. This is the point of scientific research and inference; we do not need to take the time or endure the cost necessary to obtain information relevant to our research from all elements of the population before we can draw conclusions. Statistical techniques allow us to estimate population parameters within precisely known margins of error.

The relationship between samples, parameters, populations, and statistics is presented graphically in Figure 1.1. In the example shown in the figure, we are attempting

FIGURE 1.1.   The relationship between populations, samples, parameters, and statistics.

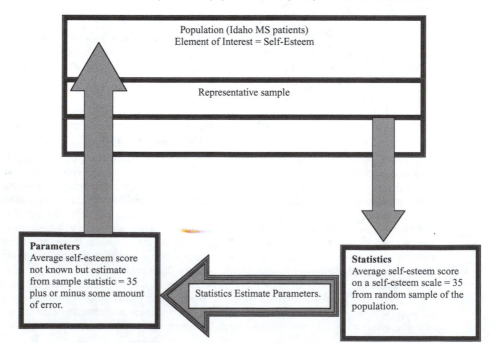

to estimate the average self-esteem score of all multiple sclerosis patients in the state of Idaho (the parameter) from the average self-esteem score (the statistic) of a random sample of those patients. Keep in mind that a statistic is to a sample as a parameter is to a population.

Assuming that our sample of multiple sclerosis patients is representative of all such patients in Idaho, we can say that our best prediction of the average level of self-esteem among the population is 35, and we can then place some margin of error around this prediction.

STATISTICS AND ERROR

Any time we measure something, particularly in the social and behavioral sciences, some degree of error is almost inevitable. **Error** in measurement is basically a function of two things: the accuracy of our instruments and the size of our samples. Obviously, the instrument used to measure self-esteem is not as reliable as is a well-calibrated scale used to measure weight, or a yardstick used to measure height. A person's feeling about his or her self-worth varies from time to time, and people sometimes fake high or low self-esteem. Fortunately, these fluctuations tend to cancel one another. That is, we might reasonably assume that for every person we catch on a bad day, we catch another on a good day, and that for every person faking high, there is another faking low.

Sample size is the other factor influencing the degree of error. The larger the sample, the smaller the error. If we wanted to determine the height of all men in the U.S. Marine Corps, a sample size of 1,000 would be better than one of 150, which is better than a sample of 50. This should be obvious, because the larger the sample taken, the more likely some rare or atypical cases (such as male marines shorter than 5′2″ or taller than 6′2″) are included. Populations always have more variability than do samples. Populations, by definition, contain all common and all rare cases. The larger the sample, the more likely it is to represent the situation as it exists in the population. But whatever the sample size, there will always be error associated with the sample statistics we use to estimate population parameters. Recognizing this, we place some margin of error around the estimates. We might conclude from our study of self-esteem among multiple sclerosis patients that the average self-esteem score is 35, plus or minus 3 points, or between 32 and 38. Statistical procedures for assessing the degree of error are addressed later in this book.

PARAMETRIC AND NONPARAMETRIC STATISTICS

Statistical methods that enable us to estimate population parameters are known as **parametric statistics,** which make certain assumptions about the population parameters. **Nonparametric statistics** are a second family of statistics that requires no assumptions about the population parameters. Many advantages and disadvantages surround the use of these two types of statistics. These issues will be addressed in more detail in Chapter 9.

OPERATIONALIZATION

The measurement of such physical constructs as height and weight is not problematic. But what about measuring such social science concepts as self-esteem, religiosity, or alienation? No one has yet invented an "alienation meter" that accurately measures all the ingredients of that concept. If we are serious about the social science enterprise, first we have to be clear about what we want to measure. Then we have to design a series of operations that yields suitable measurements of it. Clarifying what it is we wish to measure, that is, the process of refining and sharpening our conceptualizations of a phenomenon, does not concern us here. Designing a series of operations to measure those conceptualizations does. Such a design is called "operationalizing the ingredients of the concept."

The process of **operationalization** is often a difficult one to grasp. Let us first distinguish between a conceptual definition and an operational definition. A conceptual definition is a verbal statement relating our understanding of a phenomenon. For instance, we can conceptually define blood pressure as "the pressure exerted on the arterial walls by the pumping action of the heart." This is an accurate verbal definition, but what if I want to compare the blood pressure of a number of individuals in an attempt to determine whose pressure is higher (more) or lower (less)? The ideas of *higher* and *lower* and *more* and *less* are at the heart of measurement. As we all know, a well-established series of operations is used to measure the ingredients of the concepts of the more and less of blood pressure, which is measured by a sphygmomanometer. The operational definition of blood pressure is "The height of a column of mercury in standard units recorded at the first Korotkoff phase (the first audible sounds) and the fifth Korotkoff phase (termination of audible sounds)." The Korotkoff phases give us systolic and diastolic readings, respectively. We now have measured numbers that we can compare and contrast with other numbers obtained by the same operations. Thus, an **operational definition** is *the definition of a concept in terms of the operations used to measure it.*

Suppose a social science researcher makes the proposition that people with high self-esteem tend to be successful. Contained in the proposition are two concepts, self-esteem and success, that have to be operationally defined if the researcher is to test the proposition. *Self-esteem* can be defined operationally as the scores individuals obtain on a questionnaire that asks various questions relating to how people feel about themselves. Such scales usually contain multiple indicators of the concept they are attempting to measure. *Success* may be operationally defined in terms of occupational prestige, amount of money in the bank, the kind of house lived in, or many other indicators.

Figure 1.2 shows how the courts in Ohio operationalize the concepts of crime seriousness and prior record. Note that numbers have to be assigned to different aspects of the crime and to the offender's criminal history. Those numbers are then summed to give each individual a crime seriousness and prior record score. One of the data sets we will be using in this book includes these scores, so when we talk about *high* or *low* crime seriousness or prior record in future chapters you will know exactly to what we are referring. The felony sentencing worksheet is the operational definition of these two variables.

No matter how many indicators we use to measure a concept, we never exhaust its meaning. For instance, an IQ test is an operationalization of the concept of intelligence, but it does not necessarily get at the essence of the concept of intelligence. Nevertheless, for the purpose of research, the operational definition of the concept *is* the concept for all practical purposes. You may be an excellent student in all respects, but you will not get an A in most courses unless you achieve a cumulative score of 90% or more (the operational definition of the concept of academic excellence) on your examinations.

RELIABILITY AND VALIDITY

Researchers wish to be sure that the instruments used to measure their concepts are reliable and valid. **Validity** refers to how well the measures derived from the operation reflect the concept. **Reliability** refers to the consistency with which repeated measures

Felony Sentencing Worksheet
Ohio State Bar Foundation

CRIME SERIOUSNESS *Offense Rating*		PRIOR RECORD *Offender Rating*	
	Operational Definition		**Operational Definition**
1. Degree of Offense	The one most serious offense 1st°felony = 4 points 2nd°felony = 3 points 3rd°felony = 2 points 4th°felony = 1 points	**1. Prior Convictions**	2 points for each verified felony conviction.
2. Multiple Offenses	2 points if any of the following: (a) offender is being sentenced for 2 or more offenses committed in different incidents; (b) offender is currently under sentence; (c) present offense committed while on probation or parole.	**2. Repeat Offenses**	2 points if offense of violence, sex offense, theft offense, or drug offense and offender has one or more prior convictions for same type of offense.
3. Actual or Potential Harm	2 points if any of the following apply: (a) serious physical harm to a person was caused; (b) property damage of $300 or more; (c) there was a high risk of such harm, damage or loss; (d) gain or potential gain was $300 or more; (e) dangerous ordnance or a deadly weapon was actually used in the incidence, or its use was attempted or threatened.	**3. Prison Commitments**	2 points if offender was previously committed to a penitentiary, reformatory, or equivalent institution.
4. Culpability	2 points if any of the following applies: (a) offender was engaging in continuing criminal activity as a source of income; (b) offense was a part of a continuing conspiracy; (c) offense included shocking and deliberate cruelty.	**4. Parole and Similar Violations**	2 points if any of the following: (a) offender has previously had probation or parole revoked; (b) present offense committed while offender was on probation or parole; (c) present offense committed while offender free on bail; (d) present offense committed while offender in custody.
5. Mitigation	Deduct 1 point for each of the following: (a) substantial provocation, justification, or excuse for offense; (b) victim induced or facilitated offense; (c) offense was committed in the heat of anger; (d) the property damaged, lost, or stolen was restored or recovered without significant cost to the victim.	**5. Credits**	Deduct 1 point for each of the following as applicable: (a) offender has voluntarily made arrangements for restitution; (b) was age 25 or older at time of first felony conviction; (c) has been substantially law abiding for at least 3 years; (d) lives with his or her spouse or minor children and is a breadwinner.

FIGURE 1.2. Operational definitions of crime seriousness and prior record.

produce the same results across time and across observers. The validity of a blood pressure gauge is determined pragmatically. That is, individuals whose blood pressure is consistently high, say, 180/95, have very different cardiovascular histories than individuals whose blood pressure is normal or low, say, 120/75. Note that the concepts *high* and *low* in this context have definite numbers attached to them. This is pragmatic or predictive validity because, based on the number obtained, the physician makes treatment decisions and predictions about the consequences of not adhering to the treatment he or she prescribes. A blood pressure gauge is reliable if two or more health workers obtain the same reading with the same patient or if the same researcher obtains identical readings from a different gauge.

The assessment of reliability and validity of a social science instrument, such as a scale to measure self-esteem, is usually done mathematically. Other social science variables, such as race, sex, number of children, or whether or not an immigrant is a U.S. citizen, are straightforward and measured by simple observation or by a single question. Whatever the concept we are operationalizing, we assign numbers to our observations in order to measure them.

MEASUREMENT

Measurement is the process of assigning numbers to observations according to a set of rules. The observations being measured are **variables,** which refers to anything that can change in value from case to case. Gender is a variable because cases vary from male to female. Self-esteem is a variable because scores obtained on a self-esteem scale can be arranged on a continuum from those scoring lowest to those scoring highest. In our felony offender data, all offenders in the study are male. Although *male* is an attribute of the gender variable, gender is not a variable in this data set because all offenders are male. Therefore, gender of offender is a **constant** in this case because it does not vary from case to case.

DEPENDENT AND INDEPENDENT VARIABLES

The role variables play in research is one of the ways variables can be classified. A **dependent variable** is a variable that depends on the value of another variable or variables for its own values. The variables on which the dependent variable depends are called **independent variables.** Independent variables affect (bring about changes in) dependent variables; dependent variables are affected by independent variables. In the examples under the Thinking Statistically section, gender was the independent variable said to affect variation in TV watching, the dependent variable; a liking for rock music (independent variable) was said to affect the rate of unwed motherhood (dependent variable); and race (independent variable) was said to affect sentencing severity (dependent variable). Notice the temporal ordering of the dependent and independent variables—the independent variable always comes before the dependent variable. Many variables can be independent or dependent variables in different contexts. Gender and race obviously can never be dependent variables in the sense that they can be thought of as caused by some antecedent social variable, but liking rock music could be a dependent variable and unwed motherhood could be an independent variable in some contexts.

Variables can be **discrete** or **continuous.** Discrete variables classify observations according to the kind or quality of their characteristics. Yes/no, black/white, male/female are examples of dichotomous (division of two) variables. Discrete variables can take on more divisions than two; religious affiliation, ethnic origin, and income category are examples of multicategory discrete variables. Continuous variables can theoretically take on any value between two points on a scale and be classified according to the magnitude and quantity of their characteristics. For example, it is possible to divide age into any number of values on a continuum of years, months, days, hours, and seconds. Discrete variables, however, have sharply demarcated distinct values; you cannot have 1.5 yes answers or 2.45 males, nor can you have sold 25.35 cars last year. The rules we use to assign numbers to observations result in various levels of measurement. Information comes to us from the real world in many forms, ranging from crude to very refined. The statistics we use in our research depend greatly on the relative crudity or refinement of our measures. There are four levels of measurement with different properties that are important to understand: nominal, ordinal, interval, and ratio. These levels are hierarchical and cumulative in that each higher level, in addition to having its own special characteristic, incorporates the characteristics of those levels beneath it. Nominal and ordinal variables are qualitative variables, meaning that they differ in kind but cannot be expressed numerically except in an arbitrary or ranked fashion. Interval and ratio measures are quantitative, meaning that they can be expressed numerically. Let us look at these four levels of measurement one at a time.

NOMINAL LEVEL

The **nominal level** of measurement is the crudest form of measurement and is used only to classify, that is, to name observations that are different in some qualitative way. The categories of the classification scheme should be mutually exclusive (being in one category automatically excludes inclusion in another) and exhaustive (all possible categories of a variable should be included). For example, if we are interested in the variable of gender, both males and females should be included, and being placed in one category automatically excludes the respondent from being placed in the other.

The numbers assigned to nominal level data are arbitrary. The researcher may assign the number 0 to males and 1 to females. A nominal variable, such as gender, that includes only two categories is called a *dichotomous variable*. If the researcher is interested in religion, he or she might numerically code Catholics 1, Protestants 2, and Jews 3, or any other sensible coding system. It should be apparent that we cannot perform mathematical operations such as adding, substracting, dividing, and multiplying with this kind of nonquantitative data (e.g., you cannot multiply Catholics by Protestants and arrive at some meaningful third value). Numbers assigned to categories in this way are nothing more than labels. Statistical formulas for variables measured at this level make use of category frequencies (how many males, females, Catholics, etc., are in the data), not the numeric code value used to identify a particular category of the variable.

ORDINAL LEVEL

Variables measured at the **ordinal level** are capable of being ranked as well as classified. That is, we can put the data in an order that ranges somewhere from bottom to top, low to high, or less to more. For example, we can ask all people in the classroom to stand. We can then arrange them in a line based on descending order of height. Notice that when we do this we have a rank order, but we do not have the precise measures of the differences among the heights of the individuals. We know that the tallest person is at the top and the shortest person is at the bottom and that every other person is located in his or her proper ascending or descending location. We do not have the precise heights of the tallest person or the shortest person, or any person; we just have the right order.

Examples of ordinal-level data are class standing (freshman, sophomore, junior, senior) and social class when divided into lower, middle, and upper categories. These categories can be perceived only as *more* or *less* since we cannot validly assign an arithmetic interval separating them.

INTERVAL LEVEL

The **interval level** is the next highest level of measurement. At this level, in addition to classification and order, we have equal units of measurement. In other words, there are precisely defined intervals between and among the observations; the interval between 5 and 10 is exactly the same as the interval between 25 and 30, and both are identical in magnitude to the interval between 1,155 and 1,160. An example of an interval-level variable is IQ. Consider four individuals with IQ scores of 70, 140, 75, and 145. We can say that the differences between 70 and 140 and between 75 and 145 are exactly the same, but we cannot say that the second person is twice an intelligent as the first. All we can say is that those with the higher scores are more intelligent than those with the lower scores. What we lack with an interval scale is a stable starting point (an absolute zero) and, consequently, the scale values cannot be interpreted in any absolute sense. However, we can perform a large number of mathematical operations with interval data that are not possible with nominal and ordinal data.

RATIO LEVEL

The **ratio level** has all the properties of the lower measurement scales in addition to an absolute zero. We can classify it, we can place it in proper order, the numbers we use to measure it are of equal magnitudes, and it has a meaningful zero. Examples include feet and inches, ounces and pounds, years of education, and income. It should be obvious that we can use all sorts of mathematical procedures with ratio-level variables. Someone with an income of $50,000 makes precisely twice as much as someone with an income of $25,000, which produces a meaningful ratio of $2:1$.

It is important to be aware of the level at which you have measured your variables because the choice of statistical analysis depends on it. However, we must point out that statisticians have argued among themselves regarding level of measurement issues. The main bone of contention is whether or not it is permissible to treat certain ordinal variables as interval-level variables in order to take advantage of more advanced statistical techniques. An alienation scale ranging from a possible low of 0 to a possible high of 40 would be treated by most researchers as an interval-level scale, although such a scale only approximates the equidistant functions of true interval scales. That is, although scores on an alienation scale are continuous, they have properties that lie somewhere between ordinal and interval levels of measurement.

This does not mean that all ordinal variables can be properly treated as interval-level variables. Generally, the greater the number of ranks or categories of the measured ordinal variable, the greater confidence we have in treating the variable as an interval. Scores on an alienation scale ranging from 0 to 40, for example, can be more validly treated as an interval variable than if they were divided into low, medium, and high levels of alienation. A further consideration is the approximation to the equidistant function. A scoring system that looks like 0, 1, 2, 3, 4, 5, is much better than one that looks like 0, 8, 9, 16, 28, 42. The latter scoring system is far from equidistant and begins to look like discrete ordered categories.

The cumulative and hierarchical characters of the four levels of measurement are illustrated in Table 1.1.

TABLE 1.1   Characteristics of Levels of Measurement

	CLASSIFY	ORDER	EQUAL UNITS	ABSOLUTE ZERO
Nominal	Yes	No	No	No
Ordinal	Yes	Yes	No	No
Interval	Yes	Yes	Yes	No
Ratio	Yes	Yes	Yes	Yes

THE ROLE OF STATISTICS IN SCIENCE

As you know by now, many other considerations take place before researchers actually apply statistical techniques to their data. Figure 1.3 illustrates the place of statistical analysis in the scientific enterprise. Almost all research starts with the researcher's immersion in theory related to the proposed research. We begin with theory because theory not only tells us what is already known in a given area, it also tells us where and how to look for new information about it. To begin a research project without a thorough knowledge of theories pertaining to the subject matter of the project is like taking a trip into unknown territory without either a guide or a map. A theory is similar to the major premise in logical argumentation—"*if* this is true, *then* this should be true." Philosophers use these kinds of if–then statements to arrive at a logical conclusion derived from what is assumed to be a self-evident premise. If the major premise is true ("All men are mortal"), and if the minor premise is also true ("Plato is a man"), then the conclusion ("Plato is mortal") is logically correct. This is a deductive process, arguing from the general to the particular.

However, the conclusion for the philosopher is only the beginning for the scientist. The philosopher's conclusion based on reason is formally known as a **hypothesis** by scientists, who demand more proof than logical reasoning alone affords, because logic is only as good as the premise on which it is based. The reasoning process for scientists proceeds from theory to hypothesis, rather than from premise to conclusion. The hypothesis must then be put to the test.

The next step is the operationalization of the concepts contained in the hypothesis. As we have seen, this entails defining concepts in terms of the operations used to measure them.

The next step is to take a representative sample of individuals from the population of interest and apply our measuring instruments. We will discuss sampling at greater length in Chapter 5.

It is at this point in the scientific method that the subject matter of this book comes into play. Having taken our measurements, the next task is to apply our statistical tools to them. The results of our statistical analyses will enable us with a certain degree of probability to make decisions regarding our hypothesized assumptions; that is, do we accept or reject them? If we decide that the evidence derived from the sample supports our hypothesis, we infer that what is true for the sample is probably true in the population from which it came, although we are always aware that the possibility exists that it may not be. Further, because the hypothesis was derived from theory, we may also conclude that the theory is supported. Although theories are never proven, they are strengthened by a sort of inductive logic (arguing from the particular to the general) by the results of favorable tests of hypotheses derived from them. The circle from theory and back again is thus completed. The journey is a fascinating one, but one that is never as neat and tidy as we have presented it.

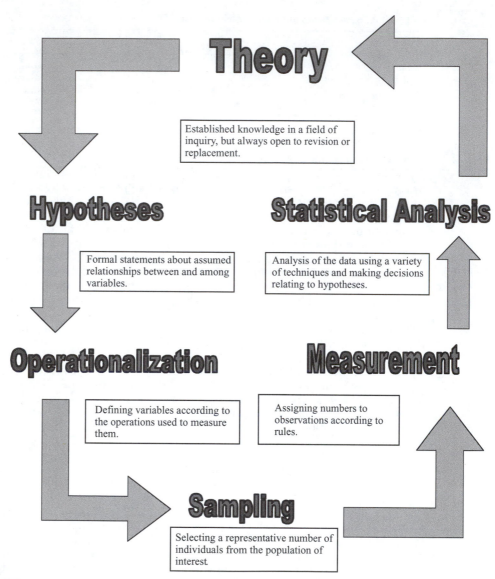

Theory

Established knowledge in a field of inquiry, but always open to revision or replacement.

Hypotheses

Formal statements about assumed relationships between and among variables.

Statistical Analysis

Analysis of the data using a variety of techniques and making decisions relating to hypotheses.

Operationalization

Defining variables according to the operations used to measure them.

Measurement

Assigning numbers to observations according to rules.

Sampling

Selecting a representative number of individuals from the population of interest.

FIGURE 1.3.   The place of statistics in the scientific enterprise.

SUMMARY

Statistics is becoming an increasingly important field of study. As a consumer of statistics you should be aware of the many ways in which the producers of statistics, either purposely or inadvertently, can mislead you. This book will make you a more sophisticated consumer, as well as a producer, of statistics.

Descriptive statistics describe data in simple and direct ways by using graphs, charts, percentages, proportions, and ratios. Inferential statistics make inferences about a population from information derived from a sample. A population is the totality of all observations that are of interest, and a sample is a subset of the population. We estimate population characteristics, called parameters, from sample characteristics, called statistics. In our estimation of parameters there will always be a certain amount of error, although we can quantify this error and take it into account. However, before we can estimate any parameter, such as the average self-esteem of a population, we have to be able to measure it. Before we can measure it we have to define it operationally, that is, in terms of the operations used to measure it.

Measurement is the assignment of numbers to observations according to rules. We measure variables, defined as some characteristic or trait that takes on different values across observations, at four different levels of measurement.

Nominal-level variables, the crudest level, have mutually exclusive and exhaustive categories that differ from one another qualitatively. There is no implied order or equality of distance between the categories. The ordinal level of measurement allows for the rank ordering of categories, but not with respect to equal distance. The interval level of measurement has categories of equal distance between continuous variables, but they lack a true zero point. The ratio level of measurement is the highest form of measurement in that it contains all the attributes of the lower levels in addition to having a true zero point. Only interval- and ratio-level variables are amenable to mathematical operations. Each level of measurement has the attributes of lower levels as well as its own.

PRACTICE APPLICATION:
VARIABLES AND LEVELS OF MEASUREMENT

A high school teacher decides to generate a statistical description of a class of eight students on four variables: sex, class standing, IQ, and weight. These measurements are made and placed in the following table:

Variable and Level of Measurement

STUDENT	SEX (NOMINAL)	CLASS STANDING (ORDINAL)	IQ (INTERVAL)	WEIGHT (RATIO)
Bill	0	2	90	200.0
Mary	1	3	110	110.5
Tony	0	3	130	152.6
Ingrid	1	2	108	100.0
Susan	1	2	120	110.4
Sam	0	4	100	165.0
Kurt	0	3	104	171.1
Alice	1	4	180	123.7

Coding Sex: 0 = male, 1 = female; class standing: 1 = freshman, 2 = sophomore, 3 = junior, 4 = senior; IQ = continuous; weight = continuous.

The first variable, sex, is a discrete, dichotomous, qualitative variable measured at the nominal level. It has no quantitative value, and all we can do arithmetically is count the numbers of males and females in the sample. The second variable, class standing, is a discrete, ordered, qualitative variable measured at the ordinal level. Alice and Sam are of higher class standing than Mary, Kurt, or Tony, who are themselves of higher standing than Bill or Ingrid. Here we can talk about higher and lower, but nothing else. If there were a direct one-to-one relationship between the number of years spent in college and class standing we could conceptualize this variable as ratio level and make statements such as "Alice has been in school twice as long as Bill." However, because the variable is presently conceptualized, we cannot even assume that Alice has been going to school as long as Bill. Her superior IQ, especially in relation to Bill's, makes it possible that she could have passed more classes than Bill in less time.

The third variable, IQ, is a continuous, quantitative variable measured at the interval level. Because we have equal units, we can say that the difference between Mary's and Tony's IQ scores (20 points) is exactly the same as the difference between Susan's and Sam's. However, even though Alice's IQ score is numerically twice that of Bill's, we cannot say that she is twice as intelligent because IQ scales lack a precise absolute zero. I should point out that some people believe that IQ is more an ordinal- than an interval-level variable. Their argument is that the substantive difference between IQ scores of 80 and 100 is much greater than the difference between 120 and 140, although mathematically the difference is still 20.

The final variable, weight, is a continuous, quantitative variable measured at the ratio level. Because weight has an absolute zero, we can validly say that Bill weighs exactly twice as much as Ingrid. Note again that the ratio level of measurement contains all the attributes of the lower levels (name, order, equal units) in addition to having an absolute zero.

PROBLEMS

1. Explain the differences between the following:
    a) Descriptive and inferential statistics
    b) Reliability and validity
    c) Statistics and parameters
    d) Sample and population

2. For each of the following, indicate whether the item is a discrete variable or a continuous variable:
    a) Age in years
    b) Gender (male or female)
    c) Annual net salary
    d) Religious affiliation
    e) Weight loss
    f) Grade point average
    g) Miles per gallon
    h) Academic major

3. Indicate whether each of the following statements exemplifies the use of descriptive or inferential statistics:
    a) A recent public opinion poll indicated that 60% of U.S. residents favor capital punishment.
    b) My score on the last test was 82.
    c) Women in managerial positions earn 79% of what men earn.
    d) In the United States, women live an average of 6.9 years longer than men.
    e) In a recent local election, candidate Berquist won by 13,236 votes.

4. Develop two hypotheses with one independent and one dependent variable. Specify the independent and dependent variable for each hypothesis.

5. Operationalize the variables in Problem 4.

6. Indicate the level of measurement for the following variables:
    a) Type of computer
    b) Coffee consumption per day
    c) Hair color
    d) Hours of computer use per day
    e) Zodiac sign
    f) Highest academic degree
    g) Net salary
    h) Pet ownership (yes or no)
    i) Pet ownership (number of pets)
    j) Type of car
    k) Number of children
    l) First, second, and third place in contest at the county fair
    m) Religious affiliation
    n) Grade point average
    o) IQ
    p) Crime rate (per 100,000 population)
    q) Occupation (professional, clerical, etc.)
    r) College major

    s) Sex (male, female)
    t) Political party affiliation (Democrat, Republican, Independent, other)

7. For each of the following variables, provide an operationalization at the interval or ratio level and one at the nominal or ordinal level:
    a) Yearly income
    b) Age
    c) City size
    d) Academic achievement

8. Specify the levels of measurement for the variables in Problem 1.

9. Give an example of a variable measured on a(n):
    a) Nominal scale
    b) Ordinal scale
    c) Interval scale
    d) Ratio scale

10. A researcher would like to examine the relationship between unemployment and crime rates. She suspects that as unemployment increases in a community so will the crime rate. She collects the percent unemployed of the workforce in 20 communities along with the number of crimes committed per 100,000 people. For this research, what is the independent variable? What is the dependent variable? How were they operationalized? What are their levels of measurement?

11. You want to determine the average number of pets per household in your county, which has 122,000 residents. Describe how you would solve this problem. In your answer, use the following terms: population, sample, parameter, statistic, descriptive statistics, and inferential statistics.

Chapter 2

Presenting and Summarizing Data

This chapter examines methods of univariate analysis, the analysis of one variable as opposed to the simultaneous analysis of two variables (bivariate) or more than two variables (multivariate). Univariate analysis allows the researcher to organize and present data and is often conducted prior to more advanced analyses.

The objective of data presentation is to communicate the informational content of the data. When researchers complete the process of collecting data, they have a mass of raw numbers that cannot tell them much unless the data are arranged and displayed in a meaningful way. Researchers cannot discern trends until some order or structure is imposed on the data. The researchers first have to organize the data into formats that can be meaningfully interpreted, and they must choose a way of summarizing data that is accurate and relevant.

The term *descriptive statistics* refers to the organization and presentation of information in simple and direct ways that better assist the presenter in describing the data. Frequency distributions, histograms, bar graphs, and pie charts are typically used to organize data. These are visual representations of data reflecting the old adage that a picture is worth a thousand words. Just as a photograph is useful in describing the characteristics of a person or place, charts and tables can serve as effective descriptors. Presenting data visually is an effective tool for highlighting particular pieces of information or presenting an overview of trends and patterns in the data. The particular graphic technique chosen by the researcher depends on a number of considerations. Four key considerations include the purpose of the research, what the researcher wants to convey, the assumed level of sophistication of the readers, and, most importantly, the type of data being described.

In addition to presenting data graphically, descriptive statistics also include the ability to summarize data numerically. Numerical summarization provides more precise descriptions of the data and complements the visual impact of the presentation. It also emphasizes the features of the data most relevant to the research. Common numeric descriptions include percentages, ratios, and proportions.

TYPES OF FREQUENCY DISTRIBUTIONS

A **frequency distribution** is simply the frequency or number of times that a particular value or class of a variable appears in a distribution of scores. Suppose we asked 20 persons to provide information about their gender and the number of children they have and we obtained the information as presented in Table 2.1.

To describe this small data set initially a researcher would say that the number of observations equals 20, therefore, the sample size equals 20 ($n = 20$). The total number of children in the families of these respondents equals 44, and there are 12 females and 8 males in the sample. We are only interested for the moment in the number of children in this data set. To obtain a clearer picture of the group, we will arrange the observations in ascending order and tally them. Each value is symbolized by *x*, and a tally is placed next to each occurrence of that value. There are two respondents with no

TABLE 2.1   Frequency Distribution of Number of Children and Gender of Respondent

RESPONDENT	NUMBER OF CHILDREN	GENDER	RESPONDENT	NUMBER OF CHILDREN	GENDER
1	1	F	11	0	M
2	0	M	12	4	F
3	2	F	13	1	F
4	2	F	14	2	M
5	2	M	15	3	M
6	3	F	16	2	F
7	3	M	17	2	F
8	4	F	18	3	M
9	3	M	19	3	F
10	2	F	20	2	F

children, two with one child, eight with two children, six with three children, and two with four children. The result of this exercise is the frequency distribution presented in Table 2.2 where f stands for frequency and Cum. f stands for cumulative frequency. The cumulative frequency is obtained by adding the number of the observations in each category to the score values preceding it. The cumulative frequency of respondents is 20, and the number of children these 20 people reported is 44.

INTERPRETING CUMULATIVE FREQUENCIES

When the data in Table 2.2 are arranged in some order (lowest to highest, smallest to largest) in the first column, it is meaningful to consider the number of individuals who have more than or less than a certain number of children. The **cumulative frequency** in the fourth column in Table 2.2 enables us to determine the number of individuals who had more than or less than a certain number of children. For example, we can see that there are 8 individuals who have 2 children. When individuals with less than two children are added, we can see at a glance that there are 12 people with 2 children or fewer. To create the cumulative frequency column, begin with the frequency of the lowest category in the first column. Each time you go down the column one category, add the frequency above to the cumulative frequency of that category. The total cumulative frequency of respondents is 20, which will always equal n, meaning that all 20 respondents had 4 or fewer children and the total number of children these 20 people reported was 44.

Table 2.3 is a computer printout of a frequency distribution representing the number of children of women participating in a community program. The computer

TABLE 2.2   Tabulation of Frequencies and Cumulative Frequencies of Respondents and Number of Children Reported

NUMBER OF CHILDREN X	TALLY	f	CUM. f	TOTAL NUMBER OF CHILDREN ($f \times x$)
0	//	2	2	0
1	//	2	4	2
2	//// ////	8	12	16
3	//// //	6	18	18
4	//	2	20	8
	$n = 20$	$n = 20$		$\Sigma(f \times x) = 44$

TABLE 2.3   Frequency Distribution of Number of Children

	NUMBER OF CHILDREN	FREQUENCY	PERCENT	VALID PERCENT	CUMULATIVE PERCENT
Valid	0	39	26.4	26.5	26.5
	1	38	25.7	25.9	52.4
	2	33	22.3	22.4	74.8
	3	21	14.2	14.3	89.1
	4	10	6.8	6.8	95.9
	5	4	2.7	2.7	98.6
	6	2	1.4	1.4	100.0
	Total	147	99.3	100.0	
Missing	System	1	0.7		
Total		148	100.0		

printout is an array of the data on number of participants' children ordered from the least number of children, zero, to the largest number of children, six. The first term we encounter identifies the variable on which the frequency distributed is based (total children). The first column represents the number of children, the second column labeled frequency is the number of participants who had the corresponding number of children. Therefore, in this sample, 39 women had no children. This represents 26.4% of the total sample. The term Valid Percent is printed out in case we have missing values in the data. Because we had one missing case, representing a participant who did not tell us how many children she had, the valid percent is calculated after subtracting the missing case from the total sample size. Therefore, the valid percent is 26.5% indicating that 26.5% of the participants, with whom we had information on number of children, had no children. The final term, Cumulative Percent, is an alternative to reporting cumulative frequencies as raw numbers and will always cap at 100%.

FREQUENCY DISTRIBUTION OF GROUPED DATA

It is sometimes desirable to group continuous data such as age, income, or educational attainment into discrete groups, or intervals. The data in Table 2.4 prior to being grouped into intervals contained 66 different values with ages ranging from 15 to 99. We can comprehend this amount of information more easily when we have fewer values for graphical presentation. In a grouped frequency distribution, a group of scores is associated with a particular frequency, whereas in a regular frequency distribution each individual score is associated with a frequency. Thus, a grouped frequency is the sum of all the frequencies in the group. For example, in looking at Table 2.3, if we wanted to place number of children 0 through 2 into a single group, the frequency for this group would be 39 + 38 + 33 = 110. This then can be interpreted as 110 of the women respondents had between 0 and 2 children. In Table 2.4, age is grouped for a study on natural disaster victims. Ages were grouped in 20-year intervals.

LIMITS, SIZES, AND MIDPOINTS OF CLASS INTERVALS

For the purposes of illustration, we have decided to divide the data in Table 2.4 into five class intervals, each containing 20 values. A **class interval** is a segment of the frequency distribution containing certain score values. Each interval has three values we need to calculate, the real lower limit, the real upper limit, and the midpoint. The apparent limits of a group of scores are the lowest and highest scores. In a class interval containing

TABLE 2.4   Grouped Frequency Distribution of the Ages of Natural Disaster Victims

	AGE	FREQUENCY	PERCENT	VALID PERCENT	CUMULATIVE PERCENT
Valid	0–19	2	0.8	0.8	0.8
	20–39	75	29.4	29.6	30.4
	40–59	88	34.5	34.8	65.2
	60–79	79	31.0	31.2	96.4
	80–99	9	3.5	3.6	100.0
	Total	253	99.2	100.0	
Missing	System	2	0.8		
Total		255	100.0		

the scores 8, 9, 10, 11, and 12, the apparent lower and upper limits are 8 and 12, respectively. The **real lower limit** of a class interval is one-half of the distance between the apparent lower limit of that interval and the apparent upper limit of the preceding class interval. Likewise, the **real upper limit** is one-half of the distance between the apparent upper limit of that class interval and the apparent lower limit of the next class interval.

Real limits of class intervals are important for accurate placement of data into the appropriate interval. Suppose we had entered the values of disaster victims' ages in years and months rather than rounding off to the nearest whole year. If an individual were 19.8 years of age, he or she would have been placed in interval 2 rather than interval 1 because we would round up to the nearest whole number. In doing so, we are implicitly recognizing that the real lower limit of the number 20 is 19.5. The practice of determining real class limits resolves the conflict of deciding in which of two adjacent class intervals a given score belongs. Figure 2.1 illustrates this process.

To obtain the size of the class interval, we simply subtract the real lower limit of the interval from its real upper limit. The size of interval one is $19.5 - (-0.5) = 20$ and the size of interval 2 is $39.5 - 19.5 = 20$. Thus, the size of each interval is 20. The midpoint of a class interval is located precisely at its center and is obtained by adding one-half of the size, $20/2 = 10$, of the class interval to the lower real limit. The midpoint for interval one is $10 + (-0.5) = 9.5$ and for interval two it is $10 + 19.5 = 29.5$.

ADVANTAGES AND DISADVANTAGES OF GROUPING DATA

Whenever you group data you must consider the advantages and disadvantages. The advantage is that grouping reduces data to manageable sizes, which presents a more

FIGURE 2.1.   Apparent and real limits of class interval 2.

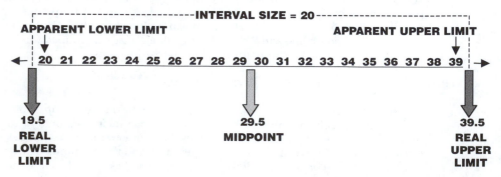

pleasing visual representation and ease of computation. A major disadvantage is that the more we reduce data in order to summarize it, the more information we lose. Returning to our discussion of levels of measurement in Chapter 1, when we group data such as disaster victims' ages, we transform a ratio variable into an ordinal variable. With ages rendered in the original metric (each person's actual age), we could validly say that a 40-year-old disaster victim is twice as old as a 20-year-old victim. However, we cannot say that the victims in grouped category 4 are twice as old as those in grouped category 2; we can only say that they are older. By grouping the data we have lost the ability to make precise statements about the data. The problem is magnified as the size of the class interval becomes larger. Some of the more powerful statistical techniques can be applied only to interval and ratio data. Therefore, if possible, the data should be collected initially in ungrouped form. We can easily group them, if necessary, for analysis and presentation.

BAR GRAPHS AND PIE CHARTS

If the data you are presenting describes the number of observations occurring in each of two or more discrete categories, that is, characteristic of the nominal level of measurement, **a bar graph** is an appropriate representational form. Bar graphs are also suitable for the visual presentation of ordinal-level data and for grouped interval- or ratio-level data. This type of graph uses vertical bars to represent the frequency, or the number of observations or occurrences for each category of a variable.

In a survey of health care needs among college students, respondents were asked to rate their satisfaction with their health care insurance coverage. The distribution of satisfaction levels is illustrated by the bar graph in Figure 2.2. When constructing a bar graph, the categories of the variable should be placed on the horizontal axis, and the frequency of occurrence should be represented on the vertical axis.

FIGURE 2.2.   Bar graph of satisfaction with health insurance.

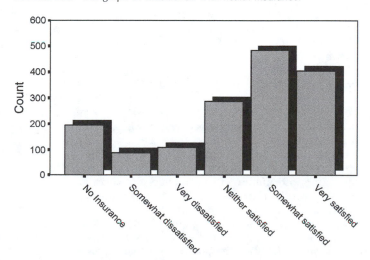

How satisfied with health insurance?

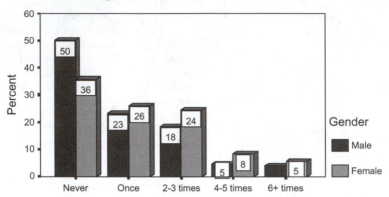

Percentage Comparison

Physician visit for primary care

FIGURE 2.3.   Bar graph of physician visits by gender.

In this particular graph, the categories represent levels of satisfaction with health insurance coverage. The graph shows that the majority of students in this survey are either satisfied or very satisfied with their health insurance. The somewhat dissatisfied group occurred the least frequently implying that if students were dissatisfied with their insurance coverage, they were likely to be very dissatisfied. The equal segments along the vertical axis are used to indicate the number of respondents who were in each category of satisfaction level. The height of the bars reflects the difference among the frequencies.

Bar graphs generally have spaces between the bars along the horizontal axis to illustrate that the bars represent discrete categories of a variable although they can also be used to visually illustrate grouped interval or ratio data. Bar graphs can also be used to illustrate percentages rather than frequencies. These are often used when making comparisons in a graph between different groups, particularly if there are different Ns for each group. Figure 2.3 illustrates the use of a bar graph to illustrate the difference between how frequently male and female students visit a physician. Fifty percent of the male students compared with 36% of the female students had not seen a physician within the past year. The table clearly illustrates that males were less likely than females to visit a physician and when they did go, they went less often than females.

If data are represented accurately by a bar graph, the bars should be of equal width, the frequency scale along the vertical axis should originate at zero, all of the equal units of the frequency should be accounted for, and the vertical size should be approximately the same length as the horizontal axis.

The **pie chart** is another visual aid used to represent the distribution of observations by discrete categories of a variable. Either a bar graph or a pie chart can be used to represent the same information. The pie chart shown in Figure 2.4 presents an alternative visual image of the data describing the class standing (e.g., freshman, sophomore, graduate student, etc.) of the students who completed the health care survey. When percentages are presented in a pie chart, a total *n* should be indicated in the table, a footnote, or in the text. The total *n* for this sample was 1,568 students.

A pie chart is constructed by, first, converting the number of respondents in each category to a proportion of the total number of respondents. This is accomplished easily by dividing the number for each category by 1,568. The Valid Percent column in

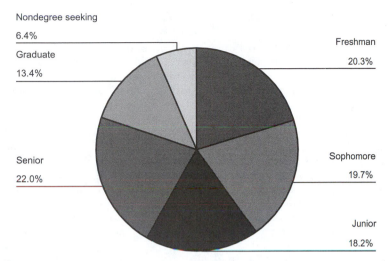

FIGURE 2.4. Pie chart of class standing.

Table 2.4 presents these proportions as percentages. Each category is represented proportionately in the circle keeping in mind that the sum of the percentages in a pie chart must always equal 100%.

HISTOGRAMS AND FREQUENCY POLYGONS

When you need to present interval- or ratio-level variables, bar graphs and pie charts generally are not appropriate. Because continuous variables have the characteristics that categories are no longer discrete, the units of measurement are numerically equal in size, and there is a continuing order among the units, histograms and frequency polygons, or line graphs, are more suitable. The histogram in Figure 2.5 represents the

FIGURE 2.5. Histogram of enrolled credit hours.

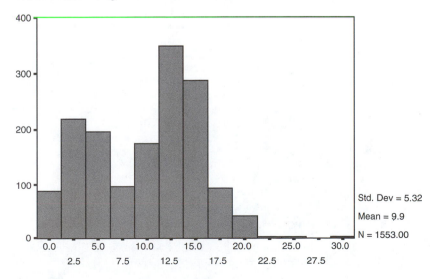

Std. Dev = 5.32
Mean = 9.9
N = 1553.00

number of credit hours in one semester taken by the group of students who completed the health survey.

It is apparent from the distribution that most of the students take between 10 and 17 credit hours. Many of them, however, were attending part time, taking 7 credits or less. Very few of the students were able to take 20 credits or more. With the number, or frequency, of students represented on the vertical (*y*) axis and the corresponding number of credit hours on the horizontal axis (*x*), the **histogram** is an efficient way to depict the distribution of values for a continuous variable.

The histogram in Figure 2.5 is different from the bar graph in Figure 2.2 in a number of ways. First, there are no spaces between the bars in a histogram. Blank spaces without corresponding values on the horizontal axis indicate that the data are not continuous or that gaps have been created artificially. Second, for each value, the bar widths represent the distance between the lower and upper real values. Finally, the units of measurement on the vertical axis increase from the bottom to the top and units on the horizontal axis increase from the left to the right. The intersection of the axes represents the point with 0 value on the horizontal axis and a frequency of 0 on the vertical axis.

Having the *x* axis always begin at zero can be cumbersome. For example, if you are researching only individuals who are 60 years of age or older, beginning the histogram at zero would make for an extremely long horizontal axis. In cases such as these, you can indicate a break in the *x* axis by inserting two lines (/ /) which signal that the continuous distance has been broken to shorten the *x* axis.

A histogram can be transformed into a **frequency polygon** by using straight lines to connect the midpoints at the top of each of the bars in a histogram. When the values on the horizontal axis do not begin with 0, the ends of the line that serve as the polygon are connected to the horizontal axis by plotting a zero frequency for the observations above and below the first and last observations in the distribution. Figure 2.6 illustrates how the histogram in Figure 2.5 can be transformed into a frequency polygon (although using a histogram as a starting point is certainly not necessary).

Frequency polygons are useful, particularly when comparing two distributions of observations of the same variable in one graph. Of the 1,553 students whose enrolled credit hours are depicted in Figure 2.6, 982 are females and 571 are males. The polygons

FIGURE 2.6.   Frequency polygon of enrolled credit hours.

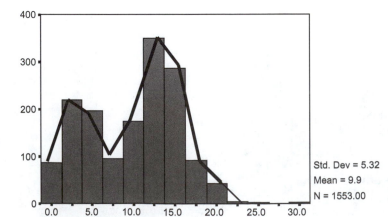

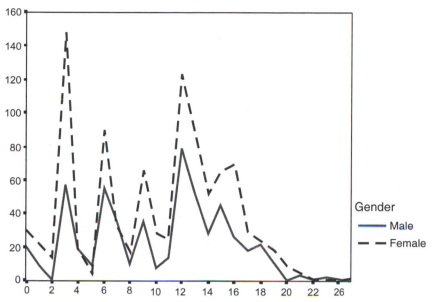

FIGURE 2.7.   Frequency polygon.

for males and females can be compared in the same graph as illustrated in Figure 2.7. The frequency polygon clearly illustrates that there is very little difference between the number of credits taken by males and the number of credits taken by females.

NUMERICAL SUMMATION OF DATA: PERCENTAGES, PROPORTIONS, AND RATIOS

In addition to the various types of graphs and distribution charts, researchers often present numerical summaries of their data. The most commonly used techniques are percentages, proportions, and ratios. **Percentages** standardize the raw data to a base of 100, **proportions** standardize to a base of 1.00, and a **ratio** is a comparison between two quantities, such as between two subsamples of a whole sample.

By standardization we mean that disparate numbers are changed to conform to a uniform scale for purposes of comparison. For instance, suppose we have a sample of 110 males and 288 females and find that 46 males and 90 females fear dental surgery. Given these numbers, we could not say that females are twice as likely to fear dentists than males since there were twice as many females in the sample. We must have a standardized total in order to fairly compare two groups. By standardizing to a base of 100, or percentage, we can say that $46/100 = 41.8\%$ of the males and $90/228 = 31.25\%$ of the females report a fear of dental surgery. This will give us a common base on which to compare the two groups.

To illustrate the numerical summation of data, we will again consider the 20 people from whom we requested information regarding family size (see Table 2.1 earlier in this chapter). A proportion compares a part of the distribution with the whole, a particular frequency divided by the total number of cases. The formula for calculating proportions is given in formula (2.1):

$$\text{Proportion } (P) = f/n \tag{2.1}$$

where f = frequency
n = total number of cases.

There are 12 females in our small data set of 20 cases. Thus, the proportion of females in our sample of 20 is $12/20 = 0.60$.

The more familiar percentage is simply a proportion multiplied by 100, as we see from formula (2.2):

$$\text{Percentage } (\%) = f/n \times 100 \tag{2.2}$$

Therefore, females constitute $(12/20) \times 100 = 60\%$ of our sample.

A ratio is a comparison of two quantities relative to one another. If we wanted to find the ratio of females to males in our data set we would divide the number of females by the number of males, as shown in formula (2.3):

$$\text{Ratio } = f_1/f_2 \tag{2.3}$$

where f_1 = frequency of females
f_2 = frequency of males.

The ratio of females to males for this sample is $12/8 = 1.5$ indicating that there are 1.5 females for every male in the sample.

The use of percentages, proportions, and ratios allows us to make clear and meaningful comparisons.

SUMMARY

The use of graphs and frequency distributions provides the researcher with the ability to communicate information visually. The appropriate mode of presentation depends first on the level of measurement: categorical, nominal, or ordinal data or continuous, interval, or ratio data. Second, the presenter should consider the audience, purpose, and setting for the presentation. When the nature of the audience and the purpose warrant a presentation that focuses on the general description of information rather than a detailed analysis, the relative or cumulative frequencies in a frequency distribution may not be appropriate. Decision-making bodies, in other cases, may want a more detailed description and presentation of data. Whether you or others present data in the form of a table, graph, or summation, you should interpret fully the information depicted.

PRACTICE APPLICATION: DISPLAYING AND SUMMARIZING DATA

The following table represents the gender and the average daily amount of time spent exercising for a group of 20 adolescents:

GENDER	EXERCISE	GENDER	EXERCISE
F	60	F	20
M	40	M	23
M	44	F	5
F	15	M	28
F	55	M	32
F	15	M	10
M	10	M	5
M	0	F	45
F	20	M	60
F	25	F	20

Construct an ungrouped frequency distribution and frequency polygon for exercise.

Average Amount of Time Exercising

MINUTES	FREQUENCY	PERCENT	CUMULATIVE PERCENT
0	1	5.0	5.0
5	2	10.0	15.0
10	2	10.0	25.0
15	2	10.0	35.0
20	3	15.0	50.0
23	1	5.0	55.0
25	1	5.0	60.0
28	1	5.0	65.0
32	1	5.0	70.0
40	1	5.0	75.0
44	1	5.0	80.0
45	1	5.0	85.0
55	1	5.0	90.0
60	2	10.0	100.0
Total	20	100.0	

Daily Average Time Exercising

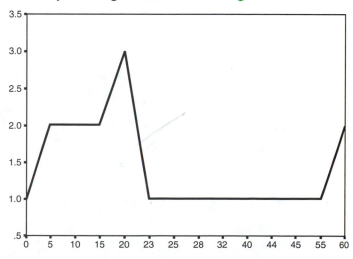

Using one frequency polygon, chart males and females separately in terms of the amount of time spent exercising.

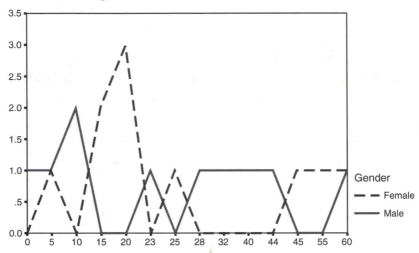

Average Daily Time Exercising
Comparing Males and Females

Group the exercise data into 10-minute intervals and construct a grouped frequency distribution and bar chart.

Average Amount of Time Exercising: Grouped

MINUTES	FREQUENCY	PERCENT	CUMULATIVE PERCENT
0–9	3	15.0	15.0
10–19	4	20.0	35.0
20–29	6	30.0	65.0
30–39	1	5.0	70.0
40–49	3	15.0	85.0
50–59	1	5.0	90.0
60–69	2	10.0	100.0
Total	20	100.0	

What is the proportion and percentage of adolescents who exercised an average of 50 minutes a day or more?

$P = f/n = 3/20 = 0.15$
Percentage $= f/n \times 100 = 3/20 \times 100 = 15.0\%$

Average Time Exercising—Grouped

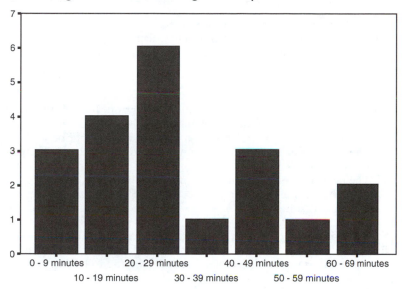

What is the ratio of males to females?

$R = f_1/f_2 = 10/10 = 1:1$

What percentage of the sample exercised less than 20 minutes a day?

$3 + 4 = 7$ individuals exercised less than 20 minutes a day
Percentage $= f/n \times 100 = 7/20 \times 100 = 35.0\%$

PROBLEMS

1. The following is a distribution of scores from a test. The highest possible score was a 20. Place the scores in a frequency distribution table and then draw a frequency polygon showing the distribution of scores.

    16, 18, 20, 15, 17, 17, 18, 20, 20, 19

2. What is the appropriate graph technique (polygon, histogram, pie chart, or bar graph) for each of the following situations?:
    a) The average daily population of a jail over a 5-year period
    b) The number of people in a community who own cats and the number of people who own dogs
    c) The percent male and the percent female in a classroom
    d) The clocked miles per hour of a sample of cars passing a speed trap in a 35-mph speed zone

3. Sally is trying to decide what type of computer to buy. She decided to survey her friends to find out what types of computers they have so that she can be "compatible" with as many as possible. She collected the following data:

COMPUTER TYPE	NUMBER OF FRIENDS
Micron	8
Apple	3
IBM	6
Gateway	7

    Construct a pie chart for these data. Using the pie chart, what type of computer should Sally purchase? Further, Sally learns that the Microns and the Gateways are identical to the IBMs. Now which computer should Sally purchase?

4. Students were asked how many pages of a 25-page assignment they had read prior to class. Anonymity was ensured to gain an honest response. The following were their responses:

0	5	0	25
25	5	0	20
15	25	5	15
15	25	10	15
10	15	20	25

    a) Construct a frequency distribution for ungrouped data.
    b) Calculate the relative frequencies.
    c) Calculate the relative frequency proportions and percents.
    d) Interpret the data patterns.

5. Place the following 30 scores in a grouped frequency distribution table using
    a) An interval width of 5
    b) An interval width of 10

60	55	62	46	98
62	92	94	40	84
85	88	86	70	85
98	88	75	72	78
46	72	75	74	77
78	75	90	76	71

c) Construct a histogram using the interval width of 5.
d) Construct a histogram using the interval width of 10.
e) Compare the two histograms.

6. Final exam scores for a sociology class are distributed as follows:

SCORE	FREQUENCY
95–99	2
90–94	4
85–89	12
80–84	14
75–79	53
70–74	48
65–69	13
60–64	4
Total	150

a) Convert the frequency distribution into relative frequency proportions.
b) Convert to a cumulative frequency distribution and then do a cumulative relative frequency distribution using proportions.
c) Graph part (a).
d) Graph part (b).
e) Find the approximate percentile rank for a score between 70 and 74.
f) What percent of students scored less than 80?

Chapter 3

CENTRAL TENDENCY AND DISPERSION

In studying social phenomena, scientists collect and evaluate data in numerous ways. Organizing the data into frequency distributions, charts, graphs, and tables is a useful way of visualizing the shape and scope of the data for a single variable, such as the numbers of births in Idaho, age at marriage for Irish males, suicides in Sweden, and homicides in Canada. However, if we wanted to compare Idaho births with California births, American suicides with Swedish suicides, and so on, we would find visual inspection of frequency distributions somewhat cumbersome and not very precise. When making such comparisons it would be more useful to have mathematically precise summary statements that would tell us the center of each distribution and how the data in each are dispersed or scattered away from their centers. We call such techniques *measures of central tendency* and *measures of dispersion*.

MEASURES OF CENTRAL TENDENCY

Measures of central tendency show the centrality of the data, where we generally find the preponderance of values in a population or sample. Measures of dispersion indicate the spread of the data away from the center. These measures sacrifice the overall view of the data provided by a frequency distribution, but more than make up for it by providing very useful numerical summaries that can be compared with distributions of other populations and samples. The three measures of central tendency are the mode, median, and mean. We will examine each measure, beginning with the mode.

MODE

The **mode** (symbolized Mo) is defined as that score that occurs most frequently in the distribution. Because the mode is the most frequently occurring score, it may appear in a distribution in places other than at the center, although it will always be under the peak of a distribution curve. It is possible to have more than one mode in a distribution; in such cases the distribution is bimodal or multimodal. The mode is the only valid measure of central tendency for nominal data, but it may also be validly used for all other levels of measurement.

Suppose we asked 30 people to reveal their annual income and we organize their responses in rounded thousands of dollars into ungrouped and grouped distributions as shown in Table 3.1.

The mode for these data is 16 because it is the income category that occurs most often (four times). The modal interval is 16–20, which represents the class interval that occurs most frequently. The mode is the least frequently used measure of central tendency in statistics because it does not lend itself to mathematical operations. It is purely a descriptive statistic that provides useful information regarding the typical case.

TABLE 3.1 Annual Income of 30 Respondents in Thousands of Dollars in Ungrouped and Grouped Form

	UNGROUPED				GROUPED	
VALUE	FREQ.	VALUE	FREQ.	CLASS	FREQ.	CUM FREQ.
12	1	28	2	9–15	4	4
13	2	29	1	16–20	7	11
14	1	30	2	21–25	4	15
16	4	32	1	26–30	6	21
18	1	35	2	31–35	3	24
19	1	36	1	36–40	4	28
20	1	37	1	—	—	28
24	1	38	1	—	—	28
25	3	40	1	95–99	2	30
26	1	97	1			
		99	1			

MEDIAN

The **median** (symbolized Md) is defined as that score in the range that divides the scores into two equal parts; it is the middle score of a set of scores that have been arranged from lowest to highest. Consider the following range of scores:

5 6 8 9 10 11 **12** 13 15 16 18 21 33

↓

median

The median score is 12 because half of the values are above that number and half are below it. Because there are 13 scores, six of the scores will be above the median and six will be below. If there are an even number of scores, the median is determined by interpolating between the two middle scores by taking their average. For instance,

two middle scores
↓
5 6 8 9 10 11 **12 13** 14 15 16 18 21 33   Md = (12 + 13)/2 = 12.5

To take another example, because there are 30 scores in our annual income data (see Table 3.1), we must interpolate between the two middle scores, which are 15 and 16. The 15th score is 25 and the 16th is 26. Thus, (25 + 26)/2 = 25.5; the median income of this group of observations is $25,500.

COMPUTING THE MEDIAN WITH GROUPED DATA

The median is not so easily computed with grouped data. By putting cases with diverse scores into a single group, such as the seven cases with incomes between 16 and 20 thousand dollars, we have lost the precision available we had in the ungrouped distribution, but sometimes grouped data are all we have available to us. We will compute an estimate of the median from the grouped data in Table 3.1 using formula (3.1):

$$\text{Md} = L + \left[\frac{N/2 - \text{CF}}{f} \right] w$$

(3.1)

where   L = the true lower limit of the class interval in which the median is located
$n/2$ = one-half of the total frequency
CF = the cumulated frequency up to but not including the median class interval
f = the frequency of the median class interval
w = the class width.

Step 1.   We proceed by first dividing the sample n by 2 ($30/2 = 15$). So 15 is the number that divides the distribution into two equal parts.

Step 2.   To determine the value of L, the real lower limit, the class interval containing the 15th score must be identified. From the cumulative frequency distribution we see that the class containing the 15th score is the 21–25 class. The median is somewhere in this class interval. The real lower limit of the number 21 is 20.5. Therefore, $L = 20.5$.

Step 3.   The value of CF is determined by adding all frequencies down to, but not including, those in the class containing the median. We note that 11 scores precede this interval, so CF = 11.

Step 4.   The value of f is defined as the value frequency of the class containing the median, so $f = 4$.

Step 5.   The value of w refers to the width of the class containing the median. The width of the interval is obtained by subtracting the real lower limit from the real upper limit of that class ($25.5 - 20.5 = 5$). The class width is 5. Substituting these values into the formula, we get

$$Md = 20.5 + \left[\frac{30/2 - 11}{4}\right] 5 = 20.5 + \left[\frac{15 - 11}{4}\right] 5$$

$$= 20.5 + (1)(5) = 25.5 \tag{3.1}$$

This is the same value previously computed from the ungrouped data. Half of our respondents have incomes below $25,500 and half have incomes equal to or above $25,500. However, the value of the estimated median calculated from grouped data will often not be the same as the median calculated from the same data in ungrouped form. This is because we are forced to make the simplifying assumption that all cases are distributed at equal distances across the class interval, which is often not true.

THE MEAN

The **mean** is symbolized in two different ways, depending on whether we are describing the population mean (μ, read *mu*) or the sample mean ($\overline{X}$ read *ex-bar*). The mean is the measure of central tendency that most of us think about when we hear the term *average*. It is simply the arithmetic average of a distribution of scores. Among the measures of central tendency the mean is most commonly used. Unlike the mode and the median, it is suited only to interval and ratio data. The mean is the focal point and entrance to more advanced statistics. Before we can calculate interval- and ratio-level statistics, we must first know the means of the variables with which we are working. Another nice characteristic of the mean is that it is quite stable across repeated random samples from the same population. The modes and medians of repeated random samples from the same population tend to fluctuate more than the means.

The common formula for the mean is given in formula 3.2, which simply requires us to add all the individual scores or values (this is what the Greek symbol Σ, *sigma*, tells us to do) and divide by the sample size.

$$\overline{X} = \frac{\Sigma X}{N} \tag{3.2}$$

where $\overline{X}$ = the mean
Σ = sigma = *the sum of*
X = the values to be summed
N = sample size.

The mean annual income is obtained from Table 3.1 by first summing all numbers in the distribution:

$$\Sigma X = 12 + 13 + 13 + 14 + \cdots + 99 = 892$$

and then dividing this sum by the number of observations:

$$\overline{X} = \frac{892}{30} = 29.733$$

COMPUTING THE MEAN FROM GROUPED DATA

Just as we computed an estimated median from grouped data, we can also compute an estimate of the mean. The formula for computing the mean from grouped data is given in formul a (3.3):

$$\overline{X} = \frac{\Sigma fm}{N} \tag{3.3}$$

where fm = the frequency of each class multiplied by its midpoint. Recall that the midpoint of a class interval is halfway between its real lower and upper limits. Therefore, the midpoint for class 1 is between 9.5 and 15.5 and is equal to 12.5. The logic of using the midpoint is that it represents our best estimate of the mean value of the scores in each class interval. There are four observations in this class. The symbol fm instructs us to multiply the frequency of the class by its midpoint, so for the first class we have $12.5 \times 4 = 50$. We continue in this way until we have computed fm for each class.

Class 1:	$12.5 \times 4 =$	50
Class 2:	$18.0 \times 7 =$	126
Class 3:	$23.0 \times 4 =$	92
Class 4:	$28.0 \times 6 =$	168
Class 5:	$33.0 \times 3 =$	99
Class 6:	$38.0 \times 4 =$	152
Class 7:	$97.5 \times 2 =$	195
	$\Sigma fm =$	882

Thus,

$$\overline{X} = \frac{\Sigma fm}{N} = \frac{882}{30} = 29.4$$

Our estimated mean computed on the basis of grouped data underestimates the true mean, which we know to be 29.733. A mean computed from group data is only an estimate of the sample mean. The formula for the mean of grouped data assumes that the class scores are uniformly distributed around the class midpoint. Our actual data tend to be on the high side of the midpoint. Take the first and last class intervals, for instance. The actual mean of the first interval is 13, not 12.5, and the actual mean of the last class is 98, not 97.5. Although the amount of misestimation is usually quite small, it is always preferable to collect data at the highest level of measurement possible.

We can further emphasize the desirability of raw over grouped data by pointing out that the mode of grouped data is simply the midpoint of the class interval with the largest frequency. It should be intuitively obvious that this is the best estimate of the mode that we could make from grouped data. The class interval with the largest frequency is class 2, and the midpoint of class 2 is 18. Thus we overestimate the value of the mode, which we know to be 16.

A RESEARCH EXAMPLE

We will now use the computer to run a frequency program in which these measures of central tendency, as well as measures of dispersion, have been calculated for us. The distribution is from our multiple sclerosis (MS) data from Idaho (Walsh & Walsh, 1987). The variable is number of years since each respondent's MS has been diagnosed. The computer results are shown in Table 3.2. From the output we see that the mode is 1, the median is 7, and the mean is 10.474. We will defer discussion of the other printed values until our discussion of dispersion. Do note, however, that if we smoothed the histogram derived from these data and stood the resulting distribution on end, we would

TABLE 3.2 Number of Years Since Multiple Sclerosis Diagnosed

CENTRAL TENDENCY	YEARS DIAG	TALLY	FREQ.	CUM. FREQ.	PERCENT	CUM. PERCENT
Mode	1	XXXXXXXXXXXXXXXXXX	18	18	13.33	13.33
	2	XXXX	4	22	2.96	16.30
	3	XXXXXXXXXXXXXXXX	16	38	11.85	28.15
	4	XXXXXXXXX	9	47	6.67	34.81
	5	XXXXXX	6	53	4.44	39.26
	6	XXXXXXXXXXXXXX	14	67	10.37	49.63
Median	7	XXXXXX	6	73	4.44	54.07
	8	XXXXXXXX	8	81	5.93	60.00
	9	XX	2	83	1.48	61.48
Mean	10	XXXXXXXXXX	10	93	7.41	68.89
	13	XX	2	95	1.48	70.37
	14	XX	2	97	1.48	71.85
	15	XXXXXX	6	103	4.44	76.30
	16	XX	2	105	1.48	77.78
	17	XXXX	4	109	2.96	80.74
	18	XX	2	111	1.48	82.22
	19	XX	2	113	1.48	83.70
	20	XXXXXXXX	8	121	5.93	89.63
	21	XX	2	123	1.48	91.11
	23	XX	2	125	1.48	92.59
	26	XXX	3	128	2.22	94.81
	29	X	1	129	0.74	95.56
	30	XX	2	131	1.48	97.04
	36	X	1	132	0.74	97.78
	40	X	1	133	0.74	98.52
	49	X	1	134	0.74	99.26
	59	X	1	135	0.74	100.00

Mean	10.474	Standard error	.938	Median	7.000
Mode	1.000	Standard deviation	10.839	Variance	118.654
Kurtosis	6.446	Skewness	2.265	C.V.	103.485
Minimum	1.000	Maximum	59.000	Range	58.000

FIGURE 3.1.   Multiple sclerosis distribution curve superimposed on normal curve.

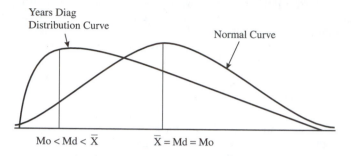

have a distribution curve that resembled a ski slope, with the mode at the top of the hill and the median and mean located more or less halfway down the hill.

In Figure 3.1, we have superimposed the normal curve (examined in the next chapter) over our MS data curve. The normal curve is perfectly symmetrical, with the mean, mode, and median all being exactly in the center of the distribution. Our MS distribution, however, is highly skewed to the right. The normal curve has no skew, with a skewness value of 0.0. A curve skewed to the right is called a *positive skew,* and a curve skewed to the left is called a *negative skew.* The computer printout indicates a **skewness** of 2.265 in the MS distribution, indicating a strong positive skew. A rough and ready indication of the skewness is the difference between the mean and the median. If that value is negative, the curve has a negative skew; if positive, a positive skew. The rightward skew of this distribution is a function of a few highly atypical cases at the high end of the distribution. These atypical cases pull the mean toward them at the tail of the distribution. As is usual in such skewed distributions, the median falls between the mode and the mean, and of the three measures the mean lies closest to the tail of the distribution.

Another measure of the shape of the distribution given in Table 3.2 is **kurtosis,** which is a measure of the relative peakedness of a curve. The normal curve has a kurtosis of 0.0. If kurtosis is positive, as it is here (6.446), the curve is more peaked or narrow than the normal curve; if it is negative it is flatter than the normal curve.

Choosing A Measure of Central Tendency

Choosing a measure of central tendency depends on the kind of information you wish to convey to the readers of your research. You should use the mode if you are referring to a variable measured at the nominal level. It makes no sense to talk about the mean sex of a sample, but we can say that the modal sex was male. We can use the mean of a dichotomous nominal-level variable that has been dummy coded as 0 and 1. In these instances, the mean represents the proportion of cases in the category coded 1. This convention is important to some of the statistical techniques we will be discussing in later chapters. You also use the mode when you wish to point out the typical. For instance, a politician is much more interested in the typical opinion than in any mean level of opinion.

The median is used when the variable to be described is measured at the ordinal level or higher. It is useful when extreme scores distort the mean, as they do in our MS distribution. In such cases the median better reflects central tendency than does the mean because it is less affected by extreme scores. The government uses the median rather than the mean to report average individual and household income in the United

TABLE 3.3 Relationship between Measures of Central Tendency and Measurement Levels

LEVEL OF MEASUREMENT	VALID TO USE		
	MEAN	MEDIAN	MODE
Nominal	No	No	Yes
Ordinal	No	Yes	Yes
Interval	Yes	Yes	Yes
Ratio	Yes	Yes	Yes

States for just this reason. The income of billionaires pulls the mean in the direction of the higher incomes in a very positively skewed distribution. Using the median gives us a better picture of incomes that fall in the middle of the distribution and better reflects the average American household.

We use the mean only with interval- or ratio-level measures. It is the only measure of central tendency that uses all the information in a distribution. Variables measured at the interval or ratio levels are not limited to the mean for description, however. It is valid to report all measures of central tendency for such variables. Table 3.3 summarizes the relationship between the measures of central tendency and levels of measurement.

Statisticians refer to the mean as the *center of deviations* or the *center of gravity.* By this it is meant that deviations from the mean in a distribution of scores, both above and below the mean, will balance each other. To illustrate, suppose we have the distribution of scores given in Table 3.4. We calculate the mean, median, and mode for these data and find them to be 9, 10, and 6, respectively. We first calculate the deviation scores for the mean. A deviation score is the raw score minus the mean ($X - \bar{X} = x$), where x is the deviation score. As illustrated, the sum of x will always be equal to zero. However, the deviations from the mode and the median will not be zero unless the distribution is perfectly symmetrical (the mean, median, and mode are identical).

As noted earlier, there is one significant problem regarding the mean. Although we have said that it is the most stable measure of central tendency across random samples from the same population, it is affected more than the mode or median by extreme scores in a distribution. In this sense it is less stable than the median. For instance, if we had a 31st respondent in our income data set who reported an income of $250,000, it

TABLE 3.4 Deviations from the Mean, Mode, and Median of a Distribution of Scores

MEAN			MEDIAN			MODE		
X	$\bar{X}$	$X - \bar{X}$	X	Md	$X -$ Md	X	Mo	$X -$ Mo
3	9	−6	3	10	−7	3	6	−3
6	9	−3	6	10	−4	6	6	0
6	9	−3	6	10	−4	6	6	0
6	9	−3	6	10	−4	6	6	0
10	9	+1	10	10	0	10	6	+4
10	9	+1	10	10	0	10	6	+4
12	9	+3	12	10	+2	12	6	+6
13	9	+4	13	10	+3	13	6	+7
15	9	+6	15	10	+5	15	6	+9
	$\Sigma (X-\bar{X}) = 0$			$\Sigma (X-Md) = -9$			$\Sigma (X-Mo) = +27$	

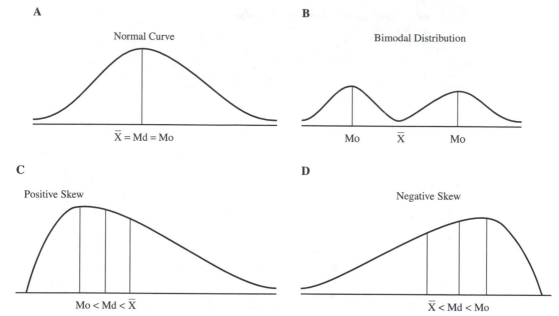

FIGURE 3.2.   Mean, mode, and median in different distributions.

would change the mean considerably (from 29.467 to 36.58), would change the median only from 25.5 to 25.6, and would leave the mode totally unchanged (16 would still be the modal category).

Figure 3.2 presents four distributions (from an infinite number of possible distributions) with the mean, mode, and median in different positions relative to each other. Note that in a positively skewed distribution, the mean is greater than the median and the median is greater than the mode. In a negatively skewed distribution, the mean is less than the median and the median is less than the mode. Our annual income data would be distributed approximately like curve C, with a mode of 16, a median of 25.5, and a mean of 29.733.

MEASURES OF DISPERSION

The measures of central tendency are very useful in relating indices of typicality or averageness of a group of scores. However, it is also useful to gain some idea of how the individuals or objects in a distribution differ from one another. A measure of dispersion or variability, coupled with the mean, allows us to compute measures indicating how different two or more individuals or groups are with regard to a variable of interest. For instance, suppose that the mean income for both a sample of college professors and a sample of car salespersons is found to be $65,000. Such information standing alone conveys a false impression without a measure of the variability within the respective samples.

RANGE

The **range** is the simplest measure of dispersion. Unlike the other measures we will be discussing, the range is not a measure of the dispersion from the mean; rather it is simply the difference between the lowest and highest scores in the distribution. In our MS distribution the lowest score is 1, the highest is 59, so the range is 58 ($59 - 1 = 58$). Even this simple measure of dispersion gives us a better feel for the data than we would have with the mean alone. In our professors/salespersons example, suppose the lowest income is \$40,000 and the highest is \$95,000 for the professors and \$15,000 and \$130,000 for the salespersons. Among the professors the highest paid person receives about 2.4 times more money than the lowest paid person, whereas the highest paid salesperson receives almost nine times as much as the lowest salesperson.

The range for the distribution of salaries for professors is \$55,000, and for the salespersons it is \$115,000. The information provided by the range thus gives us a little better feel for the data than the mean alone. We know there is large variability among the salespersons' income and relatively little among the professors'. However, the range is a very crude measure of sample variation that depends entirely on the two extreme values. One or both of these values may be so atypical as to render the range most untrustworthy as a measure of dispersion.

A somewhat better measure of dispersion is the **interquartile range** (IQR). The term *quartile* refers to the division of a distribution into four equal quarters. The first quartile (Q_1) contains the first 25% of the cases, Q_2 contains the 25% of the distribution from Q_1 to Q_2 (the median), Q_3 contains the 25% from Q_2 to Q_3, and Q_4 contains the final 25% of cases. Another way of putting it is to say that Q_1 lies at the 25th percentile, Q_2 at the 50th percentile, Q_3 at the 75th percentile, and Q_4 at the 100th percentile. The IQR is obtained by $Q_3 - Q_1$; that is, the score at the 75th percentile minus the score at the 25th percentile. The advantage of the IQR over the range is that the IQR reports the range of scores in the middle 50% of the distribution, where the great majority of cases typically fall, thus eliminating much of the bias imposed by extreme scores lying at the ends of the distribution.

You can estimate the interquartile range with grouped data by using the same process as calculating the median from grouped data. The formulas, however, are slightly different to reflect the class interval where the specific quartile is located. The formula for the median is equivalent to the second quartile:

$$Md = L + \left[\frac{N/2 - CF}{f} \right] w = Q_2 \qquad (3.4)$$

Therefore, the formula to estimate the first quartile is

$$Q_1 = L + \left[\frac{N/4 - CF}{f} \right] w \qquad (3.5)$$

where L = the real lower limit of the class interval in which the first quartile is located
     CF = the cumulative frequency up but not including the first quartile class interval
     f = the frequency of the first quartile class interval
     w = the class width.

The formula for the third quartile is:

$$Q_3 = L + \left[\frac{3N/4 - CF}{f} \right] w \qquad (3.6)$$

where L = the real lower limit of the class interval in which the third quartile
is located
CF = the cumulative frequency up but not including the third quartile
class interval
f = the frequency of the third quartile class interval
w = the class width.

Using the data from Table 3.1, we can calculate the interquartile range by estimating Q_1 and Q_3:

$$Q_1 = 15.5 + \left[\frac{30/4 - 4}{7} \right] 5 = 18$$

$$Q_3 = 30.5 + \left[\frac{3/4(30) - 21}{3} \right] 5 = 33 \tag{3.7}$$

Interquartile range = $Q_3 - Q_1$, = $33 - 18 = 15$
The range of the middle 50% of the 30 respondents is $15,000

Both the range and the IQR are quick and dirty measures of dispersion that are unsatisfactory if we want to go beyond describing a distribution. Note that the range and IQR use only two values to report dispersion. A more satisfactory measure of dispersion is one that utilizes every score in the distribution in its calculation, which minimizes the effects of any extreme scores. Such a measure is the standard deviation.

STANDARD DEVIATION

Although there are a number of other rarely used measures of dispersion, we will concentrate on the three major indices of variability used to assess the spread of interval and ratio data in a distribution about their mean. Although they are different measures, they are only made so by mathematical transformations. The most basic of the three is the sum of squares (ss). A measure called the variance (s^2) is derived from the sum of squares, and the **standard deviation** (s) is derived from the variance. All three measures are used in their various transformations in statistical analysis of interval- and ratio-level data.

A good and complete measure of dispersion should utilize all scores in the distribution and describe the typical or average deviation of the scores around their mean. Such a measure would be small in a distribution in which the scores are closely clustered around the center, and get larger as they become more scattered away from it. The standard deviation is such a measure. As illustrated in formula (3.8), if all observations had exactly the same value the standard deviation would be zero because there would be no variability in the data. As the observations become more different from one another, the standard deviation becomes progressively larger. The standard deviation, in effect, reflects the extent to which the mean represents the entire set of observations in a population or sample. If you turn back to Table 3.2 you will see that the standard deviation for *years since diagnoses* is 10.839. This value is actually larger than the mean (10.474), indicating that the mean is a poor indicator of the central tendency of this distribution.

Like the mean, there are two symbols for the standard deviation. When we talk about the population standard deviation, the lowercase Greek letter sigma (σ) is used, and when we are referring to a sample standard deviation, which is used to estimate the population standard deviation, we use the lowercase letter s. The formulas for the population standard deviation is

$$\sigma = \sqrt{\frac{\Sigma(X - \mu)^2}{N}} \qquad (3.8)$$

where N = the number of cases
X = each individual case
Σ = the sum of
μ = the population mean.

and for the sample standard deviation

$$s = \sqrt{\frac{\Sigma(X - \overline{X})^2}{N - 1}} \qquad (3.9)$$

where $\overline{X}$ is the sample mean. Formula (3.9) is the definitional formula for the standard deviation, so-called because it enables us to intuitively grasp what is going on and why the resulting value is called the standard deviation. Note that the formula instructs us to subtract the mean from each case or observation. Doing this results in some negative and some positive results. Because the positive and negative deviations cancel each other, the sum of $X - \overline{X}$ will always be 0, as we demonstrated in Table 3.4. A measure of dispersion that always equals zero is not much use to us. To avoid this inconvenience, we square each difference before we sum. Note also that when the standard deviation of a sample is calculated we use $N - 1$ rather than N, as we do when calculating a population standard deviation. We do this because s^2 (the sample variance) is a biased estimator of σ^2 (the population variance), and subtracting 1 from N corrects for that bias. The bias reflects the fact that a sample has less diversity (variance) than is found in its parent population. The correction factor is particularly important for small samples, but the difference between N and $N - 1$ becomes more trivial as the sample size gets larger.

Let us compute the standard deviation with a small data set of randomly selected physical therapy patients (Table 3.5). Each individual case (X) represents the number of physical therapy sessions in the previous year. After taking the mean from each observation, squaring the difference, and summing, we have a value known as the **sum of squares,** which is the numerator under the radical in the standard deviation formula

TABLE 3.5 Computing the Standard Deviation of Physical Therapy Sessions

X	$\overline{X}$	$(X - \overline{X})$	$(X - \overline{X})^2$
2	5.5	−3.5	12.25
4	5.5	−1.5	2.25
4	5.5	−1.5	2.25
4	5.5	−1.5	2.25
5	5.5	−0.5	.25
5	5.5	−0.5	.25
6	5.5	0.5	.25
6	5.5	0.5	.25
8	5.5	2.5	6.25
11	5.5	5.5	30.25
$\Sigma = 55$		$\Sigma = 0.0$	$\Sigma = 56.50$

$$\overline{X} = \frac{55}{10} = 5.5 \qquad \text{Sum of squares} = 56.50$$

$\Sigma(X - \overline{X}^2)$, which is equal to 56.5. The next step is to divide the sum of squares by $N - 1$, which provides us with the **variance** (s^2). The variance is the complete term under the radical in the standard deviation formula, and is equal to 6.278 for these data:

$$s^2 = \frac{\Sigma(X - \overline{X})^2}{N - 1}$$

Plugging the numbers into formula (3.9), we get

$$s = \sqrt{\frac{\Sigma(X - \overline{X})^2}{N - 1}} = \sqrt{56.5/9} = \sqrt{6.278} = 2.50$$

The variance is an important and vital statistic that will be used in many subsequent calculations. However, it is somewhat difficult to conceptualize because it represents the square of whatever it is we are measuring. For instance, when we say that the variance in physical therapy sessions is 6.278, it could easily be misinterpreted as meaning that the typical deviation from mean number of sessions is 6.278 *squared* sessions. If we performed the calculation on a distribution of number of children and told you that the typical deviation from the mean number of children is 3.5 *squared* children, you might drop the class. Such statements are not easy ideas to play around with. What we need to do is to get these values back to the same metric in which they were originally measured by taking the square root of the variance to arrive at the standard deviation, which has a value of 2.5.

COMPUTATIONAL FORMULA FOR *s*

Formula (3.9) is the definitional formula for the standard deviation, presented to give you an intuitive appreciation of what is going on mathematically. With a large number of cases it is a cumbersome and time-consuming method. Fortunately, the following computational formula requires far less time and effort:

$$s = \sqrt{\frac{\Sigma X^2 - (\Sigma X)^2/N}{N - 1}} \tag{3.10}$$

where ΣX^2 = the sum of the squared individual scores
$(\Sigma X)^2$ = the sum of the individual scores squared.

Step 1. Square each value: $2 \times 2 = 4$, $4 \times 4 = 16$, etc., and sum; $\Sigma X^2 = 359$.
Step 2. Square the sum of the individual values: $55^2 = 3055$. Plug in the numbers.

X	X^2
2	4
4	16
4	16
4	16
5	25
5	25
6	36
6	36
8	64
11	121
$\Sigma X = 55$	$\Sigma X^2 = 359$

$$s = \sqrt{\frac{359 - 3025/10}{9}} = \sqrt{(539 - 302.5)/9} = \sqrt{6.28} = 2.5$$

The mean and the standard deviation (along with its more unwieldy cousins the sum of squares and the variance) constitute the computational bedrock of statistics. The usefulness of the standard deviation will become more apparent when we use it later to compute more advanced statistics. For now let us say that it serves as a summary of the dispersion of a single variable, and most important, it is the basis for the calculation of many of the statistics we will be examining. Additionally, because the mean is the reference point for computing the standard deviation, the standard deviation is viewed as the expected (average or typical) amount of error we would make in attempting to guess any score in a distribution from its expected value (the mean). When we discuss the normal curve in the next chapter we will see that more than two-thirds of all observed values will be within 1 standard deviation on either side of their mean.

VARIABILITY AND VARIANCE

The idea of **variance** (s^2) is of great importance to us because the whole point of the vast majority of social and behavioral research is to *explain* or *account for* variance in dependent variables. Whenever we measure observations of any kind we are bound to find a degree of variability or difference in the measures from case to case. When we observe a distribution of scores and note that they are not all the same, we want to know why. We then look for theoretically meaningful variables that may help us to find out. Let's look at an example that should make the idea of *variance explained* intuitively more understandable.

    We begin with a class of 10 rookie police officers training at the academy in 1986. Because they all share the same rank and seniority, they all are paid the same salary of $24,000 per year. What will the mean, standard deviation, and variance be? Because there is no variability in salary, the mean will be $24,000, and SS, s^2, and s will be zero. Because there is no variance, there is none to explain or to be accounted for. Ten years later, we return to the same police department and to the same group of officers. We find that their salaries differ considerably this time, ranging from $36,000 to $57,000. Now we have variability, and thus variance, to be accounted for. We put these data in a table so that we can calculate the variance. We have rounded to the nearest $1,000 and eliminated the last three zeros for ease of computation:

X	X^2
36	1,296
36	1,296
38	1,444
39	1,521
40	1,600
40	1,600
42	1,764
45	2,025
46	2,116
57	3,249
419	17,911

$$\Sigma X^2 = 17,911, \quad (\Sigma X)^2 = 419^2 = 175,561$$
$$s^2 = \frac{\Sigma X^2 - (\Sigma X)^2/N}{N-1} = \frac{17,911 - 175,561/10}{9} = \frac{354.9}{9} = 39.433$$

TABLE 3.6 Computation of Standard Deviation from Grouped Data

CLASS	f	m	f(m)	fm(m)
1–4	4	2.5	10	25.00
5–8	5	6.5	32.5	211.25
9–12	1	10.5	10.5	346.50
	$\Sigma f = 10 = N$		$\Sigma f(m) = 53.0$	$\Sigma fm(m) = 346.50$

The variance (the average of the sum of the squared deviations from the mean) is thus 39.433. What do you think would explain or account for this variance? Rank (patrol officer, sergeant, lieutenant, etc.) would certainly account for a big proportion. Other variables might include overtime pay, specialist assignments, and pay given for special skills such as bilingualism. In the behavioral and social sciences, explaining variance is a major objective for researchers. Because many variables, including pure chance, affect social behavior, researchers often fall short of being able to account for even 50% of the variance in the dependent variable.

COMPUTING THE STANDARD DEVIATION FROM GROUPED DATA

If the physical therapy data came in the form of grouped data we would use formula (3.11) to compute the standard deviation. The first thing we do is to set up a table of five columns showing the class intervals, the frequencies in each class, the midpoint of the classes, the frequencies times the midpoint, and the product of the frequencies times the midpoint multiplied by the midpoint. We will assume that the data are grouped into three classes, as shown in Table 3.6. The formula for computing the standard deviation from grouped data follows:

$$\overline{X} = \frac{\Sigma f(m)}{N} = \frac{53}{10} = 5.3$$

$$s = \sqrt{\frac{fm(m)}{N} - (\overline{X})^2} = \sqrt{\frac{346.5}{10} - 5.3^2}$$

$$= \sqrt{34.65 - 28.09} = 2.56 \tag{3.11}$$

The standard deviation computed from grouped data is 2.56, or just slightly greater than the value computed from the ungrouped data.

COEFFICIENT OF VARIATION

Another useful measure of variation is the coefficient of variation (CV), which is used to assess relative rather than absolute variation. It is useful for comparing variation in two distributions of the same variable having different means, or for comparing two distributions in which the variable of interest is measured in different units. CV standardizes s by multiplying it by 100 and dividing the product by the mean:

$$CV = (s)(100)/\overline{X} \tag{3.12}$$

For instance, we will be working with IQ data from two different samples in this book. One sample is composed of juvenile delinquents and the other of adult offenders. The mean IQ for the juveniles is 92.2 with a standard deviation of 10.5. The mean for the adults is 93.56, with a standard deviation of 12.18. Let us see which sample has the most relative variation:

$$\text{Juvenile CV} = \frac{(10.5)(100)}{92.2} = 11.39 \qquad \text{Adult CV} = \frac{(12.18)(100)}{93.56} = 13.0$$

There is more variation in the adult offender population.

To give another example, suppose we had average weekly income data from the United States and France measured in dollars and francs, respectively. The average weekly wage for Americans was found to be \$412, and for the French it was ff2,320. Because there are approximately 5 francs to the dollar, we would expect the French distribution to have both a higher absolute mean and a higher absolute standard deviation. We compare the relative weekly income variation by computing CV:

$$\text{United States CV} = \frac{(91)(100)}{\$412} = 22.1 \qquad \text{France CV} = \frac{(415)(100)}{\text{ff}2,320} = 17.9$$

There is more income variation in the United States.

INDEX OF QUALITATIVE VARIATION

So far we have focused on measures of variation for interval or ratio variables. It is sometimes useful to know how a qualitative nominal or ordinal variable is dispersed. We can find this out by using a measure known as the *index of qualitative variation.*

If all values of a variable are in one category of a nominal or ordinal variable, there is no variation, and the index of qualitative variation (IQV) will be zero. If the values are distributed evenly across the categories, IQV will be 1, its maximum value. The formula for IQV follows:

$$\text{IQV} = \frac{k(N^2 - \Sigma f^2)}{N^2(k-1)} \tag{3.13}$$

where k = the number of categories
           N = the number of cases
         Σf^2 = the sum of the squared frequencies.

Let us compute and compare the IQV for the marital status variable for both our offender and MS patient data to see which group has more variation. First, we must present the category frequencies of the variable. Second, we square each of the frequencies and sum. First, the offender data:

Step 1.   Square the number of cases in each category and sum:

IQV for Marital Status (Offender Data)

MARITAL STATUS	f	f^2
Married	230	52,900
Divorced	117	13,689
Single	285	81,225
Widowed	5	25
	637	147,839

Step 2.   Substitute the numbers into the formula ($k = 4$, $N^2 = 637^2 = 405{,}769$, $f^2 = 147{,}839$) and proceed:

$$\text{IQV} = \frac{k(N^2 - \Sigma f^2)}{N^2(k - 1)} = \frac{4(405{,}769 - 147{,}839)}{405{,}769(3)} = \frac{1{,}031{,}720}{1{,}217{,}307} = 0.847$$

Now do the same for the MS data.

IQV for Marital Status (MS Data)

MARITAL STATUS	f	f^2
Married	87	7569
Divorced	28	784
Single	8	64
Widowed	12	144
	135	8561

$$\text{IQV} = \frac{k(N^2 - \Sigma f^2)}{N^2(k - 1)} = \frac{4(18{,}225 - 8{,}561)}{18{,}225(3)} = \frac{38{,}656}{54{,}675} = 0.707$$

Thus, there is more variation in marital status among the offenders than among the MS patients.

SUMMARY

Measures of central tendency indicate the centrality of the data, and measures of dispersion indicate the spread of the data away from the center. The mode, median, and mean each report a summary value of a typical or representative value of the data. The mode is the most frequent value found in the data, the median is the value that splits the distribution exactly in half, and the mean is the arithmetic average of the distribution. The mean is generally the most useful of the three measures. It is the most stable of the three, and it is the entry point for the calculation of more advanced statistics.

The range is a measure of the difference between the highest and lowest scores in the distribution. It is minimally useful because only the two extreme scores in the distribution are used in its calculation. Although the interquartile range is something of an improvement over the range, it also utilizes only two scores in its calculation. The sum of squares is the most basic of the measures of dispersion away from the mean. It is the sum of the squared differences between each score or observation and the mean. The variance is the sum of squares divided by N for populations and $N - 1$ for samples. We use $N - 1$ for samples to correct for the fact that there is more variance in populations than in samples. The standard deviation is the square root of the variance. The standard deviation plays a key role in many of the statistics we will be discussing.

The coefficient of variation is useful for comparing variation in different distributions with different means and/or when a variable being investigated is measured in different units, for example, time measured in days or months, price in dollars or francs, or temperature in Fehrenheit or Celsius. The index of qualitative variation provides a measure of variation of variables measured at the nominal or ordinal levels.

PRACTICE APPLICATION: CENTRAL TENDENCY AND DISPERSION

Compute the mean, mode, and median IQ for juvenile delinquents from the following data:

IQ Levels of Juvenile Delinquents

OBS.	X	X^2	OBS.	X	X^2	OBS.	X	X^2
1	72	5,184	11	90	8,100	21	100	10,000
2	78	6,084	12	90	8,100	22	100	10,000
3	80	6,400	13	90	8,100	23	100	10,000
4	81	6,561	14	90	8,100	24	105	11,025
5	83	6,889	15	90	8,100	25	111	12,321
6	84	7,056	16	94	8,836	26	112	12,544
7	85	7,225	17	94	8,836	27	113	12,769
8	85	7,225	18	95	9,025	28	114	12,996
9	88	7,744	19	95	9,025	29	120	14,400
10	88	7,744	20	95	9,025	30	120	14,400

Sum of $X = 2842$ Sum of $(X)^2 = 8076964$ Sum of $X^2 = 273814$

Compute the mean:

$$\bar{X} = \frac{\Sigma X}{N} = \frac{2842}{30} = 94.73$$

The mean = 94.73. The modal IQ is 90; more juveniles in the sample have an IQ of 90 than any other IQ value. Compute the median: Simply take the middle two values (90 and 94), and calculate their mean. Median = $90 + 94 = 184/2 = 92$. Half the scores are above this value and half are below it. The range is $120 - 72 = 48$, and the IQR is $Q_3 - Q_1$ ($100 - 85 = 15$).
Compute the standard deviation.

$$s = \sqrt{\frac{\Sigma X^2 - (\Sigma X)^2/N}{N-1}} = \sqrt{\frac{273,814 - 807,694/30}{29}}$$

$$= \sqrt{\frac{273,814 - 269,232.13}{29}} = \sqrt{4,581.86/29} = \sqrt{157.995} = 12.57$$

The standard deviation is 12.57 (rounded).

REFERENCE

Walsh, P. and Walsh A. (1987). "Self-Esteem and Disease Adaptation among Multiple Sclerosis Patients." *Journal of Social Psychology,* 127: 669–671.

PROBLEMS

1. Find the mean, median, and mode for the following distribution:

   3, 6, 7, 1, 2, 3, 3, 8

2. Find the mean, median, and mode for the following frequency distribution:

X	F
1	2
2	4
3	3
4	1
5	6
6	4

3. Indicate whether the following distributions would be skewed and if so, state the direction of the skew. Draw a sketch of each distribution.
   a) Income of the U.S. population
   b) Scores on a very easy test
   c) Intelligence scores for the U.S. population

4. For Problem 3, indicate whether the mean would be greater than, less than, or equal to the median.

5. Jean is thinking about buying a house. She has found one she likes but she doesn't know if she can afford the utility bills. The sellers tell her not to worry because the average bill is $50.50 per month. Calculate the median and find out if Jean should be worried.

MONTH	UTILITY BILL	MONTH	UTILITY BILL
January	75.00	July	11.00
February	72.00	August	12.00
March	70.00	September	30.00
April	56.00	October	70.00
May	53.00	November	72.00
June	10.00	December	75.00

6. The following represents the number of hours of television watched in a week by a group of sixth graders:

24	29	10	28	7
14	21	14	16	16
10	17	13	17	15
5	12	11	11	10
12	14	22	12	21

   a) Calculate the mean, median, and mode using the raw score procedure.

b) Interpret the above measures of central tendency.
c) Group the data using an interval width of 5.
d) Recalculate the mean, median, and mode.
e) Compare parts (a) and (d). Which is more accurate?

7. The following is a grouped frequency of the clocked time in minutes for runners in a race:

TIMES	FREQUENCY
18.0–18.9	2
17.0–17.9	3
16.0–16.9	5
15.0–15.9	15
14.0–14.9	16
13.0–13.9	12
12.0–12.9	2

a) Graph the distribution.
b) Calculate the median.
c) Calculate the mean.
d) Is there a skew?

8. Find the range and the standard deviation for the following sets of scores:
a) 2, 4, 17, 15, 13, 2, 1, 18
b) 422, 618, 974, 284, 367, 792
c) 16.93, 17.92, 12.31, 25.62, 12.91, 10.16
d) 2, 3, 6, 9

9. The following is a frequency distribution for the number of hours mothers spend in child care per week:

NUMBER OF HOURS (X)	FREQUENCY
50–59	3
40–49	7
30–39	14
20–29	32
10–19	13
0–9	4

a) Find the mean and the median.
b) Find Q_1 and Q_3.
c) Find the interquartile range.
d) Calculate the standard deviation.
e) Interpret your findings.

10. Calculate the standard deviation of the grouped data in Problem 7.

11. The following data represent the temperature recorded in the morning at the airport in Duluth, Minnesota, for each day in the month of May:

72	55	80	36	66	62
70	55	60	42	68	
66	66	52	51	69	
32	72	43	51	68	
41	75	42	60	62	
42	75	38	62	58	

a) Find the average May temperature.
b) Find the median May temperature.
c) Find the variance and standard deviation.
d) Find the range.
e) Interpret your findings.

12. The following data represent the scores out of a possible 100 points for a statistics class. Using the data, calculate the mean, median, and standard deviation for this sample. Draw a histogram and interpret your findings.

48	42	80	61
72	63	91	72
71	71	78	74
62	73	63	82
56	74	52	67

13. The following grouped frequency distribution represents the scores on the LSAT (Law School Entrance Exam) for a group of college juniors. The highest possible score is a 48.
a) Calculate the mean, median, and standard deviation for these data.

LSAT SCORE (X)	FREQUENCY
46–48	1
43–45	2
40–42	7
37–39	18
34–36	26
31–33	17
28–30	9
25–27	3
22–24	2

b) Calculate the interquartile range.
c) Interpret your findings.

14. The mean score on a statistics midterm exam last year was 75 with a standard deviation of 12. This year, the average score in the statistics class was 78 with a standard deviation of 10. Calculate and interpret the coefficient of variation.

15. The following table lists the frequencies of different majors for two classes of students. Calculate and interpret the index of qualitative variation.

MAJOR	CLASS 1	CLASS 2
Sociology	5	8
Psychology	12	9
Political Science	10	9
Economics	2	6
Undeclared	1	2

16. The average cost of college tuition in the northwestern United States is $2,580 per semester with a standard deviation of $430. Across the border, in Canada, the average tuition is $1,490 per semester with a standard deviation of $1,000. Does the United States or Canada have more variation in their tuition costs?

17. Sales by region for different sales teams are listed below. Which sales team wins the award for greatest variation? Which team wins the award for selling the most?

REGION	TEAM A	TEAM B	TEAM C
North	520	22	890
South	492	153	712
East	511	1720	921
West	471	155	745

Chapter 4

Probability and the Normal Curve

PROBABILITY

The mathematical basis of statistical analysis is the idea of **probability,** which provides a basis for making predictions. Statistical statements are statements of probability, not of determinism. We do not say that given A, B will occur. This is a deterministic statement. Rather, we might make a statement such as "Given A, B has a 0.33 probability of occurring." We are all familiar with probability statements such as "The chances of rolling a 6 in one throw of a fair die are 1 in 6," "There is a 60 percent chance of rain through tomorrow morning," or "The chances of a cancer patient surviving for five years after diagnosis is 75 percent."

The first probability statement, regarding a throw of a die, is an example of classical probability; the second two statements are examples of empirical probability. *Classical probability* is probability based on *a priori* knowledge of all possible numerical values. Each throw of a fair die is a random event, with any one of six die values being equally probable for any toss. The variables (dice, cards, coins, etc.) on which classical probability is based are called *random variables* because, assuming fairness, each has an equal numerical chance of occurring. That is, each of the six values of a die have a 1/6 probability of coming up, each card in a shuffled deck has a 1/52 chance of being drawn, and a head or a tail is equally likely each time a coin is tossed. This is not to say that it is impossible to get four heads in four tosses of a coin, although it is not very likely. We do expect heads to come up 50% of the time in the long run, however. There is something called the *law of large numbers*, which tells us that the observed proportion will come closer and closer to the expected proportion (in this case, 0.50) as the number of trials increases.

Empirical probability is based on observation. When meteorologists talk about a 60% chance of rain, they mean that based on previous occasions when weather patterns were similar, it rained about 60 times out of 100. Probability in the real world is empirical probability. In other words, outcomes do not rest on pure chance in the same way as does the fall of a fair coin. Although the statistics in the rest of this book result from empirical observations, classical probability is very useful for the demonstration of some basic principles of probability.

THE MULTIPLICATION RULE

Suppose we want to determine the probability of getting two heads on two tosses of a fair coin. For each toss of the coin the probability of getting a head is equal to one-half, or 0.50. Each successive toss is independent of the outcomes of previous tosses. That is, what happens on the first toss does not in any way influence what happens on the second. The probability of getting a head (or tail) remains 0.50 regardless of how many times you toss the coin. If you want to determine the probability of two independent events occurring, such as two heads in two tosses of a fair coin, you must multiply the two independent probabilities. This is known as the **multiplication rule,** which has two forms. One is based on mutually exclusive (independent) outcomes, and the other on nonindependent (conditional) outcomes. For independent outcomes, the multiplication rule is:

MULTIPLICATION RULE. The probability of two *independent* events (A and B) occurring is equal to the product of their respective probabilities.

$$P(AB) = P(A) \times P(B) \qquad \text{where A and B are independent events}$$

The probability of two heads in two tosses is $(0.5)(0.5) = 0.25$; the probability of three heads in three tosses is $(0.5)(0.5)(0.5) = 0.125$; and so on.

If the outcomes A and B are not independent of one another, the multiplication rule is:

MULTIPLICATION RULE. The probability of two *dependent* events occurring together is the product of the probability of A and the probability of B given A.

$$P(AB) = P(A) \times P(B/A) \text{ where } P(B/A) \text{ is the probability of B, given A has already occurred.}$$

Behavioral scientists often want to know the probability of joint occurrences far more complex than the simple coin-tossing experiment. For instance, suppose we have a random sample of 200 men. Of these, 120 are white and 70 are opposed to affirmative action. The other 80 men are black, 20 of whom are opposed to affirmative action. We select an individual at random from the sample: What is the probability that a person is white and an opponent of affirmative action? The probability of being white is $120/200 = 0.6$. The probability of being opposed to affirmative action, given that he is white $= 70/120 = 0.5833$. Therefore, $P(AB) = P(A) \times P(B/A) = (0.6)(0.583) = 0.35$. We can verify our answer with the general probability formula, which is

$$P = \frac{\text{Number of ways the event can occur}}{\text{Total number of possible outcomes}} = \frac{70}{200} = 0.35$$

THE ADDITION RULE

Another probability rule you should be familiar with is the **addition rule.** To take a simple example: For the roll of a die, the probability of a 3 or a 5 is simply the sum of their respective probabilities $(1/6 + 1/6 = 0.333)$. We are able to add these probabilities together because there are only six possible mutually exclusive outcomes, and each face of a die has an equal chance of coming up. The addition rule for two independent outcomes occurring is thus $P(A \text{ or } B) = P(A) + P(B)$, or the sum of their respective probabilities.

To go back to our affirmative action example, what if we wanted to determine the probability that a man selected at random from the sample is white *or* an opponent of affirmative action? We know that the probability is 0.6 that a man in our sample is white. The probability of being opposed to affirmative action is $90/200 = 0.45$. If we simply sum these two probabilities we get 1.05. This would be the same as summing the number of whites (120) and the number of men opposed to affirmative action (90) and dividing by the total sample N $(210/200 = 1.05)$. Such an outcome is a logical impossibility because the probability of anything cannot exceed 1. We have exceeded 1 because there is an overlapping of occurrences of outcomes; that is, they are not mutually exclusive outcomes. If we roll a 3 on a die, all other numbers are automatically excluded for that roll, but being white does not automatically tell us whether a man is in favor of or opposed to affirmative action.

In fact, we have counted a number of men twice. Seventy of the 90 men opposed to affirmative action are white, and we already accounted for all whites when we broke the sample down by race. We cannot count them again when we break the sample down

TABLE 4.1   Race and Affirmative Action

AFFIRMATIVE ACTION	RACE		
	White	Black	Total
Oppose	70	20	90
Favor	50	60	110
Total	120	80	200

by opposition to affirmative action. To eliminate this overlap of probabilities, we have to add the individual probabilities and subtract the probability of their joint occurrence, which we know from the previous example to be 0.35. This is known as the addition rule for nonmutually exclusive occurrences.

ADDITION RULE. The probability of either of two nonmutually exclusive events occurring is equal to the sum of their respective probabilities minus the probability of their joint occurrence.

$$P(A \text{ or } B) = P(A) + P(B) - P(A \text{ and } B)$$

where A and B are not mutually exclusive.

Thus, the probability of selecting a white male *or* an opponent of affirmative action is

$$P(A \text{ or } B) = P(A) + P(B) - P(A \text{ and } B) =$$
$$P(A \text{ or } B) = (0.6) + (0.45) - (0.35) = 1.05 - 0.35 = 0.70$$

Another way of making the idea clear is to put the observations in a table as in Table 4.1. You can then ask yourself which of the cell values satisfies the requirement of being white *or* an opponent of affirmative action. There are 120 males who satisfy the requirement of being white. A total of 90 males are opposed to affirmative action, but we can only count the 20 blacks who are opposed because we already counted the 70 whites who are opposed when we classified them by race. The only value that does not satisfy our criteria is the 60 blacks in the lower right of the table (that is, they are neither white nor opposed to affirmative action). So we count 70 + 50 + 20 = 140, and then divide the sum by the total number of males: 140/200 = 0.70. Putting a probability problem into a table such as this helps us to visualize the situation.

Let us illustrate the two rules of probability for independent outcomes with a sociological example. It has been estimated that less than 1% of marriages in the United States are interracial (Reiss & Lee, 1988, p. 297). What if there were no cultural, economic, or psychological barriers to interracial marriage? How many interracial marriages might we expect if marriages were determined simply by chance? Let us assume that the racial groups in the United States break down according to the following proportions: white = 0.76, black = 0.14, and other = 0.10. Let us also assume that there is an equal number of men and women in each race. Under these conditions the probabilities of inter- and intraracial marriages would be as shown in Table 4.2. The multiplication rule is illustrated by the probabilities of marrying either into one's own race or into another (two independent events under the conditions we have assumed). The addition rule for mutually exclusive events is illustrated in the summation of the proportion of inter- and intraracial marriages expected under the assumed conditions (marrying a person of one race automatically excludes marrying a person of another, at least at the same

TABLE 4.2   Probabilities of Inter- and Intraracial Marriages
under Assumed Conditions

RACES		PROPORTIONS
Intraracial marriages		
White/white	(0.76)(0.76)	0.5776
Black/black	(0.14)(0.14)	0.0196
Other/other	(0.10)(0.10)	0.0100
Proportion of intraracial marriages		**0.6072**
Interracial marriages		
White/black	(0.76)(0.14)	0.1064
White/other	(0.76)(0.10)	0.0760
Black/white	(0.14)(0.76)	0.1064
Black/other	(0.14)(0.10)	0.0140
Other/white	(0.10)(0.76)	0.0760
Other/black	(0.10)(0.14)	0.0140
Proportion of interracial marriages		**0.3928**
Total marriages		**1.000**

time). Because they are mutually exclusive events, we can simply sum the individual probabilities.

There is no doubt that the percentage of interracial marriages expected under conditions of pure chance (39.28%) is a long way from the situation described by Reiss and Lee. This gap might be considered an indicator of the sociocultural distance between the races in this country. We make this statement on the basis of the very large difference between the expected and observed percentages. Many statistics we will be discussing are built around comparisons of observed and expected distributions, and the tools enabling us to make such comparisons are theoretical probability distributions.

THEORETICAL PROBABILITY DISTRIBUTIONS

Another reason for discussing classical probability is its usefulness in showing how theoretical distributions of common and rare events are constructed. These distributions are actually theoretical probability distributions for random variables. They are not empirical distributions, such as the "years diagnosed" and IQ distributions shown in the last chapter. However, theoretical probability distributions are indispensable to the statistical interpretation of empirical distributions, and the most important is the normal distribution for continuous random variables. We will discuss this distribution at length later in this chapter. Another probability distribution is the binomial probability distribution for discrete random variables (*binomial* means two distinct, either/or events, such as coin tossing).

Let us construct a binomial distribution by tossing coins. If we toss three fair coins, there are eight possible outcomes: HHH, HHT, HTH, THH, TTH, THT, HTT, TTT. Suppose we want to determine the probability of getting *just* two heads (no more, no less) in three tosses. Checking our eight possibilities, we see that three of them had just two heads (HHT, HTH, and THH). As already indicated, for discrete events the probability of any random event occurring is the ratio of the number of ways the event can occur to the total number of possible outcomes. We have determined that just two heads can occur three ways, and that the total number of possible outcomes in three tosses is eight. Therefore, the probability of two heads in three tosses = 3/8 = 0.375.

This example was fairly easy to compute without resorting to a mathematical formula. But what if instead of three tosses we toss the coin 10 times, or even 100 times? Determining the possible number of unique outcomes by listing them as we did with three tosses would be a formidable task. Luckily, there is a simple formula for determining the number of possible outcomes:

$$_nC_r = \frac{N!}{r!(N-r)!} \qquad (4.1)$$

where $\quad C =$ number of combinations, outcomes, sequences, or successes
$\qquad\quad N =$ number of trials
$\qquad\quad r \,=$ number of successes
$\qquad\quad ! \,=$ factorial (the product of all positive integers from N to 1).

For purposes of illustration, let us apply the formula to the three-toss example. We have three trials, so $N = 3$. We want to determine the number of ways we can get two heads, so $r = 2$. The factorial (!) means that we start at $N(3)$ and determine the product of all positive integers from 3 to 1($3 \times 2 \times 1$). The complete calculation is

$$\frac{3 \times 2 \times 1}{2 \times (1)!} = \frac{6}{2} = 3$$

The next step is to determine the probability of observing two heads in three tosses by using formula (4.2):

$$_nP_r = \frac{N!}{r!(N-r)!}\, p^r q^{n-r} \qquad (4.2)$$

where p is the probability, $q = 1 - p$, P is the probability of success on one toss (0.5), and q is $1 - p$, or $1 - 0.5 = 0.5$. The formula applied to the problem of the probability of getting two heads in three tosses is

$$_nP_r \frac{3!}{2!(3-2)!}\, p^2 q^{3-2} = \frac{3 \times 2 \times 1}{2 \times 1 \times 1}(0.5^2)(0.5^1)$$

$$= 3(0.25)(0.5) \,=\, 3(0.125) = 0.375$$

If we were calculating the probability of getting four heads from 10 tosses, the calculations would be as follows. Note that p^4 means that the probability of a single success (0.5) is multiplied by itself four times.

$$_nP_r = \frac{10!}{4!(10-4)!}\, p^4 q^{10-4}$$

$$\frac{10 \times 9 \times 8 \times 7 \times 6 \times 5 \times 4 \times 3 \times 2 \times 1}{(4 \times 3 \times 2 \times 1)(6 \times 5 \times 4 \times 3 \times 2 \times 1)}(0.5^4)(0.5^6)$$

Canceling,

$$= \frac{\cancel{10} \times \cancel{9} \times 8 \times 7 \times \cancel{6} \times \cancel{5} \times \cancel{4} \times \cancel{3} \times 2 \times \cancel{1}}{(\cancel{4} \times \cancel{3} \times 2 \times 1)(\cancel{6} \times \cancel{5} \times \cancel{4} \times \cancel{3} \times 2 \times \cancel{1})} = \frac{210}{1}(0.0625)(0.015625)$$

$$= (210)(0.000976562) = 0.2051$$

Let us now construct a binomial distribution by the simple operation of tossing a fair coin 10 times. The discrete random variable in this exercise is the exact number of heads in 10 tosses. There are 11 possible outcomes (0 heads, 1 head, 2 heads, . . . , 10 heads). Each of these outcomes has a number of ways it can occur, and each probability is computed by formula (4.2). By the multiplication rule, each outcome has a $p^r - q^{n-r}$ probability of occurring, which is equal to 0.000976562, or 1/1024. To arrive at the probability of a given outcome, you multiply the number of ways that outcome can occur by 1/1024. For example, 5 heads in 10 tosses can occur in 252 ways. Therefore, $(252)(1/1024) = 0.2460937$ is the probability of exactly 5 heads in 10 tosses of a fair coin. Note that 0 and 10 heads have the same probability of occurrence, as does 1 and 9 heads, and so on. (Note that 0! equals 1, as does any number raised to the zero power.) The calculations have been done for you and appear in Table 4.3. The first column of Table 4.3 lists the 11 possible outcomes. The second column lists the number of ways each outcome can occur. The third column shows the probabilities for each way. Note that these probabilities are equal, as demanded by the symmetry of $(p)(q)$. The fourth column shows the probability of the outcome.

This probability distribution serves as a standard by which we can judge empirical, or real-life, outcomes. If we wanted to test the fairness of a suspect coin, for instance, we could actually toss it in the air 10 times and compare the observed outcome to the theoretically expected outcome. If the empirical outcome departs significantly (we have ways of quantifying what we mean by *significantly*, but that discussion comes in Chapter 6) from the theoretically expected outcome, we reject the notion that the coin is a fair one. As we have previously indicated, inferential statistics are built around comparisons of observed and theoretically expected outcomes.

We now display all 11 probabilities in the probability curve of Figure 4.1. Note that the curve is perfectly symmetrical, indicating that low outcomes (e.g., 0 or 1 head) are just as probable as high outcomes (e.g., 10 and 9 heads). Its highest point is the most probable outcome, and its lowest points are the least probable outcomes. As is always the case, the area underneath the probability curve is 100%, or unity.

TABLE 4.3   Binomial Probability Distribution Where $N = 10$ and $P = 0.5$

NUMBER OF HEADS	$_nC_r$	$(p^r)(q^{n-r})$	PROBABILITY
0 heads	1	$(1/2)^0(1/2)^{10} = 1/1024*$	1/1024 = 0.0009765
1 heads	10	$(1/2)^1(1/2)^9 = 1/1024$	10/1024 = 0.0097650
2 heads	45	$(1/2)^2(1/2)^8 = 1/1024$	45/1024 = 0.0439453
3 heads	120	$(1/2)^3(1/2)^7 = 1/1024$	120/1024 = 0.1171875
4 heads	210	$(1/2)^4(1/2)^6 = 1/1024$	210/1024 = 0.2050781
5 heads	252	$(1/2)^5(1/2)^5 = 1/1024$	252/1024 = 0.2460937
6 heads	210	$(1/2)^6(1/2)^4 = 1/1024$	210/1024 = 0.2050781
7 heads	120	$(1/2)^7(1/2)^3 = 1/1024$	120/1024 = 0.1171875
8 heads	45	$(1/2)^8(1/2)^2 = 1/1024$	45/1024 = 0.0439453
9 heads	10	$(1/2)^9(1/2)^1 = 1/1024$	10/1024 = 0.0097650
10 heads	1	$(1/2)^{10}(1/2)^0 = 1/1024$	1/1024 = 0.0009765

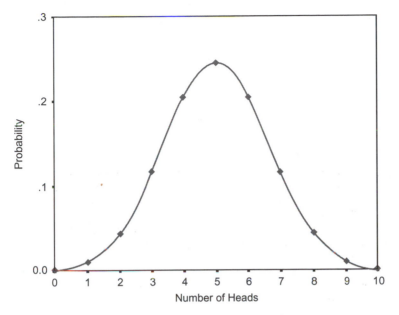

FIGURE 4.1. A probability line graph for the data in Table 4.2.

If we were to make 1,000 tosses of a fair coin rather than 10 we would have 1,001 possible values rather than 11.

THE NORMAL CURVE

As we noted in the last chapter, the mean and the standard deviation are powerful ways of describing distributions of interval- and ratio-level variables. We also noted that the means of the distributions we have examined so far fall at differing points along the horizontal axis of the frequency distributions, and that about two-thirds of the observations fall between ±1 standard deviation from their mean. It would be nice if we had some ideal distribution against which we could compare our observed distributions. As we have seen, there is such a distribution, called the normal distribution, the bell-shaped curve, or the **normal curve.**

The normal curve is a probability distribution for continuous random variables that is entirely specified by two parameters, its mean (μ) and its standard deviation (σ). By normal we do not mean that it is the typical or most often observed distribution, although we do find rough approximations with fair regularity in large samples. *Normal* is used in the sense that the curve is a norm, or idealized version, of a distribution against which we can compare the distributions we obtain in our research. It is a completely hypothetical curve, with a number of special attributes. It is perfectly symmetrical and smooth, and it is unimodal (it has only one mode). The tails of the curve never touch the horizontal axis. Technically, we say that the normal curve is asymptotic to the *x* axis. This property reflects the assumption that any score, value, or outcome is theoretically possible, although extreme values are highly unlikely.

When we say that the normal curve is perfectly symmetrical we mean that each side of a curve split in the middle by its mean occupies exactly one-half of its total area.

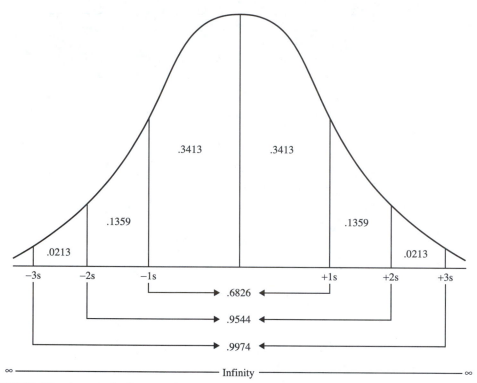

FIGURE 4.2.   Areas under the normal curve.

This means also that precisely 50% of the observations are on one side of its center and 50% are on the other side. Further, exactly 68.26% of the total area of the curve falls between ±1 standard deviation, exactly 95.44% of the area falls between ±2 standard deviations, and exactly 99.74% of the area falls between ±3 standard deviations. These proportions under the normal curve are not tied to any particular distribution of scores. They are strictly a distribution of probabilities that can be generalized to any empirical distribution more or less regardless of their measurement units and the number of observations involved. Figure 4.2 presents the distribution of the area under the normal curve.

Summing these proportions under the curve, you will note that you get 0.9974 rather than unity. This result reflects the fact that scores that deviate from the mean further than ±3 standard deviations are possible. Such highly unlikely scores account for the remainder of the area (0.0026, or 0.0013 on either side). In a sample of 10,000 we would expect only 13 cases more than 3 standard deviations below the mean and 13 cases more than 3 standard deviations above the mean.

It might help you to understand if we conceptualized these proportions or percentages of the area under the normal curve as numbers of observations in a sample. Suppose that we had a random sample of 1,000 observations of male heights (a variable that is roughly normally distributed). In such a sample we should find about 683 cases within ±1 standard deviation of the mean, about 954 between ±2 standard deviations, and about 997 within ±3 standard deviations. If our mean is 5 feet 9 inches and our standard deviation is 3 inches, we would observe the distribution of cases shown in Figure 4.3. With a truly representative sample of all males in the population we would

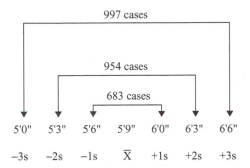

FIGURE 4.3. Number of cases in a normal distribution of male heights (*N* = 1,000).

expect to find only about three males that were either shorter than 5 feet 0 inches or taller than 6 feet 6 inches. The unlikelihood of finding extreme cases or scores beyond 2 or 3 standard deviations is something you should thoroughly digest for future reference.

The smoothness of the curve is based on the theoretical assumption of an infinite number of observations. Because the normal curve is a distribution of probabilities rather than empirical frequencies, we observe no peaks, valleys, or gaps in the normal distribution as we did in the empirical distributions in Chapters 2 and 3. This fact has an important implication for research in that it suggests that the larger the sample size, the more the distribution of scores will approximate the normal curve if the underlying population is normally distributed.

DIFFERENT KINDS OF CURVES

A curve may be perfectly symmetrical (i.e., each side of the curve may be the same size and shape) but not be normal. In fact, there are theoretically an infinite number of different symmetrical curves, although they all contain the same proportion of observations within their standard deviation units regardless of their height or width. As mentioned earlier, the shape of the curve is determined entirely by the mean and standard deviation. The formidable-looking equation for the curve might convince you of this if you are a fair mathematician. Note that π and e are constants (they do not vary), so the only values that do vary are μ and σ.

$$Y = \frac{1}{\sigma\sqrt{2\pi}}\, e^{-(x-\mu)^2/2\sigma^2} \quad \text{Normal curve equation}$$

Fortunately, you will never have to construct a normal curve for yourself, but the formula should convince you that curves can differ infinitely according to their means and standard deviations. They may be tall and thin relative to the theoretical normal curve, indicating a small amount of variation around the mean. Such a curve is called **leptokurtic** (from the Greek term *lepto*, meaning *thin*), as shown in the top curve of Figure 4.4. A curve that is wide and flat relative to the theoretical normal curve, indicating a great deal of variation around the mean, is called **platykurtic** (*flat*), as in the bottom curve of Figure 4.4. A **mesokurtic** (*middle*) curve is a curve with a normal scatter of observations about its mean, as is the theoretical normal curve shown in Figure 4.2. Notice that the curves in Figure 4.4 have the same mean but different standard deviations. The reason why these curves differ in height is that the area under the curve is unity (100%). Therefore, it follows that as the base of the curve expands

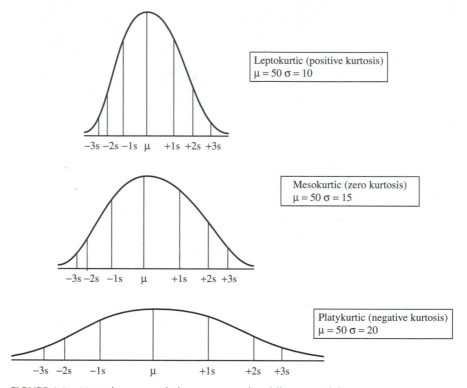

FIGURE 4.4.   Normal curves with the same mean but different variability.

(indicating a large σ) or shrinks (indicating a small σ), the height must decrease or increase accordingly to keep the area constant.

THE STANDARD NORMAL CURVE

The **standard normal curve** is a special case of the normal distribution curve in that it has a mean of zero and a standard deviation of 1. The utility of the standard normal curve is that any normally distributed variable can be transformed into a standardized distribution, allowing a single reference distribution for comparing otherwise noncomparable statistics. For instance, if we wished to compare the IQ of one of our juvenile delinquents with the IQ of one of our adult criminals it would be difficult because the two different distributions have different means and standard deviations. Standardizing both distributions to a mean of zero and a standard deviation of 1 renders such comparisons meaningful. To do so we will compute what are called z *scores*. But first we will look at the distribution of IQ scores in our offender data. Because we have 376 cases for which we have IQ data, we can expect a good approximation of the normal curve. The distribution of IQ scores for the offender data is presented in Table 4.4.

A visual inspection of the distribution in Table 4.4 suggests that this distribution is very close to normal. If we rounded the mean to the nearest whole number, the mean, median, and mode would all be 94, and the skewness and kurtosis statistics values are quite small.

TABLE 4.4   Distribution of Offender IQ

IQ	TALLY	FREQ.	CUM. FREQ.	PERCENT	CUM. PERCENT
60	X	2	2	0.53	0.53
66	XX	2	4	0.53	1.06
68	XXXXX	5	9	1.33	2.39
70	XXXXXXXX	8	17	2.13	4.52
72	XXX	3	20	0.80	5.32
74	XXXXXXX	7	27	1.86	7.18
76	XXXXXXXXXXXXX	13	40	3.46	10.64
78	XXXXXXXXXX	10	50	2.66	13.30
80	XXXXXXXXXXX	11	61	2.93	16.22
82	XXXXXX	6	67	1.60	17.82
84	XXXXXXXXXXXXXXXXXXXXXXXXX	25	92	6.65	24.47
86	XXXXXXXXXXXXXXX	15	107	3.99	28.46
88	XXXXXXXXXXXXXXXX	16	123	4.26	32.71
90	XXXXXXXXXXXXXXXXXXXXXXXXXXXXXXX	31	154	8.24	40.96
92	XXXXXXXXXXXXXXXXXXXXXXXXXXXXXXX	31	185	8.24	49.20
94	XXXXXXXXXXXXXXXXXXXXXXXXXXXXXXXXXX	34	219	9.04	58.28
96	XXXXXXXXXXX	12	231	3.19	61.44
98	XXXXXXXXXXXXXXXXXXXXXX	22	253	5.85	67.29
100	XXXXXXXXXXXXXXXXXXXXXXXXXXXXXXX	31	285	8.51	75.80
102	XXXXXXXXXXXXXXXXXXXXX	21	306	5.59	81.38
104	XXXXXXXXXXXXXXXXXXXXX	21	327	5.59	86.97
106	XXXXX	6	333	1.60	88.56
108	XXXXXXXXXXXX	12	345	3.19	91.76
110	XXXXXXXXXXXX	12	357	3.19	94.95
114	XXXXXXX	7	364	1.86	96.81
116	X	1	365	0.27	97.07
118	X	1	366	0.27	97.34
120	XXXXX	5	371	1.33	98.67
122	X	1	372	0.27	98.94
124	X	1	373	0.27	99.20
126	X	1	374	0.27	99.47
140	XX	2	376	0.53	100.00

N	376	Sum	35,179	Mean	93.561
Variance	148.359	Std Dev	12.180	Kurtosis	0.743
Skewness	0.182	Range	80	Mode	94
Median	94				

THE Z SCORES

The **z scores** are a way of tying the theoretical probability distribution to empirical raw scores. When we convert raw scores into z scores, the distribution of scores is standardized to the theoretical normal curve. There is nothing esoteric about standardizing scores. Banks do it when they standardize or convert foreign currency to the U.S. dollar so that they can have a common basis for comparing the value of British pounds, German marks, French francs, Mexican pesos, and so on. The point is that standardizing does not in any way alter the value of the underlying variable. The distance from point A to point B is the same whether rendered in miles or kilometers. The formula for converting raw scores to z scores is

$$z = \frac{x - \overline{X}}{s}$$

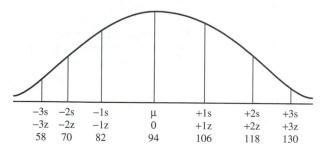

FIGURE 4.5. Standard deviations and *z* units of the standardized normal curve and equivalent raw scores from the offender IQ data.

where *x* is an individual score. A *z* score tells us the number of standard deviations a score lies above or below its mean. A positive *z* score is above the mean, and a negative *z* score is below the mean. In essence, *z* scores are synonymous with standard deviation units. Figure 4.5 graphically demonstrates this equivalence, using the offender IQ data and rounding the mean and standard deviations.

To demonstrate the usefulness of *z* scores, let us take an individual from our offender data with an IQ of 106 and transform this raw score into a *z* score:

$$z = \frac{x - \overline{X}}{s} = \frac{106 - 94}{12} = \frac{12}{12} = 1.00$$

A *z* score of 1.00 means that this individual has a score that lies 1 standard deviation above the mean. We saw in Figure 4.2 that 0.3413 of the total area under the normal curve lies between the mean and $+1s$. Below the mean lies 0.50 of the total area. To find the total area of the curve corresponding to a *z* score of 1.0, we simply sum those two proportions to get 0.8413. This strategy is demonstrated graphically in Figure 4.6.

What this means in substantive terms is that an offender with an IQ score of 106 has an IQ higher than 84.13% of the offenders in the sample. Conversely, his IQ score is lower than 15.85% of the sample. In other words, he scores higher than about 316 of the other subjects in the sample and lower than about 60.

Let us now take an individual from our sample of juvenile delinquents who also has an IQ of 106 and compute his *z* score. The mean IQ for the juvenile delinquents is 92.2 and the standard deviation is 10.5. We will not round our figures this time.

$$z = \frac{x - \overline{X}}{s} = \frac{106 - 94.2}{10.5} = \frac{13.8}{10.5} = 1.31$$

FIGURE 4.6.

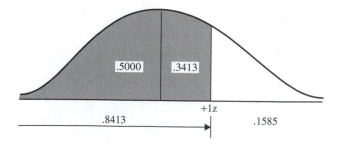

TABLE 4.5   Section of the Area under the Normal Curve Table

z	0.00	0.01	0.02	0.03	0.04	0.05	0.06
1.0	.3413	.3438	.3461	.3485	.3508	.3531	.3554
1.1	.3643	.3665	.3686	.3718	.3729	.3749	.3770
1.2	.3849	.3869	.3888	.3907	.3925	.3944	.3962
1.3	.4032	**.4049**	.4066	.4083	.4099	.4115	.4131
1.4	.4192	.4207	.4222	.4236	.4251	.4265	.4279
1.5	.4332	.4345	.4357	.4370	.4382	.4394	.4406
1.6	.4452	.4463	.4474	.4485	.4495	.4505	.4515

A *z* score of 1.31 is not readily converted to an area under the curve by visual inspection. Luckily, there is a table in which areas under the curve for any *z* score have been precisely determined. This **normal curve table** is presented in Appendix A. Table 4.5 reproduces a small portion of this table for our present use. The four-digit numbers in the body of the table represent areas of the curve falling between a given *z* score and the mean. The numbers in the column at the far left are the first two digits of the *z* score, and the numbers in the top row correspond to the third digit of the *z* score. A *z* score of 1.0, for instance, is located at the top left-hand corner of the table (0.3413). To find the area corresponding to our computed *z* score of 1.31, go down the column until you reach the value of 1.3. Then go across that row until you come to the third digit of 1.31, which is 0.01. The value you find there is 4049. You can read this as either a proportion (0.4049) or a percentage (40.49%) of the area under the normal curve from the mean. The total area under the curve corresponding to a *z* score of 1.31 is this value plus the area below the mean (0.5000 + 0.4049 = 0.9049). Our juvenile delinquent with an IQ of 106 has a score that exceeds 90.49% of all the other scores in the sample (see Figure 4.7). An important point for you to remember is that the probability of finding a juvenile delinquent with an IQ score of 106 or higher is only about 10% (only about 10% of the area of the curve contains scores that high or higher).

We now have a basis for comparing similar IQs across two different samples. Although both the juvenile and the adult had an IQ of 106, the juvenile scores better relative to his peers in the sample. We could also compare scores of an individual on different attributes by using *z* scores. For instance, we might want to know if our delinquent's number of years of schooling is as high relative to his delinquent peers as his IQ is. In other words, do his years of schooling exceed the mean number of years of schooling for the sample by as many *z* units as his IQ exceeds the mean IQ?

FIGURE 4.7.

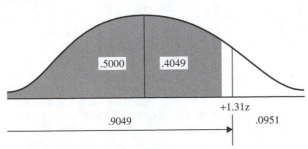

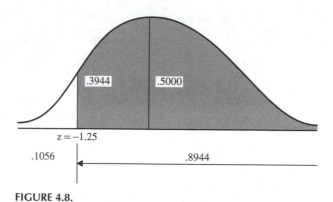

FIGURE 4.8.

FINDING AREA OF THE CURVE BELOW THE MEAN

What if an adult offender scored 79 on an IQ test? How many of his peers would score higher or lower than he did? His z score would be $(79 - 94)/12 = -1.25$. Ignoring the negative sign for the moment, we see that the area corresponding with a z score of 1.25 is 0.3944. Because the sign is negative, this figure corresponds with 39.44% of the area *below* the mean. Note that in the negative case the z-score area is subtracted from 0.5000 rather than added to it. An offender with an IQ of 79 scores higher than only about 10% of his peers in the sample and lower than about 90% (see Figure 4.8).

On occasion you may wish to determine the area under the curve between two scores rather than simply the area above or below the mean. For example, suppose that we wanted to determine what proportion or percentage of our adult offenders had IQ scores considered to be in the normal range between 90 and 110. The first thing you would do is convert these two raw scores (90 and 110) into z scores:

$$\text{Raw score } 90: \quad z = \frac{90 - 94}{12} = \frac{-4}{12} = -0.33$$

$$\text{Raw score } 110: \quad z = \frac{110 - 94}{12} = \frac{16}{12} = 1.33$$

Since we have not included z scores as low as 0.33 in Table 4.5 you will have to turn to Appendix A to complete this exercise. The first two digits are 0.3. Tracing along this row until you reach the final digit (0.03), you will find an area of 0.1293, which corresponds to the area below the mean. For our second z score of 1.33, the area is 0.4082, which corresponds to the area above the mean. To find the total proportion of the area corresponding to IQ scores of 90 and 110, you simply sum the two areas $(0.1293 + 0.4082 = 0.5375)$. Thus, 53.75% of our offenders had IQs in the normal range (see Figure 4.9).

If you wanted to find the area between two positive z scores, say, 0.50 and 1.55, you would first find the areas lying between the mean and 0.50 (0.1915) and 1.55 (0.4394). Having done so you would then subtract the smaller area from the larger $(0.4394 - 0.1915. = 0.2479)$. The area of the curve between z scores of 0.50 and 1.55 is 24.79% (see Figure 4.10). A similar strategy would be followed if both z scores were negative.

In our examples so far we have started with a known score, computed z, and then found the corresponding area of the curve. We will now illustrate the reverse process. Suppose, for instance, we wish to know between what two IQ scores in our offender data do the middle 50% of the cases fall. If we start from the mean, a figure of 50% means that 25%

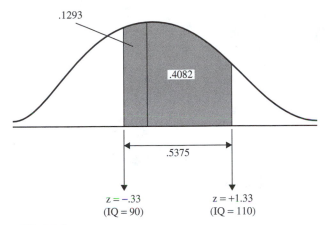

FIGURE 4.9.

of the cases will be below the mean and 25% will be above the mean. We turn to Appendix A to find what z score is associated with an area of 0.2500. The closest value in the table is 0.2486, which is associated with a z score of 0.67. A z score of 0.67 is 67% of 1 standard deviation $(0.67)(12) = 8.04$. Adding and subtracting 8 (rounded) from the mean, we find that the middle 50% of the cases fall between IQ values of 86 and 102 (see Figure 4.11).

Let us sum up some of the things we have learned about the normal curve. First, it is a probability distribution in which the total number of observations under it equals 100%. It contains a central area, under which most of the observations are to be found, and increasingly smaller areas on both sides of the central area, where fewer and fewer observations are found. The normal curve is basically a distribution of probabilities analogous to the probability line graph of Figure 4.1.

We can even calculate an approximate standard deviation and mean for binomial events like coin-tossing outcomes. Suppose we flip a fair coin 400 times and observe that it falls heads 220 times and tails 180 times. If only chance is operating we would, of course, expect 200 heads and 200 tails, or something very close to it. The mean of the binomial distribution (μ_b) is equal to $(N)(p)$, in the present case, $400(0.5) = 200$. We now have to ask ourselves what the probability is of observing 220 heads and 180 tails in

FIGURE 4.10.
Area of the curve between $z = +0.50$ and $z = +1.55$: $0.4394 - 0.1915 = 0.2479$

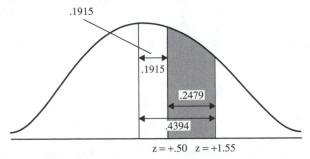

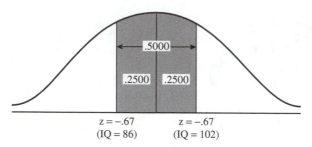

FIGURE 4.11.

400 tosses. Before we can determine this figure we have to calculate the standard deviation according to the formula

$$s = \sqrt{N(p)(q)} \qquad \text{where } p = \text{proportion of heads}$$
$$q = \text{proportion of non-heads (i.e., proportion of tails)}$$

$$s = \sqrt{N(p)(q)} = \sqrt{400(0.55)(0.45)} = \sqrt{400(0.2475)} = \sqrt{99} = 9.95$$

We calculate z to determine the probability of our finding. We accomplish this by subtracting the value we would expect (E) under conditions of pure chance (200), or the mean, from what we actually observed (O), which was 220, and then dividing by the standard deviation.

$$z = \frac{O - E}{s} = \frac{220 - 200}{9.95} = \frac{20}{9.95} = 2.01$$

Turning to the table of z scores, we find that a z of 2.01 is equal to an area under the normal curve of probabilities of 0.4778. We add 0.500 to this figure as demanded by the symmetry of the curve to arrive at 0.9778, and we find that such an outcome could happen by chance $(1 - 0.9778) = 0.0222$, or about 2 times out of a series of 100 coin flip trials of 400 flips each. We may conclude that this is probably not a fair coin.

    The probability of observing a given score or value in a normal distribution of cases for any variable is obtained in exactly the same manner. If we randomly select an individual from the sample of offenders, the probability that he would have an IQ further than 2 standard deviations above or below the mean (94 ± 24) is about 0.05. Stated another way, the chances of finding an offender with an IQ equal to or less than 70 $(94 - 24)$ or equal to or greater than 118 $(94 + 24)$ are theoretically about 5 in 100. If you turn back to Table 4.4 and count the actual number of observations that are either equal to or less than 70 or equal to or greater than 118, you will find 28 such cases. Twenty-eight is 7.4% of the 376 cases in the distribution. Thus, our empirical distribution is quite close to the theoretical expectation. It is important to remember, then, that small deviations from the mean are a lot more common than large deviations from the mean, that very large deviations from the mean are rare, and that positive and negative deviations from the mean occur in roughly identical proportions.

SUMMARY

Probability is a ratio of an event or outcome to the total number of possible events or outcomes. Probability is a vital concept to the understanding of statistics. We have discussed some basic ideas of probability, such as computing probabilities by using the addition and multiplication rules for independent and dependent events. We will discuss these concepts again as the need arises. We also showed how a theoretical binomial probability distribution curve is generated.

The normal curve is a very useful tool in statistical analysis. There are many different normal curves, the shapes of which are determined by their means and standard deviations. Curves with small standard deviations are leptokurtic, and curves with large standard deviations are platykurtic. Normal curves are perfectly symmetrical, with 50% of the area falling on one side of the mean and 50% falling on the other side of the mean. One standard deviation on either side of the mean contains 68.26% of the area, 2 standard deviations on either side contain 95.4%, and 3 standard deviations on either side contain 99.74%.

A standardized normal curve is one that has been standardized to a mean of zero and a standard deviation of 1. It is a model by which we compare chance events in an empirical distribution by the use of z scores, which give us the proportion of the normal curve corresponding to a given raw score. The larger the value of the computed z score (either positive or negative), the rarer the value of the raw score. We find the area corresponding to a z score in the table of z scores in Appendix A. This is an important use of the normal curve and z scores because inferential statistics are concerned with estimating the probabilities of events.

PRACTICE APPLICATION: THE NORMAL CURVE AND z SCORES

Suppose we have a population of women in which 50% are married. We draw a random sample of 4 women from this population and determine if they are married. There are five possibilities: 0 married women, 1 married woman, 2 married women, 3 married women, or 4 married women. Construct a probability table of these outcomes. (Remember, the probability of a randomly selected women being married is 0.5.) We will start with the probability of getting 0 married women in a randomly selected sample:

$$
\begin{aligned}
{}_nP_r &= \frac{N!}{r!(N-r)!}\, p^r q^{n-r} \\
&= \frac{4 \times 3 \times 2 \times 1}{0!(4 \times 3 \times 2 \times 1)}(0.5^0)(0.5^4) = -\frac{1}{1}(0.5^0)(0.5^4) = 1 \times 0.0625
\end{aligned}
$$

Remember, $0! = 1$, and any number raised to the 0 power is also 1. Now fill in the rest of the following table:

NUMBER MARRIED WOMEN	$_nP_r$	$p^r q^{n-r}$	PROBABILITY
0	1	$(0.5^0)(0.5^4) = 1/16$	$1/16 = 0.0625$
1			
2			
3			
4			
	16		$16/16 = 1.0000$

You have a random sample consisting of 80 men and 70 women; 50 men and 25 women are smokers. What are the probabilities of:

A randomly selected person being a man? $80/150 = 0.533$
A randomly selected person being a woman? $70/150 = 0.466$

A randomly selected person being a smoker? 75/150 = 0.500

A randomly selected person being a man *and* a smoker? $P(A \text{ and } B) = P(A) \times P(B/A) = P(AB) = (0.533)(0.625) = 0.333$

A randomly selected person being a woman *or* a nonsmoker? $P(A \text{ or } B) = P(A) + P(B) - P(A \text{ and } B) = (0.466 + 0.500) - 0.30 = 0.966 - 0.30 = 0.666$

A psychologist in the process of assessing various juvenile delinquents for the courts wants to determine the relative standing of selected members on IQ from our sample of juvenile delinquents, for which the mean IQ is 92.2 with a standard deviation of 10.5.

Johnny and LeRoy are particularly troublesome children. Johnny's IQ score is 75 and LeRoy's is 120. Calculate their z scores.

$$\text{Johnny:} \quad z = \frac{75 - 92.2}{10.5} = \frac{-17.2}{10.5} = -1.64$$

$$\text{LeRoy:} \quad z = \frac{120 - 92.2}{10.5} = \frac{27.8}{10.5} = 2.65$$

Graph their positions on the normal curve:
What percentage of the juveniles scored higher and lower than Johnny?

Higher: 0.4495 + 0.5000 = 0.9495 = 94.95%

Lower: 1 − 0.9495 = 0.0505 = 5.05%

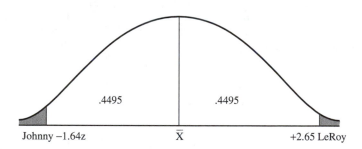

Total: 1.000 = 100%

What percentage of the juveniles scored higher and lower than LeRoy?

Higher: 1 − 0.9956 = 0.0044 = 0.44%
Lower: 0.4956 + 0.5000 = 0.9956 = 99.56%
Total: 1.000 = 100.00%

What percentage of the cases falls between Johnny's and LeRoy's scores?

0.4495 + 0.4956 = 0.9451 = 94.51%

REFERENCE

Reiss, I. and Lee, G. (1988). *Family Systems in America.* New York: Holt, Rinehart and Winston.

PROBLEMS

1. Find the area under the normal curve between the mean and the z score for the following z scores:
   a) +2.00
   b) −1.00
   c) +2.52
   d) −0.33
   e) +3.12
   f) −2.96
   g) +0.50
   h) −1.15

2. Draw a diagram shading in the designated area under the curve for parts (a), (b), (f), and (h) from Problem 1.

3. Find the area under the curve that lies beyond (above or below) the following z scores:
   a) −1.65
   b) −0.50
   c) +2.96
   d) +1.15
   e) −1.00
   f) −1.96
   g) +1.96
   h) +0.75

4. Draw a diagram shading in the designated area under the curve for parts (b), (c), (f), and (h) in Problem 3.

5. Find the area under the normal curve that lies between the following z scores:
   a) −1.65 and +1.65
   b) −1.15 and +0.65
   c) −1.96 and +1.96
   d) −0.75 and +0.75
   e) −0.95 and +0.50
   f) +1.15 and +2.15
   g) −2.25 and −3.00
   h) −0.10 and +0.50

6. Draw a diagram shading in the designated area under the curve for parts (a), (c), (e), and (f) in Problem 5.

7. Given that $\mu = 200$ and $\sigma = 50$, find the z score for each of the following z values:
   a) 210
   b) 150
   c) 100
   d) 300
   e) 315
   f) 225
   g) 50
   h) 125

8.   Calculate the percentile rank for parts (b), (d), (e), and (h) in Problem 7.

9.   Grades from a large (500 students) criminology lecture class approximate a normal curve. The mean score was 75 with a standard deviation of 10.
     a) How many students scored less than 60?
     b) The professor stated that the top 5% of the class would receive an A. What minimum score must a student receive to get an A?
     c) What percentage of students scored 90 or above?
     d) What percent of students scored between 80 and 90?
     e) How many students scored between 60 and 80?

10. At the local county fair, 100 people entered the pie eating contest. On average, it took the contestants 42 seconds to eat their pie with a standard deviation of 9 seconds.
     a) How many contestants ate their pie in less than 30 seconds?
     b) How many contestants ate their pie in less than one minute?
     c) How many contestants ate their pie in less than one minute but longer than 30 seconds?
     d) What percentage of contestants ate their pie in less than 20 seconds?
     e) Prizes were awarded to the fastest 10 pie eaters. How fast was the slowest of the top 10 pie eaters?
     f) What percentage of participants took longer than one minute to finish their pie?
     g) How fast did the slowest 20% eat their pie?
     h) How fast was the 95th percentile rank?
     i) Second place awards were given to the second 10 fastest pie eaters. The second place awards went to contestants who ate their pies in__seconds to__seconds.

11. Find the probability of each of the following events assuming a well-shuffled deck of cards is used:
     a) Drawing the ace of spades
     b) Drawing the ace of spades and any king
     c) Drawing the 3 of diamonds or the 2 of spades
     d) Drawing a king or a club
     e) Drawing the ace of spades and the ace of diamonds
     f) Drawing any two aces

12. Given a random sample of 500 voters, 300 are white and 200 are black. Of the white voters, 200 voted Republican and 100 voted Democrat. Of the black voters, 50 voted Republican and 150 voted Democrat.
     a) What is the probability that an individual selected at random is white and voted Republican?
     b) What is the probability that an individual selected at random is black and voted Republican?
     c) What is the probability that an individual selected at random is white and voted Democrat?
     d) What is the probability of selecting a black or a Democrat?

13. Find the value for each of the following combinations:
     a) $_{20}C_2$
     b) $_{18}C_{12}$

    c) $_{42}C_4$
    d) $_8C_8$
    e) $_{10}C_4$
    f) $_{50}C_4$
    g) $_3C_2$
    h) $_{16}C_4$

14. Calculate the following probabilities:
    a) Getting four heads in five flips of a coin
    b) Getting five tails in ten flips of a coin
    c) Getting two ones in five rolls of a die
    d) Getting four sixes in ten rolls of a die

15. Calculate the binomial probability distribution for the number of heads in six flips of a coin.
    a) Using the binomial probability distribution, find the probability of four or more heads.
    b) Find the probability of three or fewer heads.
    c) Find the probability of no heads.
    d) Find the probability of two or fewer heads.
    e) Find the probability of two or fewer heads and five or more heads.
    f) Find the probability of no heads and six heads.

16. Find the mean and the standard deviation of the following binomial distributions:
    a) $N = 526, p = 0.25$
    b) $N = 12, p = 0.60$
    c) $N = 900, p = 0.05$
    d) $N = 320, p = 0.75$

17. Using the binomial distribution in part (a) of Problem 16, calculate the z scores for the following values of r:
    a) 150
    b) 100
    c) 125
    d) 145
    e) 131.5
    f) 135
    g) 110
    h) 160

Chapter 5

THE SAMPLING DISTRIBUTION AND ESTIMATION PROCEDURES

SAMPLING

In Chapter 1 we noted that populations of interest to the social scientist are usually much too large to be studied as a whole. Social researchers have to study small subsets of the population, called *samples,* and from the information derived from these samples they draw conclusions about the population from which the samples were taken. In other words, we use statistics to estimate parameters. The present chapter extends this discussion.

Assume that we have a defined population of 10,000 individuals and know that their mean (μ) income is $25,000. If we took a representative sample of 100 individuals from this population and calculated the mean ($\overline{X}$) income for this sample, what would you expect that value to be? You would expect it to be about $25,000. Now suppose you had such a defined population but did not know what their mean income was. Suppose that you drew a representative sample of 100 individuals from that population and calculated the mean income and found it to be $25,000. Then what would you expect the population income to be? You would expect it to be about $25,000 also. Few people have problems with the first example (estimating $\overline{X}$ from μ), but considerably more have problems with the reverse (estimating μ from $\overline{X}$), although the logic is really no different.

To make inferences about population parameters from sample statistics, we must make sure that our sample is representative of the population. This is easily accomplished in the physical sciences since one piece of tungsten, for instance, is probably fully representative of every other piece of tungsten in the universe. It is less easily accomplished in the social and behavioral sciences because, unlike inanimate substances, human beings and situations vary enormously. Because of this variability we cannot make general statements about the elements of interest unless we have a truly representative sample of the population of interest. It would be of no value to obtain the mean height of a college basketball team, just because its members were readily available, to estimate the height of all males at the college. Such a sample is obviously biased and would greatly overestimate the population's height, since basketball players are not physically representative of all males, and the researcher could not generalize beyond that sample.

But how do researchers know if their sample is representative unless they already know what the population parameters are? And if the population parameters are known, why bother to sample? In a great many instances we can never know the population parameters, so however methodologically correct we are able to be, some degree of uncertainty will always remain. However, we can collect samples that are as representative as possible, which will allow us to generalize cautiously to the population of interest. An exhaustive discussion of sampling techniques more properly belongs in a research methods text. However, we will briefly discuss some of the more usual methods of sampling.

SIMPLE RANDOM SAMPLING

Simple random sampling is the ideal method of achieving representativeness, although it does not guarantee it. Simple random sampling is based on probability. A probability sample is one in which the probability of selecting any case in the population is known or is ascertainable prior to selection. *Random* does not mean haphazard or coincidental sampling. Rather, random sampling relies on very precise methods in which every member of a defined population has an equal chance of being included in the sample. For instance, if a random sample consists of 100 divorced women from a dating service known to have 1,000 divorced women among its members, each divorced woman should have a 0.10 probability of being included in the sample.

Examples of nonrandom sampling abound. Magazines and newspapers often invite their readers to send in their answers to questionnaires. These requests often result in much larger samples than the typical social science researcher is able to collect. Samples of more than 10,000 are not uncommon. Take, for instance, *Redbook*'s survey of female sexuality and the now famous Ann Landers question asking whether women would rather cuddle or have sex. Despite the numerically overwhelming responses to these requests, the results are extremely unreliable because respondents were self-selected and thus perhaps captured only those respondents who have a certain grievance or who are particularly interested in the topic. The readers of *Redbook* and the Ann Landers column constitute special populations that we cannot assume to be representative of all American females. Furthermore, those readers who are willing to talk about their sex lives are a subset of even these unique populations. This is not to say that the results were inherently uninteresting, but they cannot be generalized beyond their respective samples.

A random sample requires three things: (1) a defined population, for example, all multiple sclerosis (MS) patients in Idaho, (2) an exhaustive list of all members of the population, and (3) a selection process that ensures that every case or group of cases in the population has an equal probability of being selected. The first two requirements constitute a **sampling frame,** that is, a kind of operational definition of the target population. Ideally, the sampling frame and the target population should be identical, but this is rarely possible. No lists are ever completely exhaustive. For instance, if we wanted to poll the citizens of Waterloo, Iowa, probably the best list we could obtain would be the telephone directory. But because we know that some people have unlisted numbers and others do not have a phone, we would have to rely on an incomplete list to conduct our poll. In countries where a telephone is considered a luxury, such a sampling procedure would be useless because we would presumably be polling only the wealthy.

Assuming that a list of the population exists, the selection process can begin. The usual way of approaching case selection is to begin with a randomly selected number from a table of random numbers (lists of number without any pattern to them) such as Table 3 in Appendix A. The researcher then selects the case on the list that corresponds to the randomly selected number, repeating this process until the desired sample size is selected. If you are lucky enough to have a sampling frame stored in a computer, you can have the computer generate a random sample for you. This was the procedure used to select the sample of MS patients mentioned in Chapter 1. However, we are not assured of complete representativeness even with this procedure, because even though our procedure may select a subject, that subject may well decide not to participate in the research. Even the most assiduous attempts to select a truly random sample are not free of research design and sampling problems that are beyond the power of the researcher to control.

STRATIFIED RANDOM SAMPLING

The second kind of probability sampling is **stratified random sampling.** This type of sampling design subdivides a heterogeneous population into homogeneous subsets (strata) and randomly selects cases from each subset as in simple random sampling. A stratified random sample can be proportional or disproportionate.

Suppose you are interested in determining the mean income in your city of each of four racial groups based on a sample of 400 cases. Further suppose that Asians make up only 5% of the population. If you want proportional representation in your sample, you would have to select the sample in such a way as to ensure that Asians constitute 5%. So with your proposed sample of 400 cases you would randomly select 20 cases from the Asian population of your city.

Another type of stratified sampling is disproportionate stratified sampling, which is used when the researcher wishes to get an equal number of cases from each list regardless of the proportion of cases in each sublist. For instance, the 20 Asian cases in the preceding example may not be adequate for interstratum comparisons of income, and you might find it necessary to select disproportionately more Asians in order to make such comparisons. As long as disproportionate substrata are analyzed comparatively, the disproportionate sampling method can be effective. However, if the subgroups are to be combined and then analyzed to obtain an income picture of the entire city, we must take the sampling method into consideration. We would have to adjust for the disproportionate number of Asians by a process known as *weighting*. This process is simple and is discussed in texts on sampling and research methods.

There are many other ways to select a sample, but we have no room to discuss them here. All of them in one way or another are attempts to compensate for the inability to select a truly representative sample. As the population to which we want to generalize becomes larger and more diverse, the difficulties of selecting a representative sample increase. We could easily select a truly random sample from the population of coeds at a college. But if the population to which we wanted to generalize is "American woman," our sampling task would be monumental since every woman in America would have to have an equal probability of being selected. Such a sample would require a sampling technique known as *multistage cluster sampling*, whereby the researcher would sample clusters, or subpopulations, of women living in various areas in the United States.

Whatever the sampling design, whether relatively simple or complex, the basic steps of listing and randomly sampling are always the same. The main obstacle to truly random sampling is the unavailability in many instances of the exhaustive lists we mentioned. In many cases such lists simply do not exist, and if they do exist they may not be freely supplied to researchers. Even if lists exist and are available, we still must confront the problem of nonresponse. We have to be very careful not to make generalities beyond those warranted by the data.

THE SAMPLING DISTRIBUTION

Suppose that we have a large amount of information from a random sample. How is it that we are justified in making inferences about the population from it? For instance, we saw in Chapter 3 that the mean IQ of our adult felony offenders was 93.561. If we want to estimate the population parameter (the population mean IQ), this would be our best estimate. But, we have only a sample. What if we took another sample and found the mean to be 95.5 or a number of samples and found that the mean differed each time? We would almost certainly find different means with each sample, since means vary across samples just as scores within them vary from their mean. In fact, we took 60 different random samples of 30 cases each from the IQ data and not once did we find exactly the same mean. How then do we know that our single sample mean is our best estimate?

This apparent dilemma is solved by a theoretical probability distribution known as the **sampling distribution of means.** The sampling distribution of means is a frequency distribution of all possible unique sample means of constant sample size that we could draw from the same population. The number of possible unique samples is almost infinitely large when the population is large. To determine the number of possible unique samples of size n from a population of size N we use the combinations formula we used in Chapter 4:

$$C = \frac{N!}{n!(N-n)!}$$

where N = size of population and n = sample size. You can see that the possible number of samples from a population of any decent size would soon become huge. If we were to take a population of only 100 units and draw small samples of size 5, the number of possible samples would be 75,287,520.

If we were able to take all possible sample means, sum them, and divide by the number of samples, we would have the exact value of the population mean. As with all distributions, the distribution of sample means has a mean, that is, a **mean of means,** symbolized as $\mu_{\bar{X}}$ (read *"mu sub-X bar"*). As you might guess, the sampling distribution of sample means is a purely theoretical mathematical construct, not something that researchers have to calculate. What this theoretical distribution tells us is that we are justified in using sample statistics to estimate parameters.

Let us take a very simple example. Suppose we have a population of five men, with height being the element of interest. Instead of simply adding their heights and dividing by five (as sane people would do), we decide to do it the hard way and select all possible samples of size 3 from this population of five men. Using the combinations formula we find that we can form 10 unique samples of size 3 from a population of 5. The data for this exercise are presented in Table 5.1.

The mean height for the population is 70 inches with a standard deviation of 1.4 inches. The 10 unique samples of size 3 that can be formed by these five men are then presented. The sum of these sample means is 700, and when divided by the number of samples (10) we have a *mean of means* ($\mu_{\bar{X}}$), which is the same as the population mean (70). We then calculate the standard deviation of the distribution of sample means and find it to be 0.578. How can the standard deviations be so different (1.41 versus 0.578) when $\mu_{\bar{X}}$ is the same as μ? Look at the range of individual heights in the population ($72 - 68 = 4$ inches). Compare this with the range of the sample means ($71 - 69 = 2$ inches). This illustrates an important point: The sampling distribution is always less variable than the population from which the samples were taken. The special symbol for the standard deviation of the sampling distribution is $\sigma_{\bar{X}}$, which is also called the **standard error** of the sampling distribution.

We will use an adult offender data from earlier chapters to illustrate this further. Figure 5.1 is a distribution of sample means consisting of 60 computer-selected random samples of size 30 taken from our adult offender IQ data. Random selection means that every unit or case has an equal probability of being selected in each of our 60 samples of 30 cases. There are 376 cases with IQ data, so each case has a $30/376 = 0.08$ probability of

TABLE 5.1   Standard Error of the Sampling Distribution ($\sigma_{\bar{x}}$)

POPULATION ($\mu = 70$, $\sigma = 1.4$)

Name	Allan	Bill	Carl	Dennis	Edward
Height (inches)	68	69	72	71	70

ALL POSSIBLE SAMPLES OF n = 3

	SAMPLE VALUES	$\bar{X}$	$(\bar{X} - \mu_{\bar{x}})^2$
Allan, Bill, Carl	68, 69, 72	69.7	0.09
Allan, Bill, Dennis	68, 69, 71	69.3	0.49
Allan, Bill, Edward	68, 69, 70	69.0	1.00
Allan, Carl, Dennis	68, 72, 71	70.3	0.09
Allan, Carl, Edward	68, 72, 70	70.0	0.00
Allan, Dennis, Edward	68, 71, 70	69.7	0.09
Bill, Carl, Dennis	69, 72, 71	70.7	0.49
Bill, Carl, Edward	69, 72, 70	70.3	0.09
Bill, Dennis, Edward	69, 70, 71	70.0	0.00
Carl, Dennis, Edward	72, 71, 70	71.0	1.00
		$\Sigma = 700.0$	$\Sigma = 3.34$

$$\mu_{\bar{x}} = \frac{\Sigma_{\bar{x}}}{N} = \frac{700.0}{10} = 70 = \mu$$

$$\sigma_{\bar{x}} = \sqrt{\frac{\Sigma(\bar{X} - \mu_{\bar{x}})^2}{N}} = \sqrt{3.34/10} = .578$$

being included. We are treating the sample distribution of offender IQs as a population distribution for the purpose of making our point, but you should realize that the population mean is generally unknown and probably unknowable. The "population" mean IQ has been rounded to 94, and each mean was rounded to the nearest whole number for ease of diagraming.

As we see from Figure 5.1, the distribution of sample means clusters around the known population mean. The mean of these means (calculated prior to rounding) is 93.280, which only differs from the unrounded population mean by 0.281 (93.561 − 93.280 = 0.281). If we took more random samples and plotted them on Figure 5.2 we would come even closer to the true population mean. Realistically, we can only approximate the sampling distribution since it is a purely theoretical distribution based on all possible unique samples of size *N* from the population.

The beauty and elegance of the sampling distribution is such that even if the population, and hence the samples drawn from it, is not normally distributed, repeated representative samples will generate means that are approximately normally distributed. Because we have no population distribution we will again have to suspend reality and use a sample distribution to make the point. In Chapter 3 we saw that the sample distribution of MS patients is highly skewed. We had the computer generate 30 random samples of size 30 from this distribution and plotted them in Figure 5.2. You can see that with just 30 samples the distribution of sample means is beginning to approximate the normal curve. The mean of the means is 10.306, which is only 0.195 away from the population mean of 10.111. Once again, we are only assuming the sample to be a population to illustrate the point.

Distribution of Sample Means
Population mean $\mu = 93.561$; Calculated mean of means $\mu_{\bar{x}} = 93.280$

89	90	91	92	93	94	95	96	97	98	99
				$\bar{X}$						
				$\bar{X}$						
				$\bar{X}$						
			$\bar{X}$	$\bar{X}$						
			$\bar{X}$	$\bar{X}$	$\bar{X}$					
			$\bar{X}$	$\bar{X}$	$\bar{X}$					
			$\bar{X}$	$\bar{X}$	$\bar{X}$	$\bar{X}$				
		$\bar{X}$	$\bar{X}$	$\bar{X}$	$\bar{X}$	$\bar{X}$				
		$\bar{X}$	$\bar{X}$	$\bar{X}$	$\bar{X}$	$\bar{X}$				
	$\bar{X}$		$\bar{X}$	$\bar{X}$	$\bar{X}$	$\bar{X}$	$\bar{X}$	$\bar{X}$		
	$\bar{X}$	$\bar{X}$	$\bar{X}$	$\bar{X}$	$\bar{X}$	$\bar{X}$	$\bar{X}$	$\bar{X}$		
	$\bar{X}$	$\bar{X}$	$\bar{X}$	$\bar{X}$	$\bar{X}$	$\bar{X}$	$\bar{X}$	$\bar{X}$	$\bar{X}$	
$\bar{X}$	$\bar{X}$	$\bar{X}$	$\bar{X}$	$\bar{X}$	$\bar{X}$	$\bar{X}$	$\bar{X}$	$\bar{X}$	$\bar{X}$	$\bar{X}$

FIGURE 5.1.   Distribution of 60 sample means ($n = 30$) of offender IQ population.

We rarely take more than one sample to estimate population parameters, which means that we will almost certainly be in error when making our estimations. The difference between a sample statistic and its corresponding population parameter is known as **sampling error.** Each mean in Figure 5.2 whose value is not 10.111 is in error. Fortunately, because of simple random sampling, we are able to consider the error to be random due to the variability that occurs from random sample to random sample. Nevertheless, if we use the sample mean as an estimate of the population mean, we will make an error of less magnitude than if we use any other value. Just as there are fewer and fewer raw scores in a frequency distribution as we move away from the mean toward the tails of the distribution, Figures 5.1 and 5.2 demonstrate that fewer and fewer samples have means that are much larger or much smaller than the population mean in the sampling distribution. In both of these figures, the means are clustered around their

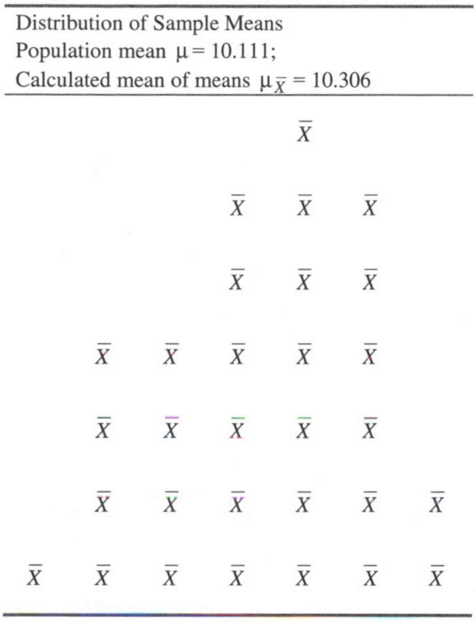

Distribution of Sample Means
Population mean $\mu = 10.111$;
Calculated mean of means $\mu_{\bar{X}} = 10.306$

$$\bar{X}$$

$$\bar{X} \quad \bar{X} \quad \bar{X}$$

$$\bar{X} \quad \bar{X} \quad \bar{X}$$

$$\bar{X} \quad \bar{X} \quad \bar{X} \quad \bar{X} \quad \bar{X}$$

$$\bar{X} \quad \bar{X} \quad \bar{X} \quad \bar{X} \quad \bar{X}$$

$$\bar{X} \quad \bar{X} \quad \bar{X} \quad \bar{X} \quad \bar{X} \quad \bar{X}$$

$$\bar{X} \quad \bar{X} \quad \bar{X} \quad \bar{X} \quad \bar{X} \quad \bar{X} \quad \bar{X}$$

FIGURE 5.2.   Distribution of 30 sample means from samples of size 30 from highly skewed distribution of years since diagnosis for multiple sclerosis patients.

population means and have peaked at these values. Some sample means missed the mark, but the frequency of the misses is reduced as the magnitude of the difference becomes larger and larger.

THE CENTRAL LIMIT THEOREM

We can summarize much of what we have discussed so far in this chapter in an important statistical concept known as the **central limit theorem:**

> If repeated random samples of size N are drawn from a population having a mean μ and a standard deviation σ, as N becomes large, the sampling distribution of sample means will approach normality with a mean μ and a standard deviation (standard error) $\sigma/\sqrt{N}$.

The central limit theorem is the most important concept in statistical theory. It tells us that we can make inferences from samples to populations regardless of the shape of their distributions and regardless of whether the population values are discrete or continuous. Further, it tells us that we can do so with relatively small samples, providing they are randomly selected. The theorem states "as N becomes large," but "large" is usually considered to be any number over 30, although this is a somewhat arbitrary rule of thumb that is sometimes distinguished from the central limit theorem as the *law of large numbers*. It should be intuitively reasonable that as sample sizes become larger, the data will come closer to the true population values. The "as N becomes large" statement also removes the constraint of the assumption of normality of the parent population distribution, as we saw from the demonstration in Figure 5.2.

STANDARD ERROR OF THE SAMPLING DISTRIBUTION

As with all distributions, the sampling distribution has a standard deviation. As we have already pointed out, the mean of the sampling distribution will be the same as the population mean, but the standard deviation of the sampling distribution will be smaller than the population standard deviation. As we have already seen, the standard deviation of the sampling distribution has a special name: the **standard error,** or sometimes the *standard error of the mean*. The standard error is so called because it represents error due to sampling variation and is equal to the sample standard deviation divided by the square root of the sample size. The smaller the standard error, the more confident we can be that the sample mean is close to the population mean. The standard error is found in formula (5.1):

$$s_{\overline{X}} = \frac{s}{\sqrt{N}} \qquad\qquad (5.1)$$

From formula (5.1) we note that the standard error of the sampling distribution is a function of sample size. As mentioned in our discussion of the standard deviation in Chapter 3, and in our discussion of the sampling distribution earlier in this chapter, there is less variability in a sample than there is in the parent population since the population, by definition, includes all extreme scores. The smaller the sample, the less likely it is to include extreme scores because they are rare relative to scores closer to the mean.

Before we see how the standard error is used in estimate parameters, it is a good idea to distinguish between the symbols used for the different types of distributions (populations, samples, and sampling) we have discussed (see Table 5.2).

POINT AND INTERVAL ESTIMATES

There are two kinds of estimates of population parameters from sample statistics: point estimates and interval estimates. A **point estimate** is a single value, and an **interval estimate** is a range of values. When we say that the mean IQ of our offenders is 93.561, this is a point estimate of the population parameter, the mean IQ of all criminal offenders. When a pollster says that 60% of the American population is pro-choice on the issue of abortion, this is a point estimate of the percentage of people in the population who are so inclined. An interval estimate would be of this kind: "The mean IQ of criminal defendants is between 90.5 and 95.5," or "Between 57 percent and 63 percent of the American population is pro-choice on the issue of abortion."

A statistic used to estimate a parameter should be unbiased, consistent, and efficient. For instance, a sample mean is an **unbiased estimate** of the population mean if the mean of the sampling distribution (the mean of means) is equal to the population

TABLE 5.2   Symbols for Means and Standard Deviations for the Population, Sample, and Sampling Distribution

DISTRIBUTION	MEAN	STANDARD DEVIATION
Population	μ	σ
Sample	$\overline{x}$	s
Sampling	$\mu_{\overline{x}}$	$\sigma_{\overline{X}}$

mean. We know from our discussion of the central limit theorem that sample means are unbiased estimates of population means if the sample is randomly selected. However, the sample standard deviation(*s*) is a biased estimator of the population standard deviation σ, as we saw in Chapter 3. We also saw that the sample *s* is considered an unbiased estimator of σ, if $N - 1$ is used rather than N to calculate it. Unbiasedness only means that over the long run the average sampling error is zero.

A **consistent estimate** is one in which there is agreement between the value of the sample statistic and its parameter. The larger the sample size, the greater the consistency of these values. As sample size increases, the standard error decreases, meaning that the potential for sampling error decreases. If two random samples are drawn from the same population of size $N = 50$ and $N = 500$, the consistency will be greater in the larger sample.

The efficiency of a statistic refers to its relative superiority as a point estimate compared to alternative estimates. The mean, for instance, is a more **efficient estimate** of central tendency than is the median or the mode because of its greater stability in a normally distributed population. The standard error of the mean is less than the standard errors of the median or mode, making for less sampling error. This concept was demonstrated in Chapter 3.

CONFIDENCE INTERVALS AND ALPHA LEVELS

To establish the range of interval estimates, we use the standard error. We establish the interval range for the population mean of offenders by using our sample mean, ceasing at this point to use it as an assumed population mean and again treating it as what it actually is, a sample mean. Now we calculate the standard error. We know that the sample mean IQ is 93.561 and that $N = 376$. Since we do not know the population standard deviation, we estimate it with the sample standard deviation, which we know from Table 4.3 to be 12.18. Putting these numbers into the formula for the standard error, we get

$$\sigma_{\overline{x}} = \frac{s}{\sqrt{N}} = \frac{12.18}{\sqrt{376}} = \frac{12.18}{19.39} = 0.628$$

We know that the sampling distribution performs the same function for samples that the normal distribution performs for raw scores. With a distribution of raw scores, approximately 68% of all scores lie between ± 1 standard deviation, approximately 95% lie within ± 2 standard deviations, and approximately 99% lie within ± 3 standard deviations. Similarly, the same percentages of sample means lie within the respective standard errors. That is, if an infinite number of sample means were calculated, 68% of them will be between ± 1 standard error of the population mean. Assuming our sample IQ mean is the population mean once again, 68% of all sample means from this population will be within ± 0.628 of 93.561. So, 68% of the sample means in the sampling distribution will fall within the range of 92.933 to 94.189. Ninety-five percent of sampling means in the sampling distribution will fall within ± 2 standard errors of the mean ($\pm 0.628 \times 2 = 1.256$), and 99% within $0.628 \times 3 = 1.884$ on either side of the mean. This range of values constructed around the point estimate is known as the **confidence interval.** Thus, we are 99% confident that the population parameter (μ_{IQ}) lies within the range of 2.58 standard errors on either side of our point estimate ($\overline{X}_{IQ}$).

TABLE 5.3   Relationship between Confidence Levels, Alpha Levels, z Scores and Areas under the Curve

CONFIDENCE LEVEL (%)	ALPHA LEVEL (α)	z SCORE	AREA FROM MEAN TO z SCORE	AREA × 2	AREA BEYOND z SCORE (α)
95.0	0.05	1.96	0.4750	0.95	0.05
99.0	0.01	2.58	0.4950	0.99	0.01
99.9	0.001	3.30	0.4995	0.999	0.001

An interval estimate is wrong if it does not contain the population parameter. How do we know if it does or does not? We never do, although we can state that the interval estimates contain the parameter with a given level of confidence. Confidence levels correspond to probabilities, which are conventionally set at 0.95, 0.99, and 0.999. These values represent researchers' confidence that the confidence interval contains the population parameter. A value called an *alpha* (symbolized α) *level*, represents the probability that the confidence interval does not contain the parameter ($1 - $ confidence interval $= \alpha$). Researchers select their alpha levels depending on how confident they wish to be that their confidence interval contains the population parameter. By selecting an alpha level of $0.05 (1 - 0.95)$, for instance, the researcher is saying that he or she is willing to run the risk of being wrong (concluding that the confidence interval contains the parameter when it does not) 5 times out of 100. At the $0.01 (1 - 0.99)$ level, the risk of being wrong is 1 time out of 100.

In Table 1 of Appendix A we note that the area under the normal curve that corresponds to the 95% confidence level has a z value of 1.96. To refresh your memory, turn to Table 1 in Appendix A and locate the area of the curve above a z score of 1.96. We find this value to be 0.4750. Doubling this value to take in both sides of the curve, we get 0.95, or 95%. The area beyond this value ($1 - 0.95 = 0.05$) is the alpha level. Table 5.3 presents the areas under the curve and the corresponding alpha levels and z scores for three different confidence levels. Note that the alpha level corresponds to the area beyond the z score representing the rare events.

CALCULATING CONFIDENCE INTERVALS

If $\overline{X}$ is within 1.96 $\sigma_{\overline{X}}$ of μ 95% of the time, and if we start at $\overline{X}$ and go 1.96 $\sigma_{\overline{X}}$ in either direction, that interval should include μ. We are now in a position to calculate confidence intervals for our population mean. We determine the risk we are willing to take that we are wrong by specifying the z score corresponding to a given alpha level in the following formula:

$$\text{CI} = \overline{X} \pm z(s/\sqrt{N}) \tag{5.2}$$

Where   CI = confidence interval
        $\overline{X}$ = sample mean
        s = sample standard deviation.

We know that the sample mean and standard deviation for our offender data in Chapter 4 are 93.561 and 12.18, respectively. All that remains is to select a level of confidence.

We choose the 95% level ($z = 1.96$) Therefore, the confidence intervals for the population mean are

$$CI = \bar{X} \pm z(s/\sqrt{N}) = (1.96)\,12.18/\sqrt{376}$$
$$= (1.96)(12.18/19.391) = (1.96)(0.628) = 1.231$$
$$= 93.561 \pm 1.231$$

Lower confidence interval (LCI) $= 93.561 - 1.231 = 92.330$

Upper confidence interval (UCI) $= 93.561 + 1.231 = 94.792$

Thus, we are 95% confident that the population mean is somewhere between 92.33 and 94.792. More precisely, if we took an infinite number of random samples from the same population and constructed confidence intervals for each one, the confidence interval would contain μ 95 out of 100 times. If we want more confidence, we substitute the z value for the desired level. What this does not say is that there is a 95% chance that the mean IQ for the total population of criminal offenders falls between our upper and lower limits. The population mean either falls between 92.330 and 94.792 or it does not, which means it has a probability of falling between these estimates of either 0 or 1. Remember that it is the statistic that we place confidence intervals around, not the parameter.

If we want to be 99.9% confident, meaning we wish only to run the risk of being wrong 1 time in every 1,000, we set z at 3.3:

$$CI = (3.30)(0.628) = 2.072$$
$$= 93.561 \pm 2.072$$

$LCI = 93.561 - 2.072 = 91.489$ $UCI = 93.561 + 2.072 = 95.633$

Note that as confidence that our sample mean includes the population mean increases, the intervals widen. There is a constant trade-off in statistics between confidence and precision of estimates. You could be absolutely sure, for instance, if you estimated the population mean IQ of offenders to be between 80 and 120, but it wouldn't be very useful. Conversely, the narrower the confidence intervals, the less confident we are that they include the population mean.

One way to narrow the range of the interval estimates without sacrificing confidence or precision is to increase sample size. As we have seen, the larger the sample, the smaller the standard error. For instance, if our sample were doubled, all other things being equal, the standard error would be 0.444 rather than 0.628. With a standard error of 0.444 our confidence intervals would be smaller at the 99% confidence interval than they are at the 95% interval with a standard error of 0.628. You can verify this result for yourself as an exercise.

Some of you may have looked at Figure 5.1 after our discussion of confidence intervals and wondered how many of the computer-generated samples actually fell within 1.96 standard errors of the mean. We hope that you realize by now that it should be about 5%. Since 5% of 60 is 3, that's about how many samples should theoretically have means falling outside ± 1.96 standard errors. The standard error for each sample is identical because the known population standard deviation is the numerator and the square root of 30, which is the constant sample N, is the denominator in each case. Thus, the standard error is $12.18/\sqrt{30} = 2.224$ and 1.96 times this is 4.395. The LCI and UCI are $94 - 4.395 = 89.6$ and $94 + 4.359 = 98.359$, respectively. Only the two extreme means (89 and 99) fall beyond 1.96 standard errors.

SAMPLING AND CONFIDENCE INTERVALS

Could we use this sample mean of 93.561 IQ points to estimate the mean IQ of the general American population? (Not that we would want to because IQ is one of the few population parameters actually known; IQ has a μ of 100 and a σ of 15.) Your first guess is that we probably could not, because even with z set at 3.3, we saw that the upper confidence level is only 95.633, which is a long way from 100. Thus we know that it would require a very large z to encompass the population mean. We know that the difference between the mean population IQ and the mean IQ of our sample of offenders is 6.44 IQ points. We can rearrange formula (5.2) to find out how large a z would be required to encompass this difference. In this case, z is the unknown, and the interval between $\overline{X}$ and μ is known (6.44). Rearranging the confidence interval formula $CI = \overline{X} \pm z\,(s/\sqrt{N})$ to find z, we get

$$z = \frac{CI}{s/\sqrt{N}} \tag{5.3}$$

Since we know the population standard deviation is 15, we no longer have to estimate it with our sample standard deviation. Inserting the number, we get

$$z = \frac{6.44}{15/\sqrt{376}} = \frac{6.44}{15/19.39} = \frac{6.44}{0.774} = 8.32$$

Thus, we would need to choose a z of 8.32 in order to calculate a confidence interval large enough to include the population parameter. Since z scores correspond with areas under the normal curve, and since area corresponds with probabilities, our calculated z tells us that it is extremely improbable (8.32 standard deviations between the ordinate at the mean of the normal curve and the ordinate at z) that criminal offenders and the general population are from the same IQ population.

INTERVAL ESTIMATES FOR PROPORTIONS

The procedure for estimating population proportions from sample proportions is similar to that for estimating population means from sample means. Based on the central limit theorem, sample proportions have sampling distributions that are normal in shape. We can thus construct confidence intervals for population proportions based on sample proportions by using formula 5.4:

$$CI = P_s \pm z\sqrt{(P_p)(Q_p)/N} \tag{5.4}$$

where P_s = sample proportion
          P_p = population proportion
          $Q_p = 1 - P_p$.

Since we select the value of z depending on how confident we wish to be, and P_s and N are sample values, we are left only with one value to estimate (P_p). By definition P_p is an unknown, so we simply use the sample proportions as our best estimates.

Suppose that we want to estimate the proportion of California's females who voted for Proposition 209 (the anti-affirmative action proposition). A sample of 500 women resulted in a proportion of 0.42. We now place confidence intervals around these proportions, using the 95% level of confidence:

$$\text{CI} = 0.42 \pm 1.96\sqrt{(0.42)(0.58)/500} = 0.42 \pm 1.96\sqrt{0.2436/500}$$
$$= 0.42 \pm 1.96\sqrt{0.0004872} = 0.42 \pm 1.96(0.0221)$$
$$= 0.42 \pm 0.0433$$
$$\text{LCI} = 0.42 - 0.0433 = 0.3767 \qquad \text{UCI} = 0.42 + 0.0433 = 0.4633$$

Our best estimate of the proportion of Californian women who voted for Proposition 209 is 0.42, or 42%. The 95% confidence intervals are approximately 0.38 to 0.46, meaning that in the long run the population proportion will be within these intervals 95% of the time.

ESTIMATING SAMPLE SIZE

The answer to the question "How big should my sample be?" depends on three things: (1) the degree of precision desired in estimating the parameter, (2) the desired level of confidence, and (3) some estimate of the parameter standard deviation. The first two requirements are easily met because the researcher determines them. The last requirement is problematic, because if we knew the population standard deviation we would also know the mean, and sampling the population to get a value we already know would be redundant. What we do in effect is to make an enlightened guess about the unknown population standard deviation. Suppose that we wish to estimate the mean IQ for offenders with 95% confidence and that we want to be wrong by only 1 IQ point on either side of the population mean. An enlightened guess would have to be derived from previous studies or a pilot study (a small-scale study done to provide a larger study with guidelines) of our own. Assume that our offender study was a pilot study. In that case we can use the standard deviation derived from it (12.18) to estimate the population standard deviation. Under these conditions we can determine the required sample size by the following formula:

$$N = \left[\frac{(z)(\sigma)}{E} \right]^2 \tag{5.5}$$

where z = desired level of confidence
σ = population standard deviation estimated from sample s
E = desired accuracy (amount of error we are willing to accept).

Formula (5.4) is a by-product of the theory of the standard error in that the standard error is an estimate of how much an estimated mean will be off (E), the value of the population mean. Thus, we could write E, with the 95% confidence level, as $E = (1.96)(s/\sqrt{N})$, which for our offender data is the confidence interval at the 95% confidence interval (1.231) we previously calculated. If, for instance, we were willing to tolerate an estimation error of no more than 1 IQ point, we know then that a sample size of 376 is inadequate.

To obtain an estimation of the desired sample size that would allow us to say that our sample mean accurately estimates the population mean ±1 IQ point, we substitute our tolerable error (1) for E in formula (5.4) and solve for sample size:

$$N = \left[\frac{(z)(\sigma)}{E}\right]^2 = \left[\frac{(1.96)(12.18)}{1}\right]^2 = \left[\frac{23.8728}{1}\right]^2$$
$$= (23.8728)^2 = 570 \text{ (rounded)}$$

We would need a sample of 570 cases if we wanted to have an error of 1 IQ point on either side of the population mean with a confidence level of 95%. Verify for yourself that if we are willing to be wrong by 2 IQ points with the same level of confidence, our sample size of 376 is more than adequate.

ESTIMATING SAMPLE SIZE FOR PROPORTIONS

We can estimate the sample size required to estimate a population proportion from the sample proportion. Again, the researcher determines the confidence level and the amount of error he or she is willing to tolerate. Suppose we wanted a closer estimate of the proportion of Californian women who voted for Proposition 209. We will consider our sample of 500 women as a pilot study and the 4% interval estimate too large for us to tolerate. We want to be wrong by no more than 2 percentage points in either direction. We can determine the required sample size by the following formula:

$$N = \frac{z^2(P_s)(Q_s)}{E^2}$$

where z^2 = selected alpha squared and E^2 = tolerable error squared. The researcher sets the alpha level (we choose 0.05) and the error he or she will tolerate (0.02 in either direction). The values for P_s and Q_s are derived from the sample. Putting in the numbers, we get

$$N = \frac{1.96^2(0.42)(0.58)}{0.02^2} = \frac{(3.8416)(0.2436)}{0.0004} = \frac{0.9358}{0.0004} = 2,340$$

We would need a sample of at least 2,340 cases if we desired an interval estimate no larger than 2% with 95% confidence. Determine if this is so by substituting this N for the N of 500 in our example of California females voting for Proposition 209.

SUMMARY

When we estimate population parameters from sample statistics we assume that the sample is representative of the population. A simple random sample is one in which every element in the population has an equal chance of being included. There are other types of samples such as proportionate and nonproportionate stratified samples. Although our statistical tests assume representative samples, you should be aware of the difficulties of collecting such samples in social science.

When making inferences from samples to populations we are actually dealing with three kinds of distributions: sample, population, and sampling distributions. The sampling distribution is a theoretical distribution of an infinite number of sample means of equal size taken from a population. This distribution of sample means has a mean, and we take this *mean of means* to be the mean of the population from which the infinite samples were selected. An interesting observation of the sampling distribution is that even if the underlying distribution of some characteristic is not normally distributed, repeated sampling from this population will result in a sampling distribution of means that is approximately normally distributed.

As with any other distribution, the sampling distribution has a standard deviation. We call the standard deviation of a sampling distribution the *standard error.* The smaller the standard error the more confident we can be that the sample mean is a good estimate of the population mean.

The central limit theorem is a pivotal concept in inferential statistics. It states that if repeated random samples of size N are drawn from a population, the sampling distribution of sample means will approach normality as N becomes large. *Large* can be as few as 30.

We can estimate two types of parameters from statistics: point and interval estimates. A point estimate is a single value, and an interval estimate is a range of values. We use sample statistics and the standard error to place confidence intervals around interval estimates. We have shown in this chapter how confidence intervals are placed around means and proportions. Confidence intervals become smaller, and therefore more precise, as sample size increases because the larger the sample the smaller the standard error. We discussed techniques for estimating required sample sizes for given confidence levels and amount of error the researcher is willing to tolerate.

PRACTICE APPLICATION: THE SAMPLING DISTRIBUTION AND ESTIMATION

An office manager collects the annual salaries of all administrative assistants in her company and obtains the following list of 30 salaries rounded to the nearest thousand dollars and computes the mean, standard deviation, standard error, and range. Because she has included all administrative assistants in the company, she has a population, not a sample.

**Annual Salary for Administrative Assistants
(In Thousands of Dollars)**

16	18	25	28	32
18	20	26	29	32
19	24	26	30	35
20	24	27	30	36
23	25	27	31	40
24	25	28	32	40

$\bar{X} = 27.00$ $s = 6.159$ SE $= 1.124$ Range $= 24$

From this population, take 10 random samples of various sizes and compute means, standard deviations, and ranges.

SAMPLE	N	$\bar{X}$	s	RANGE	SAMPLE	N	$\bar{X}$	s	RANGE
a	8	30.37	2.56	8	f	8	25.50	5.88	16
b	7	27.71	5.22	16	g	9	28.89	4.86	16
c	10	28.70	4.99	16	h	13	25.92	4.17	22
d	4	24.75	6.18	14	i	8	25.62	6.45	14
e	9	24.56	5.43	16	j	7	27.57	6.83	21

The ranges of the samples are smaller than the range in the population. The population range is 24, the smallest sample range is 8, and the largest is 22.

Compute the mean of means:

$$\bar{X}_1 + \bar{X}_2 + \cdots + \bar{X}_{10}/N = (30.37 + 27.71 + \cdots + 27.57)/10 = 26.959$$
$$= 30.37 + 27.71 + \cdots + 27.57/10 = 26.959$$

The mean of means only differs from the population mean by 0.041. The mean of means will equal the population mean in the long run.

Compute 95% confidence intervals for sample mean *a*:

$$\text{CI} = \bar{X}_a \pm z(s/\sqrt{N}) = (1.96)(2.56/\sqrt{8}) = (1.96)(2.56/2.828) = (1.96)(0.905) = 1.774$$
$$\text{LCI} = 30.37 - 1.774 = 28.596 \quad \text{UCI} = 30.37 + 1.774 = 32.144$$

Mean *a* misses the population mean at the 95% confidence interval. Only means *i, h, j,* and *b* fall within 2 standard errors of the mean. Sample sizes are too small to adequately estimate the population mean.

Imagine that our population of administrative assistants is a random sample of administrative assistants from all companies in the state. How big should our sample be if we are willing to tolerate an error of plus or minus $500 in estimating the population mean with 95% confidence?

$$N = \left[\frac{(z)(\sigma)}{E}\right]^2 = \left[\frac{(1.96)(6.159)}{0.5}\right]^2 = \left[\frac{12.0716}{0.5}\right]^2 = 24.1433^2 = 583$$

PROBLEMS

1. A class has 30 students. Using the random numbers table in Appendix A, select a simple random sample of five students.

2. For each of the following hypothetical situations, indicate which sample design would be most appropriate and why:
   a) A university president is interested in student attitudes about the university core program.
   b) A candidate in a local election wants to know what issues are most critical to voters in the community.
   c) A medical researcher is interested in knowing whether taking aspirin every day helps prevent heart attacks in men and women equally.
   d) The governor's office wants to know whether residents from different counties have significantly different attitudes toward pollution control regulations.

3. A local telephone directory contains 328 pages with approximately 120 names per page.
   a) Explain how you would choose a simple random sample from these names. Using the random numbers table in Appendix A, select ten numbers that could be used in selecting such a sample.
   b) How would you obtain a systematic sample of 200 names from the directory?
   c) Would cluster sampling be applicable to this situation? How could it be carried out and what would be the advantages and disadvantages?

4. Following an episode of *Saturday Night Live,* Larry the Lobster's life was on the line. Callers were given two phone numbers, one to call to save Larry the Lobster and one to call to have him cooked and eaten. More callers called the line to have Larry cooked. Thus ended Larry the Lobster.
   a) Comment on whether or not this was a random sample.
   b) How might this poll have been improved?

5. I want to collect data on a sample of state prison inmates in the United States. I obtain a list of all U.S. state prisons. I assign each prison a unique number. Beginning randomly, I choose every 8th prison on the list. I then obtain a list of all current inmates housed at the selected prisons. I select a simple random sample from each list.
   a) What kinds of sampling have I used?
   b) Would there be a more efficient way to sample this population?

6. Determine the mean and the standard deviation of the sampling distribution of the mean for the following:
   a) $\mu = 25$; $\sigma = 0.60$; $N = 30$
   b) $\mu = 13$; $\sigma = 1.29$; $N = 9$
   c) $\mu = 268$; $\sigma = 38$; $N = 100$
   d) $\mu = 170$; $\sigma = 22$; $N = 25$
   e) $\mu = 90$; $\sigma = 8.21$; $N = 100$
   f) $\mu = 45$; $\sigma = 15$; $N = 1,000$

7. The following numbers represent an entire population: 3, 5, 7, 9, 11.
   a) Take all possible samples, with replacement, of a sample size equal to 2.
   b) Calculate the mean of each sample.

    c) Calculate the mean and standard deviation of the population.
    d) Calculate the mean and standard deviation of the 25 sample means.
    e) Compare parts (c) and (d).

8. Find the 95% confidence intervals for the following:
    a) $\bar{X} = 30$; $\sigma = 5.45$, $N = 24$
    b) $\bar{X} = 65$; $\sigma = 1.38$, $N = 50$
    c) $\bar{X} = 268$; $\sigma = 38$, $N = 100$
    d) $\bar{X} = 125$; $\sigma = 24.24$, $N = 9$
    e) $\bar{X} = 82$; $\sigma = 2.38$, $N = 19$

9. Find the 99% confidence intervals for the following:
    a) $\bar{X} = 50$; $\sigma = 5.00$, $N = 9$
    b) $\bar{X} = 65$; $\sigma = 1.42$, $N = 15$
    c) $\bar{X} = 12$; $\sigma = 1.98$, $N = 40$
    d) $\bar{X} = 250$; $\sigma = 24.12$, $N = 100$
    e) $\bar{X} = 125$; $\sigma = 12$, $N = 5$

10. Ten households were selected at random and asked how many televisions they had in their household. The following data were collected: 1, 1, 2, 2, 2, 2, 3, 3, 5, 6. Calculate the point estimate of the population mean and the standard deviation.

11. Given the research correlating grade point average (GPA) and IQs of students, a school counselor claims that she is 95% confident that Miguel, who holds a 3.35 GPA, will have an IQ between 104 and 140. Are the following statements true or false?:
    a) Ninety-five percent of the time, Miguel's IQ will be between 104 and 140.
    b) We can be reasonably confident that Miguel's IQ is between 104 and 140.
    c) We can be reasonably confident that Mary, who also has a GPA of 3.35, has an IQ between 104 and 140.
    d) Ninety-five percent of all the students in Miguel's school have an IQ between 104 and 140.
    e) Approximately 95% of Jamal's classmates with GPAs of 3.35 have IQs between 104 and 140.

12. One hundred widows were selected at random and asked how many times they had been hospitalized within the past year. The results are listed below:

NUMBER OF HOSPITALIZATIONS	FREQUENCY
0	55
1	25
2	7
3	4
4	3
5	3
6	0
7	2
8	1

a) Calculate the point estimate μ.

b) Calculate the point estimate σ.
c) Construct a 95% confidence interval for μ.
d) Construct a 99% confidence interval for μ.

13. What is the maximum variance of a proportion?

14. What is the z score that corresponds to:
    a) A 98% confidence interval?
    b) An 80% confidence interval?
    c) A 50% confidence interval?

15. In a large national survey of U.S. homeowners, 620 respondents favored the death penalty, 410 opposed it, and 125 had no opinion.
    a) What is the point estimate of the proportion of U.S. homeowners who favor the death penalty?
    b) Find a 95% confidence interval for the population proportion.

16. We asked a random sample of 100 families in a Midwestern town how many own two or more automobiles. The survey showed that 42% of the sample owned more than one car.
    a) Form a 99% confidence for the proportion of all families in this town that own two or more cars.
    b) Recalculate the confidence interval assuming a sample size of 50.
    c) Recalculate the confidence interval assuming a sample size of 400.
    d) Compare parts (a), (b), and (c). What happens to the confidence interval as your sample size increases?

17. A researcher is interested in estimating the proportion of traffic accidents that involved alcohol. The researcher would like the estimate to be accurate to within 0.05 with probability 0.90. What sample size will the researcher need?

18. A study is being developed that will estimate the proportion of women with children who are also caring for their elderly parents. How large a sample size is required to estimate the proportion correcting within:
    a) 0.01 with probability 0.99?
    b) 0.01 with probability 0.95?
    c) 0.05 with probability 0.99?
    d) 0.05 with probability 0.95?
    e) 0.10 with probability 0.99?
    f) 0.10 with probability 0.95?
    g) Compare parts a–f. What conclusions can you draw about sample size, precision and confidence?

Chapter 6

HYPOTHESIS TESTING: INTERVAL/RATIO DATA

Chapters 4 and 5 concentrated mainly on a seemingly endless discussion of theoretical probability curves. We also talked a lot about means, standard deviations, and z scores and how we use sample statistics to estimate population parameters. We have been, and will remain so for most of the rest of the book, heavily dependent on the normal curve, in which most observations cluster around their mean and become rarer and rarer as we approach the tails of the curve. We build on this knowledge in this and subsequent chapters to help us make decisions about how well sample statistics accurately reflect population parameters. We saw that they are quite likely to reflect them well if randomly selected, although we also saw that even random samples are subject to sampling error. Sample statistics either do or do not reflect their respective population parameters. Fortunately, we have a system to help us to decide which of these two alternatives is *probably* correct called **hypothesis testing.** Recall from Chapter 1 that *hypotheses* are hunches or educated guesses that researchers make about relationships between or among variables. These educated guesses are derived from previous research and theory, or perhaps from some assertion that the researcher does not believe.

THE LOGIC OF HYPOTHESIS TESTING

Suppose a Michigan State politician argues for the passage of a gun control bill because 56% of the Michiganders say they support such a bill. We decide to check this claim by conducting a telephone survey of 500 randomly selected Michigan homes and find that only 48% support the bill. What do we conclude? We do not know how the politician arrived at her figure, but we know how we arrived at ours. There are two possible explanations for the difference between the politician's claim and our survey results (excluding fibbing, which we know we're not doing, and which we know politicians *never* do):

1. Sampling error caused us to underestimate the true magnitude of the support for the gun control bill in Michigan, which really is 56%.
2. Our survey accurately reflects the state's sentiments regarding gun control, and thus the true magnitude of support for the bill is not 56%.

To take another example, suppose we are interested in the psychosocial precursors of hypertension. Theories of stress tell us that long-term stress will eventually manifest itself in elevated blood pressure. On the assumption that African-Americans suffer more stress in our society than whites, we decide to study 500 randomly selected males and then divide them into black and white racial categories and find that blacks have a mean diastolic blood pressure of 89, and whites have a mean of 81. There is an observed sample difference of 8 points, which can be interpreted in two ways:

1. The difference is not an accurate reflection of the population difference, but is rather the result of sampling error. There is no difference between black and white diastolic blood pressure means.

2. The difference accurately reflects population differences; the blacks' diastolic blood pressure mean is really higher than the white mean.

The process of hypothesis testing involves testing the first of each of these competing explanations (i.e., the Michigan politician is correct, and that black and white blood pressure means do not differ). The test of *no difference* is referred to as the **null hypothesis,** symbolized as H_0. The researcher states the null hypothesis and subjects it to rigorous testing procedures. The null hypothesis is stated symbolically according to the kind of test being conducted. For our gun control example, H_0 would be stated as:

$H_0: P = 0.56$

This means that the percentage of Michiganders who support the gun control bill really is 56, and that any difference we will find in our survey will be due to sampling error. In our blood pressure example, H_0 would be stated as:

$H_0: \mu_1 = \mu_2$

This means that the diastolic blood pressure mean of African-American males is equal to the mean of white American males.

Of course, we don't really believe either null hypothesis. If we did, we would not have conducted our studies. So why do we test for *no difference* when we clearly don't believe it? The answer is that we wish to be cautious. Testing the null hypothesis is similar to the logic of the criminal trial process in the Anglo-American common law tradition. The police and the prosecutor have educated guesses concerning the relationship between the crime committed and the accused, namely, that he or she is guilty. The jury is analogous to the scientist's sample in that it is supposed to be representative of the population. The assumption that the accused is not guilty is identical to the null hypothesis. The alternative assumption (the accused is guilty) is put to a stringent test in that his or her guilt must be *proved beyond a reasonable doubt.* If the null hypothesis of *not guilty* cannot be rejected, the accused is set free.

Prosecutors are also really interested in the alternative to their operating assumption. If they did not have very good reasons for believing in the accused's guilt, they would not have bothered with the indictment in the first place. The assumption of innocence is a cautionary mechanism to maximize the probability that a person who is innocent will not be unjustly punished. Nevertheless, prosecutors believe that the truth is contradictory to the assumption of innocence. Likewise, researchers are really interested in the opposite of the null hypothesis, which is called the **alternative** or **research hypothesis.** For our gun control bill example, the research hypothesis is symbolized as

$H_1: P \neq 0.56$ (the percentage of Michiganders who support gun control bill is not 56)

For our blood pressure example it would be stated as:

$H_1: \mu_1 \neq \mu_2$ (the black blood pressure mean is not equal to the white mean)

If the sample results can be shown not to be a function of sampling error, we can reject the null hypothesis just as a jury, after examining the evidence, may reject the assumption of the accused's innocence. In both cases, however, the operating assumptions are considered true until the evidence suggests otherwise.

THE EVIDENCE AND STATISTICAL SIGNIFICANCE

In a court of law the accused is found guilty because the evidence supposedly points to the conclusion that he or she committed the crime *beyond a reasonable doubt*. This does not mean beyond all possible doubt, only beyond *reasonable* doubt. What constitutes *beyond reasonable doubt* for the researcher that will allow him or her to reject the null hypothesis? In Chapter 4, we showed that by marking off standard units of distance under the normal curve we were able to determine the percentage of the area that was within and beyond those points. The measures used to mark off the units are z scores. We saw that a z score of ± 1.96 marks an area of the normal curve beyond which 5% of the area lies (2.5% on each side).

We can think of differences between means in the same way. Just as there are distributions of raw scores and of sample means, there are distributions of mean differences. Such a distribution, like the sampling distribution, is purely theoretical. Let us suppose that we take an infinite number of pairs of samples of equal size from the same population, compute their means, and note the difference between the means of each pair. Each of these differences is then graphed in a distribution of mean differences. It should not surprise you that such a distribution would be normal. The mean of the distribution of mean differences will be zero since negative and positive differences will cancel one another out in the long run. There will be a few large mean differences toward the tails of this distribution, but as always, the great bulk of them will be in the center.

To help illustrate this point, we computer generated 100 paired samples (200 separate samples) of size 30 from our offender IQ data and plotted the mean difference of each pair (rounded to the nearest whole number) in Figure 6.1. Small differences are clustered around the center, and larger differences are at the tails of the distribution. The mean of the mean differences for the distribution of 100 sample mean differences is 0.06, although in the long run it will be exactly zero. We now have a sampling distribution of mean differences with a mean of its own, but what about a standard deviation (the standard error of the mean of mean differences)? Because we know σ to be 12.18 for our IQ data, we do not have to estimate it. However, the standard error for each

FIGURE 6.1. Sampling distribution of sample mean differences.

Frequency	$\bar{X}_1 - \bar{X}_2$	Total	Distribution
3	−6.00	−18	XXX
3	−5.00	−15	XXX
4	−4.00	−16	XXXX
6	−3.00	−18	XXXXXX
8	−2.00	−16	XXXXXXXX
16	−1.00	−16	XXXXXXXXXXXXXXXX
20	0.00	00	XXXXXXXXXXXXXXXXXXXX
15	1.00	+15	XXXXXXXXXXXXXXX
10	2.00	+20	XXXXXXXXXX
4	3.00	+12	XXXX
3	4.00	+12	XXX
4	5.00	+20	XXXX
3	6.00	+18	XXX
1	7.00	+7	X

$\Sigma = 100$ $\Sigma = 6$ Mean of mean differences $= \dfrac{6}{100} = 0.06$

sample mean will not be 0.628 as calculated in Chapter 5 because $N = 30$, not 376. Thus the standard error for each mean will be

$$\sigma_{\bar{X}_1} = 12.18/\sqrt{30} = 12.18/5.477 = 2.225$$

Because we are exploring the difference between two sample means we have two standard errors to contend with because we want the *standard error of the difference*, the formula for which is given in formula (6.1):

$$\sigma_{\bar{X}_1 - \bar{X}_2} = \sqrt{\sigma_{\bar{X}_1}^2 + \sigma_{\bar{X}_2}^2}, \text{ which is the same } \sqrt{\frac{\sigma_1^2}{N_1} + \frac{\sigma_2^2}{N_2}}$$

where σ_1^2 = the variance in the first population
σ_2^2 = the variance in the second population
N_1 = the number of cases in the first sample
N_2 = the number of cases in the second sample.

Calculating, we get:

$$\sigma_{\bar{X} - \bar{X}_2} = \sqrt{2.224^2 + 2.224^2} = \sqrt{4.946 + 4.946} = \sqrt{9.892} = 3.145$$

What this means is that approximately 68.26% of the differences between means *drawn from the same population* will be within ± 1 $\sigma_{\bar{X}_1 - \bar{X}_2}$ and 95% of them will be between ± 1.96 $\sigma_{\bar{X}_1 - \bar{X}_2}$ or between ± 6.164 ($1.96 \times 3.145 = 6.164$). If samples are *not* drawn from the same population (say, samples of prison inmates and medical students compared on IQ, or Norwegians and Chinese compared on height), things, of course, will be quite different. If we find a difference between two means large enough to be 1.96 $\sigma_{\bar{X}_1 - \bar{X}_2}$ we have an event rare enough to constitute *reasonable doubt* that the null hypothesis is true, and thus we can reject it. If we wish to be more cautious about claiming the null hypothesis is false, we might decide not to reject it unless the difference between the means falls at or beyond 2.58 $\sigma_{\bar{X}_1 - \bar{X}_2}$.

Differences between two means that could have occurred as a result of sampling error fewer than 5 times in every 100 samples are called *significant* differences, meaning that the difference between them is large enough for us to bet (the rent, if not the mortgage) that it is a real difference rather than one that occurred purely by chance. The cutoff point for determining significance is called an **alpha level.** As we saw in the last chapter when discussing confidence intervals, an alpha of a given level says that the researcher is willing to be wrong alpha percent of every 100 samplings of the population. At the 0.05 level it is 5 times in 100, at 0.01 it is 1 time in 100, and at 0.001 it is one time in every 1,000. The lower we set alpha, the more difficult it will be to reject the null simply because we are moving further toward the ends of the decreasing areas of the curve where extremely rare events occur. To summarize, if a statistical test of the null hypothesis fails to achieve significance at the chosen alpha level, we do not reject the null and the status quo is maintained, just as it is in a court of law when the accused is released. We will return to this discussion later.

ERRORS IN HYPOTHESIS TESTING

Regardless of the strength of the evidence used to reject a null hypothesis, it must be understood that it remains possible that our decision to reject could be wrong. Just as

Hypothesis Testing				Jury Trial		
	Null Hypothesis Is Actually				**Defendant Is Actually**	
		False	True		Guilty	Not Guilty
Your Decision — Reject H_0	Correct decision	Type I error	*Jury Verdict* — Guilty	Justice done	Justice not done
Fail to reject H_0	Type II error	Correct decision	Not guilty	Justice not done	Justice done

FIGURE 6.2. Possible outcomes when making decisions about hypotheses and guilt or innocence of criminal defendant.

innocent people are sometimes found guilty, true null hypotheses are sometimes rejected. Wrongly rejecting a true null hypothesis is called a **Type I,** or **alpha** (α), **error.** We never really know if we have committed a type I error, but we can guard against the likelihood by requiring more stringent rules of evidence before making our decision. In science we do this by setting alpha at a lower level, thus moving the critical region further toward the tails of the normal curve. That is, a more conservative test of the null is to set the alpha level at 0.01, or even lower. The **critical region** is the area under the curve that includes unlikely sample outcomes. Again, when we select an alpha level, we are defining *unlikely* as being the selected probability level.

There is a problem with selecting lower alpha levels that should be obvious: As the critical region becomes smaller, the noncritical region necessarily becomes larger. This presents us with a problem parallel with the problem of choosing between confidence and precision that we confronted in Chapter 5. That is, as we minimize the risk of rejecting a true null, we increase the probability of failing to reject a null hypothesis that is in fact false. Failing to reject a false null hypothesis is known as a **Type II,** or beta (β), **error.** Which do we choose to minimize? A Type II error is analogous to setting free an accused person who is in fact guilty; a Type I error is analogous to imprisoning an accused person who is in fact innocent. In principle, the law would rather let the truly guilty free than imprison the truly innocent, and science would rather fail to record a result that (unknown to us) is in fact true than to claim a result that (also unknown to us) is illusory. Unfortunately, the probability of making a Type II error is not simply 1–alpha as you might expect. The two types of errors are only roughly inversely related to one another. The reason that this is so is a subject for a more advanced statistics course. Suffice to say that as the probability of one type of error decreases, the probability of committing the other increases, and that it is impossible to minimize the risk of committing both types of errors simultaneously. Within a single sample we can only minimize the risk of one type of error at the expense of the other. To minimize the probability of a Type I error without increasing the probability of a Type II error, we have to increase sample size. As we have seen, sampling error is inversely related to sample size, so increased sample size will lower the probability of making either type of error.

Figure 6.2 illustrates possible outcomes (correct decisions and errors) in hypothesis testing compared to possible outcomes for a jury trial.

ONE SAMPLE *z* TEST

This chapter deals with hypothesis testing with interval and ratio data using the z and t distributions. As we have emphasized, whenever we compare means from samples we almost always observe a difference between them. Hypothesis testing allows us to decide if the observed difference is large enough to draw the conclusion that the mean of the variable of interest is significantly different from the hypothesized population mean, or if two or more population means differ.

Both the differences between the means of two groups and the size of the variances associated with them contribute to the finding of a significant difference. The greater the absolute difference between the means, the more likely you are to find a significant difference. You are also a lot more likely to find a significant difference when groups have less variability (low standard deviations) within them. In summary, we are likely to obtain a significant difference when there are large differences between the two groups but relatively small differences among subjects or observations within them. We will now apply what we have learned using a one sample z test as an example.

In previous chapters we noted that the mean IQ for our sample of felons is 93.56, with a standard deviation of 12.18. We know from numerous testing with millions of subjects over many years that the population mean IQ (in this instance *population* refers to all Americans) is 100, with a standard deviation of 15. We immediately saw that our sample mean was 6.44 IQ points below the population mean. The question is whether or not this observed difference could have been the result of sampling error. Since we are dealing with a sample, we can never be absolutely sure that the difference is a real one, not attributable to chance. However, we provided you with a clue in Chapter 5 as to how we could decide if the two means really are different, with a low probability that we have made an incorrect decision. We saw that it would require a z value of 8.32 to calculate a confidence interval that would encompass the population mean of 100. We concluded with great confidence that our offenders and the *average American* come from two different IQ populations (in essence, we rejected the null hypothesis that there was no difference). As you may have guessed, confidence intervals and significance testing are intimately connected. We have found that students grasp the idea of significance tests more readily if we build on what they have learned about calculating confidence intervals.

In Chapter 4 we saw that we could translate a raw score in a distribution into a z score. We can also do so for a group of cases. Thus,

$$Z = \frac{x - \overline{X}}{s} \quad \text{for a single score}$$

becomes

$$z = \frac{\overline{X} - \mu}{\sigma / \sqrt{N}} \quad \text{for groups of scores}$$

(6.2)

where $\overline{X}$ = sample mean

μ = population mean

$\sigma / \sqrt{N}$ = standard error.

DECISION RULE

We will illustrate a test of a hypothesis of the form $\mu_1 = \mu_2$ by comparing the mean GRE (graduate record exam) of a sample of 400 students who took a preparatory course ($\overline{X} = 632$, $s = 47$) with the known national mean score ($\mu = 614$, $\sigma = 52$). Since we know the population σ we do not have to estimate it with s. We begin the process conservatively by assuming that the sample mean is equal to the population mean (the null hypothesis). The opposite assumption is that the observed difference is real and not due to chance (the research hypothesis). These two assumptions are stated symbolically as:

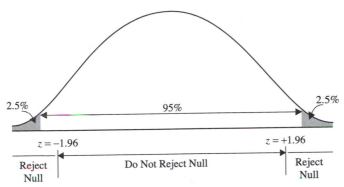

FIGURE 6.3.   Areas under the normal curve and z values necessary to reject the null hypothesis at the 0.05 level of significance.

Null hypothesis: H_0: $\mu_1 = \mu_2$ (GRE scores in both populations are equal)
Research hypothesis: H_1: $\mu_1 \neq \mu_2$ (GRE scores in both populations are not equal)

We know that there is a difference of 18 GRE points ($632 - 614 = 18$) between the preparatory students and the population mean, but we also know that this difference could have been caused by sampling error rather than the preparatory course (the independent variable). We have to establish a cutoff point to separate sample results leading to a decision to accept H_0 from sample results leading to a decision to reject it. This cutoff point is known as the *critical value*. As we have seen, the critical value is a probability value called alpha. The decision rule is that we can reject H_0 if our calculated z is equal to or greater than ± 1.96, because in such a case there is only a 5% (or lower) probability that an observed difference is due to sampling error. Prior to testing our hypotheses we have to specify our alpha level (probability of being wrong). Shown graphically in Figure 6.3, we reject the null if our computed z falls within the shaded areas (the critical regions corresponding to the critical values) on either side of the tail. Actually we know that the calculated z will be positive (because 632 is greater than 614) and will thus be located somewhere to the right of the mean. However, null hypotheses should be formulated prior to data collection to keep us honest. To continue with our criminal trial analogy, assume for now that the direction of the difference is *excluded evidence* and that we are equally interested in rejecting the null at either tail of the curve. When we are equally interested in outcomes at either end of the tail, the 0.05 rejection region is divided between the two tails of the distribution, as in Figure 6.3.

We can now proceed with the test of our hypothesis using formula (6.2):

Null hypothesis: H_0: $\mu_1 = \mu_2$
Population: $\mu = 614, \sigma = 52$
Preparatory students: $\overline{X} = 632, s = 47, N = 400$

Decision rule: The chosen alpha level is 0.05. Reject H_0 if calculated $z \geq 1.96$:

$$z = \frac{\overline{X} - \mu}{\sigma/\sqrt{N}} = \frac{632 - 614}{52/\sqrt{400}} = \frac{18}{52/20} = \frac{18}{2.6} = 6.92$$

$z = 6.92, \qquad p < 0.05$

Our computed z of 6.92 greatly exceeds 1.96. It is extremely unlikely that the observed difference between the sample and population means is due to chance (sampling error). The notation following the z value is shorthand for saying "probability (p) is less than (<) the selected alpha level (0.05)." If we had attained a z value of less than 1.96, the notation would have been $p > 0.05$ (greater than 0.05) or ns (not significant).

Keep in mind that any conclusion the researcher makes must be based on a random sample that is representative of the population. You should also remember that although we have rejected the null hypothesis, we have *not* proven the research hypothesis. We have simply made a decision based on probability that the null is untenable.

THE *t* TEST

When we have small samples, we can no longer assume that sample variances are close approximations of their population variances. We saw in Chapter 5 that the smaller the sample, the larger the standard error tends to be. For these reasons the use of the normal curve, and hence the z test based on it, would be inappropriate. Fortunately, there is a distribution that we can use when we have small samples: the t distribution. For reasons to be discussed shortly, the t distribution should be used when the combined N's of the two samples being tested number less than 120, although it is often a preferred statistic when sample sizes greatly exceed this number.

DEGREES OF FREEDOM

Before we discuss the t distribution and t test, it is necessary to briefly discuss the concept of **degrees of freedom,** which is involved in many of the statistics we will be discussing. Degrees of freedom basically represent restrictions placed on the data. Suppose that we have to select five numbers that must sum to 30. We can choose any five as long a their sum is 30, but only our first four choices are free choices since the fifth number is entirely determined by our previous choices. If we select numbers 9, 6, 5, and 4, for example, our fifth number is restricted to 6. Degrees of freedom (df) in the context of the t test refers to the size of the sample(s) minus the number of parameters being estimated. In testing the difference between two population means based on samples taken from those populations, one sample having an N of 50 and the other an N of 40, the degrees of freedom would be 49 and 39, respectively, for a total of 88 df. In such a test we have actually estimated four parameters: two population means and two population standard deviations. However, we do not lose any df in the estimation of the mean. You might want to convince yourself of this fact by again examining the formula for the mean. We must know the values of all N scores to calculate the mean, so in this sense they are all free to vary. When estimating s, on the other hand, $N - 1$ values are free to vary. That is, since we know that the sum of the deviations from the mean must always be zero, all deviations except the last one are free to vary.

A more complete explanation of the idea of degrees of freedom requires mathematical proofs. For our purposes we will be content with defining the degrees of freedom generally as some function of the number of observations from which a statistic is computed. Specific methods for determining degrees of freedom with different statistical techniques will be explained as the need arises.

THE *t* DISTRIBUTION

The *t* distribution only approximates the normal curve, being more platokurtic (flatter) than the normal curve when df are fewer than 120. For all practical purposes, when df > 120, the *t* distribution is identical with the normal curve. The *t* distribution is a continuous distribution, like the normal curve, but unlike the normal curve it is independent of μ and σ and is entirely specified by a single parameter, the degrees of freedom. Because the single factor determining the shape of *t* is the number of df, it is easy to see that as the sample size changes, the shape of the curve also changes. Unlike the normal curve, for every value of df we generate a unique *t* distribution. As sample sizes become larger and larger, the shape of the curve approaches that of the normal curve.

Figure 6.4 illustrates the *t* distribution with 20 df superimposed on the normal curve. Because the *t* distribution is flatter, its tails appear to contain more area in the critical region than the tails of the normal curve, but in actuality the area is the same. However, we must obtain higher *t* values in order to reject the null than we do for *z* at the same alpha level. The smaller the sample, the more platykurtic the *t* distribution, and the larger the *t* value required to claim significance. For instance, with two samples having a combined *t* of 22 (df = $N - 2$ = 20), the 0.05 rejection region is 2.086 rather than the 1.96 required by *z*. With df = 4, a value of 2.776 or higher is required to reject the null at the 0.05 level of significance.

The *t* test is a popular statistic for comparing means between two samples regardless of the sample size. Its popularity probably rests in the observation that, as sample size increases, the *t* distribution becomes more and more like the normal distribution. If you turn to Table 2 Appendix A you will note, with degrees of freedom greater than 120, that the critical region for rejection of the null hypothesis is exactly the same (1.96) as it is for *z*.

DIRECTIONAL HYPOTHESES: ONE- AND TWO-TAILED TESTS

If researchers have no theoretical reason to believe one group would be more alienated than the other, they would conduct what is called a **two-tailed** or **nondirectional test** of the hypothesis. In a nondirectional hypothesis test we might find a significant difference

FIGURE 6.4. *t* distributions with 20 and infinite degrees of freedom (df) and critical regions for rejecting the null hypothesis at $\alpha = 0.05$.

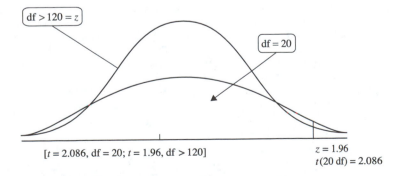

[*t* = 2.086, df = 20; *t* = 1.96, df > 120]   *z* = 1.96
t(20 df) = 2.086

at either side of the distribution curve. We refer to a nondirectional test as two tailed because we can reject the null (assuming we have chosen the 0.05 level of significance) only if our computed statistic corresponds with an area of the normal curve that contains 2.5% of the probabilities on either tail ($z \geq 1.96$). If our computed statistic corresponds with an area under the normal curve that contains 95% of the probabilities ($z < 1.96$), we cannot reject the null.

In a two-tailed test researchers are equally interested in sample outcomes that are significantly greater than or less than the population value, or in which one population value is significantly greater or less than the value of another population. However, if there are theoretical reasons for expecting a difference in a particular direction, researchers may conduct a **one-tailed** or **directional test.** In such cases researchers are concerned only with sample outcomes in one of the tails of the curve. In a one-tailed test the rejection region is $\pm 1.65z$ rather than $1.96z$. To convince yourself of this, turn to Table 1 in Appendix A, containing areas under the normal curve, and you will find that a z of 1.65 corresponds to 0.4505. If we are equally interested in sample outcomes on either side of the mean, we have to double this value to get 0.9010, leaving about 5% of the area on either side, or 10% overall, beyond this range. The 0.10 probability level is not usually considered sufficiently rare to reject the null. However, if we are only interested in outcomes in one side of the tail, we can add the entire area of the side of the curve in which we have no interest to the area of the side of the curve in which we do have interest. Thus, $0.5000 + 0.4505 = 0.9505$. There are now only about 5% of outcomes beyond this single-tailed range, so we can reject the null if our calculated value falls in this region.

What we have done by specifying direction is to locate the 5% of the area that constitutes the rejection region in one tail of the curve, and thereby increased the probability of rejecting the null. But beware. One-tailed tests should be used only when the direction of the outcome can be theoretically justified prior to conducting the test. It should not be used in exploratory research or in research that has previously produced mixed results, and it should never be used simply to increase the probability of rejecting the null hypothesis. Figure 6.5 illustrates the differences in rejection regions for two-tailed and one-tailed tests.

COMPUTING *t*

To illustrate the computation of *t*, we will use a simple example. Suppose researchers are interested in comparing the mean alienation scores of faculty and maintenance staff at a university. They take a random sample of 12 faculty members and 13 maintenance staff and find that the faculty members have a mean score of 50 and a standard deviation of 19.54, and the maintenance workers have a mean of 57.69 and a standard deviation of 14.23. Implicit in the research is the assumption that one's occupational status will affect one's alienation score. Put otherwise, the researchers believe that they can predict the level of alienation on the basis of occupation. Thus, the alienation level is viewed as being dependent on occupation. Recall that a variable considered to be dependent on some other variable is called a *dependent variable,* and a variable that is thought to influence or predict the values of the dependent variable is called an *independent variable.* In the present case, the independent variable, occupation, is assumed to affect variation in alienation scores—the dependent variable. Let us proceed with the calculation of *t*:

Faculty	Maintenance staff
$\bar{X} = 50.0s = 19.54N = 12$	$\bar{X} = 57.69s = 14.23N = 13$

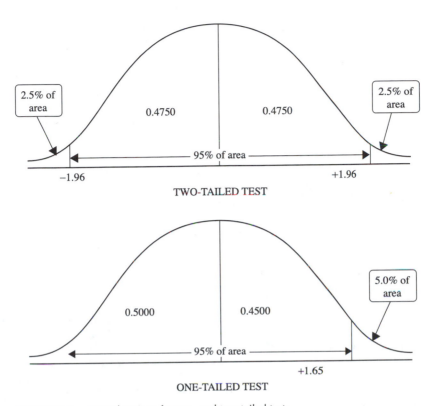

FIGURE 6.5. Critical regions for one- and two-tailed tests.

$\alpha = 0.05$, one-tailed test

$$t = \frac{\overline{X}_1 - \overline{X}_2}{\sqrt{\dfrac{N_1 S_1^{\,2} + N_2 S_2^{\,2}}{N_1 + N_2 - 2}}\sqrt{\dfrac{N_1 + N_2}{(N_1)(N_2)}}} \tag{6.3}$$

Notice that by adding the variances of our two samples together we have pooled the variance for each group after we have computed it by squaring the standard deviations. Note that $N_1 + N_2 - 2$ represents the degrees of freedom associated with the test.

$$t = \frac{50 - 57.69}{\sqrt{\dfrac{(12)(19.54)^2 + (13)(14.23)^2}{12 + 13 - 2}}\sqrt{\dfrac{12 + 13}{(12)(13)}}}$$

Step 1. Put in numbers, subtract mean 2 from mean 1, square the standard deviations:

$$t = \frac{-7.69}{\sqrt{\dfrac{(12)(381.8) + (13)(202.49)}{25 - 2}}\sqrt{\dfrac{25}{156}}}$$

Step 2. Multiply both variances by their respective Ns. Perform the multiplication and addition:

$$t = \frac{-7.69}{\sqrt{\frac{4581.6 + 2632.37}{23}} \sqrt{0.1603}}$$

Step 3. Perform the addition on the right side of the equation and divide the sum by 23. Take the square root of 0.1603:

$$t = -\frac{-7.69}{\sqrt{313.65}(0.40)} = \frac{-7.69}{(17.71)(0.40)}$$

Step 4. Take the square root of 313.65 and multiply that by 0.40. Divide −7.69 by 7.084:

$$t = \frac{-7.69}{7.084} = \frac{\text{Difference between means}}{\text{Standard error of difference}} = -1.085$$

Our calculated t value is −1.085. To determine if this value is statistically significant (if it is sufficiently large to allow us to reject the null), we turn to the table of t values in Appendix A. Because we have theoretical reasons to assume that maintenance workers would have higher alienation scores, we have specified which of these two means would be greater, and we thus use the line in the table marked "level of significance for one-tailed test." We have selected an alpha of 0.05, so we use the 0.05 column and read down the extreme left-hand column until we get to the number 23, which is our number of degrees of freedom. Where these two values intersect in the body of the table we find the number 1.714. This means that to claim a significant difference between the means with alpha set at 0.05 and using a one-tailed test, the difference between means must be equal to or greater than 1.714 times the value of the standard error of the difference. If our computed t value is equal to or greater than this value, we reject the null hypothesis. However, our calculated t value is only −1.085, which is less than 1.714 (the negative sign is ignored in reading the t table, as it is when reading areas under the normal curve). We thus conclude that there is no significant difference between the means of these two populations with regard to their alienation scores. Occupation does not predict alienation levels. The possibility remains, however, that we could have made a Type II error given the very small sizes of our samples. To reiterate:

$t_{\text{calculated}} = -1.085,$ $t_{\text{critical}} = 1.714$ (table value needed to reject H_0, $\alpha = 0.05$ one-tailed)
Conclusion: t calculated is not equal or greater than t critical at $\alpha = 0.05$
Decision: Do not reject the null.

t Test for Correlated (Dependent) Means

The t-test formulas discussed so far have assumed random samples from independent groups; that is, there was not any connection between cases in each sample or subsample. However, we sometimes have occasion to test differences between means from nonindependent groups, such as means obtained from matched pairs of subjects or from the same individuals tested twice. If we match individuals on IQ scores obtained from one test, for instance, and then compare group IQ means from a second test, we are not likely to see a very large difference between the means. Similarly, if we test individuals at time 1 and time 2, an individual who scored high at time 1 is likely also to score high at time 2. In other words, the two means being compared have a built-in connection (correlation). The correlated *t* test provides a basis for testing correlated groups because it has a factor in its formula that corrects for the built-in correlation.

Suppose we ask 10 social workers on July 20 (*time 1*) to rate a hypothetical family's need for subsidized housing. The ratings are based on a scale of 0 (no need) to 20 (extreme need). We then go back to the same social workers on December 20 (*time 2*) and present them with the same case. Since December 20 is close to Christmas, we expect them to be more charitable this time around. What we actually want to find out is how susceptible the assessment instrument is to subjective judgment. If the mean at time 2 is significantly greater than the mean at time 1 at <0.05 we conclude that the assessment instrument is subject to subjective bias. The data for the two testing times and the statistical procedure for testing our assumption are presented in Table 6.1.

In Table 6.1 we have arrayed the scores of each social worker taken at time 1 and time 2 and calculated each mean. We then take the difference between each score at time 1 and time 2 and calculate the mean difference (1.6). We then square each difference and sum to arrive at the sum of the squared differences (34). We then substitute the appropriate values into formula (6.4). Because the same subjects are tested twice, $N = 10$, not 20.

$$t = \frac{\overline{X}_1 - \overline{X}_2}{\sqrt{\dfrac{\Sigma D^2 - \dfrac{(\Sigma D)^2}{N}}{N(N-1)}}} = \frac{13.6 - 15.2}{\sqrt{\dfrac{34 - \dfrac{256}{10}}{10(9)}}}$$

$$= \frac{-1.6}{\sqrt{\dfrac{34 - 25.6}{90}}} = \frac{-1.6}{\sqrt{0.0933}} = \frac{-1.6}{0.3055} = -5.24$$

$$t = -5.24, \quad df = 9, \quad p < 0.05 \tag{6.4}$$

Table 6.1   Data on Social Worker Ratings and Summary of Procedures For *t* Test of Correlated Means

SOCIAL WORKER	TIME 1	TIME 2	DIFFERENCE D	D^2
1	17	19	2	4
2	16	17	1	1
3	14	15	1	1
4	13	16	3	9
5	12	15	3	9
6	17	19	2	4
7	16	16	0	0
8	9	11	2	4
9	9	10	1	1
10	13	14	1	1
N = 10	$\Sigma X_1 = 136$	$\Sigma X_2 = 152$	$\Sigma D = 16$	$\Sigma D^2 = 34$
	$\overline{X}_1 = 13.6$	$\overline{X}_2 = 15.2$		

The computed $t(t_{calculated}) = -5.24$. With 9 df, and $\alpha = 0.05$, the t value required to reject the null ($t_{critical} = 2.262$. *Decision:* Reject the null; the mean at time 2 is significantly greater than the mean at time 1.

If we had used the t test for independent samples with these data, do you think we would have found a significant difference between the means? Your emerging statistical intuition will tell you that with a difference of only 1.6 rating points between the mean at time 1 and the mean at time 2, you would not be likely to reject the null by using formula (6.3). The correction factor built into formula (6.4) ensures that you are more likely to pick up a difference, if one exists. Hence you are less likely to make a Type II error.

EFFECTS OF SAMPLE VARIANCE ON H_0 DECISION

Figure 6.6 illustrates the effects of sample variability in rejecting or failing to reject the null hypothesis with the same observed mean difference. In the first example there is small variability in both samples. If we compute the standard error of the difference between the means of sample A and B we get 2.84. Dividing the difference between means (10) by the computed standard error of the difference, we obtain a significant t ratio of 3.52. Now consider samples C and D. Although the means are the same as samples A and B, the variability is much greater. Computing the standard error of the difference between these two means, we obtain 6.27 for a t ratio of 1.59, which is not large enough to allow us to reject the null. The overlap of variability for samples C and D is shown in the shaded area of Figure 6.6. Clearly, both samples could have come from populations with identical means, and thus we cannot reject the null hypothesis.

LARGE SAMPLE t TEST: A COMPUTER EXAMPLE

Now that you understand the logic underlying the two-sample t test, we can present a real life example from our felony offender data. Suppose that we want to find out if sex offenders or non–sex offenders are punished more severely in this jurisdiction. Sentence severity is rendered in terms of days in prison. Thus, each offender group has a mean number of days of imprisonment. Our null hypothesis states that there is no significant difference between the sentence severity means of the two groups.

Our research hypothesis states that sex offenders receive significantly harsher penalties than do non–sex offenders. Offender type is our independent variable with two attributes (sex offender versus non–sex offender), and sentence severity is the dependent variable. The assumption is that sentence severity will change as we move from one attribute of the independent variable to the other.

INTERPRETING THE PRINTOUT

The output in Table 6.2 compares the sentence severity means of group 1 (non–sex offenders; $N = 206$) and group 2 (sex offenders; $N = 431$). The first piece of information tells us that the mean severity of sentence for non–sex offenders is 324.13, and the mean for sex offenders is 572.26. The difference between the means of the two groups is a substantial one of 248.1 sentence severity points.

Next we look at standard deviations. Their most overwhelming feature is that they are both larger than their respective means. Obviously one standard deviation below the mean in both cases is going to put us into negative sentence severity scores. We know it is not possible for an offender to have a negative sentence; and thus our curves for these

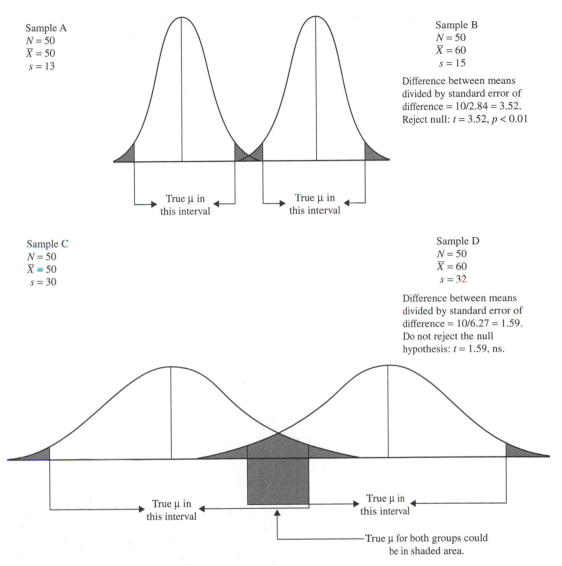

Sample A
N = 50
$\overline{X}$ = 50
s = 13

Sample B
N = 50
$\overline{X}$ = 60
s = 15

Difference between means
divided by standard error of
difference = 10/2.84 = 3.52.
Reject null: $t = 3.52$, $p < 0.01$

True μ in
this interval

True μ in
this interval

Sample C
N = 50
$\overline{X}$ = 50
s = 30

Sample D
N = 50
$\overline{X}$ = 60
s = 32

Difference between means
divided by standard error of
difference = 10/6.27 = 1.59.
Do not reject the null
hypothesis: $t = 1.59$, ns.

True μ in
this interval

True μ in
this interval

True μ for both groups could
be in shaded area.

FIGURE 6.6. Illustrating the effects of small and large variability, in the rejection or retention of the null hypothesis.

two groups are clearly very positively skewed. Because these standard deviations are larger than their respective means, we conclude that these are not normal curves. Insofar as theoretical interpretation of the result is concerned, we are not unduly alarmed about this finding. A great deal of sentencing variation is to be expected when dealing with a heterogeneous sample of criminals who have committed crimes ranging from receiving stolen property to murder.

Clearly there is a difference in sentence severity means between these two offender groups, but is the difference significant? We know immediately that our directional hypothesis corresponds to what is going on statistically. That is, we hypothesized

Table 6.2   Computer Printout Assessing the Null that Sentence Severity Does Not Differ between Groups (Non–Sex Offenders vs. Sex Offenders)

VARIABLE: SENSV = SUBJECTS SENTENCE SEVERITY SCORE

GROUP	N	MEAN	STD DEV	STD ERROR
1. Non–sex offender	206	324.136	569.997	39.714
2. Sex offender	431	572.264	779.570	37.550

VARIANCES	t	df	PROBABILITY
Unequal	−4.5399	532.5	0.0001
Equal	−4.0764	635.0	0.0001

Test for equality of variances $F = 1.87$ with 430 and 205 df Prob < 0.0001

that sex offenders were going to get more severe sentences than non–sex offenders, and they do. In other words, the independent variable does help us make predictions regarding the dependent variable, but only if the difference is significant.

Next we consider the STD ERROR, or the standard error of the mean. Again, this is the standard deviation divided by the square root of N, computed for each of our two categories. As we saw in Chapter 5, we can use the standard error to place confidence intervals around the means of our two offender groups.

Next in the listing we encounter variances. You will recall from Chapter 3 that variance is a measure of how the scores are dispersed around the mean. The larger the spread of scores around the mean, the larger the variance. The computer calculates two t tests based on equal and unequal variance. The t test assumes equality of group variances, which makes sense because if two groups are sampled from the same population, we should expect only random variance difference. Although homogeneity of variance is an assumption of the t test, the test is quite robust. **Robustness** refers to the ability of a test to withstand violations of its assumptions without seriously impairing its interpretation.

At this point we must make a decision about which of these two tests we are going to use. All statistical packages use some variation of the F test to help us with this decision. We will discuss the F test in greater detail in the next chapter, but for now just think of it as simply another test of the significance. In this case it is a test of the significance of difference between sample variances. The part of the printout that addresses the issue of whether or not the two group variances differ reads, "Test for equality of variances $F = 1.87$ with 430 and 205 df Prob < 0.0001." This means that under the null hypothesis that the variances are equal, F with 430 and 205 degrees of freedom (the degrees of freedom associated with each group) was calculated to be 1.87, and the probability that the variances are equal is 0.0001, or one chance in 10,000. What this statement means practically is that when the F value falls below 0.05 we must use the unequal variance test to determine whether or not t is significant. To obtain the F value, we square the standard deviations for each of the groups to get the variance and then divide the larger variance by the smaller variance. Presented symbolically,

$$F = \frac{s^2(\text{larger variance})}{s^2(\text{smaller variance})} = \frac{779.6^2}{570^2} = \frac{607776.2}{324900.0} = 1.87$$

Thus, in our example, the larger variance is 1.87 times greater than the smaller variance.

Because our F value is significant, we have unequal variances and must use the t value based on unequal variance. This t value is given as −4.5399, which is significant at the 0.0001 level with degrees of freedom equal to 532.5. The nice thing about these computer listings is that they give us the exact probability of the *t* test and we do not have to use a table. We conclude that there is a significant difference between the sentence severity score of sex offenders and non–sex offenders. We accept our directional hypothesis: Sex offenders receive significantly more severe sentences.

We should point out that most computer printouts give us the two-tailed level of significance. If we are conducting a directional hypothesis we would simply divide the given probability value by 2. It makes no difference in the present example, but if the probability level was, say, 0.0650, knowing this value would prevent you from correctly rejecting a false null since 0.0650/2 = 0.0325.

CALCULATING *t* WITH UNEQUAL VARIANCES

Notice that we can obtain two different *t* values based on the same data. This is possible because two different formulas were used. The first is formula (6.3), used to calculate *t* for our alienation example. We calculated our example under the assumption of equal variances, an assumption that allowed us to pool the variances of both samples and treat them as a single variance. If the variances are unequal we cannot pool them, and they must be considered separately. Because we treat unequal variances separately, we require a different formula, formula (6.5). Compare this formula with formula (6.3) for pooled variance. We will demonstrate the use of the separate variance formula by using the sentence severity/group data.

$$
t = \frac{\overline{X}_1 - \overline{X}_2}{\sqrt{\dfrac{s_1^2}{N_1 - 1} + \dfrac{s_2^2}{N_2 - 1}}}
$$

$$
= \frac{324.1 - 572.2}{\sqrt{\dfrac{570.0^2}{205} + \dfrac{779.6^2}{430}}} = \frac{-248.1}{\sqrt{\dfrac{324900}{205} + \dfrac{607776.2}{430}}}
$$

$$
= \frac{-248.1}{\sqrt{1584.9 + 1413.4}} = \frac{-248.1}{\sqrt{2998.3}} = \frac{-248.1}{54.76} = -4.53
$$

$$
t = -4.53, \qquad p < 0.0001 \tag{6.5}
$$

Our computed *t* of −4.53 matches the printout. Notice that the computer also adjusts the degrees of freedom when the variances are unequal. The formula used to accomplish this computation is formidable, and it is not really necessary for you to know at this stage in your statistical education. Do note that if we had based our decision on the assumption of equal variances, we would have had extra protection against rejecting a true null hypothesis, as reflected by the smaller *t* value. When the larger sample is associated with the larger variance, as is the case here, the *t* test is conservative with respect to committing Type I errors. In other words, the deck is stacked in favor of the null hypothesis in such instances.

TESTING HYPOTHESES FOR SINGLE-SAMPLE PROPORTIONS

Let us return now to our gun control issue mentioned at the beginning of the chapter. Recall that the politician claimed that 56% of Michiganders supported a particular gun control bill, and that we found that only 48% supported it in our random telephone sample of 500 Michiganders. We wish to determine if there are sufficient grounds to question the validity of the politician's claim. We are actually testing a claim about a supposedly known population parameter with a sample statistic, hence the term *single-sample test*. The formula for a single-sample test of hypotheses for proportions is given in formula (6.6). Because we want to be really confident before claiming that the politician's figure is incorrect, we set alpha at 0.01.

$$z = \frac{Ps - Pp}{\sqrt{\dfrac{Pp(1 - Pp)}{N}}} \qquad\qquad (6.6)$$

where Pp = population proportion
Ps = sample proportion
N = sample size.

H_0: $Pp = 0.56,$ $\alpha = 0.01.$ Reject if $z_{calculated} \geq 2.58$

Now we compute the test statistic:

$$z = \frac{0.48 - 0.56}{\sqrt{\dfrac{(0.56)(0.44)}{500}}} = \frac{-0.8}{\sqrt{\dfrac{0.2688}{500}}} = \frac{-0.8}{\sqrt{0.0005376}} = \frac{-0.8}{0.0232} = 3.45$$

Our computed z of 3.45 is greater than the value of z needed to reject the null at the 0.01 level of significance (2.58). Thus, we reject the null and conclude that the percentage of Michiganders who support the gun control bill is not 56%.

STATISTICAL VERSUS SUBSTANTIVE SIGNIFICANCE, AND STRENGTH OF ASSOCIATION

The point should be strongly made that statistical significance is not necessarily the same as substantive or theoretical significance, although, of course, it may be. Statistical significance tells us when some difference is large enough to be consistently and reliably found, not whether the difference is theoretically important. With a large enough sample, even small differences, if they exist in the population, will be found. A particular research finding may be like an old penny on the floor. You may be able to find it but be unwilling to pick it up. To avoid the confusion over statistical and theoretical significance, the term *statistically reliable,* or perhaps *statistically dependable,* would be a better one to use. However, we are not about to tamper with the time-honored terminology of statistics.

One strategy to determine if a statistically significant finding is worth picking up is to compute a measure of association in conjunction with every test of significance. We will more fully discuss the concept of association in Chapter 9. It is enough to say now that a measure of association quantifies the degree to which two variables are related, linked, or associated. These measures range within fixed limits between −1.0 and +1.0, or sometimes between 0.0 and 1.0. The closer the value to −1.0 or +1.0, the closer the two variables are related to one another. Measures of significance do not range within fixed limits because the computed values depend greatly on sample size, and are thus not comparable across different samples. Measures of association are comparable across different samples because they adjust the value of the computed significance test to its maximum attainable value for a given sample size. The logic is similar to computing percentages or rates, which enables us to compare samples and populations that differ in size.

The measure of association typically calculated in conjunction with difference between means tests is eta squared (η^2), the simple formula for which is given in formula (6.7):

$$\eta^2 = \frac{t^2}{t^2 + \mathrm{df}} \qquad (6.7)$$

where $t^2 = t_{\mathrm{calculated}}$ squared and df = degrees of freedom associated with the t test. Applying this to our felony offender example, we get

$$\eta^2 = \frac{-4.0764^2}{-4.0764^2 + 635} = \frac{16.62}{16.62 + 635} = \frac{16.62}{651.62} = 0.0255$$

This means that offender group accounts for 2.5% of the variance in sentence severity. In other words, the **variance** represents 100% of the variability in sentence severity in our sample. Certain factors *account for* or *explain* portions of that variance. In the present example, the *group* variable accounts for a mere 2.5% of that variance, leaving 97.5% to be accounted for by other variables. Offender group thus plays a relatively minor role in determining sentence severity.

We cannot compute a measure of association with our Michigan gun control example. Computing a measure of association is possible only when two or more variables are thought to be linked in some way, such as is in the case with the sex offender data where we hypothesized that *group* was associated with *sentence severity*. In the gun control example we had only one variable, *attitude toward gun control,* and simply wanted to determine if two proportions purporting to measure it were similar or different.

Although significance testing is a valuable tool, you should constantly be aware of the shortcomings of your sampling procedures, of the distinction between statistical and theoretical significance, and of the need to compute a measure of association with each test. Do not generalize beyond the population from which the sample was drawn. For instance, do not make assumptions about all Democrats from a sample of Democrats drawn only from Toledo, Ohio. (This is not to say, however, that a dozen small, well-designed studies of single communities around the country will not tell you a great deal about Democrats in general when the studies are viewed in their entirety.)

SUMMARY

Hypothesis testing is a process of testing propositions derived from theory according to rigorous rules. We begin with a hypothesis about parameters in one or more populations and test it with sample statistics. The hypothesis to be tested is the null hypothesis of equality, or *no difference*. We reject the null hypothesis only if our computed statistics achieve a given level of significance. A level of statistical significance is known as an alpha level, conventional alpha levels being 0.05 and 0.01. These levels correspond with areas under the standard normal curve known as critical regions.

Two types of errors, Type I (alpha) and Type II (beta), were identified. A Type I error is the wrongful rejection of a true null hypothesis, and a Type II error is the failure to reject a false null hypothesis. The two errors are roughly inversely related, although the probability of β is not simply $1 - \alpha$. Scientists try to minimize the probability of a Type I error by moving the rejection region closer to the tail of the normal curve, a strategy that simultaneously increases the risk of a Type II error. Increasing sample size is one method of decreasing the probability of making either type of error.

We use the z distribution to test the hypothesis that some population mean estimated by a sample mean is equal to some constant (a known mean) or that two population means estimated from sample means are equal. When sample Ns are 120 or fewer we use the t distribution. The t distribution is more platykurtic than the normal curve, but it is identical with it when df are greater than 120.

Tests of hypotheses can be either nondirectional or directional. A nondirectional hypothesis is one in which the direction of any difference between means is not predicted from prior theoretical knowledge and in which the researcher is equally interested in outcomes in either tail of the distribution. This type of test is also known as a two-tailed test. A directional, or one-tailed test, is conducted when there are good theoretical reasons for expecting differences to occur only in one tail of the distribution. The effect of a one-tailed test is to move the rejection region closer to the mean. At the 0.05 level a one-tailed test will reject the hypothesis at z (or t if df are greater than 120) = 1.65, rather than the 1.96 required for a two-tailed test.

Depending on whether or not there are equal variances in the two groups, t tests are computed differently. Equality of variance is computed by obtaining the ratio of the larger variance to the smaller variance. If the variances are determined to be equal with the F ratio, t is computed by pooling the variances. If the variances are not equal, t is computed by the separate variance formula.

We tested a hypothesis for single-sample proportions and noted that we cannot compute a measure of association when only one variable is involved.

Statistical significance and substantive significance are not necessarily the same thing, although it can be. One way to assess the substantive significance of an independent variable is to compute a measure of association directly from the computed value of the significance test. The measure typically computed in conjunction with the t test is eta squared, a measure that ranges between 0.0 and 1.0, and which standardizes a calculated t by dividing it by the maximum possible t for a given sample size.

PRACTICE APPLICATION: *t* TEST

Researchers are interested in determining whether or not differential socialization of males and females leads to a differential acceptance of their bodies. They asked 125 females and 85 males to express their level of satisfaction with their bodies on a five-point scale ranging from 0 for complete acceptance to 5 for complete lack of acceptance. The null hypothesis is that there is no difference between males and females in the acceptance of their bodies. The researcher obtains the following data:

Female: $N = 125$, $\overline{X} = 2.75$, $s = 1.40$
Male: $N = 85$, $\overline{X} = 1.50$, $s = 1.30$

Use the t-test formula for equal variances and set alpha at 0.05. The null hypothesis is that there is no sex difference in the acceptance of one's body.

$$t = \frac{\overline{X}_1 - \overline{X}_2}{\sqrt{\dfrac{N_1 S_1^2 + N_2 S_2^2}{N_1 + N_2 - 2}} \sqrt{\dfrac{N_1 + N_2}{(N_1)(N_2)}}}$$

$$= \frac{2.75 - 1.5}{\sqrt{\dfrac{(125)(1.96) + (85)(1.69)}{125 + 85 - 2}} \sqrt{\dfrac{125 + 85}{(125)(85)}}}$$

$$= \frac{1.25}{\sqrt{\dfrac{245 + 143.65}{208}} \sqrt{\dfrac{210}{10625}}}$$

$$= \frac{1.25}{\sqrt{1.8685}\ \sqrt{0.01976}} = \frac{1.25}{(1.3669)(.1406)} = \frac{1.25}{0.1922} = 6.5$$

The critical value of t with df above 120 (at infinity) at the 0.05 critical value is 1.96. Thus if our computed t is equal to or larger than 1.96, we reject the null hypothesis and accept the research hypothesis. Because 6.5 is larger than 1.96 we reject the null and find that males, in general, are more accepting of their bodies than females.

Compute eta squared:

$$\eta^2 = \frac{t^2}{t^2 + df} = \frac{6.5^2}{6.5^2 + 208} = \frac{42.25}{250.25} = 0.1688$$

Gender accounts for 16.88% of the variance in acceptance of one's body, leaving 83.12% of the variance accounted for by other factors.

PROBLEMS

1. A large sample test of a hypothesis is conducted about the value of a mean. The observed z value is 1.80. Find the p value when the alternative hypothesis is the following:
   a) $H_a: \mu < \mu_0$
   b) $H_a: \mu \neq \mu_0$
   c) $H_a: \mu > \mu_0$

2. The p value for a large sample test about a mean is reported to be $p = 0.10$. Find the value of the z-test statistic for each of the alternative hypotheses:
   a) $H_a: \mu < \mu_0$
   b) $H_a: \mu \neq \mu_0$
   c) $H_a: \mu > \mu_0$

3. Indicate whether the following statements are true or false:
   a) If the 0.05 level is used, there are, on average, 5 or fewer chances in 100 of making a Type I error.
   b) If the null hypothesis is rejected, one can be certain that the alternative or research hypothesis is true.
   c) As the probability of making a Type I error is reduced, the probability of making a Type II error is increased.
   d) Rejecting the null hypothesis when it is actually true in the population is called a Type I error.

4. A conclusion is to be made in a test of $H_0: \mu = \mu_0$ against $H_a: \mu > \mu_0$, using the $\alpha = 0.05$ level. For a value five units above the null hypothesis value of the mean, the probability of a Type II error is determined to be .10.
   a) Explain the meaning of this last sentence.
   b) If the test were conducted at the $\alpha = 0.01$ level, would the probability of a Type II error be less than, equal to, or greater than 0.10?

5. You need to make a decision about whether to reject H_0 in a statistical test, but are worried about the possibility of making a Type I error. Explain how you can control the probability of a Type I error.

6. If a jury convicts an innocent person, would this most likely be a Type I or a Type II error? If a jury finds a defendant not guilty when in fact they truly are guilty, would this be a Type I or a Type II error?

7. For each of the following situations, indicate whether H_0 should be retained or rejected.
   a) Given a two-tailed test with $\alpha = 0.05$ and
      ■ $z = 1.74$
      ■ $z = 0.13$
      ■ $z = -2.51$

b) Given a one-tailed test, lower tail critical with $\alpha = 0.01$ and
- ■ $z = -2.34$
- ■ $z = -5.13$
- ■ $z = 4.04$

c) Given a one-tailed test, upper tail critical with $\alpha = 0.05$ and
- ■ $z = 2.00$
- ■ $z = -1.80$
- ■ $z = 1.61$

8. A local school district recently implemented an experimental program for science education. After 1 year, the 36 children in the special program obtained an average score of 61.8 on a national science achievement test. This test is standardized so that the national average is 60 with a standard deviation of 6. Did the students in the special program score significantly above the national average? Use a one-tailed test with $\alpha = 0.05$.

9. A recent national survey reported that the general population gave the president an average rating of $\mu = 60$ on a scale of 1 to 100, with 1 being most unfavorable and 100 being most favorable. A researcher hypothesizes that college students are likely to be more critical of the president than people in the general population. To test her hypothesis, she selects a random sample of college students and has them rate the president. She collects the following scores:

44	57	61	59	66	19
50	25	56	48	45	55
24	90	80	88	35	21
45	78	66	36	95	92
39	54	53	51	22	60

On the basis of this sample, can the researcher conclude that college students rate the president more critically?

10. An affluent nation has a mean household income of $43,700 in 1996. A sample of 800 families drawn from a single state has a mean income of $38,200 with a standard deviation of $5,110. Could this state be considered poorer than the national average?

11. The mean number of children per family in a South American country was 3.2 in 1984, with a standard deviation of 2.0. In 1995, a sample of 100 families has a mean of 2.8 children per family. Is this decrease statistically significant?

12. A fundraiser for a charitable organization has set a goal of averaging $25 per donation. To see if the goal is being met, a random sample of recent donations is selected. The data are as follows:

25	10	15	30	10
10	10	30	10	15
25	50	100	10	15
100	5	5	15	25

Do the contributions differ significantly from the goal of the fundraiser?

13. A study of University professors indicates that males with 5 years experience earn a base salary of $42,500 with a standard deviation of $5,000. Females with 5 years experience earn an average of $40,000 with a standard deviation of $7,000. The samples consist of a random selection of 50 male and 35 female professors. Do males earn significantly more than females in this occupation?

14. An experiment was conducted to evaluate the effect of two dosage levels of a drug designed to relieve allergy symptoms. One group of allergy sufferers was given a 25-mg dose of the drug each day and another group of allergy sufferers was given a 50-mg dose of the drug each day. After 1 month, each participant was rated on a scale of 1–80 with high scores indicating more allergy symptoms present and a low score indicating relief from allergy symptoms. The data are listed below. Did the 50-mg dose provide significantly more relief than the 25-mg dose?

25-MG DOSE			50-MG DOSE		
62	30	45	50	60	33
70	80	59	48	32	48
66	40	60	63	75	23
54	49	75	39	30	23

15. A mathematics aptitude test is taken by 10 college freshman selected at random both before and after undergoing an intensive training course designed to improve their performance on the test. The paired scores are listed below:

STUDENT	BEFORE	AFTER
1	60	70
2	73	80
3	42	40
4	88	94
5	66	79
6	77	86
7	90	93
8	63	71
9	55	70
10	96	97

a) Compare the mean scores before and after the training course by finding and interpreting the p value for testing whether the mean change equals 0.
b) Compare the mean scores before and after the training course by constructing and interpreting a 90% confidence interval for the population mean difference.
c) Give a couple of other examples where it would be sensible to compare means using dependent samples rather than independent samples.

Chapter 7

ANALYSIS OF VARIANCE

The z and t tests allow us to compare differences between two group means. **Analysis of variance (ANOVA)** is an extension to these tests that allows us to compare more than two group means for significant differences simultaneously. There are many forms of ANOVA, ranging from the relatively simple to the complex. In this chapter we will examine the most basic form of ANOVA, one-way analysis of variance, and then briefly discuss two-way ANOVA. In one-way ANOVA we are interested in the mean values of an interval- or ratio-level dependent variable within three or more categories of an independent variable.

ASSUMPTIONS OF ANALYSIS OF VARIANCE

ANOVA takes advantage of the following assumptions:

1. Independent random samples
2. Interval or ratio level of measurement
3. Independent subjects in each group (i.e., not the same subjects tested twice and not matched subjects)
4. Homogeneity of variance
5. Normal sampling distribution.

ANOVA tests the equality of means under the assumption that all category, group, or sample means come from a random sample of independent subjects from the same population. If we are testing the equality of three category means, the null hypothesis would be presented symbolically as

$$H_0: \mu_1 = \mu_2 = \mu_3$$

The research hypothesis would be that at least two of the means differ.

THE BASIC LOGIC OF ANOVA

ANOVA is based on a comparison of two sources of variance in the dependent variable: between- and within-group variance. The **between-group variance** is often referred to as the explained variance because it is accounted for by the grouped or categorized independent variable. The **within-group variance** is referred to as the unexplained variance because it is the proportion of the variance left unexplained by the groupings. The first of these sources of variance is an estimate of the variance between the group means. (It would be more grammatically correct to say *among* the groups, but *between* is the convention.) If there is no difference between the means other than that attributable to chance, the null hypothesis is true. The second source of variability is due to differences among the individual observations within the groups. The null hypothesis testing the equivalence of these two sources of variance is tested with the F distribution (F is capitalized because it is named after its originator, the British statistician Ronald Fisher).

The logic of ANOVA is that if the variance between groups is significantly greater than the variance within the groups, the populations from which the groups came can also be considered to be different with regard to the dependent variable.

In a *t* test, the difference between two group means constitutes the numerator, and the denominator is the standard error of the difference of means, which is a measure of the differences within the two groups being compared. The larger the *t* ratio, the greater the probability of rejecting the null hypothesis. The logic of ANOVA is analogous, and with only two groups to compare, ANOVA provides the same answer as the *t* test. The difference is that *t* focuses on means, whereas ANOVA focuses on variances, although, of course, means and variances are used in the calculation of both statistics. The comparison is made for you symbolically below. Note that both formulas describe a ratio of between- and within-group differences.

$$t = \frac{\text{Difference of means}}{\text{Standard error of difference}} \qquad F = \frac{\text{Between–group variance}}{\text{Within–group variance}}$$

THE IDEA OF VARIANCE REVISITED

As we indicated in Chapter 3, *variance* refers to the extent to which values on some attributes for individuals or objects differ from their mean. The objective of science is to determine the source of this variability. We ask questions like "What is it that 'causes' or accounts for the observed differences between this group of people and that group of people?" The hypothetical distributions in Figure 7.1 should reinforce your understanding of *accounting for variance*. Both samples are composed of three different groups or subsamples divided according to the social class of their members. The numbers represent individual scores on some sort of test. There is considerable variation in both samples, with individual scores ranging from 30 to 54 in sample A, and from 12 to 70 in sample B, although their grand means (the mean of the group means) are identical at 42. Group means in both samples are also identical at 52, 42, and 32, so the dispersion of group means (between-group variance) around their grand means will be identical in both samples.

Within-group variance refers to the extent to which observations vary *within* a group. Which of the two samples has greater within-group variance? Obviously, it is sample B. In sample A the maximum difference within any group (among individual group members) is 4, whereas in sample B the maximum difference is 43 (55 − 12 = 43). In sample A the variance attributable to social class (between-group variance) is larger than the variance attributable to individual differences within those class categories (within-group variance). In sample B we observe the opposite situation, in which between-group variance, although identical with sample A, is less than the variance *within* social class groups. The distribution curves of each subsample further help you to visualize the difference between between- and within-group variance. Notice that the leptokurtic curves in sample A have no significant overlap (no overlapping within-group variance). The overlapping platykurtic curves in sample B reflect the greater variability of the scores within them.

Substantively, we would conclude from sample A that variation in social class (between-group variation) appears more important in accounting for variation in test scores than variation in any individual attributes (within-group variation) members of the groups may possess. We would conclude the opposite from sample B; that is, individual differences are more important in accounting for test scores than is one's social class category.

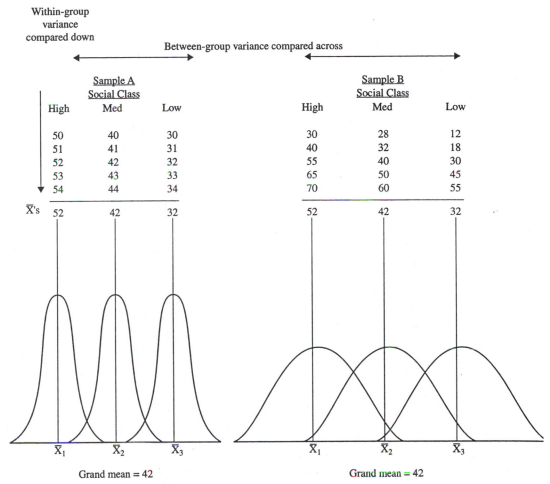

FIGURE 7.1. Illustrating between- and within-group variance.

THE ADVANTAGE OF ANOVA OVER MULTIPLE TESTS

You might wonder why we do not simply calculate separate t tests between all possible pairs of groups rather than bother with another test. The simple answer is that it would be inefficient and misleading to do so. The number of pairwise group comparisons is determined by the formula $N(N-1)/2$. If we were comparing four group means we would have to run $(4)(3)/2 = 6$ separate t tests. With ANOVA we have to perform only one test. Further, if we run six separate t tests they would not all be independent comparisons and the resulting probabilities would overlap, thus increasing the probability of making a Type I error. Remember, if we are looking for a difference that is statistically significant at the 0.05 level, we would falsely reject a true null hypothesis in the long run in 1 out of every 20 comparisons. The more separate tests we conduct, the more likely it becomes that we will claim that some difference is real when it is actually due to chance. For instance, with six separate t tests, each with an alpha of 0.05, the actual combined alpha would be

$$\text{Actual alpha} = 1 - [(1 - \alpha)(1 - \alpha)(1 - \alpha)(1 - \alpha)(1 - \alpha)(1 - \alpha)]$$

$$= 1 - [(.95)(.95)(.95)(.95)(.95)(.95)] = 1 - .73509 = .2649$$

From the preceding we see that the probability of one or more Type I errors in using a series of t tests where each is set at 0.05 is about 0.2649. In short, the more tests we perform, the more we increase the risk of rejecting a true null hypothesis. So in addition to being a more parsimonious test for comparing multiple means, the problem of overlapping probabilities is avoided with ANOVA.

THE *F* DISTRIBUTION

The variance ratios in ANOVA are tested for significance with the **F distribution,** a family of distributions that, like the t distribution, vary in shape according to the number of degrees of freedom used in calculation. The F distribution begins to look something like the normal curve as df increases, but it always remains positively skewed (we cannot have a negative F value). Unlike other distributions, the F distribution is described by two types of df: the degrees of freedom between groups (df_b) and the degrees of freedom within groups (df_w). The former (df_b) are determined by $k - 1$, where k is the number of groups or categories being compared. We had three social class categories in Figure 7.1, so df_b would be $3 - 1 = 2$. Within-group degrees of freedom (df_w) are determined by $N - k$, where N is the total number of cases in all groups. If we were examining four groups of 25 members each, df_w would be $100 - 4 = 96$. Figure 7.2 illustrates F distributions with various degrees of freedom.

An Example of ANOVA

Suppose a researcher wants to study the effects of class standing in college on levels of general knowledge. He or she randomly selects six sophomores, six juniors, and six seniors and administers a general knowledge test. Null hypothesis H_0 is that the means of the three groups will not differ among themselves, and H_1 is that at least two group

FIGURE 7.2.   *F* Distribution with different pairs of df.

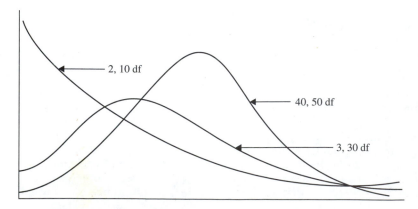

TABLE 7.1   Preliminary ANOVA Computations

SOPHOMORES		JUNIORS		SENIORS	
X_1	X^2	X_2	X^2	X_3	X^2
73	5329	72	5184	83	6889
75	5625	78	6084	86	7396
77	5929	74	5476	89	7921
75	5625	80	6400	85	7225
78	6084	83	6889	90	8100
75	5625	80	6400	95	9025
453	34217	467	36433	528	46556
$\overline{X}_1 = 75.5$		$\overline{X}_2 = 77.83$		$\overline{X}_3 = 88.0$	

means will be significantly different. To determine if there is any effect of class standing on general knowledge, it is necessary to sum the scores of each member in each group and divide by the number of members in the group to arrive at a group mean. The three group means have been calculated for you in Table 7.1. The means represent the average performance in each group and the basis of the calculation of the between-group variance. Next, we determine the overall average performance, that is, the sum of the performances of all subjects divided by the total N. The total mean serves as the basis for calculating the total variance. If the between-group variance exceeds the within-group variance by a specified amount, we will be in a position to reject the null hypothesis.

The computation of ANOVA utilizes the sum of squares (SS), which we examined in Chapter 3. Recall that SS is expressed as $\Sigma(X - \overline{X})^2$. However, in ANOVA we have separate group means and a total or grand mean, and thus separate sums of squares. To avoid confusion about which mean has to be included in the formula for determining the **total sum of squares** (SS_{total}), the formula is written as

$$SS_{total} = \Sigma(X - \overline{X}_t)^2 \tag{7.1}$$

where $\overline{X}_t$ is the total or grand mean. Recall from Chapter 3, that the business of subtracting the mean from every score, squaring the difference, and then summing is a tedious and error-prone process. Worse yet, in ANOVA we have to calculate between- and within-group sums of squares as well as the total sum of squares. Happily, the computational formula for the standard deviation is applicable to ANOVA. The computational formula for SS_{total} is given by formula (7.2), which is exactly the same as the formula in Chapter 3. We will calculate SS_{total} using the data from Table 7.1.

$$SS_{total} = \Sigma X_t^2 - \frac{(\Sigma X_t)^2}{N_t} \tag{7.2}$$

where ΣX_t^2 = the sum of the squared X scores totaled over all groups and $(\Sigma X_t)^2$ = the square of the sum of the X scores totaled over all groups.

Step 1.   Compute ΣX_t, ΣX_t^2, and $(\Sigma X_t)^2$:

ΣX_t $= 453 + 467 + 528 = 1448$ Grand mean $= \overline{X}_t = 1448/18 = 80.444$
$(\Sigma X_t)^2 = 1448^2 = 2096704$
ΣX_t^2 $= 34217 + 36433 + 46556 = 117206$

Step 2.   Substitute these values in formula (7.2) to obtain SS_{total}:

$$SS_{total} = \Sigma X_t^2 - \frac{(\Sigma X_t)^2}{N_t} = 117206 - \frac{2096704}{18} = 117206 - 116483.5 = 722.5$$

$$\boxed{SS_{total} = 722.5}$$

Step 3.   Partition SS_{total} into $SS_{between}$ and SS_{within}, starting with $SS_{between}$. The formula for computing $SS_{between}$ is formula (73):

$$SS_{between} = \Sigma \left[\frac{(\Sigma X_g)^2}{N_i} \right] - \frac{(X_t)^2}{N_t} \qquad (7.3)$$

where $(\Sigma X_g)^2$ = the square of the sum of the X scores in each group
   N_i = the number of observations in each group
   $(\Sigma X_t)^2$ = the square of the sum of the X scores totaled across all groups.

$$SS_{between} = \left[\frac{453^2}{6} + \frac{467^2}{6} + \frac{528^2}{6} \right] - \frac{2096704}{18}$$
$$= (34201.5 + 36348.2 + 46464) - 116483.5$$
$$= 117013.7 - 116483.5 = 530.2$$
$$SS_{between} = 530.2$$

Step 4.   Calculate SS_{within}. Because $SS_{between}$ plus SS_{within} must equal SS_{total}, we could simply subtract $SS_{between}$ from SS_{total} to find SS_{within}. However, we will calculate SS_{within} with formula 7.4 as a check on our other computations made so far:

$$SS_{within} = \Sigma \left[\Sigma X_g^2 - \frac{(\Sigma X_g)^2}{N_i} \right] \qquad (7.4)$$

where ΣX_g^2 = the sum of the squared observations in each group
   $(\Sigma X_g)^2$ = the sum of the observations in each group squared
   N_i = the number of observations in each group.

Substituting,

$$SS_{within} = \left[34217 - \frac{453^2}{6} \right] + \left[36433 - \frac{467^2}{6} \right] + \left[46556 - \frac{528^2}{6} \right]$$
$$= (34217 - 34201.5) + (36433 - 36348.2) + (46556 - 46464)$$
$$= 15.5 + 84.8 + 92 = 192.3$$

$$\boxed{SS_{within} = 192.3}$$

$$SS_{between} + SS_{within} = SS_{total}$$
$$530.2 + 192.3 = 722.5$$

DETERMINING STATISTICAL SIGNIFICANCE: MEAN SQUARE AND THE *F* RATIO

The next step is to determine if our finding is statistically significant. What we have at this point are two sum of squares values, but ANOVA is based on variance ratios. In

Chapter 3 we defined variance as the sum of squares divided by $N - 1$. We cannot do so here because we have partitioned the sums of squares. Instead, we must divide each of the SSs by their respective degrees of freedom to arrive at a value called the **mean square** (MS), which is the ANOVA term for variance. We previously defined the degrees of freedom for $SS_{between}$ as $k - 1$, and for SS_{within} as $N - k$. We have three categories of the dependent variable and 18 observations. The degrees of freedom for $SS_{between}$ are therefore $3 - 1 = 2$, and for SS_{within} df is $18 - 3 = 15$. The mean square values are calculated as follows:

$$\text{Mean square between} = \frac{SS_{between}}{df} = \frac{530.2}{2} = 265.1$$

$$\tag{7.5}$$

$$\text{Mean square within} = \frac{SS_{within}}{df} = \frac{192.3}{15} = 12.82$$

We are now in a position to test for significance with the F distribution. The **F ratio** is determined by the ratio of the mean square within to the mean square between, as in formula (7.6). If there are no differences among the groups, the between-group and within-group variances will be approximately equal, and the value of F will be about 1. The more the between-group variance exceeds the within-group variance, the greater the probability that the groups represent different populations.

$$F = \frac{MS_{between}}{MS_{within}} = \frac{265.1}{12.82} = 20.68 \tag{7.6}$$

This F value means that the between-group variance is 20.68 times larger than the within-group variance. We now have to make our decision regarding H_0 by comparing our computed F with the critical F found in the F-distribution table in Appendix A. As with the other distributions we have examined, the value of critical F depends on the selected alpha level and the degrees of freedom. However, there are two sets of degrees of freedom in the F distribution corresponding to the denominators of the mean square formula (in the present example, df = 2 and 15). Because the F-distribution table involves two sets of degrees of freedom, it has separate tables for the 0.05 and 0.01 alpha levels. We reproduce a small portion of the F-distribution table for alpha = 0.05 in Figure 7.3. Note that $df_{between}$ (the numerator) entries run across the top of the table

FIGURE 7.3. Reading the F-distribution table with 2 and 15 df, alpha = 0.05.

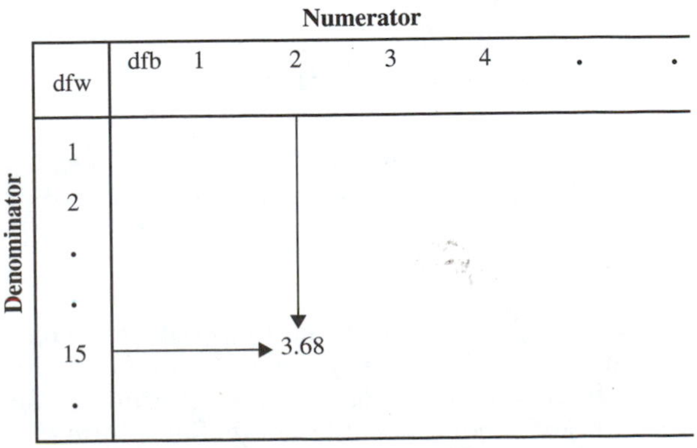

and df$_{within}$ (the denominator) entries run down the side. To read this table, start at the top and find the degrees of freedom between (df$_b$ = 2); then trace the column down until you come to degrees of freedom within (df$_w$ = 15). At the intersection of these two values is the minimum value of F necessary to reject the null. This value is 3.68 at the 0.05 level (the corresponding value at the 0.01 level is 6.36). Our computed F of 20.68 greatly exceeds both of these values. We may reject the H_0 and accept the research hypothesis: There is a real difference in the levels of general knowledge among the three groups.

ETA SQUARED

The measure of association computed with ANOVA is eta squared (η^2), which is the ratio of explained to total variance:

$$\eta^2 = \frac{SS_{between}}{SS_{total}} = \frac{530.2}{722.5} = 0.7338 \tag{7.7}$$

As we noted in Chapter 6, eta squared is interpreted as the amount of variance in the dependent variable explained by the independent variable. When we talk about *variance explained,* we mean in the statistical rather than causal sense. Class standing does not *cause* variation in general knowledge; it does statistically account for about 73.4% of the variance in general knowledge.

Multiple Comparisons: The Scheffé Test

Because we have rejected the null hypothesis, we know that at least two means differ significantly, but we don't know which two, or even if all three means differ from one another. There are a number of ways to go about determining which means differ. We prefer the Scheffé multiple comparison method because it is both the most conservative and the most versatile method. It is the most conservative because it yields fewer significantly different pairs than other methods; it is the most versatile because it can be used with unbalanced designs (unequal sized groups).

The formula for the Scheffé test is

$$\text{Scheffé contrast} = [\sqrt{(K-1)(F_{crit})}] = \left[\sqrt{\frac{1}{N_1} + \frac{1}{N_2}}\,(MS_{within})\right] \tag{7.8}$$

where $K - 1$ = number of categories or groups minus 1
F_{crit} = the critical F ratio for a given alpha and given pair of df
N_1, N_2 = number of subjects in groups to be contrasted
MS_{within} = mean square within.

From the formula you can see that the Scheffé test has to be computed for each unique pair being contrasted if group sizes are unequal. In our case we need only compute it once since all groups are of equal size. Note that F_{crit} in the formula is the F value required to reject the null with 2 and 15 degrees of freedom. Substituting,

TABLE 7.2   ANOVA Summary Table

SOURCES OF VARIANCE	SS	df	MEAN SQUARE	F	SIG.	η^2
Between groups	530.2	2	265.1	20.66	<0.001	0.734
Within groups	192.3	15	12.82			
Total	722.5	17				

MULTIPLE COMPARISON OF MEANS

Sophomore 75.5 − junior 77.83 = 2.33, ns
Sophomore 75.5 − senior 88.00 = 12.5, $p < 0.05$
Junior 77.83 − senior 88.00 = 10.17, $p < 0.05$

$$\text{Scheffé contrast} = [\sqrt{(2)(3.68)}]\left[\sqrt{\frac{1}{6} + \frac{1}{6}}(12.82)\right]$$

$$= \sqrt{7.36}\sqrt{4.848} = (2.7129)(2.067) = 5.61$$

Thus, the minimum difference between a pair of means in our sample must be 5.61 or greater in order to claim significance. We identify the significantly different group means in Table 7.2, which summarizes our results.

TWO-WAY ANALYSIS OF VARIANCE

Two-way ANOVA examines the effects of two independent variables on the dependent variable. In experimental research the researcher randomly assigns subjects to experimental and control groups and then manipulates the independent variable. Because subjects are randomly assigned, the researcher is reasonably assured that any post-test difference in the dependent variable is accounted for by the independent variable. The random assignment of subjects into one of the groups essentially means that all potentially confounding additional variables are evenly distributed across all groups. In experimental research, a one-way ANOVA is sufficient to test the null hypothesis. In nonexperimental research, however, we cannot be confident that all subjects are similar in terms of other variables that may influence scores on the dependent variable. This being the case, researchers have to attempt to eliminate the influence of additional variables by statistical control. This is done by incorporating one or more additional variables that are theoretically meaningful into an ANOVA.

Suppose we add gender to class standing to determine if gender has any effect on levels of general knowledge and whether the effects of class standing on general knowledge are the same regardless of gender. With three levels of class standing and two genders, we have $3 \times 2 = 6$ different combinations or conditions. Table 7.3 presents the raw data within each of the six conditions. We have calculated the cell, column, row, and grand means.

In one-way ANOVA we partitioned SS_{total} into two parts: between- and within-group components. In a two-way ANOVA things get more complicated because we now have two classification schemes, class standing (a) and gender (b). Each individual is classified according to both of these variables. We will thus have two between-group contrasts to examine: between-group class standing (SS_a) and between-group gender (SS_b). Additionally, the effects of class standing on general knowledge may differ across cate-

TABLE 7.3 Preliminary Calculations for ANOVA of General Knowledge by Class Standing and Gender

FACTOR 2: GENDER	FACTOR 1: CLASS STANDING			ROW TOTALS AND MEANS
	SOPHOMORE	JUNIOR	SENIOR	
Male	73	72	83	
	75	78	86	
	77	74	89	
	225	224	258	707
	$\bar{X} = 75$	$\bar{X} = 74.7$	$\bar{X} = 86$	$\bar{X} = 78.6$
Female	75	80	85	
	78	83	90	
	75	80	95	
	228	243	270	741
	$\bar{X} = 76$	$\bar{X} = 81$	$\bar{X} = 90$	$\bar{X} = 82.3$
Column totals	453	467	528	
				$\bar{X}_t = 80.44$ (grand mean)
Column means	$\bar{X} = 75.5$	$\bar{X} = 77.8$	$\bar{X} = 88$	

gories of gender. That is, although unlikely, class standing may effect general knowledge differently for males and females. This means that we have yet another source of variance. In a two-way ANOVA, SS_{total} is partitioned four ways: SS_a, SS_b (the separate **main effects** of the two variables; SS_{ab} (the **interaction** effects), and SS_{within}. Symbolically, $SS_{total} = SS_{between\ (a)} + SS_{between\ (b)} + SS_{ab\ interaction} + SS_{within}$

Step 1. The first step is to compute the total sum of squares. Obviously, SS_{total} will not differ simply because we have now taken note of the gender of our respondents. Therefore, $SS_{total} = 722.5$ The next step is to calculate $SS_{between}$. However, $SS_{between}$ now has three components: $SS_{class\ standing}$, SS_{gender}, and $SS_{class\ standing \times gender}$. All three sources of between-group variance are referred to collectively as $SS_{explained}$ (explained sum of squares).

Step 2. Compute $SS_{explained}$ ($SS_a + SS_b + SS_{ab}$) by the following formula:

$$SS_{explained} = \Sigma \left[\frac{(\Sigma X_c)^2}{N_c} \right] - \left[\frac{(\Sigma X_t)^2}{N_t} \right] \tag{7.9}$$

where c = cell means and cell Ns and t = total cell means and total N.

$$= \left[\frac{225^2}{3} + \frac{228^2}{3} + \frac{224^2}{3} + \frac{243^2}{3} + \frac{258^2}{3} + \frac{270^2}{3} \right] - \frac{1448^2}{18}$$

$$= 16875 + 17328 + 16725.3 + 19683 + 22188 + 24300 - 116483.5 = 615.8$$

$$\boxed{SS_{explained} = 615.8}$$

Step 3. Partition $SS_{explained}$ into components beginning with SS_a (class standing). Note that this computation is exactly the same as computing $SS_{between}$ in the one-way ANOVA:

$$SS_{\text{class standing}} = \Sigma \left[\frac{(\Sigma X_a)^2}{N_a} \right] - \left[\frac{(\Sigma X_t)^2}{N_t} \right] \qquad (7.10)$$

where a = class standing column means and Ns.

$$= \left[\frac{453^2}{6} + \frac{467^2}{6} + \frac{528^2}{6} \right] - \frac{1448^2}{18}$$

$$= 34201.5 + 36348.2 + 46463 - 116483.5 = 530.2$$

$$\boxed{SS_{\text{class standing}} = 530.2}$$

Step 4. Compute SS_{gender}. Note that in the computation of SS_{gender} we use the sum of squares summed across the rows:

$$SS_{\text{gender}} = \Sigma \left[\frac{(\Sigma X_r)^2}{N_g} \right] - \left[\frac{(\Sigma X_t)^2}{N_t} \right] \qquad (7.11)$$

where r = row means and N = number of subjects in each gender category.

$$= \left[\frac{707^2}{9} + \frac{741^2}{9} \right] - \frac{1448^2}{18}$$

$$= 55538.8 + 61009 - 116483.5 = 64.3$$

$$\boxed{SS_{\text{gender}} = 64.3}$$

Step 5. Compute main effects (combined effects of class standing and gender):

$$SS_{\text{main}} = SS_{\text{class standing}} + SS_{\text{gender}} = 530.2 + 64.3 = 594.5$$

$$\boxed{SS_{\text{main}} = 594.5}$$

Step 6. Compute $SS_{\text{class standing}} \times SS_{\text{gender}}$ (class standing $\times$ gender interaction). The main effects constitute the sum of squares jointly accounted for by the two factors in the model minus the interaction effects. Stated another way, the explained sum of squares (or simply what we called SS_{between} in one-way ANOVA) combines $SS_{\text{class standing}}$, SS_{gender}, and $SS_{\text{class standing} \times \text{gender}}$ interaction. Thus, $SS_{\text{class standing} \times \text{gender}}$ is obtained by subtracting SS_{main} from $SS_{\text{explained}}$:

$$SS_{\text{class standing} \times \text{gender}} = SS_{\text{explained}} - SS_{\text{main}} = 615.8 - 594.5 = 21.3$$

$$\boxed{SS_{\text{class standing} \times \text{gender}} = 21.3}$$

Step 7. Compute SS_{within}

$$SS_{\text{within}} = SS_{\text{total}} - SS_{\text{explained}} = 722.5 - 615.7 = 106.7$$

$$\boxed{SS_{\text{within}} = 106.7}$$

Notice in this example that the sum of squares accounted for by class standing, plus gender, plus the interaction of these two factors, equaled the explained sum of squares. This nice additive property, whereby $SS_{\text{rows}} + SS_{\text{columns}} + SS_{\text{rows} \times \text{columns}} + SS_{\text{within}} = SS_{\text{total}}$, holds true only for the classical ANOVA case in which we have equal cell numbers.

When we have unequal cell Ns, as is almost always the case in nonexperimental research, SS_{total} no longer defines completely separate (nonoverlapping) sources of variance.

DETERMINING STATISTICAL SIGNIFICANCE

Having partitioned the SS into their various components, we now have to determine if the observed effects are significant. As we have seen, the F ratio is calculated by first dividing the sums of squares by their respective degrees of freedom to obtain the between and within mean squares, and then dividing $MS_{between}$ by MS_{within}. We know that degrees of freedom in ANOVA are $N - 1$ for SS_{total} and $k - 1$ for a given condition. Determining the degrees of freedom for interaction effects is not quite so simple. Calculating interaction effects involves row and column means. As we know, degrees of freedom are the number of values free to vary. To determine the degrees of freedom, we ask ourselves how many cell means are free to vary, given the grand mean and all row and column means. Table 7.4 reproduces the grand mean and the row and column means for the present ANOVA problem. We have arbitrarily placed two cell means in the table: the male sophomore mean in cell A and the female senior mean in cell F. Any two cells not in the same column will do. Notice that if we fill cell A we need not fill the tied cell D since knowing the value of cell A and the column mean renders D no longer free to vary. Once any two cell means not in the same column in a 3 × 2 table are known, the values of the other cells are automatically determined (not free to vary).

Therefore, df for interaction effects are always determined by the number of rows minus 1 multiplied by the number of columns minus 1 $(r - 1)(c - 1)$. In a 3 × 2 table such as ours it is $(2 - 1 = 1)(3 - 1 = 2)$, and $(1)(2) = 2$. A 2 × 2 design would have 1 df, and a 3 × 4 would have 6 df.

SIGNIFICANCE LEVELS

The $SS_{between}$ values for class standing are exactly the same as they were in the one-way ANOVA. However, the F ratio will not be the same because the addition of a second variable has changed SS_{within}. The F ratio for class standing is now

$$MS_{between} = \frac{SS_{between}}{df} = \frac{530.2}{2} = 265.1$$

$$MS_{within} = \frac{SS_{within}}{df} = \frac{106.7}{12} = 8.89$$

$$F = \frac{MS_{between}}{MS_{within}} = \frac{265.1}{8.89} = 29.82, \quad p < 0.0001$$

TABLE 7.4 Determining df for Interaction Effects

				ROW $\overline{X}$s
a 75	b	c		78.6
d	e	f 90		82.3
Col. $\overline{X}$s	75.5	77.8	88	80.4

We now compute F for gender:

$$MS_{between} = \frac{SS_{between}}{df} = \frac{64.3}{1} = 64.3$$

$$MS_{within} = \frac{SS_{within}}{df} = \frac{106.7}{12} = 8.89$$

$$F = \frac{MS_{between}}{MS_{within}} = \frac{64.3}{8.89} = 7.23, \qquad p < .02$$

We now compute F for the interaction of class standing and gender:

$$MS_{interaction} = \frac{SS_{interaction}}{df} = \frac{21.3}{2} = 10.6$$

$$MS_{within} = \frac{SS_{within}}{df} = \frac{106.7}{12} = 8.89$$

$$F = \frac{MS_{interaction}}{MS_{within}} = \frac{10.6}{8.89} = 1.20, \quad ns$$

The F ratios for both variables are statistically significant. We now determine the F ratio for their combined effects, which are called the **main effects.** The main effects are equal to the sum of the SS for class standing and gender ($SS_{main} = 530.2 + 64.3 = 594.5$). Then SS_{main} is divided by the degrees of freedom used in calculating both separate effects to obtain the mean square value. We used 2 df for class standing, and 1 df for gender. Therefore, the df used to calculate the mean square for the main effects is 3. The mean square obtained by dividing the main effects by its associated df is $594.5/3 = 198.2$. Dividing this value by the mean square of the within-group mean square, we get an F ratio of 22.29 ($198.2/8.89 = 22.29$). Again, this indicates that the between-group variation is 22.29 times larger than the within-group variation. The critical region for rejecting H_0 at the 0.05 level with 3 and 12 df is 3.49, and at the 0.01 level it is 5.95. Our computed F exceeds both of these values by a wide margin. Table 7.5 summarizes the partitioning of variance for each condition and gives their F ratios.

Thus, class standing and gender jointly account for 82.3% of the variance in general knowledge scores, with class standing being by far the most important variable of the two. Eta squared is not computed for the interaction effect because it is not significant ($F = 1.20$, $p = 0.333$). Let us look more closely at this concept of interaction.

TABLE 7.5 Analysis of Variance (ANOVA) Summary Table

SOURCE OF VARIANCE	SUM OF SQUARES	df	MEAN SQUARE	F RATIO	SIG.	η^2
Main effects	594.5	3	198.2	22.29	0.0001	0.823
Class standing	530.2	2	265.1	29.82	0.0001	0.734
Gender	64.3	1	64.3	7.23	0.020	0.089
Two-way interaction	21.3	2	10.6	1.20	0.333	
Within group	106.7	12	8.9			
Total (between + within + interaction)	722.5	17	42.5			

UNDERSTANDING INTERACTION

When we examine the effects of two or more independent variables on a dependent variable, we must be aware of the possibility of *interaction effects*. Interaction occurs when the effects of an independent variable on the dependent variable differ significantly across different levels of a second independent variable. In our class standing/gender example, we did not observe a significant interaction effect, which means that the effects of class standing were identical, within the bounds of random error, over both levels of the gender variable. If the interaction effect had been significant, we could not interpret the main effects without first understanding the nature of the interaction effects.

Let us suppose that although females increase their general knowledge as their class standing increases, males actually decrease theirs (an improbable situation but useful to make our point). Since ANOVA combines the data from males and females to determine the effects of class standing, the increase in general knowledge among females would be largely canceled by the decrease among males. That is, the averageeffect of class standing would be about the same over the three conditions of the variable. Such a situation would suggest to us that we should run separate analyses for males and females if we want to understand the effects of class standing on general knowledge.

Since the concept of interaction is somewhat difficult to grasp, a simple example in which there are no main effects but substantial interaction may help. Suppose we have 10 males and 10 females taking a test. One section of the test favors verbal abilities and the other favors visual/spatial (VISPAT) abilities, but test results are rendered in terms of a composite. However, since we have a test representing two kinds of abilities, we would like to know if males and females differ on them. To find out, we break down the scores by subtests and perform a two-way ANOVA. Table 7.6 provides hypothetical data for such a test.

It is obvious from the summary of means table within Table 7.6 that there are no main effects for gender on composite test scores. The mean test score is identical for both males and females at 90. Neither are there any main effects for test type averaged over tests; both tests resulted in an average score of 90. There is, however, substantial interaction. Females scored higher than males on the verbal test, and males scored higher on the VISPAT test. Although we cannot calculate any main effects (because we know there are none for the *composite test*), the interaction effects should tell us a lot about the effects of gender on the subtests.

We begin by calculating SS_{total}:

$$SS_{total} = \Sigma X_t^2 - \frac{(\Sigma X)^2}{N_t} = 164592 - \frac{3240000}{20} = 2592$$

Because we know there are no between-group effects for gender, we can simply calculate SS_{within}:

$$SS_{within} = \Sigma \left[\Sigma X_g^2 - \frac{(\Sigma X_g)^2}{N_i} \right]$$

$$= \left[32082 - \frac{400^2}{5} \right] + \left[50208 - \frac{500^2}{5} \right] + \left[50052 - \frac{500^2}{5} \right] + \left[32250 - \frac{400^2}{5} \right]$$

$$= (32082 - 32000) + (50208 - 50000) + (50052 - 50000) + (32250 - 32000)$$

$$= 82 + 208 + 52 + 250 = 592.$$

TABLE 7.6 Demonstrating Two-Way ANOVA with No Main Effects and Significant Interaction

SUBTEST SCORES AND COMPUTATIONS

	VERBAL		VISPAT	
	X	X^2	X	X^2
Male	84	7056	110	12100
	76	5776	102	10404
	85	7225	98	9604
	75	5625	90	8100
	80	6400	100	10000
	400	32082	500	50208

$$\overline{X} = 80 \qquad \overline{X} = 100$$

	VERBAL		VISPAT	
Female	105	11025	85	7225
	95	9025	75	5625
	100	10000	70	4900
	99	9801	90	8100
	101	10201	80	6400
	500	50052	400	32250

$$\overline{X} = 100 \qquad \overline{X} = 80$$

SUMMARY OF MEANS TABLE

	VERBAL	VISPAT	ROW $\overline{X}$s
Male	80	100	90
Female	100	80	90
Column $\overline{X}$s	90	90	90

Calculating, we have

$$\Sigma X_t = 400 + 500 + 400 + 500 = 1800$$
$$(\Sigma X_t)^2 = (1800)^2 = 3240000$$
$$\Sigma X_t^2 = 32082 + 50208 + 50052 + 32250 = 164592$$

Since $SS_{total} = 2592$ and $SS_{within} = 592$, $SS_{subtest \times gender}$ interaction $= 2000$.
We can now compute mean square for SS_{within} and $SS_{subtest \times gender}$:

$$MS_{within} = \frac{SS_{within}}{df} \qquad \text{where } df_{within} = N - k = 20 - 4 = 16$$
$$= 592/16 = 37$$

$$MS_{interaction} = \frac{SS_{interaction}}{df} \qquad \text{where } df_{interaction} = (r-1)(c-1) = (2-1)(2-1) = 1$$
$$= 2000/1 = 2000$$

We can now compute the F ratio for interaction effects:

$$F = \frac{MS_{interaction}}{MS_{within}} = \frac{2000}{37} = 54.054, \qquad p < 0.00001$$

We can conclude from the preceding that although composite test scores did not differ by gender, the interaction between gender and subtest type was highly significant: Males showed greater VISPAT ability and females showed greater verbal ability. Thus, the effect of gender on scores on the composite test depends on which level of the test (which subtest) we examine.

A RESEARCH EXAMPLE OF A SIGNIFICANT INTERACTION EFFECT

The following serves as a further discussion of interaction effects and as a guide to interpreting two-way ANOVA computer output. Suppose we wish to determine the effects of the relationship a convicted sex offender has with his victim and probation officers' sentencing recommendations. We also want to find out if probation officers' ideology affects their sentencing recommendations. The recommendations are given as number of days incarceration. There are eight categories of victim/offender relationships in our data which we collapsed into three more general categories: (1) family, (2) acquaintances, and (3) strangers. The probation officers were divided into two ideological groups according to scores on a questionnaire measuring liberalism/conservativism. The output produced is shown in Table 7.7

Interpretation. Starting at the top of Table 7.7, we see that the grand mean recommendation for all 351 offenders is 520.99. This is followed by the mean recommendation scores

TABLE 7.7   Research Example of Two-Way Analysis of Variance (ANOVA)

POREC BY RELAT IDEOL		RECOMMENDATION OF PROBATION OFFICER RELATIONSHIP OF SUBJECT TO VICTIM OFFICER IDEOLOGY				
		CELL MEANS				
TOTAL	FAMILY	ACQUAINTANCE	STRANGER	LIBERAL	CONSERVATIVE	
520.99 (351)	311.30 (92)	410.27 (166)	926.05 (93)	362.98 (202)	735.21 (149)	

RELATIONSHIP	IDEOLOGY	
	LIBERAL	CONSERVATIVE
Family	287.74 (51)	340.61 (41)
Acquaintance	318.73 (108)	580.72 (58)
Stranger	563.33 (43)	1238.00 (50)

SOURCE OF VARIATION	SUM OF SQUARES	df	MEAN SQUARE	F	SIGNIF.
MAIN EFFECTS	29858903.689	3	9952967.896	22.218	0.000
RELAT	17977288.719	2	8988644.359	20.065	0.000
IDEOL	8519771.725	1	8519771.725	19.019	0.000
2-WAY INTERACTION	4656985.602	2	2328492.801	5.198	0.006
EXPLAINED	34515889.291	5	6903177.858	15.410	0.000
RESIDUAL	154549331.683	345	447969.077		
TOTAL	189065220.974	350	540186.346		

for the family (311.30), acquaintance (410.27), and stranger (926.05) categories, and the mean recommendations for the liberal (362.98) and conservative (735.21) officers. This line is followed by six different categories listing the mean recommendations of liberal and conservative officers broken down by victim/offender relationship (for instance, liberal officers recommended an average of 318.73 days for offenders who were acquaintances of their victims). The numbers in parentheses are category Ns.

Turning to the ANOVA results, we note that the separate main effects of RELAT and IDEOL are both significant. Note in this example that the sums of squares associated with each of the separate main effects do not sum to the value labeled MAIN EFFECTS as they did in our computational example. This is because we have unequal group Ns. Note also that the term RESIDUAL is used to denote SS_{within}.

The interaction effect is significant ($F = 5.198$, $p = 0.006$), meaning that although the effects of both RELAT and IDEOL are significant, we cannot get an accurate picture of their effects unless we explore the interaction effects further.

A further understanding of the concept of interaction is facilitated by viewing it as synonymous with parallelism. There is no significant interaction if lines drawn between means of the dependent variable (Y) across values of the first independent variable (X) for fixed values of the second independent variable (V) are parallel. If the lines linking the values of Y on X remain generally parallel regardless of the value of V, there is no X-by-V interaction. If there is significant X-by-V interaction, the lines will not be parallel. We have plotted the recommendation means for each victim/offender category for both the liberal and conservative officers in Figure 7.4.

Having plotted the means across categories of victim/offender relationships in Figure 7.4, we see that the lines drawn between the means for the liberal and conservative officers are not parallel. Although there is clearly a linear relationship between recommendation severity and victim/offender relationship for both sets of officers, the severity of the effects depends quite a lot on the probation officers' ideology. This type of interaction is not as difficult to interpret as one in which the levels of the second independent variable produce opposite results. For example, if the plot of means for the liberal officers remained the same as seen in Figure 7.4, but the ranking of the con-

FIGURE 7.4. Plot of sentence recommendation means for categories of victim/offender relationship by probation officer ideology.

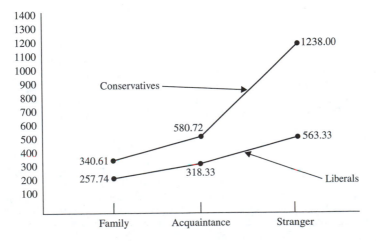

TABLE 7.8   **ANOVA Results for Sentencing Recommendations Made by Liberal and Conservative Officers, and by Combined Officers**

CONDITION	F	SIG.	η^2	N
Combined	37.765	0.0000	0.150	351
Liberals	4.163	0.0169	0.040	202
Conservatives	14.701	0.0000	0.168	149

servative officers' recommendation means were stranger, acquaintance, and family, we would have a crossover effect that would render the main effects uninterpretable.

The preceding results suggest that we could get a more accurate picture of recommendation severity and victim/offender relationship if we examined it within separate categories of probation officers' ideology. We ran three separate ANOVAs with our data to demonstrate: one with conservative officers only; and one with liberal officers only; and one combining the officers, that is, without taking ideology into account. This exercise produced the results shown in Table 7.8.

Table 7.8 shows that if we compute a one-way ANOVA for recommendation means for categories of the victim/offender relationship, ignoring probation officers' ideology, we obtain a significant F ratio and account for 15% of the variance in probation officers' recommendations. We also see from the eta-squared values that the effects of victim/offender relationship on officers' recommendations are more than four times as great for offenders processed by conservative officers (16.8% of the variance) as for offenders processed by liberal officers (4%). We now have a more complete picture.

The two separate (liberal and conservative) ANOVAs give us essentially the same results as the ANOVA with both sets of officers combined, in the sense that the relationship between officers' recommendations and victim/offender remains significant across both categories of probation officers' ideology. However, we have also specified that the relationship is particularly strong in the conservative officer category. The F ratio is stronger in the combined condition than it is in the conservative condition, whereas the eta-squared value is smaller because the combined condition is based on a larger sample.

SUMMARY

ANOVA is a statistical technique used for comparing the significance of difference among multiple means. It is based on the comparison of two sources of variance: between- and within-group variance. Between-group variance is the variance attributed to categories of the independent variable, and within-group variance is attributable to individual differences. Within-group variance is also known as error or residual variance.

The statistical significance of ANOVA result is determined by the use of the F ratio, the ratio of the mean square within to the mean square between. *Mean square* is the ANOVA term for variance, and is simply the sum of squares by their respective degrees of freedom. The F-distribution table has two sets of df, one for between- and the other for within-group variance. Like the t distribution, the F distribution is defined by df, and there is a unique distribution for each pair of degrees of freedom.

ANOVA only tells us if two or more means differ, not which ones. One of the ways to determine which pair or pairs of means differ is the Scheffé test, which is the most efficient and most conservative test for most analyses of variance.

Eta squared is defined as the ratio of $SS_{between}$ to SS_{total} and is a measure of the amount of variance in the dependent variable explained by the independent variable.

Two-way analysis of variance is an extension of one-way ANOVA to include the effects of a second independent variable. In a two-way ANOVA SS_{total} is partitioned four ways: $SS_{between(a)} + SS_{between(b)} + SS_{interaction} + SS_{within}$.

Interaction is a very important concept. If the effects of one independent variable differ significantly over levels of the second independent variable, we have interaction. Interaction renders the interpretation of the main effects problematic. If the interaction effects are significant, you must dig further into the data to understand what is happening. One way to do so is to plot a table of means and check for parallelism.

PRACTICE APPLICATION

A statistics instructor randomly divides her class of nine into three groups to test the hypothesis that a combination of instructional methods is a superior method of teaching statistics. Group 1 has lectures, a textbook, and a student workbook. Group 2 has lectures and a textbook, and group 3 has lectures only. After 1 month of instruction each group is given identical tests containing 10 questions. The following number of correct answers is obtained by each group. Are these differences statistically significant?

GROUP 1		GROUP 2		GROUP 3	
X_1	X^2	X_2	X^2	X_3	X^2
9	81	4	16	2	4
6	36	3	9	5	25
7	49	3	9	2	4
22	166	10	34	9	33

$\overline{X}_1 = 7.33$ $\overline{X}_2 = 3.33$ $\overline{X}_3 = 3.0$

Grand mean $= \overline{X}_t = 41/9 = 4.55$

Compute ΣX_t, ΣX_t^2, and $(\Sigma X_t)^2$:

$$\Sigma X_t = 22 + 10 + 9 = 41$$
$$(\Sigma X_t)^2 = 41^2 = 1681$$
$$\Sigma X_t^2 = 166 + 34 + 33 = 233$$

Compute SS_{total}:

$$SS_{total} = \Sigma X_t^2 - \frac{(\Sigma X)^2}{N_t} = 233 - \frac{1681}{9} = 233 - 186.8 = 46.2$$

$$\boxed{SS_{total} = 46.2}$$

Partition SS_{total} into $SS_{between}$ and SS_{within}, starting with $SS_{between}$:

$$SS_{between} = \Sigma \left[\frac{(\Sigma X_g)^2}{N_i} \right] - \frac{(\Sigma X_t)}{N_t}$$

$$= \left[\frac{22^2}{3} + \frac{10^2}{3} + \frac{9^2}{3} \right] - \frac{1681}{9}$$
$$= (161.33 + 33.33 + 27.0) - 186.8 = 221.66 - 186.8 = 34.86$$

$$\boxed{SS_{between} = 34.86}$$

Calculate SS_{within}:

$$SS_{within} = \Sigma \left[\Sigma X_g^2 - \frac{(\Sigma X_g)^2}{N_i} \right]$$
$$= \left[166 - \frac{22^2}{3} \right] + \left[34 - \frac{10^2}{3} \right] + \left[33 - \frac{9^2}{3} \right]$$
$$= (166 - 161.33) + (34 - 33.33) + (33 - 27) = 4.67 + 0.67 + 6.0 = 11.34$$

$$\boxed{SS_{within} = 11.34}$$

Check: Does $SS_{between} + SS_{within} = SS_{total}$? $34.86 + 11.34 = 46.2$. Then compute mean squares:

$$\text{Mean square between} = \frac{SS_{between}}{df} = \frac{34.86}{2} = 17.43$$
$$\text{Mean square within} = \frac{SS_{within}}{df} = \frac{11.34}{6} = 1.89$$
$$F = \frac{MS_{between}}{MS_{within}} = \frac{17.43}{1.89} = 9.22$$

With 2 and 6 df, the critical value at the 0.05 level is 5.14. The computed F exceeds this value, therefore reject the null that there is no difference between the instructional methods.

Compute eta squared:

$$\eta^2 = \frac{SS_{between}}{SS_{total}} = \frac{34.86}{46.2} = .754$$

Compute the Scheffé test:

$$\text{Scheffé contrast} = \left[\sqrt{(K-1)(F_{crit})} \right] \left[\sqrt{\frac{1}{N_t} + \frac{1}{N_2} (MS_{within})} \right]$$
$$= \left[\sqrt{(2)(5.14)} \right] \left[\sqrt{\frac{1}{3} + \frac{1}{3} (1.89)} \right]$$

$$= (3.21)(1.122) = 3.6$$

The minimum difference between group means for significance at 0.05 is 3.66. Group 1 ($\overline{X} = 7.33$) differs from both group 2 ($\overline{X} = 3.33$) and group 3 ($\overline{X} = 3.0$) by at least this amount. Groups 2 and 3 do not differ significantly from each other.

PROBLEMS

1. The following table lists income for three educational groups, high school graduates, college graduates, and advanced degree graduates:

	EDUCATION LEVEL		
	HIGH SCHOOL	COLLEGE	ADVANCED DEGREE
Income (in thousands)	17	30	43
	18	31	44
	20	33	45
	21	34	47
	22	35	48

    a) Without calculating F, is there more variance between the educational level groups or within the groups?
    b) Compute the total sum of squares, the between sum of squares, and the within sum of squares. Verify that $SS_{between} + SS_{within} = SS_{total}$.
    c) Specify the null hypothesis. Calculate F and test.
    d) Calculate η^2.
    e) Using the Scheffé test, compare all possible pairs of means for statistically significant differences.
    f) Complete the following ANOVA summary table and interpret your findings:

SOURCE OF VARIANCE	SS	df	MEAN SQUARE	F	SIG.	η^2
Between groups						
Within groups						
Total						

2. A researcher conducts an experiment to determine the effect of alcohol on reaction time. Three groups were tested on how quickly they responded to a sudden stimulus. The first group had consumed no alcohol, the second group consumed two beers 30 minutes prior to the experiment, and the third group consumed four beers 30 minutes prior to the experiment. The following results were obtained:

	AMOUNT OF ALCOHOL CONSUMED		
	NONE	2 DRINKS	4 DRINKS
Reaction time (in seconds)	2	3	7
	1	7	9
	3	4	5
	2	9	12
	2	5	9

a) Without calculating F, is there more variance between the groups or within the groups?
b) Compute the total sum of squares, the between sum of squares, and the within sum of squares. Verify that $SS_{between} + SS_{within} = SS_{total}$.
c) Specify the null hypothesis. Calculate F and test.
d) Calculate η^2.
e) Using the Scheffé test, compare all possible pairs of means for statistically significant differences.
f) Complete the following ANOVA summary table and interpret your findings:

SOURCE OF VARIANCE	SS	df	MEAN SQUARE	F	Sig.	η^2
Between groups						
Within groups						
Total						

3. A research class is interested in the question of whether there are any differences in the emotional maturity of people born under different signs of the zodiac. To test their hypothesis, they selected people with three different signs of the zodiac and administered a standardized test of emotional maturity. The scores from this test, with high scores indicating more emotional maturity, are given here:

	ZODIAC SIGN		
	CANCER	LEO	SAGITTARIUS
Emotional Maturity	23	17	16
	26	16	15
	24	20	16
	20	21	20
		24	21
			19

a) Compute the total sum of squares, the between sum of squares, and the within sum of squares. Verify that $SS_{between} + SS_{within} = SS_{total}$.
b) Specify the null hypothesis. Calculate F and test.
c) Calculate η^2.
d) Use the Scheffé test to test for statistical differences.
e) Complete the following ANOVA summary table and interpret your findings:

SOURCE OF VARIANCE	SS	df	MEAN SQUARE	F	SIG.	η^2
Between groups						
Within groups						
Total						

4. A new nursing employee suspects that the administrative personnel at the hospital where he works are guilty of racial bias in hiring. He ranked the occupations in the following format:

1 = Nurses aide
2 = LPN
3 = Diploma RN
4 = Baccalaureate RN
5 = Nurse supervisor
6 = Physician assistant

He then gathered the following information from the personnel files:

	RACE		
	BLACK	WHITE	ASIAN
Occupation	2	4	2
	1	5	1
	3	3	3
	1	6	4
	1	5	
		4	
		5	

Does the evidence support this employee's suspicions? Specify the null and test for significance.

Chapter 8

Hypothesis Testing with Categorical Data: Chi-Square Test

One of the most useful techniques in social science research is cross-tabulation using a statistic known as the chi-square statistic. The **chi-square test of independence** is a test of significance that is used for discrete data in the form of frequencies, percentages, or proportions. Chi-square is one of a number of tests of significance and measures of association known as **nonparametric** statistics. This terminology does not mean that the populations from which the data are gathered do not have parameters—a logical impossibility. The term simply means that unlike their parametric counterparts, such as z, t, and F, nonparametric statistics do not require any assumptions to be made regarding the underlying population. These assumptions, you will recall, are that the population is normally distributed or has a known standard deviation.

In other words, nonparametric tests are less restrictive than parametric tests. The trade-off for this characteristic is that they are less powerful than their parametric counterparts, which means that when using such tests we are less likely to reject a null hypothesis that should be rejected since they have a slightly larger probability of making a Type II error. Nevertheless, if our data do not meet the stringent demands of parametric tests, nonparametric tests are useful substitutes. This observation should not lead to dismissal of nonparametric tests as poor relatives of parametric tests. In fact, a popular science magazine (*Science 84*) listed the development of chi-square as one of the 20 most important advances in science of the twentieth century (Hacking, 1984, p. 69).

A 2 × 2 chi-square analysis is perhaps the most fundamental inferential statistical technique. Many of the variables in the social sciences deal with only two values— yes/no, agree/disagree, male/female, for/against, and so on—and two variables is the minimum number we can test for relatedness. Thus, joint contingency analysis deals with the minimum number of variables that can be related (2), each of which has the minimum number of values that a variable can have (2). In such an analysis, variables measured at the nominal and ordinal levels are displayed in rows and columns in a table to determine their joint frequency. Let us look at a very simple example to illustrate joint frequency.

TABLE CONSTRUCTION

Suppose we are interested in determining whether men and women differ in their stated willingness to vote for a woman for president of the United States regardless of her political party. We collect data from 10 men and 10 women and ask them if they would vote for a woman for president of the United States. Having done so, we have two nominal-level variables called *gender* and *vote,* each having two attributes, male/female, and yes/no. The research hypothesis states that willingness to vote for a female candidate is dependent on gender. The null hypothesis assumes that these two variables are independent of one another, meaning that willingness to vote for a female candidate and gender of voter are unrelated; that is, men are just as likely as women to report that

**TABLE 8.1   Tally of Males and Females Who Would
and Would Not Vote for a Female Candidate
for President**

MEN	WOMEN
no	yes
no	no
yes	yes
no	yes
no	yes
yes	no
no	yes
yes	no
no	no
yes	yes

they would vote for a female candidate. In other words, the classification of a case into a particular category of one variable (in this case, gender) does not affect the probability that the case will fall into a particular category of the other variable (willingness to vote for a woman). Having selected our sample we find the distribution shown in Table 8.1.

After our responses are counted, we discover that four men would vote for a female candidate and six men would not. In addition, six women would and four would not vote for a female candidate. We now put these figures into a bivariate table to show their joint distribution on the two variables.

There are a few rules of thumb for constructing a bivariate table. Conventionally, the independent variable is placed at the top of the table and summed downward in the columns, and the dependent variable is placed at the side and summed across the rows. The sums of each row and column are reported and placed in the marginals, and the total number of cases is also reported. Let us put our data into a bivariate table, as shown in Table 8.2.

We now have four mutually exclusive categories or cells informing us of the joint distribution of the two variables. We have labeled the categories of both variables and reported the marginals. All marginals happen to be equal in size in this example, and the two sets of marginals sum to 20. (If your row marginals do not sum to the same figure

TABLE 8.2   Vote by Gender

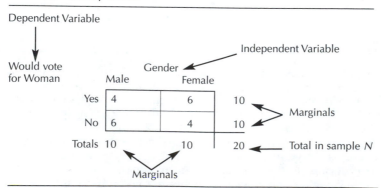

TABLE 8.3   Putting Percentages in Table and Rules for Comparing

Would Vote for Woman	Gender Male	Female			Independent Variable
					Compare Across
YES	4 40%	6 60%	10 (50%)	DEPENDENT Variable	
No	6 60%	4 40%	10 (50%)		
Totals	10% (100%)	10 (100%)	20 (100%)		(100%) (100%) Percentage Down

as your column marginals you have made an error in addition.) Gender is listed as the independent variable since being male or female can conceivably influence one's willingness to vote for a female, but willingness to vote for a female obviously cannot influence one's gender.

PUTTING PERCENTAGES IN TABLES

It is always useful to report percentages in the tables. What percentage of men would vote for a female? Four men out of a total of 10 would. Therefore $4/10 = 0.4 \times 100 = 40\%$. Similarly, $6/10 = 0.6 \times 100 = 60\%$ of the women in the sample would do so. We then place these cell percentages in the table (Table 8.3). When putting percentages in tables the basic rule is to compute percentages in the direction of the independent variable (down the columns). This rule applies because we want to compare the distribution on the dependent variable within our categories of the independent variable. In the present example, we see that four males and six females would vote for a female for president (the affirmative category of the dependent variable). Thus, we percentage down and compare across. Column percentages will, within rounding error, always sum to 100%; that is, each column represents 100% of each category of the independent variable.

Percentages are reported because they standardize the distribution, making interpretation easier. The interpretation of Table 8.3 is easy because of the equal marginal values and the fairly equal cell frequencies. We can see that gender is somehow related to willingness to vote for a female candidate for president of the United States. If we had highly unequal cell frequencies, the interpretation would be ambiguous if we did not report cell percentages along with raw numbers.

ASSUMPTIONS FOR THE USE OF CHI-SQUARE

The following assumptions are used with the chi-square test:

1. We have independent random samples.
2. The data are nominal or ordinal level.
3. No expected cell frequency is less than 5.

We now want to determine if the difference between the sexes in their willingness to vote for a woman could have occurred by chance. That is, is willingness to vote for a woman *independent* of gender? There are two possibilities: (1) The observed difference in willingness to vote in our sample is also true in the population, and (2) There is no gender-based difference in willingness to vote in the general population. The null hypothesis specific to this issue is expressed symbolically as

$$H_0: P_m = P_f$$

where $P_m =$ probability of males willing to vote and $P_f =$ probability of females willing to vote. The null hypothesis being tested is that the same proportion of males and females would be willing to vote for a female candidate. Put another way, we are testing the hypothesis that the *observed* frequencies in the table equal the frequencies we would *expect* under conditions of random chance. To test the null hypothesis we compute chi-square, the formula for which is

$$\chi^2 = \Sigma \frac{(O - E)^2}{E} \tag{8.1}$$

where $O =$ observed cell frequency and $E =$ expected cell frequency under the assumption that the null hypothesis is true. We already know the observed frequencies, which are the frequencies actually seen in each cell in the table. The expected frequencies are computed by formula (8.2):

$$E = \frac{(\text{Column marginal } N)(\text{Row marginal } N)}{\text{Total } N} \tag{8.2}$$

This formula tells us that to get the expected frequency for each cell, we multiply the relevant column marginal N by the relevant row marginal N and then divide the product by the total number (N) of cases in the sample. Given the equal marginals in our example, we do not really need to do any computations to determine what the expected cell frequencies would be if chance alone were operating. With an N of 20 with equal marginals we would expect five cases in each of the four cells.

This extremely simplified set of data is presented so that you might intuitively grasp the idea that given a sample of 10 individuals of one type and 10 individuals of another type, and given that 10 individuals, regardless of gender, would vote for a woman and 10 would not, we would expect 5 cases in each cell if chance alone were operating.

A table with a more reasonable sample size is presented in Table 8.4. How would we expect the frequencies to be distributed in this table if the null hypothesis were true? If willingness to vote for a female were independent of gender, we could conclude from the percentage of people (both genders) who were willing ($128/236 = 54.2$), that 54.2% of males and 54.2% of females would be willing. What is the expected frequency of cell A (males who are willing)? What we are actually asking is "What is the probability of two independent events (the probability of being willing, and the probability of being a male) occurring simultaneously?" We already have the probability of being

TABLE 8.4   Willingness to Vote For Woman by Gender

Would Vote for Woman	Gender Male	Female	
Yes	**A** 47 (40.5%)	**B** 81 (67.5%)	128 (54.2%)
No	**C** 69 (59.5%)	**D** 39 (32.5%)	108 (45.8%)
Totals	116 (100%)	120 (100%)	236

TABLE 8.5   Table of Expected Frequencies

Would Vote for Woman	Gender Male	Female	
Yes	A 62.9	B 65.1	128
No	C 53.1	D 54.9	108
Totals	116	120	236

willing (0.542); the probability of being male is $116/236 = 0.491$. As we saw in Chapter 4, the probability of two independent events occurring together is the product of their respective probabilities. Thus, the probability of being male *and* being willing to vote for a woman is $(0.542)(0.491) = 0.266$. To determine the expected frequency in cell A, we multiply this probability by the total number of cases: $(0.266)(236) = 62.9$.

Although this is a good process for gaining an intuitive understanding of the process, there is a simpler way to calculate the remaining expected frequencies. Given that 54.2% of the sample report a willingness to vote for a woman, we would expect $116 \times 54.2\%/100\% = 62.9$ males, and $120 \times 54.2\%/100\% = 65.1$ females to report a willingness to vote for a female candidate. Note that

$$\frac{(116)(54.2\%)}{100\%} = \frac{(116)(128)}{236} = \frac{(\text{Column marginal } N)(\text{Row marginal } N)}{\text{Total } N}$$

Let us compute each expected cell frequency:

Expected frequency for A = $(116 \times 128)/236 = 14848/236 = 62.9$
Expected frequency for B = $(120 \times 128)/236 = 15360/236 = 65.1$
Expected frequency for C = $(116 \times 108)/236 = 12528/236 = 53.1$
Expected frequency for D = $(120 \times 108)/236 = 12960/236 = 54.9$

These frequencies are shown in Table 8.5.

Now that we have both the observed and actual cell frequencies, we can calculate chi-square. A handy way to keep track of all the different calculations is to set up a table such as Table 8.6 with a column for each operation. We must first subtract O from E, square the difference, and then divide by E. (The sum of $O - E$ should always be zero; make sure you check that this is so before going on.) When we have done this for each cell in the table, we sum $(O - E)^2/E$ to obtain our χ^2 value.

TABLE 8.6   Calculating Chi-Square

CELL	OBS.	EXP.	$(O - E)$	$(O - E)^2$	$(O - E)^2/E$
A	47	62.9	−15.9	252.81	4.02
B	81	65.1	15.9	252.81	3.88
C	69	53.1	15.9	252.81	4.76
D	39	54.9	−15.9	252.81	4.60
236	236	00.0			$\Sigma (O - E)^2/E = 17.26$

Our computed chi-square is 17.26. To determine if this value is significant, we must first determine the degrees of freedom. We defined degrees of freedom in Chapter 6 as the number of values free to vary. In the case of tabular analysis we are estimating expected cell frequencies from a given set of marginals, and $df = (r - 1)(c - 1)$. The logic is identical with that discussed in Chapter 7.

For our 2×2 table we have $df = 1$. We now have to turn to Table 5 in Appendix A where we find the chi-square distribution table to determine if our computed chi-square value of 17.26 is statistically significant. We look at the column labeled *df* to find the place where $df = 1$ (this is the very first row). We then trace across the row until we get to the spot designated by 0.05, where you will find the critical value of chi-square at the 0.05 alpha level (3.841). If our computed value exceeds 3.841, we can say that our chi-square value is significant at the 0.05 level, and we can reject the null. Our computed chi-square greatly exceeds this value, so we are fairly confident that our sample was not drawn from a population in which our two variables are unrelated.

We can be even more confident than at the 0.05 level because our computed value exceeds the 0.01 alpha level (6.635), which means that we could expect a similar result by chance only once in every 100 samples. Therefore, we are extremely confident that the relationship between gender and willingness to vote for a female found among the respondents in our sample is also true within the general population from which it was drawn. In other words, females are significantly more likely than males to report that they would vote for a female candidate.

If we wish to go a little further to determine whether our computed value is a function more of female willingness to vote for a female or male unwillingness, we merely have to examine the relative magnitude of the four components for the major departures from independence. Male unwillingness (cell C) departs most from independence, with a component value of 4.76, whereas female willingness (cell B) departs least from independence, with a value of 3.88. Thus our computed value of chi-square is a function more of male unwillingness than female willingness.

THE CHI-SQUARE DISTRIBUTION

As is the case with the *t* and *f* distributions, the shape of the **chi-square distribution** is entirely determined by the degrees of freedom, and each df value describes a unique distribution. Figure 8.1 gives examples of the chi-square distribution at 1, 4, and 8 degrees of freedom. Note that the chi-square distribution is asymmetric and is skewed to the right. This does not mean that we are performing a one-tailed or directional test. Chi-square testing yields only positive results because it is arrived at by squaring the differences between observed and expected frequencies. The chi-square distribution

FIGURE 8.1.   Chi-square distributions at 1, 4, and 8 degrees of freedom.

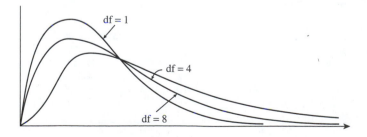

df = 1

df = 4

df = 8

becomes more and more symmetrical as the degrees of freedom increase, and it begins to look like the normal curve with df greater than 30.

We saw earlier that the *t* distribution becomes identical in shape to the *z* distribution when df > 120. To give you a further appreciation of the symmetry of statistics, it is also true that the chi-square critical value of 3.841, with df = 1, is equal to the square of the critical *z* value of 1.96. Put otherwise, *z* squared is equal to chi-square under these conditions. Thus, our computed chi-square of 17.26 is equivalent to a *z* value of 4.15. In fact, all the distributions we have examined are related in the following fashion:

$$z = t \infty \text{ df} = \sqrt{F 1; \infty \text{ df}} = \sqrt{\chi^2 ; 1 \text{ df}}$$

(*z* = *t* with infinite df, which equals the square root of *F* with 1 and infinite df, which equals the square root of χ^2 with 1 df.)

YATES' CORRECTION FOR CONTINUITY

As indicated earlier, if there are fewer than five cases in any of the cells in a table of expected frequencies (not observed frequencies), we violate one of the assumptions of chi-square. If such a condition exists, we correct the chi-square value by using **Yate's correction for continuity,** given by formula (8.3):

$$\chi^2_{corrected} = \Sigma \frac{(|O - E| - 0.5)^2}{E} \tag{8.3}$$

Correction for continuity has the effect of reducing the value of chi-square since it reduces the *absolute value* of $O - E$ for each cell by 0.5. This means that only the size, not the sign of the difference is considered. For example: $(|2 - 6| - 0.5) = 4 - 0.5 = 3.5$, not $2 - 6 = -4 - 0.5 = -4.5$. Some statisticians recommend using Yates' correction for any 2 × 2 table, whereas others believe that it overcorrects. The decision whether or not to use the correction for continuity with any 2 × 2 table depends on how conservative the researcher wishes to be when testing hypotheses. Computer printouts for 2 × 2 tables give both the corrected and uncorrected chi-square values. As is the case with all correction factors, this correction becomes less meaningful as the sample size becomes larger.

CHI-SQUARE DISTRIBUTION AND GOODNESS OF FIT

The chi-square distribution can be used when we have prior knowledge of expected values. Mendel's laws of genetics, for example, tells us that crossbreeding of organisms with certain genotypical characteristics will yield phenotypical combinations of those characteristics in a 9:3:3:1 ratio. The **chi-square goodness-of-fit test** can be used to test whether or not a given genetic experiment yields an observed distribution that fits the theoretical expected distribution.

The logic applies to sociological data also. Suppose we know that the racial composition of a given community is 88% white, 10% African-American, and 2% Hispanic, and we want to examine violent crime victimization in the community. Our *a priori* expectation is that in a sample of victims we would observe the racial/ethnic groups to be represented in proportion to their numbers in the population. That is, if race is irrelevant to victimization, we would expect 88% of the victims to be white, 10% to be black, and 2% to be Hispanic. However, if race is *not* independent of the probability of becoming a victim, we will observe some other percentage breakdown.

TABLE 8.7   Crime Victimization Data

WHITE	BLACK	HISPANIC	TOTAL
	OBSERVED		
322 (67.4%)	134 (28.0%)	22 (4.6%)	478 (100%)
	EXPECTED		
$478 \times 0.88 = 420.6$	$478 \times 0.10 = 47.8$	$478 \times 0.02 = 9.6$	478 (100%)

GROUP	OBS.	EXP.	$(O - E)$	$(O - E)^2$	$(O - E)^2/E$
White	322	420.6	−98.6	9721.96	23.11
Black	134	47.8	86.2	7430.44	155.45
Hispanic	22	9.6	12.4	153.76	16.02
	478	478	00.0	$\Sigma (O - E)^2/E = 194.58$	

$\chi^2 = 194.58$, df = 2, $p < 0.000001$

From our offender data we observe that out of 478 victims of violent crime, 67.4% are white, 28% are African-American, and 4.6% are Hispanic. The research question is: "Is violent victimization in the community in proportion to racial composition in the community, or are people of different races significantly more likely to be victimized?" Stated more formally, "Does the proportion of victims of violent crime fit the racial composition of this jurisdiction?" The null hypothesis is that the observed ratio equals the 88:10:2 expected ratio. The data set is presented in Table 8.7. Note that 322 whites (67.4%), 134 blacks (28.0%), and 22 (4.6%) Hispanics were victims of violent crimes in this community during the time period. This is different from the expected ratio, but is the difference real or simply a function of chance? The first thing we have to do is calculate the expected frequency if the null hypothesis is true. As illustrated in Table 8.7, this is accomplished by multiplying N (478) by the relevant proportion of each of the racial/ethnic groups.

It is immediately obvious that whites are underrepresented among victims of violent crimes and that blacks and Hispanics are overrepresented. To determine if these observed differences could be attributed to chance, we use the chi-square distribution. We have 2 df because we have three categories that have to sum to 478. Two of these categories can vary, but the size of the third is fixed (not free to vary) by the size of the other two. Degrees of freedom are always $k - 1$ (where k is the number of categories) in this type of chi-square.

We note from the chi-square table in Appendix A that chi-square critical at the 0.01 level with 2 df is 9.21. Our calculated chi-square greatly exceeds this value, so we reject the null hypothesis. The observed violent crime victimization does not fit the expected ratio based on knowledge of the racial composition of the community. Violent victimization depends on race. Blacks and Hispanics, particularly blacks, are victims of violent crime significantly more often than their proportions in the community would lead us to suspect.

CHI-SQUARE-BASED MEASURES OF ASSOCIATION

If the chi-square test of independence leads to the rejection of the null, the two variables are not independent of one another and are therefore associated. But chi-square does not reveal the strength of the relationship. In addition to knowing if there is a real difference between variables, we would also like to know how strongly they are related to one another. Although we will be discussing the concept of association more fully in the next chapter, it is appropriate to introduce chi-square-based measures at this point. The measure based on a 2 × 2 chi-square is *phi*. Measures of association usually range between −1.0 and +1.0. However, when computed directly from chi-square, phi, like eta squared, is always positive, ranging between zero and +1.0. The formula for computing phi directly from the chi-square is

$$\phi = \sqrt{\frac{\chi^2}{N}} \qquad \textit{Tested} \tag{8.4}$$

Applying phi to our computed chi-square, we obtain

$$\phi = \sqrt{\frac{17.26}{236}} = \sqrt{0.073} = 0.27$$

We can interpret this value in variance-explained terms if we square it ($\phi^2 = 0.27^2 = 0.073$). The proportion of variance in willingness to vote for a female for president accounted for by gender is 7.3%, leaving 92.7% accounted for by other variables. It is statistically significant because the chi-square on which it is based is significant. Although the finding is statistically significant, its importance depends on the context of the inquiry. If this were a real research finding, it may or may not be considered substantively significant, but interpretation must be done in the context of the research question. Because the question posed was "Would the respondent vote for a female candidate regardless of party affiliation?," a pollster interested in promoting a particular candidate might find the results significant for targeting political supporters regardless of party. Statistics only inform us of the situation as it exists; the researcher must carefully interpret them.

To take the statistical versus substantive discussion a little further, suppose that we had found the same results by using *liking for red cars* as the dependent variable and *gender* as the independent variable. We suspect that the substantive significance of such a finding would be, for the most part, uninteresting. On the other hand, if you were a car dealer with a large number of red cars to get rid of, and if you were considering spending a substantial amount of money on advertising, you may be interested in targeting your advertisements to a particular gender. It may also be of some theoretical importance to the sex-role researcher if he or she is convinced that such a finding is a valid indicator of consumer trends. Substantive significance, we emphasize, depends more on the theoretical context of the inquiry than on the magnitude and significance of the computed statistics.

SAMPLE SIZE AND CHI-SQUARE

Another reason for computing a measure of association in conjunction with chi-square is that the value of chi-square is extremely sensitive to sample size. Indeed, if all cell frequencies in a 2 × 2 table are multiplied by a constant percentage, it is directly proportionate to sample size. Chi-square values are thus not directly comparable across different sample sizes, but phi values are. It is quite possible with very large samples to attain a high level of significance when the variables are so weakly related that we are tempted to ask "so what?" The chi-square-based measures of association help us to decide if the significant difference is really worth attending to. To illustrate, in Table 8.8 we compute three chi-squares based on *N*s of 20, 200, and 2,000 while maintaining a constant 40/60 percentage difference across the cells.

TABLE 8.8   Comparison of χ^2 with Different Sample Sizes

N = 20			N = 200			N = 2000		
4	6	10	40	60	100	400	600	1000
6	4	10	60	40	100	600	400	1000
10	10	20	100	100	200	1000	1000	2000

$\chi^2 = 0.8$, ns, $\phi = 0.20$ $\chi^2 = 8.0$, $p < 0.01$, $\phi = 0.20$ $\chi^2 = 80.0$, $p < 0.0001$, $\phi = 0.20$

Note that, as sample size increased by a factor of 10, chi-square also increased by a factor of 10. However, phi remained constant at 0.20 because the percentage change across the cells remained constant. In effect, chi-square-based measures of association standardize the calculated chi-square by the maximum attainable chi-square. The maximum attainable chi-square in a 2 × 2 table is equal to N (the sample size) and is only attained when all cases fall in one of the diagonals, as in the following example:

	A	B	Total	
A	50	0	50	Expected frequency for each cell
B	0	50	50	$= (50 \times 50)/100 = 25$
Total	50	50	100	$(O - E)^2/E$ for each cell $= 25$

Therefore, $\chi^2 = 25 + 25 + 25 + 25 = 100 = N$, and $\phi = \chi^2/N = 100/100 = 1.00$. By dividing χ^2 by its maximum attainable value, we standardize it to a true range (between 0 and 1) to render different values based on different Ns comparable.

CONTINGENCY COEFFICIENT

Another chi-square-based measure of association is the **contingency coefficient** (C), which is appropriate for nominal and ordinal variables having more than two categories. A problem with C is that its upper range depends on the size of the table. The upper limit of C is determined by the formula $\sqrt{\frac{(r - 1)}{r}}$, where r equals the number of rows in the table. In a 3 × 3 table, for instance, the upper limit of C is $\sqrt{\frac{(3 - 1)}{3}} = 0.816$. Even in a 10 × 10 table, the upper limit is only 0.949. The interpretation of C does not go beyond that given by chi-square, that is, the concept of deviation from independence, except to give us a rough idea of the magnitude of the relationship. We cannot square C as we did with phi to arrive at a variance explained interpretation. The formula for C is

$$C = \sqrt{\frac{\chi^2}{\chi^2 + N}} \tag{8.5}$$

Applying this formula to the computer printout in Table 8.9, we obtain

$$C = \sqrt{\frac{25.073}{25.073 + 585}} = \sqrt{\frac{25.073}{610.073}} = \sqrt{0.0411} = 0.2027$$

TABLE 8.9 A 3 × 2 Chi-Square Table: Violent Offense by Birth Order

COUNT
  ROW PCT
  COL PCT

VIOLENCE	FIRST	BIRTH ORDER MIDDLE	LAST	ROW TOTAL
NO	A 101 42.3 54.3	B 82 34.3 30.8	C 56 23.4 42.1	239 40.9
YES	D 85 24.6 45.7	E 184 53.2 69.2	F 77 22.3 57.91	346 59.1
COLUMN TOTAL	186 31.8	266 45.5	133 22.7	585 100.0

CHI-SQUARE	D.F.	SIGNIFICANCE		
25.07277	2	0.00001		

| CRAMER'S *V* | | | 0.20703 | |
| CONTINGENCY COEFFICIENT | | | 0.20273 | |

CRAMER'S *V*

Cramer's *V* is the other chi-square-based measure given in Table 8.9. This statistic is a modification of the phi statistic that allows for the analysis of tables that are larger than 2 × 2. Note from formula (8.6) that *V* is identical to phi except that *N* is multiplied by *L* − 1, where *L* is the lesser of either the number of rows or columns. Note that in a 3 × 2 table, *V* turns out to be identical to phi. Cramer's *V* is superior to the contingency coefficient for tables greater than 2 × 2 because it can attain a value of 1.

$$V = \sqrt{\frac{\chi^2}{N(L-1)}} \qquad (8.6)$$

where *L* − 1 = lesser of (*r* − 1) or (*c* − 1). Table 8.9 has 2 − 1 = 1 rows and 3 − 1 = 2 columns; thus we multiply *N* by 1:

$$V = \sqrt{\frac{25.073}{585(1)}} = \sqrt{\frac{25.073}{585}} = \sqrt{0.04286} = 0.207$$

A COMPUTER EXAMPLE OF CHI-SQUARE

We will now compute chi-square from data arranged in a 3 × 2 table. From our juvenile delinquent data we generate the hypothesis that birth rank (first/middle/last born) is associated with whether a juvenile has ever committed a violent offense (no/yes). We have asked the computer for chi-square, the contingency coefficient, and Cramer's *V*. The results are presented in Table 8.9. To verify our results, we can compute chi-square as follows:

TABLE 8.10   Calculating the Chi-Square

CELL	OBS.	EXP.	$(O - E)$	$(O - E)^2$	$(O - E)^2/E$
A	101	75.99	25.01	625.50	8.23
B	82	108.67	−26.67	711.29	6.54
C	56	54.34	1.66	2.75	0.05
D	85	110.01	−25.01	625.50	5.69
E	184	157.33	26.67	711.29	4.52
F	77	78.66	−1.66	2.75	0.04
	585	585	0.00	$\Sigma\ (O - E)^2/E = 25.07$	

Expected frequency for A $= (186 \times 239)/585 = 44454/585 = 75.99$
Expected frequency for B $= (266 \times 239)/585 = 63574/585 = 108.67$
Expected frequency for C $= (133 \times 239)/585 = 31787/585 = 54.34$
Expected frequency for D $= (186 \times 346)/585 = 64356/585 = 110.01$
Expected frequency for E $= (266 \times 346)/585 = 92036/585 = 157.33$
Expected frequency for F $= (133 \times 346)/585 = 46081/585 = 78.66$

Using the expected frequencies we calculated above, Table 8.10 outlines the remaining process for deriving the chi-square from the data in Table 8.9. There is a significant relationship between birth order and the commission of a violent crime. It is highly unlikely that our data come from a population in which the probability of committing a violent crime is the same for each birth-order group. We see that 239 (40.9%) of our 585 juvenile delinquents had not been convicted of a violent crime and that 346 (59.1%) had. Firstborn children were the least likely to have committed a violent crime (45.7%), and middle-born children were the most likely (69.2%).

We can use this table to reinforce the discussion of probability in Chapter 4. What is the probability that a delinquent drawn at random from the sample will be firstborn *and* will have committed at least one violent crime? These two events (birth order and violent crime) are not independent events, as we have seen. We must use the multiplication rule for dependent events, which, you recall, is given as $P(AB) = P(A) \times P(B/A)$. The probability that a delinquent drawn from the sample at random will be firstborn is obtained by dividing the number of delinquents who are firstborn by the total number of delinquents in the sample. Therefore, $P(A) = 186/585 = 0.318$. The probability of having committed a violent crime given firstborn status is obtained by dividing the number of first-borns who have committed a violent crime by the total number of firstborns. Therefore, $P(B/A) = 85/186 = 0.457$. Multiplying the probability of A by the probability of B given A gives us $(0.318)(0.457) = 0.145$.

Can you think of a faster way to obtain this result? Of course you can. You can simply divide the lower left-hand cell by the total sample size ($85/585 = 0.145$). This is the application of the general probability rule:

$$P = \frac{\text{Number of ways an event can occur}}{\text{Total number of possible outcomes}}$$

As you can plainly see, determining probabilities is a lot simpler and more direct if the data are set up in contingency tables.

KRUSKAL-WALLIS ONE-WAY ANALYSIS OF VARIANCE

The **Kruskal-Wallis one-way ANOVA test** (H) is a nonparametric version of the parametric ANOVA discussed in Chapter 7. It is suitable for data measured at the ordinal level and permits a test of significance by using the chi-square distribution among groups ranked according to some ordinal attribute. The Kruskal-Wallis test can be used to compare two groups, but its special utility is that it can be used to test the significance of difference between more than two rank-ordered groups.

Suppose we ask five randomly selected political science professors from each of three different countries to rank their country on degree of respect for civil liberties as they perceive it on a scale of 0 through 100. The responses of these 15 professors are

Country 1:	75, 74, 52, 74, 55
Country 2:	65, 80, 70, 90, 80
Country 3:	74, 92, 85, 82, 95

Rather than working with raw scores, H substitutes the rankings of the items in each group. Thus, the last score (95) would be ranked number 1, and the middle score of country 1 (52) would be ranked 15. Table 8.11 sets up these scores by rank. Note that there is a tie for the sixth rank, where there are two scores of 80. To break the tie, we assign those scores the mean of the two ranks they would have occupied if no tie existed ($6 + 7/2 = 6.5$). Similarly, we have a three-way tie on a score of 74 for ranks 9, 10, and 11. We assign the mean of the three ranks to these three scores ($9 + 10 + 11/3 = 10$). After we arrange the ranks we sum the ranks for each country.

When we have summed the ranks, we then substitute these values into formula (8.7) to compute H. The null hypothesis is that the samples come from the same population, and thus the ranked perceptions regarding civil liberties are identical.

$$H = \frac{12}{N(N+1)}\left[\frac{s_1^2}{N_1} + \frac{s_2^2}{N_2} + \frac{s_3^2}{N_3}\right] - 3(N+1) \tag{8.7}$$

where s_1^2 = sum of the rank of country 1, etc., and 12 and 3 are constants. Thus,

$$H = \frac{12}{15(16)}\left[\frac{22^2}{5} + \frac{41^2}{5} + \frac{57^2}{5}\right] - 3(16)$$

$$= \frac{12}{240}\left[\frac{484}{5} + \frac{1681}{5} + \frac{3249}{5}\right] - 48$$

$$= (0.05)[96.8 + 336.2 + 649.8] - 48$$

$$= (0.05)(1082.8) - 48 = 54.14 - 48 = 6.14$$

TABLE 8.11   Professors' Rankings of Civil Liberties

COUNTRY 1		COUNTRY 2		COUNTRY 3	
x	Rank	x	Rank	x	Rank
95	1	90	3	75	8
92	2	80	6.5	74	10
85	4	80	6.5	74	10
82	5	70	12	55	14
74	10	65	13	52	15
	22		41		57

We test H or significance when sample sizes are greater than 5 with the chi-square distribution, entering the chi-square table with $k - 1$ degrees of freedom. Since we have three categories, df = 2. The critical chi-square value with 2 degrees of freedom is 5.991 at the 0.05 level of confidence. Our computed $H(6.14)$ exceeds this critical value; we can therefore reject the null hypothesis.

The measure of association that can be directly computed from H is the now familiar eta squared. The simple formula for this computation is

$$\eta^2 = \frac{H}{N-1} = \frac{6.14}{14} = 0.439 \tag{8.8}$$

Thus, perceptions of civil liberties are rather strongly related to the country from which the professor comes, with country of origin accounting for 43.9% of the variance.

SUMMARY

Chi-square is a popular and much-used technique for testing statistical independence and goodness of fit with tabular data. A test for independence is essentially testing whether or not the distribution of scores on one attribute in a table is independent of the distribution on another attribute. In other words, we are testing whether or not the two attributes or variables are related in the population. We do so by examining and comparing the observed bivariate cell frequencies with the cell frequencies we would expect if the two variables were unrelated. A test of goodness of fit is asking whether or not an observed distribution of scores "fits" a theoretically expected distribution. A significant chi-square indicates a poor fit between theoretical expectations and empirical actuality. A nonsignificant chi-square indicates a good fit.

The significance of the chi-square statistic depends on the value of the computed statistic and its associated degrees of freedom. Because chi-square is very sensitive to sample size, the larger the sample, the more likely we are to observe a statistically significant difference if a difference actually exists in the population. Phi is a statistic suitable for 2×2 tables that measures the strength of association between two variables. When squared, phi gives the proportion of variance in the dependent variable accounted for by the independent variable. Phi standardizes chi-square by dividing it by the maximum attainable chi-square for a given sample, which is always N, the sample size.

The Kruskal-Wallis one-way analysis of variance test is a nonparametric version of ANOVA suitable for ordinal-level data. This test tells us of any significant difference among two or more groups that have been rank ordered on some attribute using the chi-square distribution. Eta squared can be computed directly from H, giving us the proportion of variance in the dependent variable accounted for by the independent variable.

PRACTICE APPLICATION: CHI-SQUARE

We asked a sample of 89 residents of an upper-middle-class apartment complex to identify themselves as being primarily either liberal or conservative in their political orientation. We also ask them their opinion on an issue raging on the university campus at present: "Do you think that the university should be allowed to fire a professor who advocates a communistic form of government for the United States?" The answer categories are no and yes. We place their answers into a 2×2 table and compute chi-square and phi:

SHOULD BE ALLOWED TO FIRE PROFESSORS	IDEOLOGY CONSERVATIVE	LIBERAL	
Yes	40 (75.5%)	12 (33.3%)	52 (58.4%)
No	13 (24.5%)	24 (66.7%)	37 (41.6%)
Totals	53 (100%)	36 (100%)	89

Compute χ^2:

$$\chi^2 = \Sigma \frac{(O - E)^2}{E} \qquad \text{where } E = \frac{r \times c}{N}$$

Expected A = 53 × 52/89 = 31.0
Expected B = 36 × 52/89 = 21.0
Expected C = 53 × 37/89 = 22.0
Expected D = 36 × 37/89 = 15.0

CELL	OBS.	EXP.	$(O - E)$	$(O - E)^2$	$(O - E)^2/E$
A	40	31	9	81	2.61
B	12	21	−9	81	3.86
C	13	22	−9	81	3.68
D	24	15	9	81	5.40
	89	89	00.00	$\Sigma (O - E)^2/E = 15.55$	

Chi-square is significant at less than 0.001. We are confident that a person's opinion on this matter is not independent of his or her political orientation. We reject the null hypothesis.

Compute phi:

$$\phi = \sqrt{\frac{X^2}{N}}$$

$$= \sqrt{\frac{15.55}{89}} = \sqrt{0.175} = 0.418$$

Phi is moderately strong. Political orientation is moderately strongly associated with one's opinion about the university's right to fire professors who advocate the communistic form of government for the United States. The percentage of variance in a respondent's opinion accounted for by political orientation is 0.418 squared = 0.175, or 17.5%.

Let us assume that our class standing/general knowledge ANOVA example in Chapter 7 was based on rank order rather than raw scores and compute the Kruskal-Wallis H. The scores follow and are converted into ranks:

x	RANK	x	RANK	x	RANK
73	17	72	18	83	6.5
75	14	78	10.5	86	4
77	12	74	16	89	3
75	14	80	8.5	85	5
78	10.5	83	6.5	90	2
75	14	80	8.5	95	1
	81.5		68.0		21.5

Compute H:

$$H = \frac{12}{N(N+1)} \left[\frac{s^2_1}{N_1} + \frac{s^2_2}{N_2} + \frac{s^2_3}{N_3} \right] - 3(N+1)$$

$$= \frac{12}{18(19)} \left[\frac{81.5^2}{6} + \frac{68^2}{6} + \frac{21.5^2}{6} \right] - 3(19)$$

$$= \frac{12}{342} \left[\frac{6642.25}{6} + \frac{4624}{6} + \frac{462.25}{6} \right] - 57$$

$$= (0.0351)[1107.04 + 770.67 + 77.04] - 57$$

$$= (0.0351)(1954.75) - 57 = 68.12 - 57 = 11.61$$

Entering the chi-square table with 2 df, we find that the critical value needed to reject the null at the 0.01 level of significance is 9.21. Our computed value exceeds the critical value: We reject the null.

Compute eta squared:

$$\eta^2 = \frac{H}{N-1} = \frac{11.61}{17} = 0.683$$

The percentage of variance computed from the H test for these data is 68.3, which is approximately 5% less than using ANOVA (73.4%). This result illustrates the greater utility of using interval-level statistics and measures over ordinal-level statistics and measures if it is valid to do so.

REFERENCE

Hacking, I. (1984). "Trial by number." *Science* 84 (November), 69–72.

PROBLEMS

1. A teacher believes there is a relationship between spelling ability and how much students read on their own over the summer. Following a spelling test, he surveyed all the fourth graders in his school and came up with the following results:

Observed Frequencies: Spelling Test Scores

NO. OF BOOKS READ	A	B	C	D	ROW TOTALS
4 or more	15	8	4	4	31
2–3	3	12	12	15	42
0–1	2	7	15	15	39
Column Totals	20	27	31	34	112

Complete the following table by calculating the expected frequencies for this group of students:

Expected Frequencies: Spelling Test Scores

NO. OF BOOKS READ	A	B	C	D	ROW TOTALS
4 or more					31
2–3					42
0–1					39
Column Totals	20	27	31	34	112

Specify the null hypothesis to determine if spelling scores are independent of the amount of summer reading. Calculate χ^2 and test the null hypothesis.

2. At an intersection near an elementary school, local parents are lobbying to have a stop sign replaced with a traffic light. To determine the extent of public opinion on this issue, the city transportation office conducted a survey of the neighborhood asking residents whether they "favored," "opposed," or had "no opinion" concerning putting in a traffic signal. The following table illustrates the results of the survey. Is opinion concerning putting up a traffic light independent of gender? Interpret your results. Using Cramer's *V*, calculate the strength of the relationship.

GENDER	OPPOSE	FAVOR	NO OPINION	Row tot.
Males	150	120	130 73.03	400
Females	102	220	48 26.97	370
column tot.	252	340	178	

3. A previous market analysis in a midsize community found that residents preferred shopping at store A twice as much as at stores B and C, with 50% favoring store A, 25% favoring store B, and 25% favoring store C. Store C, wanting to improve its image, embarked on an expensive advertising campaign. Afterwards, they conducted a survey and got the following results:

SHOPPING PREFERENCE			
	A	B	C
Observed Frequency	120	48	82

Is there a significant difference between the distribution before the advertising campaign and after the advertising campaign?

4. Maria, an elementary school teacher, noticed that children who brought their lunches in a lunch box (usually decorated with colorful cartoon characters) tended to eat more of their lunch than did students who brought their lunch in a lunch bag. She observed students over the lunch period and came up with the following results:

	ATE ALL OR MOST	ATE ABOUT HALF	ONLY ATE A LITTLE
Box	30	22	8
Bag	19	21	20

Using the data given, determine whether how much a child eats is independent of the type of lunch box or bag they carry. Using a contingency coefficient, calculate the strength of the relationship.

5. A researcher would like to determine if attitudes about postgraduation plans differ as a function of year in college. A random sample of college students is selected. The students fill out a questionnaire, specifying year in school and what they intend to do when they complete college. Their responses are classified and recorded in the following table. Do attitudes about future plans for students differ as a function of their year in school? Calculate the strength of the relationship.

	WORK	GRADUATE SCHOOL	UNDECIDED
Freshman	22	20	48
Sophomore	37	26	29
Junior	58	31	15
Senior	56	35	9

6. A sample of 50 students was classified as to whether or not they had voted in the last student election. Is voting behavior independent of academic status? Since three of the cells in the table are less than five, calculate Yate's correction for continuity.

	VOTED	DID NOT VOTE
Freshman	4	6
Sophomore	7	8
Junior	8	2
Senior	13	2

7. A survey of male and female working parents was taken to determine if they pre-
    ferred day-care facilities or in-house babysitters to care for their children during
    the day. Is gender independent of attitudes concerning use of day care versus in-
    house babysitting? Use phi to calculate the strength of this relationship.

	PREFER DAY CARE	PREFER IN-HOUSE BABYSITTER
Mothers	16	34
Fathers	29	21

8. Three groups of dogs were used in a study of a new dog food designed to en-
    courage weight loss. Group A was fed the regular dog food, group B was given a
    50/50 mix of regular dog food combined with the new lite dog food, and group
    C was only fed the new lite dog food. After 6 months, each dog was weighed and
    their weight was compared with their weight when the program began. The re-
    sults shown below indicate the amount of weight lost or gained in ounces.

GROUP A	GROUP B	GROUP C
+3	−16	−21
−1	−24	−20
+2	0	−38
+1	−7	−22
−3	−23	−32
−14	−2	−12

   a) Use the Kruskal-Wallis test to determine whether the groups differ in terms of
      weight loss.
   b) Use η^2 to determine the strength of the relationship.
   c) Write a short statement interpreting your results.

9. An elementary English teacher wanted to determine if repeated writing of words
    would improve performance on a spelling test. A list of 25 new words was dis-
    tributed to his class. Group 1 was asked to write the new words correctly 10 times,
    the second group was asked to write the words five times, group 3 repeated the
    exercise three times, and group 4 wrote the words correctly once. The following
    table indicates the number of words each student misspelled on the spelling test.
    Use the appropriate nonparametric test to determine whether the groups differ
    significantly in terms of their spelling scores. If significant, calculate the strength
    of the relationship and interpret your results.

GROUP 1	GROUP 2	GROUP 3	GROUP 4
0	3	2	7
1	1	4	5
0	2	3	9
0	1	3	8
2	0	5	2

Chapter 9

Nonparametric Measures of Association

THE IDEA OF ASSOCIATION

We have already discussed certain measures of association without fully developing the idea of **association.** Eta squared, a measure of association introduced in Chapter 6, requires at least one of the variables being tested to be measured at the interval or ratio level, and phi squared is a measure suitable for nominal-level variables in a 2 × 2 table. We will develop the idea of association in this chapter with nominal- and ordinal-level measures. Measures based on higher level data are discussed elsewhere in the text. The statistical tests in this chapter are all nonparametric.

In social science we ask questions such as "Why do people with less formal education tend to be more prejudiced than people with more formal education?," "Why do blacks make less money than whites?," and "Why are sex offenders punished more harshly than other kinds of offenders?" Each of these questions deals with the issue of how variables are connected, related, or associated. We are saying that the condition *being black,* for instance, is related to low income, and we saw in Chapter 6 that the condition *sex offender* was related to harsher punishment. Another way of phrasing this last sentence would be to say that income levels depend on race and that harshness of punishment depends on type of crime. Thus, income and harshness of punishment are dependent variables, and race and type of offense are independent variables. Three main questions arise in the assessment of association: (1) Does an association exist? (2) How strong is it? (3) What is its direction?

DOES AN ASSOCIATION EXIST?

Before we can ask, for instance, why blacks make less money than whites we first have to determine if they actually do by subjecting the hypothesis to a test of statistical significance. If income is found to be dependent on race, then we can say that the two variables are associated. An association exists if values of one variable vary systematically with variation in a second variable. When we ask why blacks make less money than whites we take for granted that the value of the variable *income* changes as we move across conditions of the variable *race*. As another example, if we had five conditions of a religious affiliation variable ranging from the most fundamentalist denominations to the most liberal, we would expect levels of a *belief in evolution* variable to vary across those conditions. More precisely, we would expect levels of belief to increase as we move farther away from the fundamentalist denominations. If values of one variable do not change across conditions of another, there is no association between them.

Table 9.1 illustrates the presence and absence of an association between attending college and whether or not the respondent's father is a college graduate (hypothetical data). In distribution A we see that whether one attends college is largely a function of whether one's father is a college graduate. Ninety-five (82.6%) of the 115 respondents who attended college had fathers who were graduates and 20 (17.4%) had fathers who were not. Among the 125 respondents who did not attend college, 80 (64%) had fathers who were not college graduates and 45 (36%) had fathers who were. In

TABLE 9.1   Hypothetical Conditional Distributions Showing Association (A) and No Association (B)

ATTEND COLLEGE?	A FATHER GRADUATE YES	NO		ATTEND COLLEGE?	B FATHER GRADUATE YES	NO	
YES	95	20	115	YES	65	65	130
NO	45	80	125	NO	55	55	110
	140	100	240		120	120	240

other words, the distribution of frequencies of the variable *attend college* is conditional on the distribution of frequencies of the second variable, *father graduate*. We call such a joint frequency distribution a **conditional distribution**.

Distribution B shows a table of joint frequencies in which no association exists between the two variables. Whether or not one attends college is not conditional or dependent on whether or not one's father is a college graduate. Exactly half of those who attended college had fathers who were graduates, and half who did not attend college also had fathers who were graduates. The same is true for those who did not attend college. The values of the dependent variable do not vary across conditions of the independent variable.

WHAT IS THE STRENGTH OF THE ASSOCIATION?

Once we have evidence of a significant conditional distribution, the next step is to quantify the strength of the association. This is essentially a matter of examining the magnitude of change by moving from one condition to another. A crude measure of the strength of the association would be the simple percentage of change across cells. Take distribution A in Table 9.1 for instance. We could compare the percentage of respondents who attended college and who had fathers who graduated ($95/115 \times 100 = 83\%$) with the percentage of respondents who attended college but whose fathers did not graduate ($20/115 \times 100 = 17\%$). In this case we have a difference of 66 percentage points, whereas in distribution B the difference is zero.

One problem with this strategy is that we would have to make multiple comparisons of the percentages from cell to cell. It would be much more efficient to have a single summary value of the strength of the association that varies within fixed, or normed, limits. When we discussed percentages, ratios, and proportions, we performed norming operations, or standardizing, of the raw data. All of the statistics of association we will look at involve ratios of one quantity to another. The statistics we will discuss in this chapter have the efficient properties of being single summary indices of the strength of the association and of ranging within fixed limits. In addition, they have the property of indicating the direction of the relationship, something that becomes important when dealing with ordered variables.

WHAT IS THE DIRECTION OF THE ASSOCIATION?

Relationships or associations between variables can be either positive or negative. A **positive association** exists when the values of one variable increase with the increased values of another, that is, the values of both variables vary positively. In other words,

TABLE 9.2   Hypothetical Conditional Distributions Showing Positive (A) and Negative (B) Association

INCOME	A EDUCATION HIGH	MEDIUM	LOW	TV WATCHING	HIGH	B EDUCATION MEDIUM	LOW
HIGH	100	65	40	HIGH	35	50	80
MEDIUM	40	75	50	MEDIUM	75	65	60
LOW	30	55	100	LOW	90	55	40

Positive Association   Negative Association

high scores on one variable are associated with high scores on the other, and low scores are associated with low scores. **Negative association** exists when we observe the opposite pattern; that is, as the values of one variable increase, the values of the other decrease.

Table 9.2 illustrates positive and negative associations. In distribution A we see that income varies positively with level of education: High scores tend to go with high scores and low scores tend to go with low scores. In this distribution the highest category Ns are found on the main diagonal (top left-hand cell to bottom right-hand cell). In distribution B we have the opposite pattern, in which high scores on the education variable are negatively associated with low scores on TV watching, and low scores on education are associated with high scores on TV watching. In this distribution the higher category Ns are found in the secondary diagonal (top right-hand cell to bottom left-hand cell). Another way of stating a negative relationship is to say that the variables are *inversely related*.

A normed measure of association generally ranges between -1.0 and $+1.0$. An association of -1.0 is a perfect negative association, and a value of $+1.0$ is a perfect positive association. An association of zero means that there is no association between the two variables. Normed measures allow for the comparison of computed values across tables and across samples, something that could not be done if the measures were not restricted to defined ranges.

Unfortunately, there are no hard rules for interpreting the numerical values of the computed statistics unless they have a variance-explained interpretation, which most of the statistics discussed in this chapter do not. How strong does an association have to be before it is considered worth our attention? And what do we mean by *strong*, anyway? The answers to these questions depend on the specific context of the research. In one context an association of 0.50 might produce nothing more than a shrug of the shoulders; in another it might set the heart pounding. Rules of thumb for interpreting the strength of association are presented in Figure 9.1. Be aware that it only makes sense to interpret a measure of association as weak, moderate, or strong if it is found to be statistically significant.

We next discuss some of these normed statistical techniques for assessing the existence, strength, and direction of association.

PROPORTIONAL REDUCTION IN ERROR

As you might have guessed, if two variables are associated we can use one of them to predict the other. We saw in the last chapter that males and females differed significantly in their willingness to vote for a female for president of the United States. This being the case, knowing a person's gender will help predict his or her willingness to vote for

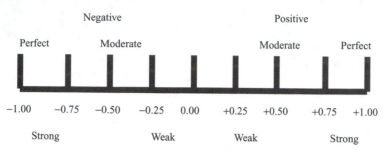

FIGURE 9.1.   Rule-of-thumb scale for interpreting statistically significant strength of association for measures with fixed limits of −1.0 and +1.0

a female president. Of course, your predictions will not be infallible. There will be a number of errors in your predictions since not all women indicated such a willingness, and not all males indicated an unwillingness. However, there will be fewer prediction errors armed with knowledge about the independent variable than without. This is formally called **proportional reduction in error (PRE),** which refers to the reduction of errors made as we move from predicting scores on the dependent variable without knowing the distribution of the independent variable to predicting scores on the dependent variable knowing how the independent variable is distributed.

Lambda is very useful for gaining a grasp of the concept of PRE because it uses the general formula for PRE, which is

$$\text{PRE} = \frac{\text{Errors using rule 1} - \text{Errors using rule 2}}{\text{Errors using rule 1}} \tag{9.1}$$

Rule 1 predicts the values of the dependent variable without knowledge of how the independent variable is distributed, and rule 2 predicts the values of the dependent variable with knowledge of how the independent variable is distributed. If there is perfect association between the two variables, knowledge of the independent variable will reduce prediction errors to zero, and lambda will be 1.0. If there is no association, knowledge of the independent variable will be of no predictive value, and lambda will be zero.

Lambda is an asymmetric measure of association (which means that is can produce different values according to which variable is considered dependent) with values ranging between 0.0 and 1.0, and it is best suited to distributions in which both variables are nominal level. Lambda is not a particularly popular statistic in actual research because it has a strange quirk, which will be discussed later, but it is very useful for illustrating the important concept of PRE. Let us compute lambda from the data in Table 9.3.

Suppose we want to determine the association between recommendations made by prison psychologists that prisoners either be released or not released and the parole board's actual release decision. From Table 9.3 we see that psychologists recommended release for 110 inmates, and the parole board released 85 of them, meaning that they disagreed with the psychologists in 25 cases. Psychologists recommended against releasing 85 inmates, and the parole board concurred in 75 instances. Altogether, 195 inmates went before the parole board, and the board agreed with the psychologists' recommendation in 160 cases. These data are set up in a 2 × 2 table.

What if we attempted to predict parole board decisions without knowledge of the psychologists' recommendations? Under conditions of ignorance about the independent

**TABLE 9.3 Psychologists' Recommendations
by Parole Board Decisions**

PAROLE BOARD'S DECISION (Y)	PSYCHOLOGISTS' RECOMMENDATIONS (X)		
	RELEASE	NO RELEASE	
RELEASE	85	10	95
NO RELEASE	25	75	100
	110	85	195

variable, our best guess would be the modal category of the dependent variable. The modal category for the parole board's decision is the *no release* row ($N = 100$). We would make fewer errors if we predicted no release for every inmate than if we predicted release for every inmate, or half for release and half for no release. If we chose the modal category, there would be 95 errors (the number of inmates who were released). Therefore, $E_1 = 95$. E_1 is thus defined as N − modal category of the dependent variable (in the present case, $195 - 100 = 95$).

Having found the number of prediction using rule 1, we now determine the number of errors using rule 2, which provides us with the knowledge that psychologists recommended releasing 110 inmates and not releasing 85. Knowing this we will make fewer errors if we predict that the board will release all 110 who were recommended for release, and release none of those not recommended for release. Our errors are those cases in which the board disagreed with the recommendations. To determine the number of errors we will make with knowledge of the independent variable (rule 2), we simply subtract the modal cell frequency in each condition from its column total and sum the differences as follows:

For release: $110 - 85 = 25$
For no release: $85 - 75 = \underline{10}$
Total $E_2 = \overline{35}$

A total of 35 errors are made when taking the independent variable into account. Because prediction errors have been reduced considerably, the variables are associated. To find the proportional reduction in error, we substitute the values of E_1 and E_2 into the formula:

$$\lambda = \frac{E_1 - E_2}{E_1} = \frac{95 - 35}{95} = .632$$

Thus, we have *proportionately* reduced our error in predicting inmate release with knowledge of the psychologists' recommendations by 63.2%. Do not confuse this with an absolute percentage reduction in error. Without knowledge of the psychologist's recommendations we made 95 errors, which is a percentage error rate of $95/195 = 0.487$, or 48.7%. When we used psychologist's recommendations we reduced our errors to 35, for an error rate of $35/195 = 0.179$. Thus, we reduced error by $0.487 - 0.179 = 0.308$, or 30.8%. The *proportional* reduction in error is the ratio of the absolute percentage reduction in error divided by the initial error ($0.308/0.487 = 0.632$). There is a moderate to strong association between the two variables.

THE CONCEPT OF PAIRED CASES

Because the remaining statistics to be discussed in this chapter rely on comparisons of various types of paired cases, we should discuss the topic before proceeding further. By **paired cases** we mean all possible pairs of cases that can be found in a given set of cases. Suppose we have the following small data set of 10 students who are categorized according to whether they scored high or low on an IQ test and on the SAT test.

STUDENT	IQ	SAT
Jim	low	low
Tanya	low	low
Guang-Yu	low	high
Frank	high	high
Andre	low	low
Janelle	high	high
Max	high	low
John	low	low
Jose	high	high
Ann	high	low

The possible number of paired cases that could be made up from any data set is determined by the formula: total pairs = $N(N - 1)/2$. For our student data there are $(10)(9)/2 = 45$ possible pairs. Let us display the data in a bivariate table (Table 9.4).

Clearly, we could predict a student's SAT score from his or her IQ score from these data. A student who scores high on an IQ test is likely to score high on the SAT also. Similarly, a student who scores low on an IQ test is likely to score low on the SAT. The seven observations conforming to this pattern can be considered to be in agreement with what we might logically hypothesize from our knowledge of the similarity of cognitive mechanisms underlying scoring high or low on both tests. There are three departures (Guang-Yu, Max, and Ann) from this general pattern. These three cases are discordant with our expectations. It is the comparison of agreement to disagreement (similar to dissimilar pairs) in a data set that constitutes the basis for assessing the degree of association that exists between two nominal or ordinal variables. Let us now look at the various kinds of pairs we could make from our data. There are five possible pair combinations in any data set:

1. Similar pairs, denoted by N_s. These are pairs that are ranked in the same order on both variables. Jose, Frank, Janelle, Tanya, Andre, John, and Jim constitute similar pairs (either high–high or low–low). The product of the N_s in these categories ($3 \times 4 = 12$) constitute similar pairs.

TABLE 9.4   Cross-Tabulation of IQ and SAT Scores

	IQ	
SAT	HIGH	LOW
HIGH	Jose Frank Janelle	Guang-Yu
LOW	Max Ann	Tanya Andre John Jim

2. Dissimilar pairs, denoted by N_d. Guang-Yu (high–low) and Max and Ann (low–high) constitute dissimilar pairs. There are $1 \times 2 = 2$ dissimilar pairs.
3. Pairs tied on the independent variable (down the columns) but not on the dependent variable, are denoted by T_x. Jose, Frank, Janelle, Max, and Ann are tied on the high category of the independent variable ($3 \times 2 = 6$ pairs), and Guang-Yu, Tanya, Andre, John, and Jim are tied on the low category ($1 \times 4 = 4$ pairs). There are thus 10 T_x pairs.
4. Pairs tied on the dependent variable (across the rows) but not on the independent variable, are denoted by T_y. Jose, Frank, Janelle, and Guang-Yu are tied on the high category ($3 \times 1 = 3$ pairs) of the dependent variable, and the remaining six students are tied on the low category ($2 \times 4 = 8$ pairs). There are thus 11 T_y pairs.
5. Pairs tied on both the dependent and independent variables, are denoted by T_{xy}. These are the pairs that can be formed from the cases in the same cell. For instance, from the three cases in the high–high cell we could obtain $(3)(2)/2 = 3$ pairs; from the low–low cell we could obtain $(4)(3)/2 = 6$ pairs. Max and Ann form a single pair, and since Guang-Yu is all alone, we cannot form a pair in his cell. There are thus 10 T_{yx} pairs. These different pairs are presented below.

N_s	3×4	$= 12$
N_d	1×2	$= 2$
T_x	$(3 \times 2) + (1 \times 4)$	$= 10$
T_y	$(3 \times 1) + (2 \times 4)$	$= 11$
T_{xy}	$3 + 1 + 6$	$= 10$
Total pairs		$= 45$

A COMPUTER EXAMPLE

Computer programs for nominal- and ordinal-level variables supply a variety of statistics. The partial printout in Table 9.5 is based on our multiple sclerosis (MS) data and will serve to illustrate some of the ordinal-level measures of association we will discuss in this

TABLE 9.5   Cross-Tabulation of Social Isolation by Physical Restriction

	PHYSICAL RESTRICTION			
SOCIAL ISOLATION	LOW	MEDIUM	HIGH	ROW TOTAL
LOW	(A) 20	(B) 14	(C) 8	42
MEDIUM	(D) 14	(E) 23	(F) 14	51
HIGH	(G) 4	(H) 24	(I) 14	42
COLUMN TOTAL	38	61	36	135

$\chi^2 = 15.10207$, df = 4, $p = 0.0045$

STATISTIC	SYMMETRIC	WITH SOCIAL ISOLATION DEPENDENT	WITH PHYSICAL RESTRICTIVENESS DEPENDENT
Lambda	0.08228	0.08333	0.08108
Somer's *d*	0.24979	0.25332	0.24636
			Significance
Cramer's *V*	0.23650		
Contingency coefficient	0.31719		
Kendall's tau-b	0.24981		0.0006
Gamma	0.37231		0.0006

chapter. We have hypothesized that an association exists between the degree of physical restrictiveness suffered by MS patients and their level of social isolation; that is, the more physically restricted an individual is by the disease, the more he or she is socially isolated. We have three conditions of physical restrictiveness: (1) those who never use a walking aid, (2) those who occasionally use a walking aid, and (3) those who always use a walking aid or wheelchair. We will call these three categories low, medium, and high, respectively. Our measure of social isolation is Neal and Groat's (1974) social isolation scale, a nine-item scale with a four-point continuum, from strongly agree to strongly disagree. The minimum score is 0, indicating a complete lack of social isolation, to 36, indicating a maximum level of social isolation. Social isolation is the dependent variable and physical restriction is the independent variable.

Note that the chi-square value given in Table 9.5 is significant with the probability being given as 0.0045. This means that we can be confident that an association exists between these two variables because we could only get the observed pattern of cases by chance 45 times out of every 10,000 samples of similar size and composition. The other reported statistics inform us of the strength and direction of the association.

GAMMA

We will begin our discussion of ordinal-level statistics with gamma because it is perhaps the most popular statistic applied to this type of analysis. Gamma ranges between -1.0 and $+1.0$ and compares similar pairs of scores with dissimilar pairs but ignores tied pairs. By ignoring tied pairs, gamma informs us that as one variable increases in value the other increases, decreases, or stays the same. When the number of similar pairs is greater than the number of dissimilar pairs, the association is positive. When the reverse is true, the association is negative.

The formula for computing gamma is

$$\gamma = \frac{N_s - N_d}{N_s + N_d} \tag{9.2}$$

where N_s = number of similar pairs and N_d = number of dissimilar pairs. From a visual inspection of Table 9.5 we note that a low level of physical restriction is associated with a low level of social isolation, and that a high level of restriction is associated with a high level of isolation. We would know before looking at the statistics, then, that the association is positive. If we were to predict a person's position in terms of low, medium, and high on social isolation, it helps to know his or her level of physical restriction. For those low on physical restriction we predict the same rank order on social isolation, that is, low. Of the 38 individuals who are low on physical restriction, 20 are low on social isolation (cell A). We cannot pair this group of 20 people with people in any of the other cells sharing the same row (low isolation) or column (low physical restrictiveness) because these cells are tied, and gamma does not consider tied pairs in its computation.

The first thing to do is to determine the similar and dissimilar pairs. To reiterate, similar pairs are all pairs that are not tied on one or the other of the conditions of the two variables. Thus, all those cells that are below and to the right of the upper left-hand cell constitute similar pairs because they are not tied in any way with those cells. We compute the number of similar pairs by multiplying the value of the upper left-hand cell with the sum of all cells below and to the right of it. This procedure is repeated for every cell in the table that has cells both below it and to the right. The following table indicates the first set of pairs to be calculated, starting with the *target cell* (low physical restriction/low social isolation) and the cells below and to its right that are to be summed.

$$N_s \text{ for cell } A = (A)(E + F + H + I) = (20)(23 + 14 + 24 + 14) = (20)(75) = 1500$$

The next step uses cell D as the target cell:

$$(D)(H + I) = (14)(24 + 14) = (14)(38) = 532$$

The next step uses cell B as the target cell:

A	B 14	C
D	E	F 14
G	H	I 14

$$(B)(F + I) = (14)(14 + 14) = (14)(28) = 392$$

The final step uses cell E as the target cell (the only cell left with a cell that is both below and to the right of it):

A	B	C
D	E 23	F
G	H	I 14

$$(E)(I) = (23)(14) = 322$$

We now sum these quantities:

$$N_s = 1500 + 532 + 392 + 322 = 2746$$

We now have to find the dissimilar pairs by working in reverse. This time we start with the upper right-hand cell (cell C) and sum the values found in the cells below and to the left of it. For the target cell:

$$
\begin{aligned}
\text{cell C} &= (8)(23 + 14 + 24 + 4) = (8)(65) = && 520 \\
\text{cell B} &= (14)(14 + 4) = (14)(18) && = 252 \\
\text{cell F} &= (14)(24 + 4) = (14)(28) && = 392 \\
\text{cell E} &= (23)(4) && = \underline{\hphantom{0}92} \\
&\text{Total } N_d = && 1256
\end{aligned}
$$

We now put the values of N_s and N_d into the formula for gamma:

$$
\gamma = \frac{N_s - N_d}{N_s + N_d} = \frac{2746 - 1256}{2746 + 1256} = \frac{1490}{4002} = .372
$$

There is a weak to moderate positive relationship between the degree of physical restriction and feelings of social isolation. Since we are dealing now with ordinal variables with an inherent ordered structure, direction of association has a definite meaningful interpretation. We are saying that as physical restriction gets more severe on an ordered scale, there is a tendency for MS patients to feel a greater degree of social isolation.

LAMBDA

As we see from the computer printout of Table 9.5, the value of **lambda** varies with which variable is taken as dependent. Lambda is thus an asymmetric statistic. Because the degree of physical restriction is obviously not dependent on social isolation, we calculated lambda with social isolation as the dependent variable. The third value of lambda in the computer printout, *symmetric lambda* can be thought of as an average of the two asymmetric lambdas.

We will not repeat the computation of lambda with these data. Instead we will consider a particularly vexing liability. The problem is that lambda can yield a value of zero when there is, in fact, an association between the variables. This result occurs when the category modes of the independent variable occur in the same category of the dependent variable. Take the following bivariate distribution in which all modal column scores occur in the same row:

100	90	60	250
40	50	60	150
140	140	120	400

$$
\begin{aligned}
E_1 &= 400 - 250 = 150 \\
E_2 &= 40 + 50 + 60 = 150 \\
\lambda &= \frac{E_1 - E_2}{E_1} = \frac{150 - 150}{150} = 0.0
\end{aligned}
$$

If we compute gamma for these data we find there is indeed a relationship:

$$
\begin{array}{ll}
N_s = (100)(50 + 60) = 11000 & N_d = (60)(40 + 50) = 5400 \\
 (90)(60) = 5400 & (90)(40) = \underline{3600} \\
 \text{Total} = 16400 & \text{Total} = 9000
\end{array}
$$

$$
\gamma = \frac{N_s - N_d}{N_s + N_d} = \frac{16400 - 9000}{1640 + 9000} = \frac{7400}{25400} = .291
$$

SOMER'S *d*

Somer's *d* is a measure of association that, although quite similar to gamma, is more restrictive in that it takes into account pairs that are tied on the dependent variable. Taking the tied pairs into account has the effect of weakening the numeric value of the association, as will be seen from the formula. By taking into account pairs tied on the dependent variable, we gain more information than gamma reveals. Somer's *d* is an asymmetric statistic, which means that its value will depend on which variable is taken as the dependent variable. The formula for Somer's *d* is

$$
d = \frac{N_s - N_d}{N_s + N_d + T_y} \tag{9.3}
$$

where T_y = pairs tied on the dependent variable. Since the dependent variable is arrayed across the rows, pairs that are tied on Y are located across the rows. Taking cell A as our first target cell, we find that pairs to the right of it with values of 14 and 8 are tied with it. We calculated T_y by multiplying the value of the target cell by all tied cases to the right of it. For the target cell:

$$
\begin{array}{lll}
\text{cell A} = (20)(14 + 8) & = & 440 \\
\text{cell B} = (14)(8) & = & 112 \\
\text{cell D} = (14)(23 + 14) & = & 518 \\
\text{cell E} = (23)(14) & = & 322 \\
\text{cell G} = (4)(24 + 14) & = & 152 \\
\text{cell H} = (24)(14) & = & \underline{336} \\
\multicolumn{2}{r}{\text{Total } T_y =} & 1880
\end{array}
$$

We already have N_s and N_d values from gamma so all that we have to do is put T_y into the formula:

$$
d = \frac{N_s - N_d}{N_s + N_d + T_y} = \frac{2746 - 1256}{2746 + 1256 + 1880} = \frac{1490}{5882} = .2533
$$

Our computed value matches the computer value taking social isolation as the dependent variable.

TAU-B

Tau-b is even more restrictive than Somer's d in that it includes pairs tied on X but not on Y and pairs tied on Y but not on X; that is, ties on one variable or the other but not on both. What this means it that tau-b can only reach -1.0 or $+1.0$ when all the frequencies fall on the diagonal. Tau-b is appropriately used when the number of rows and columns in a table are equal, as in the present case. Like gamma and Somer's d, tau-b uses the difference between N_s and N_d as the numerator. The formula for tau-b is

$$\text{tau-b} = \frac{N_s - N_d}{\sqrt{(N_s + N_d + T_y)(N_s + N_d + T_x)}} \tag{9.4}$$

We have already calculated all values except T_x, which is calculated just like T_y except that now we work down the columns of the independent variable instead of across the row of the dependent variable. Again taking cell A as the target cell, we multiply cell A by the pairs in each cell immediately below it. For the target cell:

$$
\begin{aligned}
\text{cell A} &= (20)(14 + 4) &=& 360 \\
\text{cell B} &= (14)(23 + 24) &=& 658 \\
\text{cell C} &= (8)(14 + 14) &=& 224 \\
\text{cell D} &= (14)(4) &=& 56 \\
\text{cell E} &= (23)(24) &=& 552 \\
\text{cell F} &= (14)(14) &=& 196 \\
\end{aligned}
$$
$$\text{Total } T_x = 2046$$

Putting in the values we get

$$\text{tau-b} = \frac{N_s - N_d}{\sqrt{(N_s + N_d + T_y)(N_s + N_d + T_x)}} = \frac{2746 - 1256}{\sqrt{(2746 + 1256 + 1880)(2746 + 1256 + 2046)}}$$

$$= \frac{1490}{\sqrt{(5882)(6048)}} = \frac{1490}{\sqrt{35574336}} = \frac{1490}{5964.422} = .2498$$

Because the printout of Table 9.5 supplies a probability that tau-b $= 0.0$, we take this opportunity to reinforce your knowledge of probability and the normal curve. We test tau-b for significance using the z distribution according to the following formula:

$$z = \frac{\text{tau-b}}{\sqrt{\dfrac{4(r + 1)(c + 1)}{9N_{rc}}}} \tag{9.5}$$

where $r =$ number of rows and $c =$ number of columns. Substituting the numbers, we get

$$= \frac{.2498}{\sqrt{\dfrac{4(3 + 1)(3 + 1)}{9(135)(3)(3)}}} = \frac{.2498}{\sqrt{\dfrac{4(16)}{9(1215)}}} = \frac{.2498}{\sqrt{.005853}} = \frac{.2498}{.0765} = 3.26$$

A *z* of 3.26 is associated with an area of 0.4994. Adding this figure to the 0.5000 from other side of the curve, we get 0.9994; $1 - 0.9994$ leaves only 0.0006, or 0.06% of the area under the normal curve beyond a *z* of 3.26. Note that this value of 0.0006 is the significance level for tau-b given in the computer printout.

THE ODDS RATIO AND YULE'S *Q*

A statistic known as the **odds ratio** is a very useful additional measure that can be computed from tabular data. The odds ratio is associated with an advanced method of contingency table analysis known as *logistic regression,* and thus rarely addressed in elementary statistics texts. However, it is a simple statistic to compute and it provides valuable additional information concerning the relationship between two variables. Moreover, if we were attempting to explain our findings to someone without any statistical training, it is much easier to talk about odds for or against than to talk about them with chi-square values, levels of significance, and measures of association.

As all gamblers know, the "odds" is simply the ratio of the probability of an event occurring versus the probability of it not occurring. Symbolically, it is expressed as

$$\text{Odds} = P/Q \qquad \text{where } P = \text{probability of the event, and } Q = 1 - P$$

For instance, the odds of throwing a 4 or a 5 with one throw of a fair die is a ratio formed by the probability of the stated event occurring (2/6 or 0.333) and the probability of the event not occurring (4/6 or 0.666). The ratio formed by these two probabilities is the odds (0.333/0.666. = 0.5, or 2:1 against).

It is important not to confuse odds with probability, as it is in everyday speech. The probability of a head in a single toss of a fair coin is 0.5, but the odds are $0.5/0.5 = 1$ (even, because a head or a tail is equally probable). Similarly, the probability of drawing a diamond out of a deck of cards is $13/52 = 0.25$, but the odds are $0.25/0.75 = 0.333$, or three-to-one against.

The odds ratio is the ratio of the two conditional odds obtained from the categories of the independent variable in a table. Although the odds ratio is applicable to data in any size table, the idea comes more easily if we look at it in a 2×2 table first. To illustrate the computation of the odds ratio and its meaning, look back at Table 9.3. From this table, what are the odds that an inmate will be released, regardless of a psychologist's recommendation? We determine this figure by computing the marginal probability: $95/195 = 0.487$. If $P = 0.487$, then $Q = 1 - 0.487 = 0.513$. The ratio of these two values is 0.949. Let us just say that the odds of being released versus not released are close to even. The *conditional odds* are the odds of being released given that a psychologist recommended for or against it. The odds of being released given a positive recommendation is $85/25 = 3.4:1$ in favor. Given a negative recommendation the odds are $10/75 = 0.133:1$, or $7.5:1$ against. The odds ratio (OR) provides a summary statistic that is the ratio of the two conditional odds. Thus, $OR = 3.4/0.133 = 25.5:1$.

Rather than compute multiple probabilities and risk too many rounding errors, it is more efficient to work directly from the table. The first odds value is obtained by A/C or 85/25, and the second by B/D or 10/75. The odds ratio is the ratio of these two odds: A/C ÷ B/D. By the rules of division of fractions, we invert and multiply, thus

$$= \frac{A/C}{B/D} = \frac{A}{C} \times \frac{D}{B} = \frac{(A)(D)}{(B)(C)} = \frac{(85)(75)}{(10)(25)} = \frac{6375}{250} = 25.5 \qquad (9.6)$$

This value indicates that an inmate who receives a favorable recommendation from a psychologist is 25.5 times more likely to be released than an inmate who receives an unfavorable recommendation. This is a lot more understandable to the lay reader than saying there is a 62.3% proportional reduction in error knowing what the psychologists recommended over not knowing what they recommended.

A further useful property of the odds ratio is that it can be easily converted into the traditional measure of association for 2 × 2 tables, Yule's Q. Yule's Q is simply a special case of gamma applicable to 2 × 2 tables. It may also be considered a standardized or normed odds ratio that is constrained to range between -1.0 and $+1.0$, which the odds ratio is not. As with gamma, the computation of Q involves only cell frequencies, ignoring marginal frequencies. The formula is identical in that the value of Q is derived from dividing the preponderance of similar or dissimilar cases by the total number of similar and dissimilar cases. Note that the letters refer to the cell frequencies. From the data in Table 9.3, Yule's Q is

$$Q = \frac{AD - BC}{AD + BC} = \frac{(85)(75) - (10)(25)}{(85)(75) + (10)(25)} = \frac{6375 - 250}{6375 + 250} = \frac{6125}{6625} = .925$$

We may interpret the computed value of Q as indicating a very strong relationship between our two variables. It is apparent that Q is related to the odds ratio. To obtain Yule's Q directly from the odds ratio, we use formula (9.7):

$$Q = \frac{OR - 1}{OR + 1} = \frac{24.5}{26.5} = .925 \tag{9.7}$$

This value can be interpreted as a 92.5% proportional reduction in error given knowledge of the independent variable. You may ask why there is such a big difference between the value of lambda and the value of Q for these data. The difference is that Q does not consider tied cases to be either correct predictions or errors; it is simply a ratio of similar minus dissimilar ordered pairs to the total number of untied pairs.

The computation of odds ratios is not limited to 2 × 2 tables. We can make multiple comparisons from large tables as long as we identify four cells with two columns and two rows. For instance, how much more likely than a person in the high category of education is a person in the low category of education to be high on TV watching? We used the data from Table 9.2 to illustrate our response. Because we are asking only about high and low levels on both variables, all medium cells are excluded and we are left with the 2 × 2 table, Table 9.6, formed by the four corner cells.

Calculating the odds ratio, we get (A)(D)/(B)(C) = 1400/7200 = 0.194, which indicates that people high on education are about one-fifth less likely than people low on education to be high on TV watching. This explanation in terms of a fraction is not too easily understood; nor did we ask how *less* likely is it that people high on education would be high on TV watching, we asked how much *more likely*. We arrived at our answer because of the way the table is set up. Anytime we have a negative relationship (the

TABLE 9.6   Education by TV Watching

	EDUCATION	
TV WATCHING	HIGH	LOW
High	35	80
Low	90	40

majority of the cases on the secondary diagonal), we will calculate an odds ratio of less than 1. We can rectify the problem by reversing the formula to read:

$$OR = \frac{(B)(C)}{(A)(D)} = \frac{(80)(90)}{(35)(40)} = \frac{7200}{1400} = 5.14$$

Because we have reversed the formula, we reverse the substantive interpretation to read: "People low on education are about 5 times more likely than people high on education to be in the high category of TV watching," which is what we wanted to know. Thus, if we invert the values, we must invert the substantive interpretation. Note that to say "A is less than B" is entirely consistent with saying "B is more than A."

Computing Yule's Q from both odds ratios we get $0.194 - 1/0.194 + 1 = -0.674$ in the first case, and $5.14 - 1/5.14 + 1 = 0.674$ in the second case. Thus, the strength of the relationship is each case is identical. The negative or positive sign merely informs us how we must substantively interpret the relationship between the two variables.

SPEARMAN'S RANK ORDER CORRELATION

Sometimes social science data are in the form of rankings. **Spearman's rank order correlation (rho)** is ideal for measuring association between two variables with values that have been ordered into ranks on a case-by-case basis rather than into categories, as are the other measures discussed here. We are essentially asking if a case's rank on one variable can predict its rank on another variable.

Suppose that we have 10 high school students who have taken the ACT college entrance exam in math and English and have obtained the scores given in Table 9.7. Our first task is to rank order these scores from highest to lowest. Jane's score of 20 on the math test is the highest, so she is ranked number 1 on this variable. Her score of 17 in English is the third highest, so she is ranked number 3 on this variable. Each student is so ranked. Kurt, Ahmed, and Joyce all scored 10 on the math exam. In the case of tied ranks such as these, we assign each case the average of the three ranks they would have occupied had their scores not been tied. These three subjects would have occupied ranks 7, 8, and 9. The average of these three ranks is 8, so they are all assigned this rank.

TABLE 9.7   Rank Order of Students on ACT English and Math Scores

	MATH		ENGLISH			
	x	RANK	x	RANK	D	D^2
Jane	20	1	17	3	−2.0	4.00
Frank	19	2	20	1	1.0	1.00
Jose	17	3	13	4	−1.0	1.00
Ray	14	4	18	2	2.0	4.00
Sheila	12	5	8	7.5	−2.5	6.25
Tony	11	6	8	7.5	−1.5	2.25
Kurt	10	8	10	5	3.0	9.00
Ahmed	10	8	9	6	2.0	4.00
Joyce	10	8	6	10	−2.0	4.00
Martin	7	10	7	9	1.0	1.00
Sums					0.0	36.50

Similarly, Sheila and Tony both scored 8 on the English test and are assigned the average of the two ranks they would have occupied had they not tied: $(7 + 8)/2 = 7.5$.

After we have determined the appropriate rankings, we subtract the rank on the English exam from the rank on the math exam for each case and enter that value under D for *rank difference*. Note that the sum of D is always zero. This is analogous to subtracting the mean from each raw score, as we did in Chapter 3. The positive and negative differences will cancel each other. We then square the differences to arrive at the D^2 values, which are then summed. This value is entered into formula (9.8):

$$r_s = 1 - \frac{6(\Sigma D^2)}{N(N^2 - 1)} = 1 - \frac{6(36.5)}{10(100 - 1)} = 1 - \frac{219}{990}$$
$$= 1 - .2212 = .779 \tag{9.8}$$

where N = number of paired observations
ΣD^2 = sum of the squared differences
6 = a constant.

Spearman's rho ranges from -1.0 to $+1.0$ and is an index of the strength of association between two rank-ordered variables. A perfect positive association would exist in the case of perfect agreement among the ranks, and a perfect negative association would exist for perfect disagreement among the ranks. Rho has a PRE interpretation when squared. If we square 0.779 we get 0.607, which means that our error is reduced by 60.7% when predicting rank with knowledge of one variable from rank on the other, as compared to predicting rank without knowledge of the other variable.

Assuming that these 10 cases are a random sample from the population, we can determine whether the sample finding can be generalized to the population. Since we have only 10 cases, the z distribution would not be appropriate for our test of significance. Fortunately, when the number of cases is 10 or more, the distribution of rho approximates the t distribution. We now test for significance with the t distribution:

$$t = r_s\sqrt{\frac{N - 2}{1 - r_s^2}} = .779\sqrt{\frac{8}{1 - 0.607}} = .779\sqrt{\frac{8}{0.393}} = .779\sqrt{20.356}$$
$$= (.779)(4.512) = 3.51 \tag{9.9}$$

Turning to the t-distribution table in Appendix A with 8 df $(N - 2)$, we see that a t value of 2.896 is required to reject the null hypothesis with a one-tailed test and alpha set at 0.01. Our computed t exceeds this critical value, so we can reject the null and conclude that it is unlikely that these data came from a population in which Spearman's rho is zero.

WHICH TEST OF ASSOCIATION SHOULD WE USE?

We suffer from such an embarrassment of riches when it comes to measures of association for nominal and ordinal data (and there are certainly many more than those presented here) that it is understandable to ask "Which one shall we use?" There are no hard and fast rules to guide us in answering that question except to say that you should choose the measure according to substantive theoretical context and to the type of data. In the case of a 2 × 2 table we strongly favor phi because when squared (ϕ^2) it has both PRE and variance-explained interpretations. We also highly recommend including the odds ratio with such tables because of the intuitive interpretation it provides.

For tables larger than 2 × 2, we favor tau-b with square tables (equal number of rows and columns) and tau-c (not discussed in this book) with rectangular tables. Because gamma ignores ties in its computation, we do not recommend it if there are a large number of ties in the data. Somer's *d* is an excellent choice if the researcher has hypothesized a strictly one-way asymmetric relationship between two variables in which one is clearly dependent and the other clearly independent. Nevertheless, tau measures may be preferable because they are more conservative in that they consider ties on both the independent and dependent variables. We do not favor any measure (such as the contingency coefficient discussed in Chapter 8) that does not have a PRE interpretation.

Finally, with rank-ordered data Spearman's rho is an excellent measure. However, if the data are ranked on the basis of accessible raw scores it is better to use the Pearson correlation coefficient, which we discuss in Chapter 11. What we do when we transform interval- or ratio-level data (such as math and English scores in our example) into ranks is to commit a statistical sin. Techniques applied to rank-ordered data are less powerful than techniques we can apply to interval or ratio data, so unless there is a very good theoretical reason for applying less powerful techniques to the data, we should not.

SUMMARY

Association refers to the connectedness or relatedness of two or more variables. We use various statistics to determine whether or not an association exists, its strength, and its direction. We have examined various techniques for making these determinations in cases where the variables are measured at the nominal and interval levels. Most of these techniques are based on simple ratios of similar and dissimilar pairs (agreement to disagreement) of cases. Lambda is rarely used, but it is useful for illustrating the logic of proportional reduction in error. PRE means, in essence, that knowing how one variable is distributed improves our ability to predict values on another variable. Any PRE measure is a ratio of errors made in predicting values of one variable made without knowledge of a second variable to errors made with knowledge of the second variable.

The gamma, Somer's *d*, and the tau measures differ in their computations depending on how they deal with tied cases. Gamma ignores them completely, and thus yields the most liberal index of association, and tau-b yields the most conservative index. All the measures are valid, but before choosing one you should be concerned with the theoretical context of your research and with the form and nature of the association. Choosing a measure simply to maximize the strength of the association is dishonest, and choosing one for no other reason than to be conservative is naive.

Chi-square-based measures of association (phi, contingency coefficient, and Cramer's *V*) standardize chi-square to its maximum attainable value. When squared, phi has a PRE interpretation, but *C* and *V* do not. Phi is used for 2 × 2 tables, *C* and *V* are used for larger tables.

Spearman's rho is an index of the strength of association between two variables that have been rank ordered on a case-by-case basis on some attribute. When squared it is a PRE measure. All measures of association should be tested for statistical significance.

PRACTICE APPLICATION:
NONPARAMETRIC MEASURES OF ASSOCIATION

What difference does the victim's sex make in the sentencing of sex offenders? We have 368 offenders who offended against females and 63 who offended against males. A low sentence is defined as one in which the offender was placed on probation with from 0 to 90 days in jail. A medium sentence is defined as probation with any jail sentence less than 6 months, and a high sentence is defined as any prison sentence. We find the following statistically significant distribution:

SENTENCE	VICTIM'S SEX FEMALE	MALE	
LOW	128	8	136
MEDIUM	57	13	70
HIGH	183	42	225
	368	63	431

$$\chi^2 = 12.15, p < 0.01$$

Calculate lambda: Since all the modal cell category scores are in the same category of the independent variable, lambda will be zero.

$$E_1 = 206, \qquad E_2 = 185 + 21 = 206 \qquad 206 - 206/206 = 0$$

Compute gamma:

$$N_s = 128(13 + 42) = 7040 \qquad N_d = 8(57 + 183) = 1920$$
$$57(42) = 2394 \qquad \qquad 13(183) = 2379$$
$$\text{Total} = 9434 \qquad \qquad \text{Total} = 4299$$

$$\gamma = \frac{N_s - N_d}{N_s + N_d} = \frac{9434 - 4299}{9434 + 4299} = \frac{5153}{13733} = .374$$

Compute Somer's d: We have N_s and N_d; compute T_y.

$$(128)(8) = 1024$$
$$(57)(13) = 741$$
$$(183)(42) = 7686$$
$$\text{Total } T_y = 9451$$
$$d = \frac{N_s - N_d}{N_s + N_d + T_y} = \frac{9434 - 4299}{9434 + 4299 + 9451} = \frac{5135}{23184} = .221$$

Compute tau-b: We have N_s, N_d, and T_y; compute T_x.

$$128(57 + 183) = 30720$$
$$57(183) = 10431$$
$$8(13 + 42) = 440$$
$$13(42) = 546$$
$$\text{Total } T_x = 42137$$

$$\text{tau-b} = \frac{N_s - N_d}{\sqrt{(N_s + N_d + T_y)(N_s + N_d + T_x)}}$$

$$= \frac{9434 - 4299}{\sqrt{(9434 + 4299 + 0451)(9434 + 4299 + 42137)}}$$

$$= \frac{5135}{\sqrt{(23184)(55870)}} = \frac{5135}{\sqrt{1295290080}} = \frac{5135}{3590.1} = .143$$

Test tau-b for significance, with alpha $= 0.05$, two-tailed test. H_0: tau-b $= 0$:

$$z = \frac{\text{tau-b}}{\sqrt{\dfrac{4(r+1)(c+1)}{9N_{rc}}}}$$

$$= \frac{.143}{\sqrt{\dfrac{4(3+1)(2+1)}{9(431)(3)(2)}}} = \frac{.143}{\sqrt{\dfrac{4(12)}{9(2586)}}} = \frac{.143}{\sqrt{.0020624}} = \frac{.143}{.0454} = 3.15$$

Reject the null: Computed z (3.15) exceeds critical z (1.96).

All computed measures indicate a weak but statistically significant association between the victim's sex and sentence type.

The odds ratio: Let us recode offenders who were not sentenced to prison (the low and medium categories) into one category and compute the odds ratio for receiving probation for offenders who offend against males versus against females.

SENTENCE	VICTIM'S SEX FEMALE	MALE	
LOW	185	21	206
HIGH	183	42	225
	368	63	431

The odds of receiving probation for all 431 offenders is 0.915, or $1.09:1$ against. For those who offended against females ($185/183 = 1.01$), the odds are essentially even, but for those who offended against males ($21/42 = 0.5$) or $2:1$ against. The ratio of these two odds is $1.01/0.5 = 2.02$. Computing straight from raw numbers:

$$OR = \frac{(A)(D)}{(B)(C)} = \frac{(185)(42)}{(183)(21)} = \frac{7770}{3843} = 2.02$$

Compute Yule's Q:

$$Q = \frac{OR - 1}{OR + 1} = \frac{1.02}{3.02} = .338$$

Sex offenders with female victims are twice as likely to receive probation than those who offended against males. Conversely, those who offended with male victims are about twice as likely to be imprisoned.

Use Spearman's rho to determine the strength of the following relationship: A researcher asks a number of men and women to rank the seriousness of 11 crimes, with a 1 indicating their perceptions of the most serious and as 11 indicating their perceptions of least serious. The researcher notes that although males tend to rank property crimes higher, females tend to rank personal crimes as more serious. Compute Spearman's rho to determine how these rankings agree or disagree.

CRIME	MALES RANK	FEMALES RANK	D	D^2
Robbery	1	6	−5	25
Burglary	2	7	−5	25
Child molesting	3	2	1	1
Auto theft	4	11	−7	49
Rape	5	1	4	16
Drug trafficking	6	10	−4	16
Assault	7	8	−1	1
Indecent exposure	8	9	−1	1
Trafficking in pornography	9	5	4	16
Wife beating	10	3	7	49
Dog fighting	11	4	7	49
Sums			0	248

$$r_s = 1 - \frac{6(\Sigma D^2)}{N(N^2 - 1)} = 1 - \frac{6(248)}{11(120)} = 1 - \frac{1488}{1320} = 1 - 1.127 = -.127$$

Test r_s for significance, with alpha = 0.05, two-tailed test:

$$t = r_s \sqrt{\frac{N-2}{1 - r_s^2}} = -.127\sqrt{\frac{9}{1 - .0161}} = -.127\sqrt{\frac{9}{.9839}} = -.127\sqrt{9.14739}$$

$$= (-.127)(3.024) = -.384$$

Do not reject null: Computed t (−0.384) is less than critical t(2.08). There is insufficient evidence that males and females differ in their rank ordering of crime seriousness.

REFERENCE

Neal A. and H. Groat (1976). "Social class correlates of stability and change in levels of alienation: A longitudinal study." *Sociological Quarterly,* 15: 548–558.

PROBLEMS

1. A researcher hypothesizes that males are significantly more likely to approve of premarital sex than are females. The researcher surveys 77 females and 85 males. The data are presented below. Compute and interpret lambda.

	GENDER	
OPINION	FEMALE	MALE
APPROVE	32	60
DISAPPROVE	45	25

2. The following data represent survey responses in a public opinion poll. Respondents were asked if they favored, opposed, or had no opinion as to whether physician-assisted suicide should be legalized. The table that follows breaks these responses down by males and females. Using lambda, determine if there is a significant difference between men and women in how they feel about this issue.

	GENDER	
OPINION	FEMALE	MALE
FAVOR	120	85
OPPOSE	60	85
NO OPINION	60	50

3. Use the tables from Problems 2 and 7 in Chapter 8 to calculate and interpret the lambdas.

4. The following table lists the general health status and gender of a randomly selected group of respondents.

	GENDER	
HEALTH STATUS	MALE	FEMALE
EXCELLENT	48	37
GOOD	59	54
FAIR	16	24
POOR	5	12

a) Do men and women differ significantly in terms of their health status? Compute gamma and test for significance using alpha = 0.05.

b) Compute Somer's *d* using health status as the dependent variable.
c) Compute tau-b and test for significant using alpha = 0.05.
d) Compute Cramer's *V*.
e) Interpret your findings. Which statistic or statistics would give you the most accurate information? Why?

5. Using the table in Problem 4, Chapter 8, answer the following questions:
   a) Do the children differ significantly in terms of how much they ate at lunch? Compute gamma and test for significance using alpha = 0.05.
   b) Compute Somer's *d* using how much the children ate as the dependent variable.
   c) Compute tau-b and test for significant using alpha = 0.05.
   d) Compute Cramer's *V*.
   e) Interpret your findings. Which statistic or statistics would give you the most accurate information? Why?

6. A sociological researcher is studying the relationship between extroversion and leadership abilities. He gathers data from a random sample of 275 employees at various levels of management in private corporations. Each person is given a standard personality inventory to determine if they are an introvert or an extrovert. The research then categorized them into lower management, middle management, and corporate leaders or CEOs. He obtained the following results:

	PERSONALITY	
MANAGEMENT LEVEL	EXTROVERT	INTROVERT
LOW	43	57
MIDDLE	84	61
CEO	28	2

a) Compute gamma and test for significance.
b) Compute Somer's *d* using management level as your dependent variable.
c) Compute Cramer's *V*.
d) Interpret your findings paying attention to existence, direction, and strength of association. Which statistics would you present in a research report? Why?

7. In the following distribution, 10 high schools are ranked on two attributes: (1) the tax-generated wealth of the community in which they are located and (2) the number of extracurricular activities (sports, band, special interest clubs) available to their students. The highest ranks (number 1) were assigned to schools in the wealthiest communities and to schools with the greatest number of extracurricular activities. Compute Spearman's rho and interpret.

SCHOOL	TAX WEALTH	ACTIVITIES
Bedford	1	3
Scott	2	1
Central	3	2
Libbey	4	5
Whiteford	5	6
Jefferson	6	4
Whitmen	7	7.5
Cassia	8	10
Northview	9	7.5
Maumer	10	9

8. A composition instructor would like to demonstrate that taking English composition classes significantly improves students' writing abilities. The instructor ranked the students' most recent essays from 1 (best) to 6 (lowest). He then compared the rankings with the number of courses that the students had completed. The results are as follows:

STUDENT	RANK OF ESSAY	NUMBER OF CLASSES
A	3	2
B	4	1
C	6	0
D	1	7
E	5	1
F	2	4

Was the instructor correct? Compute and interpret Spearman's rho.

Chapter 10

Elaboration of Tabular Data

CAUSAL ANALYSIS

Statistical methods are tools for uncovering new knowledge and reducing uncertainty. Scientists are always looking for causes of the phenomena they study. Although we never uncover real causes in statistical analysis, we do perform causal analysis. We say such things as, "A is assumed to be a causal factor of B if the presence of A increases the probability that B will occur." We are not saying in statements of this kind that changes in A will cause changes in B in a completely prescribed way. We operate in a probabilistic, not deterministic, world. Blalock states that causality is really a theoretical construct that cannot be demonstrated empirically: "But this does not mean that it is not helpful to think causally and to develop causal models that have implications that are indirectly testable" (1972, p. 6). We will examine this important concept of causality within the framework of the elaboration of tabular data.

CRITERIA FOR CAUSALITY

ASSOCIATION

The first criterion for causality is that an association must exist between presumed cause and its effect. It is obvious that if two variables do not covary, neither can be considered a candidate to exert causal influence on the other. For example, sexual intercourse increases the probability that conception will occur. That is, if sexual intercourse is associated with conception, conception must at least occasionally occur when sexual intercourse occurs. Conversely, if sexual intercourse can occur infinitely and conception has never been known to follow, it cannot be said to be a cause of conception. The sexual intercourse/conception association is a good example for examining the concept of causality because almost everyone thinks that the relationship between them is very strong. Actually there is a very weak association because there are numerous intercourse events that are not followed by conception.

As we have seen, variables are related to one another in varying degrees, which underscores the probabilistic nature of causality. A perfect positive relationship exists when we observe a one-to-one correspondence between the two variables being explored. A perfect relationship between sexual intercourse and conception would be one in which every act of intercourse, without exception, resulted in conception. A perfect negative association would be one in which every increase in event A produced a corresponding decrease in event B. The overwhelming majority of the time, however, events occur that only occasionally result in the occurrence of other events. But as long as some sort of consistency is observed between events A and B, we have a candidate for causal inference.

TEMPORAL ORDER

For variable A to be considered a causal candidate for the occurrence of B, it must occur before B in time. Causal order does not present much of a problem in the physical sciences. We can say without fear of contradiction that the sun shining on the window causes the glass to be warm, but it would be absurd to say that the warmth of the glass causes the sun to shine on it. Temporal order in the social and behavioral sciences is often obvious, but because of the feedback nature of many of the things we study, the order is not always easy to determine. Consider the relationship between achievement and self-esteem. It has been well demonstrated that these two variables vary positively together. But which is causally prior? Each variable can cause an increase in the other in a felicitous spiral of achievement and self-esteem without ever actually determining which was ultimately responsible for setting the spiral in motion.

SPURIOUSNESS

The third criterion is that the relationship must not statistically disappear when the influence of other variables is considered. For instance, there is a moderately strong positive correlation (about 0.45) between a school's average ACT or SAT scores and its proximity to Canada. In other words, the closer a U.S. school is located to the Canadian border, the better its students do on scholastic tests. Why is this? Do you think the effect is real? Should we build all our schools along the U.S./Canadian border? Could it perhaps be that the closer we move to Canada the further we are away from the mind-numbing urban centers of our nation, and that accounts for the correlation? Latitude, although associated with scholastic performance, has no causal influence on it at all; the two variables are coincidentally linked but not causally connected.

Another interesting correlation is the negative correlation between IQ and dental decay. Dentists used to tell us that tooth decay lowered a person's IQ, but then it was in their interest to interpret the correlation that way. Could it be that lower IQ individuals do not take care of their teeth as well as high-IQ people? Do we have to chose between these two alternative explanations, or is there a third variable that may explain both the state of a person's teeth and his or her IQ? What do you think?

Do note that although a variable can be dismissed as a causal explanation, we need not dismiss it as a predictor. As long as the association between them is consistently and reliably found, we can use IQ to predict level of tooth decay, or level of tooth decay to predict IQ, regardless of whether or not there is a causal connection between them. Because an association is spurious it does not mean that it is false; a measure of association is what it is. Spuriousness means that the *interpretation* of the association, not the association itself, is false.

It is useful at this point to examine some of the misunderstandings revolving around the concepts of variables and constants as they apply to causality. As we have seen, a variable is a factor that takes on a range of different values. A constant is a factor that does not vary across the phenomenon of interest. Scientific research is interested in exploring how factors that vary, either qualitatively or quantitatively, across a dependent variable produce changes in that dependent variable. If a factor is absolutely necessary to the viability of the dependent variable, but that factor does not vary, that is, it is always present (a constant) in conjunction with the dependent variable, then that factor can be safely ignored in research as a cause. For instance, if we set out to do research into what makes a great professional football player, we can safely ignore gender. Although gender is a variable, in this case it is a constant because all professional football players, great or otherwise, are males. Put otherwise, although up to the present time it has been absolutely necessary to be a male to be a professional big-league football player, we cannot include gender as a factor in determining what goes into making a great one precisely because of this nonvariability. Being a male is thus a necessary condition for being a great football player, but it is hardly a sufficient condition. Let us see what we mean by *necessary* and *sufficient*.

NECESSARY CAUSE

The substance of the following discussion is that a variable does not have to be a necessary or sufficient cause or condition of an event to be a causal candidate. A **necessary cause** or condition is one that must be present for an effect to follow. That is, if A is not present, there is no known incidence in which B has occurred. Immaculate conception and the newly developed technique of *in vitro* fertilization notwithstanding, intercourse is a necessary cause of conception. Certainly, being a female is necessary to being pregnant. And being a native-born white male over 35 with a well-padded wallet appears thus far to be a necessary cause of becoming president of the United States. Note that being a woman and experiencing intercourse does not mean that a woman will become pregnant any more than a man who fits the preceding profile will become president. They are merely necessary preconditions for the possibility.

SUFFICIENT CAUSE

A **sufficient cause** is a cause or condition that by itself is able to produce an event. If other causal agents are needed to augment the nominated cause, it is not a sufficient cause. This does not mean that a sufficient cause is also a necessary cause. For instance, being a convict or ex-convict is sufficient to cause stigma, discrimination, and a spoiled identity. But there are many other achieved and ascribed statuses, such as being a victim of some kind of deforming disease, being a carrier of the HIV virus, being crazy, and so on, that are themselves sufficient ways of acquiring a spoiled identity. Likewise, a cause can be necessary without being sufficient. Sexual intercourse is a necessary cause of pregnancy, but it is not a sufficient one. There are other variables in combination, such as the chemical environment of the womb, the absence of a contraceptive device, the fecundity of the female, the potency of the male, and so on, that are required to produce conception.

NECESSARY AND SUFFICIENT CAUSE

A cause is a **necessary and sufficient cause** if, and only if, it must be present for the effect to occur and has no help from other variables. Can you think of any nominated cause in behavioral science that meets this rigorous requirement for establishing a causal relationship between two variables? Neither can we. Yet this is the implied demand of laypersons who point out exceptions to causal statements made by social scientists when they assert a causal connection between two variables. "Poverty, prejudice, unemployment, and a brutal childhood are not causes of crime because there are millions who suffer these privations without resorting to crime," they say. What they are really saying is that if we cannot produce necessary and sufficient causes of the phenomena we study, the whole enterprise of social science is useless and cannot tell us anything of value. We cannot satisfy the necessary and sufficient criterion of causality and we never will.

A STATISTICAL DEMONSTRATION
OF CAUSE-AND-EFFECT RELATIONSHIPS

The following is a statistical illustration of a wholly mythical necessary and sufficient cause. Suppose we obtain a sample of 500 women who have experienced sexual intercourse and 500 women who have not. We then ask each woman if she had ever been pregnant. Having obtained the data, we array them in a 2 × 2 table and discover the bivariate distribution shown in Table 10.1. When we examine the relationship between just two variables, as we are doing in this case, the relationship is known as a *zero-order relationship*. The term *order* refers to the number of other variables being taken into account or being controlled for.

Table 10.1 tells us the following:

1. Every woman who had intercourse got pregnant (cell A).
2. No woman got pregnant who never had intercourse (cell B).
3. No woman who had experienced intercourse did not get pregnant (cell C).
4. No woman who never had intercourse got pregnant (cell D).

The conclusion that must be reached from this example is that sexual intercourse is a cause or condition that will bring about the effect (pregnancy) entirely by itself and without which the effect cannot occur. The computed statistics support the conclusion. We have maximum significance in that chi-square is equal to N (1,000), and perfect association in that $\phi^2 = 1.00$. Having sexual intercourse explains 100% of the variance in the pregnancy variable, leaving no variance to be accounted for by any other variables. This, of course, is nonsense, as is any other cause nominated as necessary and sufficient—no one thing is *the* cause of anything.

Let us consider a much more plausible example of what a tabular analysis would look like with the same sample of women, where sexual intercourse is a necessary but not sufficient cause of pregnancy (Table 10.2). We observe the following:

1. Twenty percent of the women who had intercourse got pregnant, indicating that the state of pregnancy does not characteristically follow an act of intercourse (cell A).
2. No woman who never had intercourse got pregnant, indicating that intercourse is perhaps a necessary cause of pregnancy (cell B).
3. Of the women who had intercourse, 80% did not get pregnant, indicating that although intercourse is a necessary condition it is far from sufficient (cell C).
4. Same conclusion as drawn from cell B: None of the 500 woman who never had intercourse got pregnant, which reinforces the notion that intercourse is a necessary condition for pregnancy (cell D). (Of course, with the advent of artificial insemination, sexual intercourse is no longer a necessary cause of pregnancy in an absolute sense.)

TABLE 10.1 Hypothetical Necessary and Sufficient Cause

| EVER PREGNANT | EXPERIENCED INTERCOURSE | | TOTAL |
	YES	NO	
YES	A 500	B 000	500
NO	C 000	D 500	500
TOTAL	500	500	1000

$$\chi^2 = 1000 \quad \phi^2 = 1.00$$

TABLE 10.2   Necessary Cause

| EVER PREGNANT | EXPERIENCED INTERCOURSE | | TOTAL |
	YES	NO	
YES	A 100	B 000	100
NO	C 400	D 500	900
TOTAL	500	500	1000

$$\chi^2 = 111.05 \quad \phi^2 = 0.333$$

The statistics illustrate two important concepts, one statistical and the other methodological/theoretical. First, the large computed chi-square indicates that the probability of randomly selecting such a sample from a population where the probability for getting pregnant for both groups is equal is about 1 million to one. Despite this extremely high probability level, the association between the two variables is only weak to moderate. The magnitude of the computed chi-square is a function of the sample size; the magnitude of the computed phi is a function of the distribution of the cases in the cell diagonals and would not be affected by sample size given constant cell percentages.

The second point is aimed at those who dismiss any variable as a cause when it is not characteristic. For instance, unemployment is often dismissed as a cause of crime (one among many) because the vast majority of those who become unemployed do not commit crimes; that is, it is not *characteristic* of the unemployed to commit crimes. As we have just seen, intercourse is not characteristically followed by pregnancy, but who among us who would dismiss sexual intercourse as *the* cause of pregnancy and would also dismiss it as *a* cause? The importance of one variable in explaining another lies not in whether or not it is characteristic but rather in how much of the variance it can uniquely account for in the dependent variable or how much it reduces prediction error.

The whole point of the preceding discussion is to demonstrate that although there are few, if any, variables in social science that must necessarily be present to produce a specific effect, we are not precluded from causal analysis. What we can do is intelligently and accurately identify clusters of variables that in combination increase the probability of an event's occurrence. This observation leads into the next topic, the elaboration of bivariate tables, or multivariate contingency analysis.

MULTIVARIATE CONTINGENCY ANALYSIS

If no one independent variable satisfactorily accounts for all the variance observed in the dependent variable, it is obvious that other variables as yet unexamined must also be affecting the distribution of the dependent variable. Perhaps it is even the case that the association observed in the bivariate table is spurious, meaning that some third variable affects both the dependent and the independent variables in such a way that if its effects were to be removed, any observed relationship between the initial two variables would disappear. The classic example of **spuriousness** is the strong association between the number of firefighters at a fire and the magnitude of the dollar loss resulting from the fire (the more firefighters at the fire the greater the dollar loss). Does this strong association mean that there is a cause-and-effect relationship operating? Of course not. A third variable, namely, the size of the fire, determines both the number of firefighters attending the fire and the magnitude of the dollar loss.

Taking the size of the fire into account is an example of what is known as *controlling for,* or *holding constant,* the effects of a third variable. We accomplish this by physically dividing our sample into subsamples based on categories of the control variable. We then examine the relationship between the original two variables within the categories of the control variable. By *controlling for* or *holding constant,* we mean that categories of the third variable are fixed so that they are no longer free to vary. The size of fire variable, for instance, is free to vary between large and small, or perhaps small, medium, and large. But once we determine categories of the third variable and then reexamine the original relationship within those categories, we have essentially controlled its variability by changing it into a constant. More correctly, we have created as many constants as we have categories of the control variable. When reexamining the basic bivariate relationship within any given category of the third variable, now no longer free to vary, we have in effect eliminated the influence of the third variable in each partial table by transforming it into two or more constants. The influence of the third variable can be ascertained only when we compare the outcomes of the bivariate relationship across its categories.

Where do control variables come from, and how do I know which one(s) to use? There is no substitute for a deep theoretical knowledge of your subject matter and good common sense when selecting control variables. In the firefighters/dollar loss example it would not make sense to control for, say, socioeconomic class of the firefighters. If you are hypothesizing something novel or controversial, you must always control for variables already known to affect the dependent variable. For instance, if you propose that Type A personalities have higher blood pressure levels than Type B personalities, your results would not be taken seriously unless you showed that you controlled for variables already known to be related to blood pressure levels, such as age, gender, weight, and so forth.

INTRODUCING A THIRD VARIABLE

To illustrate this process, we consider an example from our offender data. Let us suppose we want to examine the effects of the relationship of the offender to the victim on the type of sentence (probation or prison) among sex offenders. We are convinced that the courts deal more harshly with offenders who are acquainted with their victims because we see sexual offending against persons known to the offenders as a violation of trust. Consequently, we divide these offender/victim relationships into two gross categories, strangers and acquaintances, and compute chi square and gamma. The results are given in Part A of Table 10.3. We observe that this relationship is highly significant and fairly strong, although it is contrary to our expectation: Strangers, not acquaintances, are more likely to be imprisoned. We must now determine what else besides victim/offender relationship could influence sentence type. The most obvious answer is the seriousness of the crime. To determine this, we cross-tabulate sentence type with crime seriousness, which we also divide into two gross categories (high and low) from an original measure of crime seriousness that ranged from 1 to 10 (see the sentencing guidelines in Chapter 1 for operational definitions). We obtain the zero-order results in Part B of the table. These results show a much stronger association between crime seriousness and sentence type than between offender/victim relationship and sentence type.

We can now examine the association between sentence type and offender victim/relationship within the two categories of crime seriousness, a variable that is now no longer free to vary. Part C presents two tables assessing this association within low and high categories of crime seriousness. We see that when crime seriousness is taken into

TABLE 10.3   Demonstrating Elaboration

ZERO-ORDER TABLES

(A)

SENTENCE TYPE	OFFENDER/VICTIM RELATIONSHIP		TOTAL
	STRANGER	ACQUAINTANCE	
PROBATION	32	174	206
PRISON	83	142	225
TOTAL	115	316	431

$\chi^2 = 25.1$, $p < 0.001$

(B)

SENTENCE TYPE	CRIME SERIOUSNESS		TOTAL
	LOW	HIGH	
PROBATION	200	6	206
PRISON	102	123	225
TOTAL	302	129	431

$\chi^2 = 137.3$, $p < 0.0001$

CONDITIONAL (FIRST-ORDER) TABLES (C)

LOW CRIME SERIOUSNESS

SENTENCE TYPE	OFFENDER/VICTIM RELATIONSHIP		TOTAL
	STRANGER	ACQUAINTANCE	
PROBATION	30	170	200
PRISON	18	84	102
TOTAL	48	254	302

$\chi^2 = 0.35$, ns

HIGH CRIME SERIOUSNESS

SENTENCE TYPE	OFFENDER/VICTIM RELATIONSHIP		TOTAL
	STRANGER	ACQUAINTANCE	
PROBATION	2	4	6
PRISON	65	58	123
TOTAL	67	62	129

$\chi^2 = 0.87$ ns

ASSOCIATION BETWEEN OFFENDER/VICTIM RELATIONSHIP AND CRIME SERIOUSNESS (D)

CRIME SERIOUSNESS	OFFENDER/VICTIM RELATIONSHIP		TOTAL
	STRANGER	ACQUAINTANCE	
LOW	48	254	302
HIGH	67	62	129
TOTAL	115	316	431

$\chi^2 = 60.0$, $p < 0.0001$

account, the association between sentence type and offender/victim relationship is nonsignificant (both conditional chi-square values are far from the critical value of 3.841). Thus, the initially observed relationship was not a causal one. It appears that strangers are sentenced more harshly because they commit more serious crimes. (They tend to use force and to harm their victims more so than offenders who are known to their victims.) The table in Part D assessing the association between offender/victim relationship and crime seriousness confirms this proposition. We see that 67 of the 115 stranger assaults (58.3%) are in the high crime seriousness category as opposed to only 62 of the 316 acquaintance assaults (19.6%).

In this example, the variable crime seriousness emerges as the variable that helps us to interpret the initially observed bivariate relationship. Strangers are not punished more severely because of their relationship with their victims but because they commit more serious crimes. Note that the *N*s in the two conditions of crime seriousness sum to the *N* for the zero-order table (302 + 129 = 431) and that each of the respective cells sums to their zero-order value. Introducing a control variable obviously does not change the distribution of the cases. For instance, 142 offenders who were acquainted with their victims were shown to have been sentenced to prison in the zero-order table. When we placed these individuals into the low and high categories of crime seriousness in the conditional tables we still observe that 142 offenders who were acquainted with their victims were sentenced to prison, 84 in the low crime seriousness condition and 58 in the high crime seriousness condition. Tables produced in this manner are called *conditional* or *partial tables,* and the observed relationships are called *partial relationships.*

Of course, the results of the elaboration process are never this neat. If bivariate relationships were always explained away by the introduction of third variables, social science would be in a lot of trouble. A number of possible outcomes are derived from the introduction of a third variable.

EXPLANATION AND INTERPRETATION

When a bivariate relationship disappears (or becomes nonsignificant) after a third variable is controlled for, we see that the only reason for the initially observed relationship is that it is caused by one or more other variables. Such outcomes can be subdivided into outcomes known as *explanation* and *interpretation.* An outcome is called an **explanation** when the original relationship is explained away by an **antecedent variable,** that is, a variable that precedes both the dependent and independent variables in time. In the classical example of the number of firefighters and dollar loss, the relationship is explained away by a variable that clearly occurred before both the dollar loss and the number of firefighters dispatched, the size of the fire. The following diagram illustrates the relationship between an antecedent control variable and the dependent and independent variables in the context of this example.

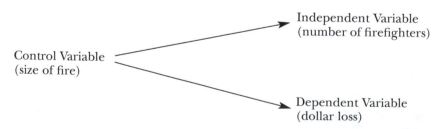

Control Variable
(size of fire)

Independent Variable
(number of firefighters)

Dependent Variable
(dollar loss)

Interpretation occurs when the initial bivariate relationship is rendered insignificant by an intervening variable. In the sentence type and offender/victim relationship it is obvious that crime seriousness is not an antecedent variable. The relationship between the two parties involved in the crime existed before the crime occurred. Crime seriousness is therefore a variable *intervening* between relationship and sentence type. Note that the association between crime seriousness and victim/offender relationship goes a long way in helping us to interpret the association between victim/offender relationship and sentence type; that is, those who offend against strangers commit more serious crimes, and more serious crimes result in more punitive sentences. Because the introduction of an intervening variable specifies a process by which the independent variable affects the dependent variable, an interpretation outcome is not a spurious one in the sense that an explanation outcome is. The independent variable "causes" the intervening control variable, which "causes" the dependent variable. In the present example, offender/victim relationship would be seen as "causing" crime seriousness, which then "causes" sentence type. The following diagram illustrates the relationship between an intervening variable and the independent and dependent variables in the context of this example.

$$\text{Independent Variable} \longrightarrow \text{Control Variable} \longrightarrow \text{Dependent Variable}$$
$$\text{(offender/victim relationship)} \quad \text{(crime seriousness)} \quad \text{(sentence type)}$$

The difference between explanation and interpretation are theoretical assumptions relating to the time ordering of the test variable. If a test variable exerts influence before both the independent and dependent variables, it is antecedent; if it exerts influence after the independent variable but before the dependent variable, it is intervening.

To give a further simple example, suppose we find a significant relationship between broken homes and delinquency rates among a sample of schoolchildren. We then introduce a theoretical variable we shall call "quality of relationship with parent(s)" as a test variable and find that the initial relationship disappears. We might then say that among children who enjoy a good relationship, delinquency rates are not affected by whether or not they come from a broken home. Similarly, we might find among children with a poor relationship that delinquency rates do not differ across categories of broken/intact homes. We thus conclude that it is the association between broken homes and quality of relationship that produced the bivariate association; that is, poor quality relationships increase the probability of delinquency *and* the probability that the home will be broken.

Let us emphasize that the difference between explanation and interpretation is theoretical, not statistical. Researchers decide what type of outcome they observe according to their understanding of what is going on theoretically within the data. The statistics will only inform us of what happens to the bivariate relationship when we control for other variables, not why it happened. For instance, the data on delinquency, broken homes, and quality of relationship could reflect processes going in any and all directions. Delinquency could actually be the cause of poor relationships between child and parents rather than the other way around. Further, a child's delinquency could lead to a broken home because of mutual parental recriminations regarding the child's behavior. Only a strong sense of theoretical ordering and the ability to dig deeply into the data will lead researchers to a reasonable conclusion.

Replication occurs when the partial relationships are essentially of similar magnitude as the bivariate relationship, meaning that the third variable has no effect on the relationship between the zero-order variables. For example, suppose we observe a strong association of 0.75 between gender and amount of time spent watching sports on television among a sample of men and women, with men watching significantly more often. We then divide the sample into subsamples based on race (white/black) and reexamine the relationship, finding an association of 0.73 in the white category and one of 0.76 in the black category. In such a case we would have replicated our original finding, controlling for race. The race variable did not affect the relationship between gender and television sports watching in any way. Men watch significantly more sports on television regardless of race.

Specification occurs when the introduction of a third variable enables the researcher to specify under what conditions the bivariate relationship is true and when it is not true. In such a case, one partial relationship may result in the replication of the bivariate correlation or even in a dramatic increase, whereas the other partial relationship is near zero or may even have changed direction (from positive to negative or vice versa). It is important to note that the specification of an intervening variable does not negate any assumed causal relationship between A and B. Rather, the intervening variable C specifies a process by which A influences B.

Some researchers use the term *interaction* to describe a specification outcome. We saw that interaction, discussed in great detail in Chapter 7 in the context of two-way ANOVA, means that the effects of the independent variable on the dependent variable differ considerably over categories of the third variable. Phrased differently, the effect of A on B depends on the level of C. *Specification* and *interaction* are really identical, but it is preferable to reserve the use of the term *interaction* for ANOVA outcomes, and to use the term *specification* when referring to cross-tabulated data.

ILLUSTRATING ELABORATION OUTCOMES

We will illustrate these outcomes using our data on the sentencing of sex offenders. We first examine the bivariate relationship between offender type (sex and non-sex offenders) and sentence (probation and prison), which is shown in Table 10.4. Only the phi and gamma measures of association are given in the table.

CONTROLLING FOR ONE VARIABLE

We see from Table 10.4 that sex offenders are significantly more likely to be sentenced to prison than are non-sex offenders. The probability of any convicted criminal being sent to prison is $281/637 = 0.441$; for a sex offender it is $225/431 = 0.522$, and for a non-sex offender it is $56/206 = 0.272$. Computing the odds ratio, we find that sex offenders are 2.9 times more likely than non-sex offenders to be sent to prison.

This does not necessarily mean that sex offenders are the victims of discriminatory sentencing because there are other variables besides the type of offense that influence sentencing. Crime seriousness is certainly one of them. We divide our crime seriousness scores into two categories. Offenders who scored 3 (the mean of the crime seriousness variable) or below are placed into a low seriousness category, and those who scored 4 or above are placed into a high seriousness category.

We then recomputed our statistics within these separate categories as in Table 10.5. We are now examining the bivariate relationship between offender type and sentence under conditions of one control variable, an operation referred to as examining the

TABLE 10.4   Cross-Tabulation of Sentence Type by Offender Group (Zero Order)

| | CATEGORIZED SENTENCE BY GROUP | | |
| | GROUP | | |
SENTENCE	NON-SEX OFFENDER	SEX OFFENDER	TOTAL
PROBATION	150 72.8	206 47.8	356 55.9
PRISON	56 27.2	225 52.2	281 44.1
TOTAL	206	431	637

$\chi^2 = 35.38,\ p < 0.0001$ $\phi = 0.24,\ \gamma = 0.49$

TABLE 10.5   Relationship Between Offender Type and Sentence Controlling for Crime Seriousness

SENTENCE TYPE	LOW CRIME SERIOUSNESS OFFENDER TYPE			SENTENCE TYPE	HIGH CRIME SERIOUSNESS OFFENDER TYPE		
	NON-SEX	SEX	TOTAL		NON-SEX	SEX	TOTAL
PROBATION	118	200	318	PROBATION	32	6	38
PRISON	13	102	115	PRISON	43	123	166
TOTAL	131	302	433	TOTAL	75	129	204

$\chi^2 = 26.6, p < 0.0001, \phi = 0.25, \gamma = 0.645$ $\chi^2 = 45.2, p < 0.0001, \phi = 0.47, \gamma = 0.8777$

first-order partial relationship. The partial relationship shows that within the low seriousness category we have replicated the original zero-order bivariate relationship. Phi has increased slightly, and gamma has increased for this conditional table from the zero-order value of 0.49 to 0.645. Note that although phi has increased, the chi-square value has decreased from 35.4 to 26.6 because the sample size has decreased. This result illustrates the principle that given a constant strength of relationship, the larger the sample size the more likely one will be to reject the null hypothesis.

The association between offense type and sentence type becomes much stronger within the high seriousness category, and slightly higher within the low seriousness category when compared with the zero-order association between sentence type and offense type. This result indicates that crime seriousness has been acting as a **suppressor variable,** hiding the true relationship between offense type and sentence type. Sex offenders tend to receive harsher sentences, but they also tend to commit less serious crimes as seriousness is defined in this jurisdiction (see sentencing guidelines in Chapter 1). The sentence type/offense type relationship is suppressed unless crime seriousness is controlled for. The outcome of this elaboration is both a replication (the original relationship and its direction remain) and a specification (the relationship is particularly true within one of the categories of the control variable).

Note that although we have substantially decreased our sample size from 637 in the bivariate table to 204 in the high seriousness partial table, our computed chi-square has increased this time from 35.4 to 45.2, thus a reduced sample size does not necessarily result in a lower probability of rejecting the null hypothesis. This result illustrates another principle of chi-square: Given a constant sample size, the stronger the relationship the more likely one is to reject the null hypothesis.

Criminal record is another variable that is considered in sentencing decisions. Criminal record is measured in this jurisdiction by an ordinal measure ranging from 0 to 27. If we did not want a 2 × 10 table, we surely do not want a 2 × 27 table. So again we collapse our ordinal variable into two dichotomous variables: first offenders and repeat offenders. We then repeat the same procedure with prior record that we went through with crime seriousness.

From Table 10.6 we observe a specification outcome. That is, we have specified that the relationship between type of offender and type of sentence is true only among repeat offenders. The low prior record partial relationship is nonsignificant, and the high prior record partial relationship has increased in magnitude over the computed bivariate phi. In other words, we observe an interactive effect because the effect of offender group on sentence type differs markedly over the two categories of the control variable. The small observed effect of offender group on sentence for first offenders could be the result of chance.

TABLE 10.6 Relationship Between Offender Type and Sentence Controlling for Prior Record

| | LOW PRIOR RECORD | | | | HIGH PRIOR RECORD | | |
| | OFFENDER TYPE | | | | OFFENDER TYPE | | |
SENTENCE TYPE	NON-SEX	SEX	TOTAL	SENTENCE TYPE	NON-SEX	SEX	TOTAL
PROBATION	69	112	181	PROBATION	81	94	175
PRISON	12	32	44	PRISON	44	193	237
TOTAL	81	144	225	TOTAL	125	287	412

$\chi^2 = 1.8$, ns $\phi = 0.09$, $\gamma = 0.243$ $\qquad$ $\chi^2 = 36.6$, $p < 0.0001$, $\phi = 0.30$, $\gamma = 0.530$

FURTHER ELABORATION: TWO CONTROL VARIABLES

Knowing the seriousness of the crime committed and the offender's criminal record will improve your ability to predict the sentence he will receive over what you would have predicted knowing only his offense type. However, each person is sentenced according to his joint distribution on both of these variables, not on either one of them alone. It is artificial, therefore, to attempt to predict sentence by either of these variables in isolation. To examine the joint effects of these variables on the offender type/sentence type relationship requires the computation of four partial relationships: (1) low crime seriousness/low prior record, (2) high crime seriousness/low prior record, (3) low crime seriousness/high prior record, and (4) high crime seriousness/high prior record. These four partial tables are presented in Table 10.7.

When the basic bivariate relationship is examined under the various conditions of two control variables, it is called a **second-order partial relationship.** Having controlled for the two legally relevant variables that are *supposed* to influence sentencing, we can now assess the effects of *group* (sex offender/non-sex offender), an extralegal variable that is not supposed to influence sentencing.

In Table 10.7 we have replicated the initial bivariate relationship. Sex offenders are significantly more likely than non-sex offenders to be imprisoned regardless of which of the four partial relationships we examine. However, we are now able to be more precise in our predictions. For instance, the relationship is particularly strong in the high crime seriousness/high prior record category but quite weak (taking phi as the measure of association) in the low crime seriousness/low prior record category. The computed odds ratio for the high/high category indicates that sex offenders are about 32 times more likely to be sent to prison than are non-sex offenders.

PARTIAL GAMMA

To summarize the relationship between offender group and type of sentence received, we have had to make four separate statements with reference to four sets of computed statistics. It would be nice if we could boil these statements down to one succinct statement about the relationship between offender group and type of sentence controlling for crime seriousness and prior record. One technique that allows us to do so is known as **partial gamma,** which is obtained by the simple method of combining the separate computations from each conditional table into a single measure of association. Recall that the formula for gamma is

TABLE 10.7   Relationship Between Offender Type and Sentence Controlling for Prior Record and Crime Seriousness

LOW CRIME SERIOUSNESS
LOW PRIOR RECORD
OFFENDER TYPE

SENTENCE TYPE	NON-SEX	SEX	TOTAL
PROBATION	56	108	164
PRISON	1	16	17
TOTAL	57	124	181

$\chi^2 = 5.7, \ p < 0.02, \ \phi = 0.18, \ \gamma = 0.785$

HIGH CRIME SERIOUSNESS
LOW PRIOR RECORD
OFFENDER TYPE

SENTENCE TYPE	NON-SEX	SEX	TOTAL
PROBATION	13	4	17
PRISON	11	16	27
TOTAL	24	20	44

$\chi^2 = 5.4, \ p < 0.02, \ \phi = 0.35, \ \gamma = 0.651$

LOW CRIME SERIOUSNESS
HIGH PRIOR RECORD
OFFENDER TYPE

SENTENCE TYPE	NON-SEX	SEX	TOTAL
PROBATION	62	92	154
PRISON	12	86	98
TOTAL	74	178	252

$\chi^2 = 22.7, \ p < 0.0001, \ \phi = 0.30, \ \gamma = 0.657$

HIGH CRIME SERIOUSNESS
HIGH PRIOR RECORD
OFFENDER TYPE

SENTENCE TYPE	NON-SEX	SEX	TOTAL
PROBATION	19	2	21
PRISON	32	107	139
TOTAL	51	109	160

$\chi^2 = 38.2, \ p < 0.00001, \ \phi = 0.49, \ \gamma = 0.939$

$$\gamma = \frac{N_s - N_d}{N_s + N_d}$$

The formula for partial gamma is

$$\gamma_p = \frac{\Sigma N_s - \Sigma N_d}{\Sigma N_s + \Sigma N_d} \qquad (10.1)$$

where ΣN_s = the similar pairs summed across all conditional tables and ΣN_d = the dissimilar pairs summed across all conditional tables. The zero-order gamma for our offender type/sentence type data was 0.490. The respective gammas for the low crime seriousness and the high crime seriousness conditional relationships were 0.645 and 0.877. We now wish to transform these separate gammas into a single summary statistic. The computations for the two separate gammas were

$$\text{Low crime seriousness} \ \gamma = \frac{12036 - 2600}{12036 + 2600} = \frac{9436}{14636} = .645$$

$$\text{High crime seriousness} \ \gamma = \frac{3936 - 258}{3936 + 258} = \frac{3678}{4194} = .877$$

To obtain partial gamma we sum as directed:

$$\Sigma N_s = 12036 + 3936 = 15972: \quad \Sigma N_d = 2600 + 258 = 2858$$

Therefore,

$$\gamma_p = \frac{15972 - 2858}{15972 + 2858} = \frac{13114}{18830} = .70$$

The first-order gamma of 0.70 indicates that knowledge of the distribution of crime seriousness, as well as knowledge of type of offense, proportionately improves our ability to predict the type of sentence by 70% over what our predictions would be without knowledge of these two variables. It is important to note, however, that crime seriousness has been controlled for in an arbitrary fashion. If we had used more categories of this variable, such as low, medium, and high, somewhat different results may have been obtained.

We will not compute the first-order partial for prior record. Rather, now that the student is aware of the logic involved, we will proceed directly to the computation of the second-order partial gamma. The computations of gamma for the four separate tables are as follows:

Low Crime Seriousness/Low Prior Record
$$\frac{896 - 108}{896 - 108} = \frac{788}{1004} = .785$$

High Crime Seriousness/Low Prior Record
$$\frac{208 - 44}{208 + 44} = \frac{164}{252} = .651$$

Low Crime Seriousness/High Prior Record
$$\frac{5332 - 1104}{5332 + 1104} = \frac{4228}{6436} = .657$$

High Crime Seriousness/High Prior Record
$$\frac{2033 - 64}{2033 + 64} = \frac{1969}{2097} = .939$$

Summing,

$$\Sigma N_s = 896 + 208 + 5332 + 2033 = 8469$$
$$\Sigma N_d = 108 + 44 + 1104 + 064 = 1320$$

Therefore,

$$\gamma_p = \frac{8469 - 1320}{8469 + 1320} = \frac{7149}{9789} = .73$$

We have now arrived at a single statistic summarizing the relationship between sentence type and offender type, controlling for crime seriousness and prior record as we have measured and categorized these variables. Since gamma is a PRE measure, we may conclude that we have proportionately reduced error in predicting type of sentence by 73% given our knowledge of offense type, crime seriousness, and prior record. Note that with knowledge of offense type only, we were able to proportionately reduce prediction errors by 49% (zero-order gamma). With the additional information provided by crime seriousness we were able to proportionately reduce errors by 70% (first-order gamma). With knowledge of prior record we were able to proportionately reduce errors by another 3%. Knowledge of offense type, crime seriousness, and prior record proportionately reduces the errors we would make in predicting an offender's sentence type without this information by 73%.

WHEN NOT TO COMPUTE PARTIAL GAMMA

In Table 10.7 all partial tables convey essentially the same information: Sex offenders are significantly more likely to be sent to prison than non-sex offenders. Given this consistency, partial gamma is a useful summary statistic. However, we would not want to compute partial gamma if we found a specification outcome. The very reason for elaboration is to uncover interesting specifications. Having gone through the process of elaboration and discovering that your control variable has an interactive effect on the bivariate relationship, we would not want to cover it up again by reporting partial gamma.

To illustrate, suppose we have a teacher concerned with inappropriate activity (fidgeting, talking, fighting, moodiness, not completing assignments, smoking, and various kinds of horseplay) in school. On the basis of various measures and other information, the teacher divides a sample of 200 boys into categories based on their activity level, coded high and low, and on whether they are considered *problem children* (see Table 10.8), and finds that the computed chi-square is insignificant at 2.66, and that the zero-order gamma is 0.263. Because chi-square was insignificant the teacher may accept the null that there is no difference in activity level between children defined as problem and non–problem children.

Suppose the teacher realizes that all children had recently completed a scale measuring extroversion/introversion. Acting on this information, the teacher divides the sample into extroverts and introverts and finds that the hypothesized relationship is strongly supported ($\chi^2 = 20.5$, $\gamma = 0.881$) among extroverts. Among the extroverts problem children are significantly more likely than non–problem children to have high activity levels. There is also a significant relationship among the introverts ($\chi^2 = 3.97$), but it is in the opposite direction ($\gamma = -0.429$). That is, whereas extroverted problem children are strongly prone to high levels of activity, introverted problem children are less prone to high activity levels than non–problem children. It is obvious that the in-

TABLE 10.8 An Illustration of When Not to Compute Partial Gamma

ZERO-ORDER RELATIONSHIP

| | PROBLEM CHILD | | |
ACTIVITY LEVEL	YES	NO	TOTAL
HIGH	80	70	150
LOW	20	30	50
TOTAL	100	100	200

$\chi^2 = 2.66$, ns; $\gamma = 0.263$

CONDITIONAL RELATIONSHIPS

| | EXTROVERTS | | | | INTROVERTS | | |
| | PROBLEM CHILD | | | | PROBLEM CHILD | | |
ACTIVITY LEVEL	YES	NO	TOTAL	ACTIVITY LEVEL	YES	NO	TOTAL
HIGH	50	20	70	HIGH	30	50	80
LOW	5	20	25	LOW	15	10	25
TOTAL	55	40	95	TOTAL	45	60	105

$\chi^2 = 20.5$, $p < 0.0001$, $\gamma = 0.818$ $\chi^2 = 3.97$, $p < 0.05$, $\gamma = -0.429$

$\gamma_p = 0.209$

dependent variable (*problem child*) has very different and interesting effects on the dependent variable under the two conditions of the control variable. The relationship attains statistical significance under both conditions, the strength of the association increases, and the relationship among the introverts is reversed. The teacher would never have uncovered these interesting findings if the analysis had ceased because of the initial insignificant bivariate result.

Computing partial gamma from these data we obtain 0.209, which provides us with a totally misleading impression of the nature of the relationship between the independent and the dependent variables. Any reader might conclude on the basis of that measure that the initial relationship is replicated, though attenuated, when controlling for the extrovert/introvert variable. Computing partial gamma after uncovering such interesting specifications is rather like digging up the pirate gold and then burying it again. The extrovert/introvert dimension is a suppressor variable masking the true nature of the relationship between activity level and the designation *problem child*.

PROBLEMS WITH TABULAR ELABORATION

As we moved from an examination of the zero-order to the second-order relationship we noted that the number of cases in each cell diminished severely. For instance, 4 of our 16 cells in the second-order examination of offender type and sentence type contained fewer than five cases, despite the fact that we have a relatively large sample. If we wished to add a further dichotomous control variable (third order), each of our four partial relationships would have to be examined under the two conditions of the added control variable. Instead of 16 cells, we would now have 32. The effect of this change on cell frequency is obvious. Results would become increasingly less meaningful as our cells became increasingly deprived of adequate frequencies. Even if we doubled our sample size, a costly and time-consuming strategy, the task of summarizing so many tables into a succinct statement about how the variables are related would be messy. The logistic problems of elaboration render it a relatively inefficient method of multivariate analysis for all but the most simple substantive problems.

A further problem arises when we collapse interval-level data into a limited number of categories. Although collapsing was necessary in order to arrive at manageable tables, doing so results in a loss of information. With crime seriousness, for instance, offenders who had 4 crime seriousness points were categorized with those who had 10 crime seriousness points. Our statistics were then computed as if these people had committed crimes of equal gravity, which they had not. In other words, it is reasonable to suppose that an offender with 10 crime seriousness points will receive a harsher sentence than will an offender with 4 crime seriousness points. However, we cannot determine this result from the analysis we have conducted because we have artificially placed them (along with offenders with 5, 6, 7, 8, and 9 points) into a single category.

It is for this reason that collapsing data measured at a higher level into limited categories to accommodate weaker methods of statistical analysis, when the data are suitable for more efficient and powerful techniques, is often problematic because you potentially lose valuable variation in the data. Other methods to be examined in Chapter 12 are far more efficient methods of multivariate analysis because they do not require the physical placement of cases into subtables, and because they utilize all cases simultaneously. However, students get a better intuitive grasp of multivariate analysis if it is first presented in tabular form because they are able to see how the cases are physically moved around into the various categories of the control variable(s).

SUMMARY

The concept of causality is a difficult one. The three basic criteria for establishing causality are (1) a statistically significant association, (2) temporal order, and (3) nonspuriousness. We differentiated between necessary and sufficient causes, and causes that are both necessary and sufficient. It is impossible to satisfy the necessary and sufficient criteria for causality, because no one thing is the cause of any other thing; variables often act in conjunction to bring about an effect. To explore the effects of an independent variable on a dependent variable when performing tabular analysis, we have to examine the association within categories of a theoretically meaningful control variable in a process called *elaboration.*

When we examine the effects of additional variables on the bivariate relationship we observe various kinds of elaboration outcomes: replication, explanation, interpretation, or specification. Replication means that the addition of another variable did not appreciably alter the zero-order outcome. Explanation means that the control variable completely eliminates (explains away) the initially observed relationship. Interpretation means that the introduction of the control variable weakens or eliminates the strength of the bivariate association. An explanation outcome means that the relationship observed between two variables is entirely coincidental, and that the control variable, which precedes both the dependent and independent variables in time, "causes" both. Interpretation means that the control variable intervenes between the independent and dependent variables and helps us to interpret the relationship between them.

Partial gamma, which we examined with our sex offender data, is an index of the strength of association between two variables, controlling for the effects of one or more additional variables. Partial gamma offers us a single statistic that sums the findings of multiple tables. However, if interesting specifications are uncovered by the elaboration method they should be noted, however, and not covered up again by partial gamma.

Some of the problems of bivariate elaboration include rapid depletion of cell sizes as more control variables are added and the somewhat arbitrary categories that sometimes have to be created, resulting in a loss of information.

PRACTICAL APPLICATION: BIVARIATE ELABORATION

Let us turn back to our 3×2 chi-square in Table 8.9. In it we found that birth order was significantly related to having committed a violent crime among a sample of 585 juvenile delinquents. We now wish to go a little further and see if this result is true for both boys and girls. We have to make two 3×2 tables now, one for the boys and one for the girls. We go back into the data to find the distributions on birth order/violent crime for each sex and we compute chi-square for each separate table.

VIOLENT OFFENCE	BOYS BIRTH ORDER				GIRLS BIRTH ORDER			
	FIRST	MIDDLE	LAST	TOTAL	FIRST	MIDDLE	LAST	TOTAL
NO	69	65	50	184	32	17	6	55
YES	79	174	74	327	6	10	3	19
TOTAL	148	239	124	511	38	27	9	74

Compute chi-square:

$$\chi^2 = \Sigma \frac{(O-E)^2}{E} \qquad \text{where } E = r \times c/N$$

EXPECTED FREQUENCIES BOYS	EXPECTED FREQUENCIES GIRLS
A. 148 × 184/511 = 53.29	A. 38 × 55/74 = 28.24
B. 239 × 184/511 = 86.06	B. 27 × 55/74 = 20.07
C. 124 × 184/511 = 44.65	C. 9 × 55/74 = 6.69
D. 148 × 327/511 = 94.71	D. 38 × 19/74 = 9.76
E. 239 × 327/511 = 152.94	E. 27 × 19/74 = 6.93
F. 124 × 327/511 = 79.35	F. 9 × 19/74 = 2.31

CHI-SQUARE BOYS

CELL	OBS.	EXP.	$(O-E)$	$(O-E)^2$	$(O-E)^2/E$
A	69	53.29	15.71	246.80	4.63
B	65	86.06	−21.06	443.52	5.15
C	50	44.65	5.35	28.62	0.64
D	79	94.71	−15.71	246.80	2.61
E	174	152.94	21.06	443.52	2.90
F	74	79.35	5.35	28.62	0.36
	511	511	00.00		$\Sigma(O-E)^2/E = 16.29$

$\chi^2 = 16.29$

Is it significant? With 2 degrees of freedom $[(r-1)(c-1) = 2]$, it exceeds the critical value for significance at 0.05 (5.99). It also exceeds the critical value for the 0.01 level (9.210). Therefore, it is highly unlikely that our sample comes from a population where the probability of committing a violent crime is the same for each birth-order group.

CHI-SQUARE GIRLS

CELL	OBS.	EXP.	$(O-E)$	$(O-E)^2$	$(O-E)^2/E$
A	32	28.24	3.76	14.14	0.50
B	17	20.07	−3.07	9.42	0.47
C	6	6.69	−0.69	0.48	0.07
D	6	9.76	−3.76	14.14	1.45
E	10	6.93	3.07	9.42	1.36
F	3	2.31	0.69	0.48	0.21
	511	511	00.00		$\Sigma(O-E)^2/E = 4.06$

$\chi^2 = 4.06$

With 2 df we need a chi-square value of 5.991 to reject the null hypothesis. Our computed value of 4.06 falls below this figure. Therefore, we do not reject the null. The sample could have come from a population in which the probability of committing a violent crime is the same for all three female birth-order groups. We have a specification result: The association between birth order and violent crime is true only for delinquent boys.

Compute the contingency coefficient for both subsamples:

$$\text{Boys: } C = \sqrt{\frac{\chi^2}{\chi^2 + N}}$$

$$= \sqrt{\frac{16.29}{16.29 + 511}} = \sqrt{\frac{16.29}{527.29}} = \sqrt{.0309} = .1725$$

$$\text{Girls: } C = \sqrt{\frac{4.06}{4.06 + 74}} = \sqrt{\frac{4.06}{78.06}} = \sqrt{.0520} = .228$$

The contingency coefficient is actually stronger for girls than it is for boys. If we had an equal number of boys and girls, and assuming constant cell percentages, we would conclude that the relationship between birth order and the commission of a violent offense is stronger for girls than for boys. This does not mean that girls are more violent than boys. The percentage of girls convicted of a violent offense is 25.7, but for boys it is 64. It simply means that whether or not one has ever been convicted of a violent crime is more dependent on birth order for girls than it is for boys. Remember also that this could possibly be a simple chance finding since we have a chi-square that did not attain statistical significance.

REFERENCE

Blalock, H. (1972). *Causal Inferences in Nonexperimental Research*. New York: W.W. Norton.

PROBLEMS

1. A sample of 150 respondents is classified by religion (Catholic or non-Catholic) according to their stand on abortion (pro-choice or pro-life). Calculate and interpret the strength and direction of the relationship using gamma.

	RELIGION	
ATTITUDE TOWARD	NON-CATHOLIC	CATHOLIC
PRO-CHOICE	70	20
PRO-LIFE	25	35

As a follow-up, determine if this relationship is influenced by a college education. There are 92 college graduates and 58 non-graduates in the sample. Using the tables that follow, compute by calculating the partial gamma the association between religion and attitudes toward abortion for each educational group. What kind of elaboration outcome is apparent? Interpret your findings.

	COLLEGE GRADUATE RELIGION			NON-COLLEGE GRADUATE RELIGION	
ATTITUDE TOWARD ABORTION	NON-CATHOLIC	CATHOLIC		NON-CATHOLIC	CATHOLIC
PRO-CHOICE	42	15	PRO-CHOICE	28	5
PRO-LIFE	20	15	PRO-LIFE	5	20

2. Researchers interested in assessing mental health following natural disasters noted a strong relationship between experiencing depression and post-disaster anxiety. Of 252 flood victims, their experiences with anxiety and depression following a severe flood are listed in the table below.

	DEPRESSION	
ANXIETY	YES	NO
YES	25	16
NO	27	184

a) Calculate and interpret gamma, phi, lambda, and Cramer's V.
b) Using the tables below, calculate the partial gamma and determine if the relationship is significantly different for men and women.

	MALES				FEMALES	
	DEPRESSION				DEPRESSION	
ANXIETY	YES	NO	ANXIETY		YES	NO
YES	10	5	YES		15	11
NO	12	100	NO		15	84

3. A researcher is interested in the relationship between pet ownership and blood pressure among elderly citizens. After surveying 200 residents in an independent living care facility, she collected the following data:

	BLOOD PRESSURE	
PET OWNERSHIP	NORMAL	HIGH
YES	80	30
NO	30	60

a) Using gamma, calculate and interpret the strength and direction of the relationship.
b) Compute Somer's *d* using blood pressure as your dependent variable.
c) Compute and interpret chi-square and Cramer's *V*.
d) Interpret your findings paying attention to existence, direction, and strength of association. Which statistics are most appropriate for the data?

4. Using the data in Problem 3, determine if this relationship is influenced by the respondent's gender. There were 100 males and 100 females in the study. Using the tables below, compute the association between blood pressure and pet ownership for male and females. Compute and interpret the partial gamma. What kind of elaboration outcome is apparent? Interpret your findings.

	MALES				FEMALES	
	BLOOD PRESSURE				BLOOD PRESSURE	
PET OWNERSHIP	NORMAL	HIGH		NORMAL	HIGH
YES	30	20	YES	50	10
NO	22	28	NO	8	32

Chapter 11

BIVARIATE CORRELATION AND REGRESSION

This chapter presents two powerful techniques for analyzing the linear relationship between two variables measured at the interval or ratio levels. Although these techniques differ somewhat in logic from those we have examined so far, they are designed to answer many of the same questions. Correlation and regression are the "meat and potatoes" of contemporary social science, so it is imperative to introduce students to these methods as soon as possible. Because they are fundamental, we devote proportionately more space to these than to other techniques.

Regression techniques are used to predict the value of one variable from knowledge of another. **Correlation** tells us how accurate these predictions are and describes the nature (strength and direction) of the relationship. The indispensable nature of regression to scientific research has been aptly put by Pedhazur (1982, p. 42): "The regression model is most directly and intimately related to the primary goals of scientific inquiry: explanation and prediction of phenomena." Correlation and regression techniques are more powerful than the statistics discussed in Chapter 9. Statistics such as gamma only allow us to predict a case's category on one variable given knowledge of its category on another. Correlation and regression are more precise in that they enable us to predict the specific value or score of a case on one variable from a value or score on another. Since the purpose of regression is essentially prediction, many researchers use the term *predictor variables* for independent variables and *criterion variable* for the dependent variable.

As we saw in Chapter 9, there is a positive relationship between two variables when high scores on variable Y are associated with high scores on variable X and low scores on Y are associated with low scores on X. Conversely, there is a negative relationship when high scores on Y are associated with low scores on X. With continuous data, these relationships can be approximated by a straight line. Any straight line is given by the equation $Y = a + bx$. In order for you to gain a preliminary understanding of linear relationships, we present an idealized example in which the relationship between two scores is perfect.

Consider the example of workers earning $4 per hour. A worker who works zero hours gets paid zero money, one who works two hours gets $8, and so on. The dependent variable (Y) is dollars earned and the independent variable (X) is hours worked. We have graphed this relationship in Figure 11.1.

The relationship is linear and perfect. As X increases so does Y in a perfectly linear fashion. For example, a 1.5 increase in X is associated with an increase of 6 in Y. In regression analysis, such straight lines are called **regression lines.** Depending on the distribution of the data, these lines have different **regression slopes.** The slope of a line is defined as the vertical distance divided by the horizontal distance between any two points on the line. This relationship is shown in formula (11.1):

$$b = \frac{\text{Vertical distance}}{\text{Horizontal distance}} = \frac{Y_1 - Y_2}{X_1 - X_2} \qquad (11.1)$$

Referring to Figure 11.1, let $Y_1 = 10$ and $Y_2 = 4$. These values are associated with the X_1

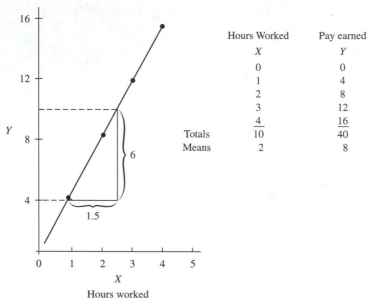

	Hours Worked	Pay earned
	X	Y
	0	0
	1	4
	2	8
	3	12
	4	16
Totals	10	40
Means	2	8

FIGURE 11.1. Illustrating the slope of a line.

and X_2 values of 2.5 and 1, respectively. We substitute these values into the formula to obtain the slope:

$$b = \frac{10 - 4}{2.5 - 1} = \frac{6}{1.5} = 4$$

The slope of the line is 4; it will be 4 for this data set regardless of which two reference points we choose. For the present example, the slope, also known as the regression coefficient or beta, informs us that for each unit increase in the independent variable there is a four-unit increase in the dependent variable

We said that the equation for a straight line is $Y = a + bx$. We have b, so all we must do now is calculate a, which is the **Y intercept,** or the point at which the slope intersects the Y axis. We can determine visually from Figure 11.1 that $a = 0$ because both Y and X scores have values of zero in the distribution, and because a score of zero on X corresponds exactly with a zero score on Y. Nevertheless, we will demonstrate that $a = 0$ by the following:

$$a = \bar{Y} - b\bar{X} \tag{11.2}$$

where a = the intercept
$\bar{Y}$ = mean of Y
$\bar{X}$ = mean of X
b = the slope

Thus,

$$a = 8 - (4)(2) = 8 - 8 = 0$$

Once we have the slope (b) and the intercept (a) for any set of data we can use the formula for a straight line to predict a Y value for any given value of X. The a and b values are constants, so all we have to do to determine a predicted Y value, symbolized as Y' (read Y *prime*) is to specify a value of X. To predict the Y value (number of dollars) for a worker who works eight hours ($8X$) we would calculate

$$Y' = a + bX = 0 + (4)(8) = \$32$$

This looks like a horribly complicated way to arrive at a value that you could easily calculate in your head (8 hours at \$4 per hour = \$32). However, realize that this is a "perfect" example designed to convey the logic of linear prediction. Social science data are never as cooperative. The intersection of Y and X scores never rises uniformly, as in this example. The plotted points representing the complexity of the real world will never fall on a straight line but will be scattered around it, so any predictions we make will be subject to error. The following example is more representative of this complexity.

PRELIMINARY INVESTIGATION: THE SCATTERGRAM

When we examined the associations between variables measured at the nominal and ordinal levels, we noted that a useful preliminary technique was to examine the pattern of frequencies and percentages in the table cells. A similarly helpful technique when examining the association between two interval/ratio variables is to examine their joint distribution in a scattergram. A **scattergram** is a plot in which the position of each observation is designated at the point corresponding to its joint value on the dependent and independent variables. The independent variable is arrayed on the horizontal axis, and the dependent variable on the vertical axis. If these plots bunch together like a thin tube along a steeply angled line, the association is strong. If they bulge out at all sides like a balloon, the association is weak or nonexistent. If the plots appear to be rising from the lower left-hand corner to the upper right-hand corner, the association is positive. If they appear to be going from the top left-hand corner to the lower right-hand corner, the association is negative. Presented in Figure 11.2 are three scattergrams illustrating possible patterns of associations between two interval/ratio-level variables. Other patterns that are nonlinear are possible, but we will not examine them here. Part of the value of examining the scattergram is to check for linearity.

We begin by constructing a scattergram for some very simple data on the number of prior felony convictions and years of imprisonment for the latest offense. Suppose we

FIGURE 11.2. Scattergrams showing various linear relationships.

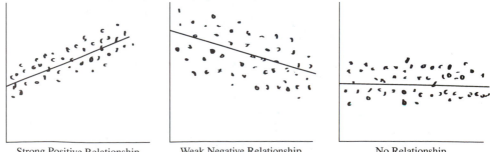

Strong Positive Relationship   Weak Negative Relationship   No Relationship

TABLE 11.1   Raw Data on Prior Convictions and Sentences

CASE	NUMBER OF PRIOR CONVICTIONS (X)	SENTENCE IN YEARS (Y)
a	1	1
b	1	3
c	2	3
d	2	4
e	2	2
f	3	3
g	3	4
h	4	6
I	5	7
j	5	5
	28	38
	$\overline{X} = 2.8$	$\overline{Y} = 3.8$

have a sample of 10 convicted felons with different criminal histories who received different sentences. We want to determine the impact that criminal record has on sentence severity. Our first task is to make a list of our 10 cases, noting the number of prior felony convictions for each individual along with the sentence he received in years for the latest offense. These data are shown in Table 11.1.

The data are plotted on the scattergram shown in Figure 11.3 according to their joint position on both variables. This pattern of dots summarizes the nature of the relationship between the two variables. We can see that the relationship is positive and

FIGURE 11.3.   Scattergram of sentence and prior convictions.

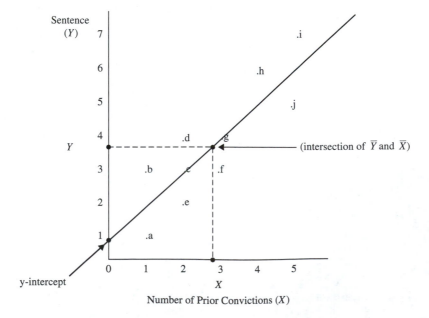

Number of Prior Convictions (X)

that it is linear; that is, as the number of prior convictions goes up, the number of years to which an individual is sentenced to prison also goes up in a constant manner. The pattern can be further clarified by drawing a straight line through the cluster of dots so that the line comes as close as possible to touching every dot. This is called *fitting the line*. To draw a line we need two reference points, the first of which is *a*, the *Y* intercept. The value of *a* has been calculated to be 0.86 (we will see the calculations later). The second reference point is the intersection of the means of the two variables. Regardless of the value of the slope, the means of the two variables are always on the regression line. The mean of *Y* is 3.8 and the mean of *X* is 2.8. When we connect the two reference points with a straight line we have what is called the *least squares regression line*. Different lines will give different *residuals* (the actual *Y* score minus the predicted *Y'* score; given symbolically as $Y - Y'$), which is regression terminology for errors from the regression line. We want the line placed where, if each residual is squared and summed, we will get the smallest value and hence the smallest prediction errors.

In other words, the *squared distance* between the regression line and an observed score is the error we make in predicting the value of that observation using the regression line. Hence the term *least squares*, and the term *ordinary least squares* (OLS) regression for the statistical technique we present here. Thus, the least squares regression line is the line that best fits the data in that it comes closer than any other possible line to touching every data point on the scattergram. This is of great importance in terms of our ability to make predictions because the *least squares* line $Y = a + bX$ is the line with such values of *a* and *b* that $\Sigma (Y - Y')^2$ is minimized.

This is a variation of a concept we addressed in Chapter 3 when we discussed the mean. Recall that the mean of any distribution of scores is the point around which the variation is minimized. The regression line functions as a kind of floating mean in that the sum of the squared deviations off the regression line is less than off any other point. We will demonstrate this to be true later in this chapter, but now we will continue with the computation of *b* and *a*.

THE SLOPE

We will begin by computing *b* because we need it to compute *a*. In addition to conceptualizing *b* as a ratio of vertical to horizontal distance we also conceptualize it as a ratio of the sum of squares of the cross-products of *Y* and *X* to the sum of squares of *X*:

$$b = \frac{SS_{yx}}{SS_x} \qquad (11.3)$$

The computational formula for *b*, however, is easier to work with:

$$b = \frac{N\Sigma XY - (\Sigma X)(\Sigma Y)}{N\Sigma X^2 - (\Sigma X)^2} \qquad (11.4)$$

where
N = number of cases (pairs of scores)
ΣXY = sum of the cross-products of the scores
ΣX = sum of the *X* scores
ΣY = sum of the *Y* scores
ΣX^2 = sum of the squared *X* scores
$(\Sigma X)^2$ = sum of the *X* scores, squared.

TABLE 11.2   Computations for *b* and *r*

CASE	X	Y	X²	Y²	XY
a	1	1	1	1	1
b	1	3	1	9	3
c	2	3	4	9	6
d	2	4	4	16	8
e	2	2	4	4	4
f	3	3	9	9	9
g	3	4	9	16	12
h	4	6	16	36	24
I	5	7	25	49	35
j	5	5	25	25	25
	$\Sigma X = 28$	$\Sigma Y = 38$	$\Sigma X^2 = 98$	$\Sigma Y^2 = 174$	$\Sigma XY = 127$

We now compute *b* from our data on imprisonment and felony convictions, which requires the five columns of figures shown in Table 11.2. The first two columns reproduce the original *X* and *Y* scores for each case. The third column lists the *X*-squared scores, and the fourth column lists the *Y*-squared scores. The fifth column lists the cross-products of *X* and *Y* (*X* multiplied by *Y*). Each column is then summed and labeled. We do not need the sum of *Y*-squared to compute *b*, but we will need it later to compute the correlation coefficient.

Putting the numbers into formula (11.4), we get

$$b = \frac{10(127) - (28)(38)}{10(98) - (784)} = \frac{1270 - 1064}{980 - 784} = \frac{206}{196} = 1.05$$

We know that *b* gives an average estimate of how much change in the dependent variable accompanies a one-unit change in the independent variable. Therefore, our computed slope of 1.05 tells us that for each unit change in *X* there is an associated average change of 1.05 units of *Y*. In this example, it means that for every additional felony conviction, an offender can expect, on the average, an additional 1.05 years of imprisonment. Take note of the repetition of the term *average*. We do not expect that an additional conviction for any particular offender will result in exactly 1.05 years of imprisonment, we only mean that averaged over all offenders the expected additional time per additional felony charge will be 1.05 years.

THE INTERCEPT

To find the intercept (*a*), we need two additional computations, the mean of *X* and the mean of *Y*. From Table 11.2, we see that the mean of *X* is 2.8, and the mean of *Y* is 3.8. Along with our computed *b*, these figures are put into formula (11.2):

$$a = \overline{Y} - b\overline{X}$$
$$= 3.8 - (1.05)(2.8) = 3.8 - 2.94 = .86$$

The regression line intercepts the *Y* ordinate at a value of 0.86. The *a* value is interpreted as the estimated average value of *Y* when *X* equals zero. It is a fixed or constant effect, which must be added to the constant effect of the slope times the varying values of *X*. In our example an offender without any prior convictions can expect, on the average, to receive 0.86 years of imprisonment. Unfortunately, we have no offender in our sample with no prior convictions. Thus we are making predictions beyond the range of the data, which is risky. Of course, in any real-life sample many times larger than our hypothetical sample, there will be many offenders with no prior felony convictions.

Now that we have all of the values for the regression line, we can use it to predict scores on the dependent variable (*Y*) for a given value on the independent variable (*X*). Because both the *a* and *b* values are constants, the only unknown value is *X*. We can give *X* any value that may be of interest to us. Suppose we wanted to predict the number of years to which an individual with six prior convictions would be sentenced (designated by *Y'* to indicate that it is a predicted value of *Y* rather than an actual value of *Y*).

$$Y' = a + bX$$
$$= .86 + (1.05)(6) = .86 + 6.3 = 7.16$$

Our hypothetical offender would expect to get 7.16 years of imprisonment. Note that for an offender with no prior convictions the *b* value would drop out of the equation, leaving 0.86 $[0.86 + (1.05)(0)] = 0.86 + 0 = 0.86$. This illustrates that the *Y* intercept (*a*) is the value of the dependent variable (*Y*) when the value of the independent variable (*X*) is zero.

Our predictions will never be completely accurate for every case. They represent only best guesses derived from the sample data we have available. However, regression minimizes the prediction error over all cases. In general, prediction error will decrease in proportion to the increase in sample size. Prediction error is also decreased when there are strong correlation coefficients. The strength of a linear relationship is measured by the Pearson product moment correlation coefficient (*r*).

THE PEARSON CORRELATION COEFFICIENT

Now that we have learned how to fit a regression line to paired data, our next step is to determine how well the line actually fits. Since *b* is a measure of the effect of *X* on *Y*, we already have some idea about the nature of the relationship. We know, for instance, that the relationship between prior convictions and sentence is positive, and we can assume with confidence that once we have computed the **correlation coefficient (Pearson's *r*),** it will be quite strong because we have minimal scatter around the regression line. We compute a further statistic because although the value of *b* is a function of the strength of the relationship, it cannot be used as a measure of the relationship as such. The computed value of *b* depends on how we have measured the variable we want to predict. For instance, if we had measured sentence severity in months instead of years, the value of *b* would be quite different. The correlation coefficient, however, would be the same regardless of how we measured sentence severity. In other words, *r* is independent on how we have measured *Y*, but *b* is not.

Figure 11.4 shows graphically how *b* can vary as correlation coefficients remain the same. This is reasonable when we realize that the value of *b* is determined by the steepness of the line and the value of *r* is determined by the scatter around it. The steeper the regression line, the greater the change in the dependent variable per unit change in the independent variable. If we had measured sentence severity in months, the value of *b* would have been 12.6 ($1.05 \times 12 = 12.6$ months) instead of 1.05. It is important to realize that although slopes take on different values according to how we measure the dependent variable, they are equivalent. This equivalence is recognized by

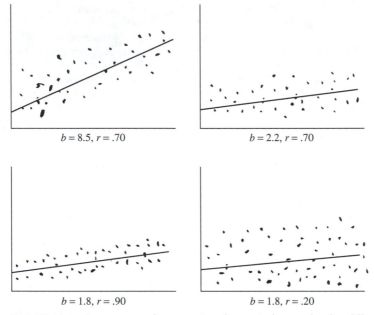

$b = 8.5, r = .70$

$b = 2.2, r = .70$

$b = 1.8, r = .90$

$b = 1.8, r = .20$

FIGURE 11.4.   Scattergrams demonstrating the equivalence of r for different values of b, and the equivalence of b for different values of r.

r since the scatter around the regression line would be exactly the same. The function of r is to indicate the strength of the relationship so that we can predict, and our prediction would be exactly the same whether we called it 1.05 years, 12.6 months, 54.6 weeks, or 382.2 days.

Another reason for computing Pearson's r in addition to b is that we cannot directly compare slopes for a number of different variables if they are all measured in different units, as we will see in the next chapter. We can compare correlation coefficients, however, regardless of how the variables they describe are measured because the squared correlation coefficient is interpreted in terms of the amount of variance explained in the dependent variable by the independent variable. This is a roundabout way of saying that b does not vary between -1.0 and $+1.0$, as do correlations. This important property of correlation coefficients renders them comparable. It is also possible, of course, to have identical slopes but different correlations.

COVARIANCE AND CORRELATION

Formula (11.5) is the computational formula for the Pearson correlation coefficient:

$$r = \frac{N\Sigma XY - (\Sigma X)(\Sigma Y)}{\sqrt{[N\Sigma X^2 - (\Sigma X)^2][N\Sigma Y^2 - (\Sigma Y)^2]}} \tag{11.5}$$

Note that the numerator of r is the same as the numerator of b, which is the **covariance** of Y and X. The covariance is the covariation of two sets of scores from their respective means. The more the two variables covary (vary together) the stronger r will be, providing that the standard deviations of the two variables remain constant. The standard deviations of the two variables being correlated constitute the denominator of the formula for r. Thus, r is defined as the ratio of the product of the standard deviations of Y and X to the covariance of Y and X.

$$r = \frac{\text{Covariance of } Y \text{ and } X}{(\text{Standard deviation } Y)(\text{Standard deviation } X)}$$

In Chapter 3 we presented the formula for the variance as

$$s^2 = \frac{\Sigma X^2 - \dfrac{(\Sigma X)^2}{N}}{N - 1}$$

Similarly, covariance is mathematically defined as

$$s^2 xy = \frac{\Sigma XY - \dfrac{(\Sigma X)(\Sigma Y)}{N}}{N - 1} \tag{11.6}$$

Calculating the covariance from the data in Table 11.2, we get

$$s^2 xy = \frac{127 - \dfrac{(28)(38)}{10}}{9} = \frac{127 - 106.4}{9} = 2.2889$$

The standard deviations of Y and X have been calculated (not shown) and found to be 1.8135 and 1.4757, respectively. Therefore

$$r = \frac{2.2889}{(1.18135)(1.4757)} = \frac{2.2889}{2.6762} = .855$$

The correlation coefficient is 0.855. The definitional formula, although very useful in explaining the concept of covariance and the relatedness of many of the techniques we have discussed, is quite cumbersome. You will find the computational formula easier to work with. Substituting the information from Table 11.2, we get

$$r = \frac{(10)(127) - (28)(38)}{\sqrt{[(10)(98) - 784][(10)(174) - 1444]}}$$

$$= \frac{1270 - 1064}{\sqrt{(980 - 784)(1740 - 1444)}}$$

$$= \frac{206}{\sqrt{(196)(296)}}$$

$$= \frac{206}{\sqrt{58016}}$$

$$= \frac{206}{240.86} = .855$$

Step 1. Work everything within parentheses: $10 \times 127 = 1270$; $28 \times 38 = 1064$; $10 \times 98 = 980$; $10 \times 174 = 1740$

Step 2. Do all subtractions: $1270 - 1064 = 206$; $980 - 784 = 196$; $1740 - 1444 = 296$.

Step 3. Multiply: $196 \times 296 = 58016$.

Step 4. Take the square root of $58016 = 240.86$ and divide: $206/240.86 = .855$.

The correlation coefficient of 0.855 indicates that there is a strong positive relationship between the number of prior felony convictions and the number of years sentenced to prison. That is, as the number of prior convictions increases, the severity of the sentence imposed increases. We remind you again that a correlation never proves causality. It is a mathematical relationship that may or may not be indicative of some underlying causal relationship. What a correlation coefficient does is support (or fail to support) an explanation that the researcher can justify on theoretical grounds.

We can go beyond the arbitrary and ambiguous method of interpreting a correlation as strong, moderate, or weak by calculating r^2, which is simply the square of the correlation coefficient ($r^2 = r \times r$). Therefore, r^2 for our data is 0.731 ($0.855 \times 0.855 = 0.731$), which is interpreted as 73% of the variance in sentence severity is accounted for by number of prior convictions. This value can also be interpreted as proportional reduction in error. That is, we can say that when knowledge of the independent variable (prior felony convictions) is taken into account, we improve our ability to predict values on the dependent variable (sentence in years) by a factor of 73.1%. We will now show this statement to be true.

Without knowledge of the independent variable, our best prediction of the number of years a given offender would receive would be the mean of the sentence distribution. As we saw earlier, the scores vary less around the mean than around any other point. In other words, we would predict a sentence of 3.8 years for all offenders, and our line of prediction would run parallel with the abscissa starting from the mean of Y. To find out how much prediction error we would have, we must compute the total variation in the same way as we do for computing ANOVA. These errors for each case are found by $Y - \bar{Y}$ because they are the difference between each person's actual sentence and our best prediction (the mean), given that we have no knowledge of the distribution of the independent variable. The total variation is the sum of all the squared errors or deviations: $\Sigma (Y - \bar{Y})^2$. In Figure 11.5 we have drawn in the line of best prediction for

FIGURE 11.5.   Scattergram showing total variation around $\bar{Y}$.

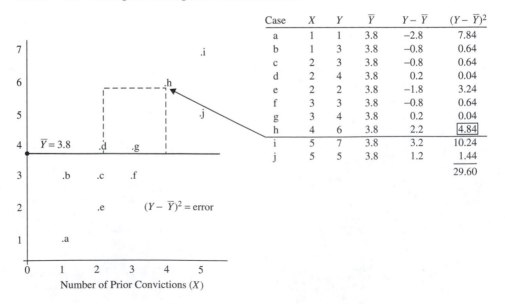

Case	X	Y	$\bar{Y}$	$Y - \bar{Y}$	$(Y - \bar{Y})^2$
a	1	1	3.8	−2.8	7.84
b	1	3	3.8	−0.8	0.64
c	2	3	3.8	−0.8	0.64
d	2	4	3.8	0.2	0.04
e	2	2	3.8	−1.8	3.24
f	3	3	3.8	−0.8	0.64
g	3	4	3.8	0.2	0.04
h	4	6	3.8	2.2	4.84
i	5	7	3.8	3.2	10.24
j	5	5	3.8	1.2	1.44
					29.60

$(Y - \bar{Y})^2 = \text{error}$

Number of Prior Convictions (X)

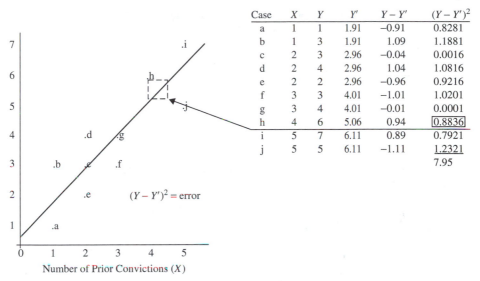

Case	X	Y	Y'	Y − Y'	(Y − Y')²
a	1	1	1.91	−0.91	0.8281
b	1	3	1.91	1.09	1.1881
c	2	3	2.96	−0.04	0.0016
d	2	4	2.96	1.04	1.0816
e	2	2	2.96	−0.96	0.9216
f	3	3	4.01	−1.01	1.0201
g	3	4	4.01	−0.01	0.0001
h	4	6	5.06	0.94	0.8836
i	5	7	6.11	0.89	0.7921
j	5	5	6.11	−1.11	1.2321
					7.95

FIGURE 11.6.   Scattergram showing total variation around Y'.

the data, given ignorance of the independent variable, and we have computed the total variance. To compute the total variance we have subtracted the mean sentence in years $(\overline{Y})$ from each person's actual sentence (Y) to get the deviation $(Y - \overline{Y})$; we then squared this figure $(Y - \overline{Y})^2$ and summed to get $\Sigma(Y - \overline{Y})^2$. The total variation in Y is 29.6 years. In ANOVA we called this value the total sum of squares.

We will now compute the error based on the regression equation, that is, the error we will make in predicting sentence severity given that we now have knowledge of the distribution of the independent variable. These errors are labeled $(Y - Y')$ and are known as residuals.

The sum of these squared residuals, $\Sigma(Y - Y')^2$, is known as the unexplained variance. To obtain this value, we compute the predicted value for each case by using the formula $Y' = a + bX$, subtract that value from the actual value, square the difference, and then sum. We have computed this value in Figure 11.6 and found it to be 7.95. Thus, knowing the distribution of X has enabled us to make smaller prediction errors. It is for this reason that some statisticians have referred to the regression line as a *floating mean*. Note the large reduction in error predicting the sentence for case h using the regression equation over using the mean.

We now have the total sum of squares (29.60) and the error sum of squares (7.95). We could calculate the explained sum of squares (the variance explained by the regression) by the same logic. But this is not necessary because once we have calculated the total sum of squares and the error sum of squares we automatically have the explained sum of squares since $SS_{explained} = SS_{total} - SS_{error}$.

Thus, r^2 represents the proportional reduction in error by moving from estimating the mean of Y for all Y values to predicting each Y value from the regression equation. We are now in a position to determine how much we have reduced our prediction error when knowledge of the independent variable is taken into consideration. We take the two components we have just computed and put them into the standard PRE formula given in Chapter 9 as

TABLE 11.3   The Relationship between *r*-Squared and ANOVA

SOURCE OF VARIATION	SUM OF SQUARES	SUM OF SQUARES AS PROPORTION OF UNITY	df	MEAN SQUARE	F RATIO
Number of convictions	21.65	0.731	1	0.731	0.731/0.0336
Unexplained	7.95	0.269	8	0.0336	$F = 21.756$*
Total	29.60	1.000	9		$p < 0.01$

* The *F* ratio (21.756) with 1 and 8 df exceeds the critical *F* at <0.01.

$$\text{PRE} = \frac{E_1(\text{total variation}) - E_2(\text{error variation})}{E_1(\text{total variation})}$$
$$= \frac{29.6 - 7.95}{29.6} = \frac{21.65}{29.6} = .731$$

Thus, we have shown how the coefficient of determination is a PRE measure because our computed PRE is exactly the same value as *r* squared; in fact it is *r* squared determined by another method. The proportion of variance in the dependent variable left unexplained by the independent variable is simply $1 - r^2$. In our present example it is $1 - 0.731 = 0.269$. In ANOVA we called the variance left unexplained by the independent variable the within-group sum of squares or the error sum of squares. The intimate relationship between correlation and regression and ANOVA is further illustrated as follows.

PARTITIONING *r* SQUARED AND SUM OF SQUARES

We calculated an r^2 for our sentencing data of 0.731, which is interpreted as the percentage of the total variance in the dependent variable (Y) that is explained by the independent variable (X). This is determined by the second step in the PRE formula for r^2, namely, the explained variation (21.65) divided by the total variation (29.6). Thus, 73.1% of the variation in sentence severity is explained by the number of prior felony convictions in our hypothetical example. This means that 26.9% ($100 - 73.1$) of the variance is explained by variables other than the number of prior convictions.

Again, we can think of r^2 in ANOVA terms as the main effects sum of squares, and $1 - r^2$ as the residual (unexplained) sum of squares. Think of the total sum of squares as unity, and r^2 ($SS_{between}$) as a proportion of unity. SS_{within} is the residual sum of squares ($1 - r^2 = 0.269$). Dividing these values (0.731 and 0.269, respectively) by their associated degrees of freedom (1 and 8), we obtain mean square values. The ratio of the mean square values is the F ratio. Table 11.3 summarizes the computation of the *F*-ratio test of significance for the coefficient of determination by using the logic of ANOVA.

STANDARD ERROR OF THE ESTIMATE

A statistic for assessing the accuracy of predictions is called the **standard error of the estimate.** This statistic informs you of the average prediction error experienced when predicting *Y* from *X*. The definitional formula for the standard error of estimate is

$$s_{y \cdot x} = \sqrt{\frac{\Sigma (Y - Y')^2}{N - 2}} \tag{11.7}$$

The formula for $s_{y \cdot x}$ is quite similar to the formula for the standard deviation except that we divide by $N - 2$ rather than $N - 1$. It is conceptually similar also in that it reflects variability, but variability around the regression line rather than about a mean. Because $s_{y \cdot x}$ involves fitting the data to a straight line, which requires the estimation of the slope and the intercept and thus the calculations of Y and X, we lose 2 df ($N - 2$). Since we already have all of the values necessary to compute $s_{y \cdot x}$, we will simply put them in as follows:

$$s_{y \cdot x} = \sqrt{\frac{7.95}{8}} = \sqrt{.99375} = .997$$

Under the assumption that the array of Y scores associated with each value of X forms a normal distribution, the standard error of the estimate may be interpreted in terms of area under the normal curve. Thus, we can say that about 68% of our predictions will be within $\pm 1 s_{y \cdot x}$, and that 95% will be within ± 2. Be aware, however, that we are talking about average error, not the error for any particular prediction of Y from X. Standard error $s_{y \cdot x}$ will underestimate the error in predicting Y from X values as X departs markedly from the mean of X. There are formulas that adjust for this error, but as with many other adjustments for error we have looked at, the amount of error becomes negligible with large samples.

STANDARD ERROR OF *r*

If we drew 10 further samples of 10 convicted felons we would not expect to get a correlation between the number of convictions and the years of imprisonment of exactly 0.855. This value is simply an estimate of the population correlation coefficient (symbolized as ρ, the Greek letter rho), and other rs will vary as a result of sampling variation. As is the case with sample means, if we draw an infinite number of random samples from the same population and computed r for the two variables of interest, we would have a sampling distribution of rs. Just as 68% of sample means will lie within ± 1 standard error of the true population mean, 68 percent of sample correlations will be within 1 standard error of the true population correlation, and 95% will fall between ± 1.96 standard errors. We can thus place confidence intervals around our sample r using formula (11.8):

$$s_r = \frac{1 - r^2}{\sqrt{N}}$$
$$= \frac{1 - .855^2}{\sqrt{10}} = \frac{.269}{3.162} = .085 \tag{11.8}$$

Our standard error of 0.085 means that 95% of the samples of the same size taken from the same population will yield a correlation of $0.855 \pm (1.96)(0.085) = 0.167$, or between 0.688 and 1.022. Because we cannot obtain a correlation of greater than unity, we would say between 0.688 and 1.00. This large confidence interval is primarily a function of the small sample size. If we obtained the same r from a sample of 100, the 95% confidence interval would be ± 0.027, a much more satisfactory interval.

SIGNIFICANCE TESTING FOR PEARSON'S *r*

As with other measures of association, we need to determine if the observed sample relationship can be assumed to exist in the general population from which the sample was drawn. Although we already know from Table 11.4 that *r* is significant at <0.01, the usual method of testing *r* for statistical significance is the *t* statistic, which is computed with formula (11.9):

$$t = r\sqrt{\frac{N-2}{1-r^2}}$$

$$= (.855)\sqrt{\frac{10-2}{1-.855^2}} = (.855)\sqrt{\frac{8}{1-.731}} = (.855)\sqrt{29.74} = (.855)(5.45) = 4.66 \tag{11.9}$$

Turning to the *t* distribution in Appendix A with 8 degrees of freedom (df = the numerator under the radical), we find that our computed *t* of 4.66 exceeds the critical value at the 0.05 level. We thus reject the null hypothesis and conclude that the variables are also related in the population from which our sample was drawn. Note that a *t* value of 4.66, when squared, results in the *F* value computed earlier, with tolerance for rounding.

We can rearrange formula (11.9) to determine the minimum *r* necessary to reject the null hypothesis that the population $\rho = 0$. The first thing we do is turn to Table 2 in Appendix A and find the critical *t* value required to reject the null with 8 degrees of freedom and a given alpha level. Let us say that we are conducting a two-tailed test and that we set alpha at 0.05. You will find the critical *t* value under these conditions to be 2.306. We then put this value into formula (11.10) to determine the critical *r*:

$$r = \frac{t_{critical}}{t_{critical^2} + df}$$

$$= \frac{2.306}{5.3176 + 8} = \frac{2.306}{13.3176} = \frac{2.306}{3.649} = .632 \tag{11.10}$$

Thus, the minimum value of *r* required to reject the null at the 0.05 level (two-tailed test) with a sample of 10 is 0.632. We leave it to you to determine what the value of *r* should be to reject the null with a sample of 100.

THE INTERRELATIONSHIP OF *b, r,* AND β

It is interesting to note that the regression slope can be expressed by

$$b = r\left[\frac{s_y}{s_x}\right] \tag{11.11}$$

The slope is equal to the correlation between *Y* and *X* multiplied by the standard deviation of *Y* divided by the standard deviation of *X*. We substitute these previously calculated values into the formula and get

$$b = .855\left[\frac{1.8135}{1.4757}\right] = .855(1.229) = 1.05$$

We can also utilize the standard deviations and the regression slope to calculate the standardized beta (β). The standardized beta, more fully explained in the next chapter, is a very useful statistic in multiple regression analysis. One basic difference between the unstandardized and standardized beta that we can introduce at this point is that the former is presented in actual units of the dependent variable and the latter is given in standard deviation units. For the time being, just think of it as being analogous to the correlation coefficient. Standardized beta is calculated with formula (11.12):

$$\beta = b\left[\frac{s_x}{s_y}\right] = 1.05\left[\frac{1.4757}{1.8135}\right] = 1.05(.8137) = .855 \tag{11.12}$$

This demonstrates that r and β are equivalent in the two-variable case.

SUMMARIZING PROPERTIES OF r, b, AND β

- r ranges between -1.0 (perfect negative relationship) and $+1.0$ (perfect positive relationship). A value of zero indicates no linear relationship between Y and X.
- The value of r is independent of the scale of measurement.
- When squared, r indicates the proportion of variance in Y accounted for by X.
- b indicates the change in Y per unit change in X.
- The value of b depends on the scale of measurement.
- β indicates the change in standard deviation units of Y per standard deviation unit change in X.
- r and β are identical in a simple bivariate regression.
- r, b, and β must have the same sign. When $r = 0$, b and $\beta = 0$.

SUMMARIZING PREDICTION FORMULAS

Table 11.4 summarizes the operations we would perform in making predictions for any score with and without knowledge of the distribution of an independent variable. Without knowledge of the independent variable, the best prediction would always be the mean. With knowledge of the distribution of the independent variable, the regression equation provides the best prediction because it minimizes the sum of squares around the regression line (the floating mean). The error in making predictions other than the mean in a univariate distribution averaged over all predictions is the standard deviation. In a bivariate distribution the error averaged over all predictions is the standard error of the estimate. We have shown that for any two variables that are linearly related,

TABLE 11.4   Summary of Prediction Computations with and without Knowledge of the Independent Variable

OPERATION	WITHOUT KNOWLEDGE OF X	WITH KNOWLEDGE OF X
Best prediction of a score	$\overline{Y} = \dfrac{\Sigma Y}{N}$ (the mean)	$Y' = a + bX$ (the regression equation)
Error of prediction of a score	$Y - \overline{Y}$ (deviation)	$Y - Y'$ (residual)
Average error in predicting a score	$\sqrt{\dfrac{\Sigma(Y - \overline{Y})^2}{N - 1}}$ (standard deviation)	$\sqrt{\dfrac{\Sigma(Y - Y')^2}{N - 2}}$ (standard error of estimate)

knowledge of their joint distributions improves our ability to predict one variable from the other.

A COMPUTER EXAMPLE OF BIVARIATE CORRELATION AND REGRESSION

We will use our sex offender data to demonstrate bivariate correlation and the versatility of regression using the example given in Chapter 6 to demonstrate the *t* test. Because we saw in Chapter 6 that the variances of the two offender groups were unequal, it is technically incorrect to perform regression with these data because regression analysis assumes equal variances. However, as is the case with the *t* test, when the larger sample has the greatest variance, as is the case here, regression is conservative with respect to committing Type I errors.

Table 11.5 presents the correlation between sentence severity and group. The first piece of information is the number of cases and the means and standard deviations of each variable. We are then given the cross-product deviation and the covariance. The cross-product deviation is divided by $N - 1$ to yield the covariance ($34584.5275/636 = 54.3782$). Dividing the covariance of XY by the product of their standard deviations results in a correlation coefficient of 0.1597, which is the value given in the table. The number beneath the coefficient is the number of cases on which the calculation is based (637), followed by the exact one-tailed significance of *r*.

We now examine the printout in Table 11.6 for the bivariate regression. We note that a one-unit change in *group* (coded 0 for non-sex offenders and 1 for sex offenders) results in a 248.128 unit change in the dependent variable (sentence severity). Note that it now becomes necessary to change the coding of the group variable. Formerly, non-sex offenders were coded 1 and sex offenders were coded 2. As we will see later, this 0 and 1 convention is important in regression analysis for ease of interpretation. If you turn back to the *t* test in Table 6.3 you will see that the difference between sentence severity means for the two offender groups is exactly the value given for *b* in Table 11.6. Also note that the *t* value based on the assumption of equal variances is the same.

We note from Table 11.6 that the *Y* intercept (CONSTANT) is 324.136. Recall that the *Y* intercept is the point at which the slope crosses the *Y* axis and is the value of *Y* when $X = 0$. Because non-sex offenders were coded zero, this represents the mean sentence severity score for them. A one-unit change in *X* (moving from non-sex offenders to sex offenders) results in a 248.128 unit increase in *Y*. If we add the value of the

TABLE 11.5   Partial Computer Printout for Pearson Correlation

VARIABLE	CASES	MEAN	STD DEV
SENSEV	637	492.0220	727.3945
GROUP	637	.6766	.4681
VARIABLES	CASES	CROSS-PROD DEV	VARIANCE-COVAR
SENSEV GROUP	637	34584.5275	54.3782

<table>
<tr><td colspan="3" align="center">Correlation Coefficients</td></tr>
<tr><td></td><td>SENSEV</td><td>GROUP</td></tr>
<tr><td>SENSEV</td><td>1.0000
(637)</td><td>.1597
(637)
P = .000</td></tr>
</table>

TABLE 11.6 Partial Printout for Bivariate Regression for the Effects of Offender Group on Sentence Severity

VARIABLE	B	SE B	BETA	T	SIG T
GROUP	248.128	60.869	.1597	4.076	.0001
(CONSTANT)	324.136	50.069		6.474	.0000

Y intercept to the value of the slope, we get the mean sentence severity score for sex offenders ($324.136 + 248.128 = 572.264$). In general terms, the formulas for calculating the means of dichotomous independent variables from the regression results are:

$\bar{Y}'_0 = a + b_0$ and $\bar{Y}_1 = a + b_1$
For non-sex offenders: $\bar{Y}'_0 = 324.136 + 0 = 324.136$
For sex offenders: $\bar{Y}'_1 = 324.136 + 248.128 = 572.264$

We have determined the respective group means from the regression analysis. Go back to Table 6.3 and check these means with those obtained from the *t*-test procedure. This illustrates that for a dichotomous independent variable subjected to bivariate regression, the difference between the means of the two categories is the value of the slope (the unstandardized beta). Figure 11.7 will help you to visualize how a one-unit change in X (moving from non-sex to sex offenders) results in a 248.1 unit change in sentence severity.

We can use the standard error to establish confidence intervals around the slope. The reported b is a specific value or point estimate around which may be placed an

FIGURE 11.7. Visualizing the slope and the intercept in the bivariate case: the effects of group on sentence severity.

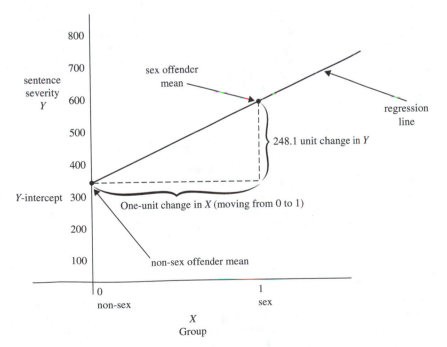

TABLE 11.7   Partial Printouts for Bivariate Regression for the Effects of Crime Seriousness and Prior Record on Sentence Severity

VARIABLE	B	SE B	(CRIME SERIOUSNESS) BETA	T	SIG T
CRSER	265.640	10.273	.716	25.859	.0000
(CONSTANT)	−303.2329	36.756		−8.250	.0000

VARIABLE	B	SE B	(PRIOR RECORD) BETA	T	SIG T
PRREC	64.3921	5.298	.4344	12.154	.0000
(CONSTANT)	235.0600	33.495		7.018	.0000

interval estimate. The logic of setting confidence intervals around the regression slope is identical to setting confidence intervals around the mean:

$$CI = b + (t)(seb)$$

where t = tabled two-tailed value for given df and alpha level and seb = standard error of b. Setting alpha at 0.05 with df >120 and $z = 1.96$:

$$CI = 248.128 \pm (1.96)(60.87) = 119.3$$

We can therefore state with 95% confidence that the parameter lies somewhere between 248.128 ± 119.3, that is, between 128.828 and 367.428.

The next value is the standardized beta (β; BETA in the printout of Table 11.6). In a bivariate regression β is equal to the zero-order correlation. Note that β is also equal to the square root of the η^2 we computed for these data in Chapter 6. Squaring β yields the same variance-explained interpretation as the squares of eta and the correlation coefficient.

The standardized beta is followed by the t value and the significance of t. In Chapter 6 we defined t as the difference between means divided by the standard error of the difference. The unstandardized beta is the difference between the means of our dichotomous variable. Therefore,

$$t = \frac{\text{Difference between means}}{\text{Standard error of difference}} = \frac{\text{Beta}}{\text{Standard error of beta}} = \frac{248.128}{60.869} = 4.076$$

Because we will need to refer back to bivariate regression values for crime seriousness and prior record when we discuss multiple correlation and regression in the next chapter, we will present these values now in the partial printouts shown in Table 11.7. Note that both crime seriousness and prior record are more powerfully related (as indicated by their respective βs) to sentence severity than is offender group. Further discussion is deferred until Chapter 12.

SUMMARY

Correlation and regression techniques are used to analyze linear relationships between interval or ratio variables. Regression is a method of predicting values on the dependent variables from knowledge of the independent variable by using the linear equation. Correlation tells us how accurate these predictions are. The regression line functions as a kind of floating mean in that predictions made on the basis of the line minimize prediction error (residuals). A preliminary stage in regression analysis is the examination of plotted values on a scattergram. The regression is a function of a (the Y intercept) and b (the slope). The Y intercept is the value of Y when $X = 0$, and the slope reveals how much the dependent variable increases or decreases in a constant manner per unit increase in the independent variable. The slope and the intercept are constants in the prediction equation and are used to make predictions about Y from a given value of X.

The correlation coefficient, an index of the strength and direction of the association, ranges from -1.0 to $+1.0$. The correlation coefficient is defined as the ratio of the covariance of Y and X to their respective standard deviations. When squared, the correlation is interpreted as the percentage of variance in the dependent variable accounted for by the independent variable, also interpreted as a PRE statistic. It is tested for statistical significance using the t distribution.

The standard error of the estimate tells us the average prediction error in predicting Y from X. It functions similarly to the standard deviation in a univariate distribution in that it gives the average deviation of scores from the regression line.

We demonstrated the diversity and usefulness of bivariate regression using our sex offender data. We saw how regression results can supply us with all the information (strength and direction of a relationship, significance of the relationship, category means with an independent variable coded 0 and 1) contained in other techniques, plus the information unique to it (the change in Y per unit change in X). The greatest utility of regression, however, lies in its ability to assess the impact of a large number of predictor variables simultaneously. This is the subject of the next chapter.

PRACTICE APPLICATION:
BIVARIATE CORRELATION AND REGRESSION

A researcher wants to determine if self-esteem is related to social distance from homosexuals. Two scales are administered to 10 subjects. The self-esteem scale ranges from 0 (low esteem) to 40 (high esteem). The social distance scale ranges from 0 (total nonacceptance of homosexuals) to 10 (complete acceptance).

CASE	SELF-ESTEEM X	SOCIAL DISTANCE Y	X^2	Y^2	XY
a	20	4	400	16	80
b	22	3	484	9	66
c	29	8	841	64	232
d	25	5	625	25	125
e	32	7	1024	49	224
f	25	7	625	49	175
g	25	5	625	25	125
h	30	9	900	81	270
I	30	8	900	64	240
j	32	8	1024	64	256
	$\Sigma X = 270$	$\Sigma Y = 64$	$\Sigma X^2 = 7448$	$\Sigma Y^2 = 446$	$\Sigma XY = 1793$
$\overline{X} = 27$	$\overline{Y} = 64$				

Compute the slope (b), the Y intercept, and the correlation coefficient. The slope (b) is

$$b = \frac{N\Sigma XY - (\Sigma X)(\Sigma Y)}{N\Sigma X^2 - (\Sigma X)^2}$$

$$= \frac{10(1793) - (270)(64)}{10(7448) - (72900)} = \frac{17930 - 17280}{74480 - 72900} = \frac{650}{1580} = .411$$

The slope of 0.411 tells us that for each one-unit change in self-esteem there is a 0.411 unit change in the acceptance of homosexuals.

The Y intercept (a) is:

$$a = \overline{Y} - b\overline{X} = 6.4 - (.411)(27) = 6.4 - 11.097 = -4.7$$

If a person has a self-esteem score of 35, what level of homosexual acceptance would you predict for him or her?

$$Y' = a + bX = -4.7 + .411(35) = -4.7 + 14.385 = 9.685$$

The correlation coefficient is

$$r = \frac{N\Sigma XY - (\Sigma X)(\Sigma Y)}{\sqrt{[N\Sigma X^2 - (\Sigma X)^2][N\Sigma Y^2 - (\Sigma Y)^2]}}$$

$$= \frac{(10)(1793) - (270)(64)}{\sqrt{[(10)(7448) - 72900][(10)(446) - 4096]}} = \frac{17930 - 17280}{\sqrt{(74480 - 72900)(4460 - 4096)}}$$

$$= \frac{650}{\sqrt{(1580)(364)}} = \frac{650}{758.37} = .857$$

Compute the significance level by using t:

$$t = r\sqrt{\frac{N-2}{1-r^2}}$$

$$= (.857)\sqrt{\frac{10-2}{1-.857^2}} = (.857)\sqrt{\frac{8}{1-.734}} = (.857)\sqrt{30} = (.857)(5.484) = 4.7$$

The variables have a strong positive association. Acceptance of homosexuals increases as self-esteem increases. The coefficient of determination is 0.734, indicating that 73.4% of the variance in the acceptance of homosexuals is explained by self-esteem. The computed t value (4.7) with 8 df exceeds the critical t (2.306) for a two-tailed test with alpha set at 0.05.

REFERENCE

Pedhazur, E. (1982). *Multiple Regression in Behavioral Research Explanation and Prediction*. New York: Holt, Rinehart and Winston.

PROBLEMS

1. An instructor believes there is a linear relationship between the number of hours spent studying for an exam and the grade one receives on that exam. She collected the following data:

STUDENT SCORE	HOURS STUDYING	EXAM
Mary	0	54
Stuart	1	62
Tyrone	4	74
Janelle	3	80
Julie	8	80
Mark	12	92
Aaron	15	98
Dwayne	4	75
Karen	9	88
Tanya	2	68

a) Draw a scattergram for the data.
b) Calculate the slope.
c) Calculate the Y intercept.
d) Compute the regression equation to predict the exam scores from the number of hours spent studying.
e) What examination score would be predicted for a student who spent 5 hours studying?
f) Using parts e and c, plot the prediction line on your scattergram.
g) Calculate the standard error of the estimate.
h) With 95% confidence, predict the range of examination scores for a student who spent 8 hours studying.
i) Calculate and interpret the correlation coefficient and its corresponding t value.

2. The following pairs of observations reflect scores on a midterm and a final exam for an introductory psychology class.

STUDENT	MIDTERM	FINAL
A	62	66
B	70	90
C	45	68
D	88	82
E	72	77
F	94	94
G	75	70
H	74	82
I	77	80
J	66	54

a) Estimate whether there exists a positive, negative, or no relationship between the midterm and the final exam.
b) Construct a scattergram. Does the scattergram confirm your estimate in part a?
c) Calculate the correlation between the midterm and the final exam.
d) Calculate the significance of the correlation coefficient.
e) Calculate and interpret the slope.
f) Compute the Y intercept and draw a line of best fit on your scattergram. Interpret the intercept.
g) For each of the following midterm exam scores, what would be their predicted final exam scores?
   1. 75
   2. 60
   3. 92
   4. 80
h) Calculate and interpret the standard error of the estimate.
i) Specify a 95% confidence interval for the predicted final exam scores in part g. How accurate were your predictions? Explain what other factors would be important in predicting final exam scores.
j) What percentage of the variance in final exam scores is accounted for by the midterm score?

3. Using the data from Problem 2, complete the following two tables. Using the data from the tables, calculate the PRE. How does this compare with your answer to Problem 2, part j?

STUDENT	MIDTERM (X)	FINAL (Y)	$\overline{Y}$	$Y - \overline{Y}$	$(Y - \overline{Y})^2$
A	62	66			
B	70	90			
C	45	68			
D	88	82			
E	72	77			
F	94	94			
G	75	70			
H	74	82			
I	77	80			
J	66	54			

$$\Sigma (Y - \overline{Y})^2 =$$

STUDENT	MIDTERM (X)	FINAL (Y)	Y'	$Y - Y'$	$(Y - Y')^2$
A	62	66			
B	70	90			
C	45	68			
D	88	82			
E	72	77			
F	94	94			
G	75	70			
H	74	82			
I	77	80			
J	66	54			

$$\Sigma (Y - Y')^2 = $$

4. Explain the meaning of the following coefficients that are the result of a regression analysis predicting salary (annual gross salary) by knowing a person's level of educational achievement (number of years of schooling completed).
   a) $a = 4{,}680$
   b) $b = 2250$
   c) $S_{y \cdot x} = 1300$
   d) $S_y = 4320$
   e) Using parts a–d, when $X = 12$ (completed a high school degree), what will Y' equal? Explain what this means.
   f) When $X = 12$, within what values of Y' on either side of the prediction line can one expect to find 98% of the observed values of Y'?
   g) When $X = 16$ (completed a college degree), what will Y' equal?

5. A health researcher believes there is a linear relationship between years of taking multiple vitamins and life expectancy. He collected the following data.

RESPONDENT	NUMBER OF YEARS TAKING VITAMINS	AGE AT DEATH
1	32	82
2	2	90
3	0	42
4	23	78
5	15	68
6	2	56
7	28	92
8	10	77
9	5	72
10	9	55
11	12	39
12	0	60

   a) Draw a scattergram for the data. Is there a relationship? What is the nature of the relationship?
   b) Calculate and interpret the slope.
   c) Calculate and interpret the Y intercept.

d) Compute the regression equation and plot the prediction line.

e) Calculate the standard error of estimate.

f) Mark has been taking vitamins for 15 years. With 95% confidence, what is his predicted life expectancy?

g) What is the correlation between number of years taking vitamins and age at death? Is this correlation significant? Calculate t and its significance. Interpret your findings.

6. a) In Problem 1, the standard error of beta (SE_b) is equal to 0.342. Calculate and interpret a 95% confidence interval for the slope.

b) In Problem 5, the standard error of beta is equal to 0.508. Calculate and interpret a 99% confidence interval for the slope.

Chapter 12

MULTIVARIATE CORRELATION AND REGRESSION

PARTIAL CORRELATION

This chapter introduces multivariate statistical techniques for variables measured at the interval/ratio level. As seen in Chapter 10, several factors typically combine to influence variation in a dependent variable in the real world. The basic logic of multivariate correlation and regression is the same as it is for partial gamma, except we mathematically control for additional predictor variables rather than physically moving cases into categories of a control variable. This enables control for any number of other variables without encountering the problems discussed in Chapter 10. The more theoretically meaningful variables that are introduced into our models the better we should be able to understand the data, and the fewer prediction errors we should make.

Let us see what happens to the zero-order correlation of 0.855 between the number of prior felony convictions and the number of years imprisonment computed in Chapter 11 when we control for a third variable, seriousness of *criminal charge*. This variable is coded 1 for the least serious charge, 2 for the next most serious, 3 for the next, and 4 for the most serious charge. The data from Table 11.1 are reproduced in Table 12.1, with the crime charge (V) variable added. There are three correlations in this data set:

Between number of convictions (X) and sentence (Y): $\quad r_{YX} = .855$
Between number of convictions (X) and charge (V): $\quad r_{XV} = .675$
Between sentence (Y) and charge (V): $\quad r_{YV} = .867$

When we examine the effect of the number of prior convictions on sentence length controlling for the effects of crime charge, it is expressed symbolically as $r_{YX \cdot V}$. The formula for partial correlation is

$$r_{YX \cdot V} = \frac{r_{YX} - (r_{YV})(r_{XV})}{\sqrt{1 - r_{YV}^2}\ \sqrt{1 - r_{XV}^2}} \tag{12.1}$$

The numerator in formula (12.1) tells us to subtract the combined effects of crime charge (V) on both sentence length and prior convictions (the product of r_{YV} and r_{XV}) from the effects of prior convictions on sentence length (r_{YX}). In effect we are considering only the covariance of sentence length and prior convictions remaining after crime charge has operated on them both. This value is then divided by what we might consider the average value of the coefficient of nondetermination, where $1 - r_{YV}^2$ equals the proportion of variance in sentence length not explained by crime charge, and $1 - r_{XV}^2$ equals the proportion of variance in crime charge not explained by prior convictions.

**TABLE 12.1   Raw Data from Table 11.1 with
Criminal Charge Added**

CASE	NUMBER OF PRIOR CONVICTIONS (X)	SENTENCE IN YEARS (Y)	CRIMINAL CHARGE (V)
a	1	1	1
b	1	3	2
c	2	3	2
d	2	4	4
e	2	2	1
f	3	3	3
g	3	4	3
h	4	6	4
I	5	7	4
j	5	5	3
	28	38	27

COMPUTING PARTIAL CORRELATIONS

Using these three correlations, we now determine the effect of prior convictions on sentence length, controlling for the effects of crime charge. Consider the correlations for a moment and try to determine logically what you think will happen. Will the correlation remain roughly the same? Will it increase? Or will it decrease?

Step 1.   From preceding correlations, put the appropriate values into formula (12.1):

$$r_{YX \cdot V} = \frac{.855 - (.867)(.675)}{\sqrt{1 - (.867)^2}\sqrt{1 - (.675)^2}}$$

Step 2.   Multiply 0.867 by 0.675 = 0.585. Subtract this value from 0.855 = 0.27.

$$= \frac{.27}{\sqrt{1 - (.867)^2}\sqrt{1 - (.675)^2}}$$

Step 3.   Square 0.867 = 0.7517. Square 0.675 = 0.4556.

$$= \frac{.27}{\sqrt{1 - .7517}\sqrt{1 - .4556}}$$

Step 4.   Subtract 0.7517 from 1 = 0.248 and 0.4556 from 1 = 0.5444.

$$= \frac{.27}{\sqrt{.2483}\sqrt{.5444}}$$

Step 5.   Take the square root of 0.2483 = 0.4983, and the square root of 5444 = 0.7378.

$$= \frac{.27}{(.4984)(.7378)}$$

Step 6.   Multiply 0.4983 by 0.7378 = 0.3676.

$$= \frac{.27}{.3676} = 0.734$$

Divide 0.27 by 0.3676 = 0.734.

TABLE 12.2   Matrix of Pearson Correlation Coefficients

VARIABLE	CASES	MEAN	STD DEV
SENSEV (Y)	637	492.0220	727.3945
GROUP (X)	637	.6766	.4681
CRSER (V)	637	2.9937	1.9611
PRREC (W)	637	3.9906	4.9073

	SENSEV	GROUP	CRSER	PRREC
SENSEV (Y)	1.000	.1597**	.7162**	.4344**
GROUP (X)		1.000	−.1666**	.0582
CRSER (V)			1.000	.3150**
PRREC (W)				1.000

* Significant at <0.05. ** Significant at <0.001.
Coding: Offender Group: non-sex = 0, sex = 1.

As we hope you anticipated from noting the high correlation between prior convictions and crime charge, the relationship between prior convictions and sentence length has diminished from 0.855 to 0.734. We will now explore partial correlation further with a more complex computer example using our sex offender data.

COMPUTER EXAMPLE AND INTERPRETATION

Table 12.2 is a correlation matrix (a row-by-column display) of zero-order correlations between all the relevant variables. In the present case, the variables are sentence severity, offender group (non-sex and sex), crime seriousness, and prior record.

The top of Table 12.2 lists the variable code names, number of cases, and means and standard deviations of all variables. Note that the mean given for the group variable is simply the proportion of sex offenders in the data set ($431/637 = 0.6766$), with non-sex offenders coded 0 and sex offenders coded 1.

Reading along the top row of the correlation matrix, we learn that sentence severity is weakly but significantly related to offender group (0.1597), that the correlation between sentence severity and crime seriousness is strong at 0.7162, and that the correlation between sentence severity and prior record is moderate at 0.4344. Given this information, we might be led to conclude that crime seriousness is the most important variable determining sentence severity, followed by prior record, and lastly by offender group. We shall see later that this conclusion is not necessarily true.

Tracing along the next row, we find that offender group is negatively and significantly related to crime seriousness (−0.1666) and positive but nonsignificantly related to prior record (0.058). That is, as these two legal variables are measured by the courts, sex offenders commit the less serious crimes but have the more serious prior records. However, since the correlation between offender group and prior record is not significant at less than 0.05, we cannot assume that this is true in the population of sex offenders in this jurisdiction.

The direction of a relationship involving a dichotomous variable depends on how we code the dichotomous variable. If we had coded group as sex = 0, non-sex = 1, the correlation between sentence severity and offender group would have been −0.1597, the correlation between offender group and crime seriousness would have been 0.1666, and the correlation between offender group and prior record would have been −0.058.

Thus, although the coding is arbitrary with nominal variables, such as offender group, and does not affect the statistical computations, it must be shown in the table so that the reader can properly interpret the results. The last correlation reported in the table is the one between crime seriousness and prior record (0.315), indicating a moderate statistically significant tendency for those with the more serious criminal histories to commit the more serious crimes.

We will now compute the partial correlation between offender group and sentence severity, controlling for crime seriousness. Given that we know that sex offenders receive significantly harsher sentences than non-sex offenders ($r = 0.1597$), but also that they commit significantly less serious crimes ($r = -0.1666$), what effect do you think that controlling for crime seriousness will have on the basic offender group/sentence severity relationship? Will the association increase or decrease?

Step 1.   From the correlation matrix, put the appropriate (rounded) values into formula 12.1:

$$r_{YX \cdot V} = \frac{.16 - (.716)(-.167)}{\sqrt{1 - (.716)^2} \sqrt{1 - (-.167)^2}}$$

Step 2.   Multiply 0.716 by $-0.167 = -0.1196$. Subtract -0.1196 from $0.16 = 0.2796$ (minus a minus is a plus). Square $0.716 = 0.5127$. Square $-0.167 = 0.0279$

$$= \frac{.2796}{\sqrt{1 - .5127}\sqrt{1 - .0279}}$$

Step 3.   Subtract 0.5127 from 1 = 0.4873, and 0.0279 from 1 = 0.9721.

$$= \frac{.2796}{\sqrt{.4873}\sqrt{.9721}}$$

Step 4.   Take the square root of $0.4873 = 0.6981$, and the square root of $0.9721 = .9859$. Multiply 0.6981 by $0.9859 = 0.6882$.

$$= \frac{.2796}{.6882} = .406$$

Step 5.   Divide 0.2796 by 0.6882 = 0.406.

If you thought that controlling for the effects of crime seriousness would increase the strength of the relationship between sentence severity and offender group, you were right. It makes sense that this should be so since offenders who were already receiving harsher sentences also had lower crime seriousness scores, a variable that contributes powerfully to sentence severity. As we pointed out in Chapter 10, crime seriousness is acting as a suppressor variable masking the true strength of the relationship between offender group and sentence severity. In other words, the punishment cost of being a sex offender rather than a non-sex offender is greater than the mean difference of 248.1 sentence severity points that separates the groups as determined by the t test in Chapter 6. The conclusion is that sex offenders, on the average, get longer sentences than can be predicted by their average lower crime seriousness score.

As an exercise, compute the correlation between sentence severity and group controlling for prior record. When you complete this task you will notice that the first-order correlation is slightly lower than the zero-order correlation at 0.15. Why is that?

SECOND-ORDER PARTIALS: CONTROLLING FOR TWO INDEPENDENT VARIABLES

As stated in Chapter 10, controlling for crime seriousness or prior record alone leaves an incomplete picture of what is going on in the sentencing world. Because they operate jointly in the real world, we have to assess their joint effects. That is, we need to determine the relationship between group and sentence severity controlling for both legal variables simultaneously—symbolically, $r_{YX \cdot VW}$. Before you can compute this second-order partial, two final first-order correlations must be computed: the relationship between sentence severity and prior record, controlling for crime seriousness ($r_{YW \cdot V}$), and the relationship between offender group and prior record, controlling for crime seriousness ($r_{XW \cdot V}$). These values have been computed as $r_{YW \cdot V} = 0.315$ and $r_{XW \cdot V} = 0.119$. We will put them into the formula along with $r_{YW \cdot V}(0.407)$, to demonstrate that the logic of computing second-order partials is the same as that for computing first-order partials.

$$r_{YX \cdot VW} = \frac{r_{YX \cdot V} - (r_{YW \cdot V})(r_{XW \cdot V})}{\sqrt{1 - r_{YX \cdot V}^2}\sqrt{1 - r_{XW \cdot V}^2}}$$

$$= \frac{.407 - (.315)(.119)}{\sqrt{1 - (.315)^2}\sqrt{1 - (-.119)^2}}$$

$$= \frac{.369}{\sqrt{1 - (.099)}\ \sqrt{1 - (.0142)}} = \frac{.369}{(.949)(.993)} = .392 \tag{12.2}$$

The relationship between offender group and sentence severity, controlling for crime seriousness and prior record, is 0.392. The simultaneous control of the two legally relevant variables (the only two variables that are supposed to determine sentencing decisions) with partial correlation analysis will allow us to make statements about the sentencing of sex offenders that other techniques just hint at. Since we have controlled for the only two variables that are legally supposed to influence sentencing decisions, we can state with confidence that sex offenders receive discriminatory sentencing relative to non-sex offenders in this jurisdiction.

THE MULTIPLE CORRELATION COEFFICIENT

A partial correlation is an estimate of the correlation between two variables in a population with the effects of one or more other variables controlled for, or partialed out. It is the correlation between Y and X uncontaminated by V, W, and so on. When using partial correlations we are only interested in the association of Y and X in a population rendered homogeneous on other variables. When we use **multiple correlation,** on the other hand, we are interested in the *combined* effects of a set of independent variables on Y. That is, we allow the population to be heterogeneous on all variables of interest and calculate the increment in variances explained over the variance explained by X alone.

In Chapter 11 we noted that the squared zero-order correlation coefficient is the proportion of variance in the dependent variable accounted for by the independent variable. In terms of our offender data, crime seriousness explains 51.3% of the variance in sentence severity ($0.716^2 = 0.513$) and offender group explains 2.56% ($0.16^2 = 0.0256$). You might think that all you have to do to determine the percentage of the variance that they jointly account for is add these percentages ($51.3 + 2.56$) to arrive at 53.86. But things are not that simple. We have already seen that when we take crime seriousness into account, the correlation between sentence severity and offender group increases. Therefore, the percentage of variance in sentence severity jointly accounted for by these two independent variables should be greater than the sum of their zero-order contributions. Formula (12.3) is used to calculate the multiple correlation coefficient (r):

$$R_{Y \cdot XV} = \sqrt{\frac{r_{YX}^2 + r_{YV}^2 - 2r_{YX}r_{YV}r_{XV}}{1 - r_{XV}^2}} \qquad (12.3)$$

where $R_{Y \cdot XV}$ = the multiple correlation coefficient (R)
   r_{YX}^2 = the zero-order correlation between sentence severity and offender group squared
   r_{YV}^2 = the zero-order correlation between sentence severity and crime seriousness squared
   r_{XV} = the zero-order correlation between offender group and crime seriousness.

$$R_{Y \cdot XV} = \sqrt{\frac{.160^2 + .716^2 - 2(.16)(.716)(-.167)}{1 - (-.167)^2}}$$

Step 1.   Perform all squaring and multiplication operations:

$$= \sqrt{\frac{.0256 + .5126 - 2(-.01913)}{1 - (.027889)}}$$

Step 2.   Add 0.0256 and 0.5126. Multiply -0.0191 by 2, and subtract 0.027889 from 1.

$$= \sqrt{\frac{.5382 - (-.03826)}{.972}}$$

Step 3.   Subtract -0.03826 from $0.5382 = 0.57646$.

$$= \sqrt{\frac{.57646}{.972}} = \sqrt{.593} = .77$$

Step 4.   Divide and take the square root of the quotient.

The multiple correlation coefficient is 0.77, and its squared value (0.593) is the percentage of the variance in sentence severity accounted for by both variables operating jointly. Note that if the correlation between offender group and crime seriousness had been zero (if they were independent events), the multiple correlation coefficient obtained from this laborious process would have been exactly the value obtained from simply adding the zero-order contributions (53.86%).

A diagrammatic illustration of a simple example may help you to visualize the nonadditivity, and hence redundancy, of some of the variance explained in Y by two correlated independent variables. In situation A in Figure 12.1 both X and V are correlated with Y but are uncorrelated with each other. We can simply sum the separate proportions of variance explained by X and V to get 16% + 16% = 32%. In situation B, X and V are correlated. We cannot sum their contributions to variance in Y because they account for a certain proportion of common variance. This shared variance, represented by the overlapped crosshatched area, is the redundant information that must be subtracted.

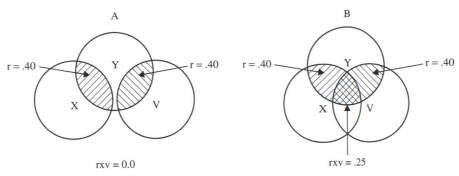

FIGURE 12.1. Overlapping and nonoverlapping variance.

The multiple correlation coefficient can be extended to include any number of independent variables, but you can safely leave the busy work to the computer as long as you understand the logic behind the process.

MULTIPLE REGRESSION

As neat and tidy as partial correlation is for summarizing the relationship between two variables controlling for a number of other variables of theoretical importance, we still need other techniques in order to fully understand our data. Which of the three variables (group, crime seriousness, or prior record) is of most or least importance in explaining variance in sentence severity, taking into consideration their simultaneous presence? How much of the variance in sentence severity do the three variables taken together explain? These questions, and more, can be answered by multiple regression. **Multiple regression** is a basic tool for evaluating the overall dependence of a variable on a set of independent variables.

THE UNSTANDARDIZED PARTIAL SLOPE

We saw in Chapter 11 that the best way to describe the linear relationship between two interval-level variables is the least squares regression line: $Y = a + bX$. This regression line can be extended to include any number of other independent variables, even those that are measured at the nominal level by the use of *dummy variables*, which are explained later. The relationship between the dependent variable sentence severity and a set of independent variables is defined by formula (12.4):

$$Y' = a + b_1X_1 + b_2X_2 + b_3X_3 + \cdots + b_kX_k \tag{12.4}$$

where $b_1, b_2, b_3, \ldots, b_k$ indicates the change in Y per unit increase in independent variables 1 through k given their simultaneous presence in the model.

We saw in Chapter 11 that a regression slope shows the amount of change in the dependent variable per unit change in the independent variable. We also saw in the bivariate regression of crime seriousness on sentence severity in Table 11.7 that each unit increase in crime seriousness resulted in an increase of 265.64 days in prison. In multiple regression, the regression slope is an **unstandardized partial regression slope,** which indicates the amount of change in the dependent variable per unit change in the independent variable controlling for the effects of all other independent variables in the equation. The partial slope is obtained by formula (12.5):

TABLE 12.4   Input Data for Calculation of the Partial Slope

SENTENCE SEVERITY (Y)	CRIME SERIOUSNESS (v)	OFFENDER GROUP (x)	CORRELATIONS (r)
$\bar{X} = 492.0$	$\bar{X} = 2.99$	$\bar{X} = 0.667$	$r_{YV} = 0.716$
$s = 727.39$	$s = 1.96$	$s = 0.468$	$r_{YX} = 0.160$
			$r_{VX} = 0.167$

$$b_p = \left[\frac{s_y}{s_x}\right]\left[\frac{r_{yx} - (r_{yv})(r_{vx})}{1 - r_{vx}^2}\right] \tag{12.5}$$

where b_P = the partial slope of V (crime seriousness) on Y (sentence severity)
   s_Y = the standard deviation of Y (sentence severity)
   s_X = the standard deviation of X (offender group)
   r_{YV} = the zero-order correlation between sentence severity and crime seriousness
   r_{YX} = the zero-order correlation between sentence severity and offender group
   r_{VX} = the zero-order correlation between crime seriousness and offender group.

The information needed to compute these partial slopes is reproduced in Table 12.4. The partial slope for crime seriousness (V) is

$$b_1 = \left[\frac{s_Y}{s_V}\right]\left[\frac{r_{YX} - (r_{YX})(r_{VX})}{1 - r_{VX}^2}\right]$$

$$= \left[\frac{727.39}{1.96}\right]\left[\frac{.716 - (.16)(-.167)}{1 - (-.167)^2}\right]$$

$$= (372.1)\left[\frac{.716 - (-.0267)}{1 - .0279}\right] = (372.1)\left[\frac{.743}{.972}\right] = (327.1)(.764) = 283.5 \tag{12.6}$$

The partial slope for offender group (X) is

$$b_2 = \left[\frac{727.39}{.468}\right]\left[\frac{.16 - (.716)(-.167)}{1 - (-.167)^2}\right]$$

$$= (1544.2)\left[\frac{.16 - (-.1196)}{1 - .0279}\right]$$

$$= (1544.2)\left[\frac{.280}{.972}\right] = (1554.2)(.288) = 447.6$$

Now that we have the partial slopes, what do they mean? The first partial slope tells us that there is a change of 283.5 units in the dependent variable (283.5 sentence severity points) per unit increase in crime seriousness points when the influence of group is held constant. When the influence of group is taken into account there is an increase of just under 20 points over the 265.4 value noted in the bivariate unstandardized slope in Table 11.7.

In the second case (b_2), there is a 447.6 unit increase in sentence severity per unit change in group (moving from 0 = non-sex to 1 = sex) when the influence of crime seriousness is held constant. This figure is an increase of 199.4 over the bivariate slope for sentence severity and group $(b = 248.1)$ noted in Chapter 11.

THE STANDARDIZED SLOPE (β)

We cannot determine from the unstandardized partial slopes which of the independent variables in the model has the most powerful impact on sentence severity. In the bivariate regressions in Tables 11.6 and 11.7, we see that the slope for crime seriousness is 265.6; for offender group, 248.1; and for prior record, 64.4. We cannot assume from these figures that since the slopes for crime seriousness and offender group are almost equal, they are approximately of equal importance in determining sentence severity, nor can we assume that either one of them is about four times more important than the prior record. This is because they are all measured differently. In Chapter 11 we explained that the value of b depends on how we measured the dependent variable. It also depends on the range of the independent variable. Recall also that the slope indicates the change in Y *per unit* increase in the independent variables(s), so if there are more units in one variable than in another we cannot directly compare their per unit impact on Y. For example, the offender group variable only has to split the sentence severity variance it explains two ways; that is, into sex or non-sex categories. Crime seriousness points range from 1 to 10, and prior record points range from 0 to 27, which means that they have to split the variance they account for 10 and 28 ways, respectively. To assess the relative importance of the independent variables in explaining variance in Y we have to convert them to a common scale, that is, standardize them. To do so we use the standard deviation to calculate the **standardized slope** (β), which informs us of the change (increase or decrease) in the dependent variable *in standard deviation units* per standard deviation change in the independent variable. The formula for standardizing a regression slope is given in formula (12.7).

For crime seriousness:

$$\beta_1 = b_1 \left[\frac{s_V}{s_Y} \right] = 265.6 \left[\frac{1.96}{727.39} \right] = .714 \tag{12.7}$$

For offender group:

$$\beta_2 = b_2 \left[\frac{s_X}{s_Y} \right] = 248.1 \left[\frac{.468}{727.39} \right] = .1595$$

A similar computation for prior record is .43. The computed values for the standardized betas are, within the limits of rounding error, analogous to the zero-order correlations between these pairs of variables given in Table 12.2. But we still cannot tell which of the three independent variables has the most important impact on sentence severity from these standardized betas any more than we could from the zero-order correlations. To do so, we must compute the **standardized partial regression slopes** for these variables.

The standardized partial regression slope, which is refered to as the *standardized beta* from now on, indicates the average standard deviation change in the dependent variable associated with a standard deviation change in the independent variable, holding constant all other variables in the equation. The formula for computing the standardized beta is given in formula (12.8):

$$\beta_{YV \cdot X} = b_{YV \cdot X} \left[\frac{s_X}{s_Y} \right] \tag{12.8}$$

where $\beta_{YV \cdot X}$ = the standardized partial beta and $b_{YV \cdot X}$ = the unstandardized partial beta. Thus,

$$\beta_{YV \cdot X} = 283.5 \left[\frac{1.96}{727.39} \right] = (283.5)(.00269) = .763$$

Note that this value of 0.763, with tolerance for rounding, is identical to the value we computed for the multiple correlation coefficient from formula (12.3). In fact, formula (12.8) is an alternative to formula (12.3). A similarly computed partial standardized beta for offender group, controlling for crime seriousness, was 0.289. We are sure at this point that crime seriousness is more important to sentencing decisions than offense type (group). However, we still do not know if *group* or *prior record* is the second most powerful predictor. The answer to this question requires us to extend the equation to include *prior record*. In the interest of brevity we will not compute this step, but the logic is analogous to that involved in computing second-order partial correlation coefficients. We will now discuss the computer readout for the regression model assessing the combined effects of offender group, crime seriousness, and prior record on sentence severity.

A COMPUTER EXAMPLE OF MULTIPLE REGRESSION AND INTERPRETATION

We are now in a position to assess the simultaneous effects of all three predictor variables on sentence severity. It is useful to look at three successive printouts so that you can see the changes in the various statistics as we add new variables and to reinforce what you have learned about regression in the last two chapters. The first printout in Table 12.5 is a simple bivariate regression of crime seriousness on sentence severity. The second printout shows the regression results with offender group added to the equation, and the third shows the full three-variable model (crime seriousness, group, and prior record regressed on sentence severity).

SUMMARY STATISTICS: MULTIPLE R, R^2, $s_{Y \cdot X}$, AND ANOVA

As seen in the two-variable regression model in printout 2 of Table 12.5, the first statistic encountered is multiple R, the correlation between a dependent variable and two or more independent variables. In the present case it is the multiple correlation between sentence severity and crime seriousness and offender group given their simultaneous presence in the model. Please note that this value is identical to the value we computed for $R_{Y \cdot XV}$.

The next statistic is R squared, which is the square of multiple $R (0.77) = 0.593$ (rounded). It is important to note the change in the R^2 value from that given in printout 1 to the value given in printout 2. It has increased from 0.51291 to 0.59299, an increment of .0801. This increase indicates that after crime seriousness has been allowed to explain all the variance that it can, offender group explains an additional 8%. In printout 3 you can see a further increase in R^2 of 0.0353, for a total R^2 for the model of 0.62829.

The next statistic is the **adjusted R squared,** a conservative estimate of explained variance that adjusts for sample size and/or number of predictor variables. It is always preferable to report this measure rather than the unadjusted R squared. The computation of the adjusted R^2 found in printout 3 of Table 12.5 is illustrated by formula (12.9):

Table 12.5　Regression Models Progressively Entering Control Variables

PRINTOUT 1.　BIVARIATE REGRESSION OF CRIME SERIOUSNESS ON SENTENCE SEVERITY

				Analysis of Variance	
Multiple R	.71618				
R Square	.51291		df	Sum of Squares	Mean Squares
Adjusted R Square	.51215	Regression	1	172599964.05	172599964.05
Standard Error	508.06003	Residual	635	163909373.64	258124.99
		F = 668.66815		SIGNIF F = .0000	

VARIABLE	B	SE B	BETA	T	SIG T
CRSER	265.640	10.273	.716	25.859	.0000
(CONSTANT)	−303.231	36.756		−8.250	.0000

PRINTOUT 2.　THE ADDITION OF OFFENDER GROUP TO THE EQUATION

				Analysis of Variance	
Multiple R	.77006				
R Square	.59299		df	Sum of Squares	Mean Squares
Adjusted R Square	.59171	Regression	2	199547814.06	99773907.03
Standard Error	64.78774	Residual	634	136961523.62	258124.99
		F = 461.85714		SIGNIF F = .0000	

VARIABLE	B	SE B	BETA	T	SIG T
CRSER	283.378	9.531	.764	29.732	.0000
GROUP	445.937	39.927	.287	11.169	.0000
(CONSTANT)	−658.059	46.260		−14.225	.0000

PRINTOUT 3.　THE ADDITION OF PRIOR RECORD TO THE MODEL

				Analysis of Variance	
Multiple R	.79265				
R Square	.62829		df	Sum of Squares	Mean Squares
Adjusted R Square	.62653	Regression	3	211424782.77	70474927.59
Standard Error	444.52889	Residual	633	125084554.92	197605.93
		F = 356.64379		SIGNIF F = .0000	

VARIABLE	B	SE B	BETA	T	SIG T
CRSER	258.685	9.656	.697	26.790	.0000
GROUP	410.668	38.456	.264	10.679	.0000
PRREC	29.548	3.811	.199	7.753	.0000
(CONSTANT)	−678.185	44.319		−15.302	.0000

$$\text{Adjusted } R^2 = 1 - (1 - R^2)\frac{N-1}{N-k-1}$$

$$= 1 - .37171\left[\frac{636}{633}\right] = 1 - (.37171)(1.004739) = .6253 \tag{12.9}$$

where N = sample size and k = number of independent variables in the model.

　　Although the R^2 value will always increase with the addition of further variables to the equation, the adjusted R^2 squared may begin to decrease in value. When there is a serious decrease, we are being warned that we have added variables that are not useful in helping us to understand our data. Notice that the adjusted R^2 value in printout 3 is only slightly less than the unadjusted R^2.

Next comes the standard error, or standard error of the estimate. Recall from Chapter 11 that this is an estimate of the average prediction error, and it is defined as the standard error of actual Y values from the predicted Y' values based on the regression equation. To understand the standard error of the estimate further, recall that it is the standard deviation of the residuals. The residual or unexplained sum of squares is printed out as 125084554.9 in printout 3. If we divide this by the df for $SS_{residual}$, defined as $N - k - 1 = 633$, we get the variance of the residuals. The square root of the residuals is the standard deviation of the residuals, or the standard error of the estimate:

$$S_{Y \cdot XVW} = \sqrt{\frac{SS_{residual}}{df}} = \sqrt{\frac{125084554.9}{633}} = 444\ 53$$

To the right of these statistics in Table 12.5 is the analysis of variance. The sum of squares explained by the regression is analogous to the term *explained sum of squares* in ANOVA, and the residual sum of squares means exactly the same as it does in ANOVA: the unexplained variance in the model. Dividing the regression mean square by the residual mean square we obtain the F ratio observed in printout 3:

$$F = \frac{70474927}{197605.93} = 356.64379$$

Clearly, our regression model explains a highly significant proportion of the variance in sentence severity.

THE PREDICTOR VARIABLES: *b*, *β*, AND *t*

Below the summary model statistics in Table 12.5 is information regarding the contributions of each specific variable in the model. Reading from left to right, the first statistic is the partial unstandardized beta for sentence severity and crime seriousness, controlling for other variables in the model, which is only offender group in printout 2. Note that the unstandardized beta has increased from 256.6 in printout 1 to 283.4 in printout 2. Within the limits of rounding error, this is the value we computed earlier. In printout 3 the partial slope for crime seriousness declines to 258.68 because prior record is significantly and positively correlated with crime seriousness. Those who commit the more serious crimes tend to have the more serious prior records.

The unstandardized partial slope of 258.68 in printout 3 means that for each unit increase in crime seriousness there is an average increase of 258.68 sentence severity points when the effects of offender group and prior record are held constant.

The next statistic is the standardized partial slope for crime seriousness, reported as 0.697 in printout 3. This value tells you how much a 1 standard deviation change in *x* will affect *y*, also in standard deviation units, controlling for the effects of the other variables in the model. This is an important statistic because, unlike the unstandardized partial slope, it is a measure of the relative importance of the independent variables in the model. The statistical significance of each variable is assessed by the *t* test. We see that all variables contribute significantly to the model.

We now move down to the second row, containing the statistics relevant to offender group. The unstandardized partial slope of 410.7 given in printout 3 indicates that the effect on sentence severity of being a sex offender as opposed to a non-sex offender is 410.7 sentence severity points. This is a dramatic increase from the 248.1 points difference observed when we did not take the two legally relevant variables into account. With the addition of prior record in printout 3, both the standardized and unstandardized betas for crime seriousness and offender group have diminished. Again, this is intuitively reasonable if we recall from the matrix of zero-order correlations that prior record is positively related to both crime seriousness and offender group. We finally know what being a sex offender versus not being a sex offender means in terms of sentence severity. It tells us more than a simple multiple correlation because we can easily translate the unstandardized partial slope into substantive terms; that is, days incarcerated.

Multiple regression allowed us to determine the ranking of the independent variables in terms of how they affect sentencing. It is now obvious from the standardized betas that offender group ($\beta = 0.264$) has a more powerful effect than does prior record ($\beta = 0.199$). We would have been misled into thinking that prior record was the more important of the two had we not performed a regression analysis. The relative importance of these three predictor variables can be determined by taking the ratio of the squares of their standardized betas. The squares (rounded to two places) of our three predictors are crime seriousness = 0.49, offender group = 0.07, and prior record = 0.04. Crime seriousness accounts for 7 times more variance ($0.49/0.07 = 7$) than offender group and just over 12 times more than prior record. Offender group accounts for 1.75 times more of the variance ($0.07/0.04 = 1.75$) than prior record.

The final statistic is the Y intercept (CONSTANT), which represents the value of Y when all of the independent variables have a value of zero. As we saw previously, the constant is used to predict the value of an individual score from given values of the independent variables in the equation. To predict the sentence severity of a sex offender with 4 crime seriousness points and 4 prior record points, we would use formula (12.4):

$$Y' = a + b_1X_1 + b_2X_2 + b_3X_3$$

Putting in the values from printout 3 of Table 12.5, we get

$$Y' = \quad -678.18 \quad + \quad 410.7(1) + 258.7(4) + \quad 29.5(4)$$
$$\text{(CONSTANT)} \quad \text{(GROUP)} \quad \text{(CRSER)} \quad \text{(PRREC)}$$
$$= -678.18 + 410.7 + 1034.8 + 118 = 885.32$$

For a non–sex offender with the same crime seriousness and prior record scores,

$$Y' = \quad -678.18 \quad + \quad 410.7(0) + 258.7(4) + \quad 29.5(4)$$
$$\text{(CONSTANT)} \quad \text{(GROUP)} \quad \text{(CRSER)} \quad \text{(PRREC)}$$
$$= -678.18 + 0 + 1034.8 + 118 = 474.62$$

A VISUAL REPRESENTATION OF MULTIPLE REGRESSION

To help you grasp the idea of multivariate regression, note what happens in Figure 12.2. The circle labeled Y is the total variance in sentence severity. The first variable to enter the equation is crime seriousness (V), which accounts for 51.29% of the variance (visually represented by the shaded area). The next most powerful predictor, offender group (X), accounts for 8.01% of the *remaining* variance. Finally, prior record (W) takes out 3.53% of the variance in Y after X and V have taken their share. Thus, the three predictor variables have taken a combined total of 62.83% of the variance in sentence severity, leaving 37.17% of the variance unexplained.

DUMMY VARIABLE REGRESSION

In Chapter 11 we looked at bivariate regression by using *group* as the independent variable. *Group* is a dichotomous variable that we dummy-coded 0 and 1. This section extends the discussion of dummy variables in regression. Some researchers have avoided the use of multiple regression under the mistaken impression that all variables must be measured at the interval or ratio level. Actually, the only requirement is that the dependent variable

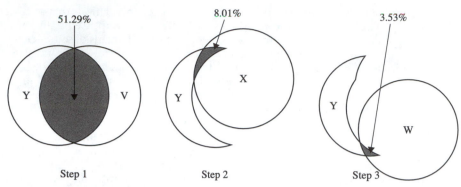

FIGURE 12.2.   Visual representation of partitioning variance in multiple regression.

be an interval or ratio measure. Nominal variables, either dichotomous or multicategory (such as religious preference), can be used in a regression format when coded as dummy variables. As previously indicated, dummy variables are variables coded 1 in the presence of a given attribute and 0 in its absence. Group is a dummy variable because offenders who committed sex offenses were coded 1 and non-sex offenders were coded 0. In this case there are only two categories of the variable; the creation of dummy variables for multicategory nominal variables is just a little more complicated.

For instance, suppose that we wish to assess the sentences for sex and non-sex offenders according to the political affiliations of the judges (Republican, Democratic, and Independent). Although there is no natural ordering of party affiliation, if we entered this nominal variable into the regression model the computer would treat it as an ordered variable and would present meaningless and uninterpretable results. Dummy variable analysis gets around this problem by creating three separate dichotomous variables from the original variable containing three categories.

Dummy variable analysis is quite similar in logic to ANOVA and may be considered a special case of ANOVA. The main difference between them is that with ANOVA, *judge* would be considered a single variable with three categories. In dummy variable regression, the nominal variable *judge* is treated as three separate dichotomous variables, scored 1 in the presence of an attribute and 0 in its absence. A Republican judge would be coded 1 on the *Republican* dummy variable and 0 on all others. A Democrat would be coded 1 on the *Democratic* dummy variable and 0 on all others. We do not need to create a dummy variable for the *Independent* category since its value is completely determined by the first $k - 1$ dummies entered into the regression equation. The excluded category serves as a reference category whose mean on the dependent variable will be the Y constant. Dummy variable analysis, then, has $k - 1$ categories. If we have three categories of an independent variable, we create $k - 1$, or two dummy variables. If we had five categories, we would create four dummy variables. The dummy variables for the judge's political affiliation are as follows:

CATEGORY	DUMMIES	
	d_1	d_2
Republican	1	0
Democrat	0	1
Independent	0	0 ← (the reference category = the Y intercept)

TABLE 12.6 Dummy Variable Multiple Regression

VARIABLE	b	β	t	SIG.
Crime seriousness	258.9	0.70	27.0	0.0000
Group	412.2	0.26	10.8	0.0000
Prior record	29.6	0.20	7.8	0.0000
Dummy1	102.9	0.07	2.1	0.0396
Dummy2	−7.3	−0.00	−0.1	0.8939
Constant	−734.8		−12.1	0.0000

ANOVA would probably be the choice of most researchers assessing the effects of categorical variables on an interval-level dependent variable, but ANOVA can deal only with categorical independent variables, whereas regression can deal with combinations of categorical and continuous variables, and ANOVA tends to become problematic as we go beyond two or three independent variables. Regression analysis, on the other hand, can deal with a large number of independent variables. A regression model assessing the effect of party affiliation on judges' sentencing of sex and non-sex offenders controlling for crime seriousness and prior record is presented in Table 12.6.

To determine the adjusted mean sentence severity scores of the judges adjusting for the effects of all other independent variables, we use the following formula:

$$Y' = a + b_1 d_1 + b_2 d_2 + b_{\text{crime ser.}} \overline{X}_{\text{crime ser.}} + b_{\text{group}} \overline{X}_{\text{group}} + b_{\text{prior rec.}} \overline{X}_{\text{prior rec.}}$$

As found in Table 12.2, the crime seriousness, prior record, and group means are 3.0, 4.0, and 0.7, respectively (all figures rounded). To determine the mean sentence for sex offenders sentenced by Republican judges (Dummy1), for example, the calculations are:

$$Y' = -734.8 + (102.9)(1) + (-7.3)(0) + (258.9)(3) + (412.3)(.7) + (29.6)(4)$$

$$= -734.8 + 102.9 + 0 + 776.7 + 288.6 + 118.4 = 551.8$$

We leave it to you as an exercise to compute predicted mean sentences for both offender groups by Democratic and Independent judges.

REGRESSION AND INTERACTION

In Chapter 7 we illustrated the concept of interaction by looking at probation officers' sentencing recommendations for sex offenders, using victim/offender relationship and probation officer ideology as independent variables. The ANOVA program indicated significant interaction between the two independent variables, thus suggesting further exploration of the data for a more meaningful interpretation of the effects of the two independent variables on recommendations. Unlike ANOVA, regression does not explicitly reveal the existence of interaction, but it can be detected with a little extra effort.

If preliminary statistical analyses of our theoretical knowledge of the subject under investigation lead us to suspect significant interaction, we should create a new variable that is a composite of the two interacting variables. For instance, we already know from the two-way ANOVA results in Chapter 7 that probation officers' sentencing recommendations are influenced by their ideology. Criminological theory tells us that conservatives are more likely than liberal officers to hold the position that punishment should fit the crime. If this is correct, we would expect to find that crime seriousness is more important in determining conservative officers' recommendations than liberal officers' recommendations. In other words, the effects of crime seriousness on recommendations will vary across officer category. To test this assumption we create an interaction term by multiplying (or rather having the computer multiply) ideology (IDEOL) by crime seriousness (CRSER). This interaction term is entered into the regression equation with its two composite variables. The regression model used to illustrate interaction in model C in Table 12.7 consists of one continuous dependent variable (POREC), one continuous independent variable (CRSER), one dummy independent variable (IDEOL), and one interaction term (CRSER × IDEOL). If the regression results indicate no significant interaction, the prediction equation is simply additive, with the form

$$Y' = a + b_1 X_1 + b_2 X_2$$

where X_1 = crime seriousness and X_2 = officers' ideology. If interaction is significant, the additive model is no longer adequate to describe the data, and the equation must take the form

$$Y' = a + b_1 X_1 + b_2 X_2 + b_3 X_1 X_2$$

where $b_3 X_1 X_2$ is the interaction term.

Table 12.7 presents three separate regression models. Models A and B are bivariate regression models of the effect of crime seriousness on recommendations for sex and non-sex offenders for liberal and conservative officers, respectively. The adjusted r^2 values (0.325 for liberals and 0.594 for conservatives) support our contention that crime seriousness has more of an impact on the recommendations of conservative officers. The impact of one additional crime seriousness unit results in an increase of 290.89 recommendation units ($b = 290.89$) for conservative officers but only 178.75 units for liberal officers ($b = 178.75$). Subtracting the slope for the liberal officers from that of the conservative officers results in a difference of 112.14 recommendation units.

TABLE 12.7   Illustrating Interaction

VARIABLE	b	(A) LIBERAL OFFICERS ONLY S.E.	β	t	SIG.
CRSER	178.75	14.66	0.572	12.20	0.0000
		Adjusted r^2 = 0.325			

VARIABLE	b	(B) CONSERVATIVE OFFICERS ONLY S.E.	β	t	SIG.
CRSER	290.89	15.92	0.772	18.27	0.000
		Adjusted r^2 = 0.594			

VARIABLE	b	(C) LIBERAL AND CONSERVATIVE OFFICERS AND IDEOLOGY × CRSER INTERACTION S.E.	β	t	SIG.
CRSER × IDEOL	112.14	21.64	0.352	5.18	0.0000
CRSER	178.74	16.43	0.502	10.87	0.0000
IDEOL	−159.04	77.64	−0.111	−2.05	0.0410
(CONSTANT)	−159.51	52.86		−3.02	0.0027
		Adjusted r^2 = 0.528			

Let us now look at model C, in Table 12.7, which is a multiple regression including both independent variables and the interaction term CRSER × IDEOL. Both independent variables are significant. The important point is the value of the unstandardized beta for the interaction term. We see that it is 112.14, the value we got from subtracting the slope in model A from the slope in model B. The test of statistical significance for the regression coefficient associated with the interaction term is a test of the statistical significance of the difference of the two slopes defined by IDEOL. The t value (5.18) for the interaction term is highly significant; thus the interaction effect is highly significant, and the additive prediction equation is inadequate. Note that IDEOL has a significant effect on recommendation severity even after the effects of the interaction term have been accounted for.

SUMMARY

Partial correlation allows us to assess the strength of the relationship between two variables controlling for the effects of one or more other variables. It is an effective technique if the researcher is concerned only with the relationship between x and y with the effects of all other theoretically relevant variables removed.

Multiple correlation is the correlation between a dependent variable and two or more variables. Squaring the multiple correlation gives the percentage of the variance in the dependent variable explained by all of the independent variables in the equation.

Multiple regression is used to make predictions of the dependent variable from two or more independent or predictor variables. The unstandardized partial slope (beta) is an index of the amount of change in the dependent variable per unit change in an independent variable, controlling for the effects of the other independent variables in the model. The unstandardized partial slope values are given in their original measurement units. The standardized partial slopes convey the same information in terms of standard deviation units rather than the original metric. By standardizing the partial slopes we render them comparable in terms of the relative strength of each variable's impact on the dependent variable. The R-squared value represents the percentage of the variance explained in the dependent variable by all independent variables operating together.

Multiple correlation and regression are remarkably powerful and robust techniques for assessing the combined effects of a series of independent or predictor variables on a dependent variable, supplying researchers with a wealth of information.

PRACTICE APPLICATION: PARTIAL CORRELATION

We will now determine if the correlation between self-esteem and acceptance of homosexuals holds up controlling for educational level (V). All the necessary information to make our computations is given in the following matrix:

	Y	X	V	$\bar{X}$	s
(Y) Social distance	1.000	857	0.769	6.3	2.01
(X) Self-esteem		1.000	0.850	27.0	4.19
(V) Level of education			1.000	13.1	2.56

What is the strength of the relationship between X and Y controlling for V?

$$r_{yx \cdot v} = \frac{.857 - (.769)(.85)}{\sqrt{1 - (.769)^2}\ \sqrt{1 - (.85)^2}} = \frac{.203}{(.639)(.529)} = .60$$

Is the partial relationship statistically significant? (Note: df = 3 because we are testing a first-order relationship.)

$$t = r_{YX \cdot V}\sqrt{\frac{N - 3}{1 - r^2}} = .60\sqrt{\frac{7}{.36}} = .60\sqrt{19.44} = 2.64$$

The t_{critical} value with 7 df at the 0.05 level (two-tail) is 2.365. Our calculated t exceeds this, so reject the null that $\rho_{yx \cdot v} = 0.0$ in the population. Thus, controlling for education level weakens the bivariate relationship because of the strong correlation between self-esteem and education level, but it remains fairly strong and is statistically significant.

We will now examine the joint effect of self-esteem and educational level on social distance from homosexuals using multiple regression.

Compute the multiple correlation coefficient:

$$R_{y \cdot xv} = \sqrt{\frac{r_{yx}^2 + r_{yv}^2 - 2r_{yx}r_{yv}r_{xv}}{1 - r_{xv}^2}}$$

$$= \sqrt{\frac{.857^2 + .769^2 - 2(.857)(.769)(.85)}{1 - (.85)^2}} = \sqrt{\frac{.734 + .591 - 2(.56)}{1 - (.722)}}$$

$$= \sqrt{\frac{1.325 - 1.12}{.2775}} = \sqrt{\frac{.205}{.2775}} = \sqrt{.739} = .86$$

Squaring multiple R we find that self-esteem and education jointly account for 74% of the variance in social distance from homosexuals. Self-esteem by itself accounted for 0.734% of the variance (0.857^2). We added practically nothing to our understanding of the self-esteem/social distance relationship by adding education to the model because education is highly correlated with self-esteem.

Calculate the unstandardized partial slope for self-esteem:

$$b_1 = \left[\frac{S_y}{S_x}\right]\left[\frac{r_{yx} - (r_{yv})(r_{vx})}{1 - r_{vx}^2}\right]$$

$$= \left[\frac{2.01}{4.19}\right]\left[\frac{.857 - (.769)(.85)}{1 - (.85)^2}\right]$$

$$= (.48)\left[\frac{.857 - .654}{1 - .7225}\right] = (.48)\left[\frac{.203}{.2775}\right] = (.48)(.7315) = .351$$

The unstandardized partial slope for education level is

$$b_2 = \left[\frac{2.01}{2.56}\right]\left[\frac{.769 - (.857)(.85)}{1 - (.85)^2}\right]$$

$$= (.785)\left[\frac{.769 - .728}{1 - .7225}\right] = (.785)\left[\frac{.041}{.2775}\right] = (.785)(.148) = .116$$

Compute the standardized partial slope for self-esteem:

$$\beta_1 = b_1\left[\frac{S_x}{S_y}\right] = .351\left[\frac{4.19}{2.01}\right] = .732$$

For education level:

$$\beta_2 = b_2 \left[\frac{S_v}{S_y} \right] = .116 \left[\frac{2.56}{2.01} \right] = .148$$

Calculate the Y intercept:

$$a = \overline{Y} - b\overline{X}_1 + b\overline{X}_2 = 6.4 - (.351)(27) + (.116)(13.1) = 6.4 - (9.48 + 1.52)$$
$$= 6.4 - 11 = -4.6$$

What social distance score would you predict for a person with a self-esteem score of 34 and 16 years of education?

$$Y' = a + b_1 X + b_2 X = -4.6 + (.351)(34) + (.116)(16)$$
$$= -4.6 + 11.93 + 1.86 = 9.19$$

PROBLEMS

1. A researcher wishes to determine the relationship between number of books read in a year and social class. He/she wishes to see if gender has any influence on number of books read with social class in the model. Books read in a year was measured simply by asking subjects how many they had read. Numbers ranged from zero to 27. Social class is scored as a composite of annual income and years of education, and ranges between 10 and 40 in the sample of 160 subjects. Gender was simply noted, and coded 0 = female and 1 = male. The matrix of zero-order correlations between these variables and their descriptive statistics follows.

VARIABLE	MEAN	STANDARD DEVIATION	N
Number of books	11.55	4.262	160
Social class	22.60	7.629	160
Gender	00.50	0.501	160

		ZERO-ORDER CORRELATIONS	
	Y	X	V
Books read (Y)	1.000	.488	−.200
Social class (X)		1.000	−.158
Gender (V)			1.000

a) Interpret the results.
b) Compute the first-order partial correlation for the association between number of books read and social class controlling for gender.
c) Compute the multiple correlation coefficient and interpret. Does the addition of gender contribute significantly to the variance explained?
d) Calculate the unstandardized partial slope for both predictor variables and interpret.
e) Calculate the standardized partial slopes for both variables and interpret.

2. The following regression models were generated using the same data set used in Problem 1. Model 1 is a bivariate analysis predicting books read in a year from social class. The second model adds gender to the equation.

MODEL 1	
MULTIPLE R	0.488
R SQUARED	0.238
ADJUSTED R SQUARED	.233
STANDARD ERROR	3.731

$$F = 49.414, \quad \text{SIG. } 0.00000$$

	VARIABLES IN THE EQUATION				
VARIABLE	*B*	SEB	BETA	*t*	SIG.
Social class	0.273	0.039	0.488	7.030	0.0000
Constant	5.388	0.925		5.826	0.0000

	MODEL 2
MULTIPLE R	0.504
R SQUARED	0.254
ADJUSTED R SQUARED	.244
STANDARD ERROR	3.704

F = 26.696, SIG. 0.00000

	VARIABLES IN THE EQUATION				
VARIABLE	*B*	SEB	BETA	*t*	SIG.
Social class	0.261	0.039	0.468	6.706	0.0000
Gender	−1.072	0.593	−.126	−1.808	0.0726
Constant	6.176	1.016		6.076	0.0000

a) What is the regression equation for Model 1? What is it for Model 2?
b) Compare the standarized betas and draw a conclusion as to the relative importance of the two predictor variables.
c) How many books (rounded to the nearest whole) would you predict a female with a social class score of 30 would read in a year?
d) How many books (rounded to the nearest whole) would you predict a male with a social class score of 12 would read?

3. The woman who runs the concession at the hockey stadium has noticed that she sells more coffee on cold days than on warm days. She wants to know if the temperature outside is more important in predicting how much coffee to have on hand if she should continue ordering based on predicted attendance. She kept records for seven games of the attendance (in thousands), the outside temperature, and coffee sales in hundreds of cups sold. The data follow.

ATTENDANCE (IN THOUSANDS)	TEMPERATURE (°F)	COFFEE SALES
6.9	42	1475
6.2	50	997
7.5	30	2135
6.5	61	1354
8.7	53	2200
7.9	38	3345
8.4	55	2127

a) Calculate the correlation between attendance and coffee sales.
b) Calculate the correlation between temperature and coffee sales.
c) Calculate the correlation between attendance and temperature.
d) Calculate the first-order partial correlation between attendance and coffee sales controlling for temperature.
e) Calculate the multiple correlation coefficient and interpret. Does the addition of temperature contribute significantly to explaining coffee sales?

4. a) Using the data in Problem 3, calculate the unstandardized partial slopes for both predictor variables and interpret.
    b) Calculate the standardized partial slopes for both predictor variables. Which is the more significant predictor of coffee sales?
    c) How many hundreds of cups of coffee would you predict the vendor would sell with an attendance of 5,500 on a day when the outside temperature was 55 degrees?

5. A researcher would like to know whether there is any relation between IQ, years of formal education completed, and salary for state employees. A random sample of 10 employees produced the following data.

IQ	EDUCATION (YEARS)	SALARY ($1,000)
104	12	23.70
126	16	38.33
148	15	45.80
105	11	16.54
122	14	30.50
97	12	29.80
135	10	25.50
128	16	44.32
96	11	19.87
108	12	25.34

a) Calculate multiple r, a, and b for the model regressing IQ and education on salary.
b) If a high school student planned to complete college (16 years of education) and had an IQ of 120, what would you predict his/her salary to be?
c) What would you predict the salary to be for someone with only a high school education (12 years) and an IQ of 105?

Chapter 13

INTRODUCTION TO LOGISTIC REGRESSION

This chapter presents a brief introduction to logistic regression without any extensive mathematical treatment of logarithms. Our intention is simply to acquaint students with an increasingly popular social science tool and to help them to interpret logistic regression computer printouts. **Logistic regression,** or logit (short for *logistic probability unit*), is suited to many kinds of data frequently found in social and behavioral research where so many of the dependent variables of interest are dichotomous (yes/no, black/white, success/failure, rural/urban, and so forth). Also, the nature of relationships between the dependent and independent variables is not linear in many instances. We have traditionally dealt with the analysis of variables measured at different levels by categorization of continuous variables, thereby losing a large amount of information. This strategy also necessitates using a weaker form of statistical analysis.

Logistic regression is "tailor-made" for social science research. Basically, logistic regression allows us to perform a regression-like analysis of data when the dependent variable is dichotomous or polychotomous (multiple categories) rather than continuous. Although ordinary least squares (OLS) regression is very robust in most of its assumptions, it is not robust against the assumption of the continuous linearity of the dependent variable.

AN EXAMPLE OF LOGIT REGRESSION

To illustrate logit regression, we will use our offender data with sentence type (probation versus prison) as the dependent variable and crime seriousness (entered in its original form, not dichotomized as in Chapter 10) as the independent variable. Using OLS regression with these data, we obtain a Y intercept of 0.055, a slope of 0.135, and a correlation coefficient of 0.510. Thus, whether or not an offender goes to prison is rather strongly associated with his crime seriousness score.

The question we must ask ourselves is whether this association can be accurately described by a straight line. OLS regression would fit the data to a straight line since by definition it fits a straight line that minimizes the sums of squared deviations from it. OLS regression also assumes a constancy of change; that is it tells us that moving from 1 crime seriousness point to 2 has exactly the same effect on sentence type as moving from 3 to 4, 9 to 10, or any other one-unit increment in the independent variable. OLS predictions under such circumstances would be highly suspect. Why? Well, we are trying to predict a sentencing outcome that is an either/or event (no-prison or prison), the probabilities for which must range between 0.0 and 1.0 (the offender either went to prison or he did not). Suppose we wanted to predict the probability of going to prison for someone with 8 crime seriousness points based on the OLS results given above. The prediction equation is

$$Y' = a + bX = .055 + .135182 = .055 + 1.08 = 1.135$$

Since the probability of a dichotomous either/or event coded 0 and 1 must range within those values (0 indicating zero probability and 1 indicating certainty), the computed probability makes no sense—we cannot be more certain than certain. Making predictions from OLS regression with a dichotomous dependent variable can often lead to predictions outside of the range of possibility, that is, less than zero or more than 1.

The best way to determine probabilities of probation or prison by crime seriousness would be to run a simple cross-tabulation. However, if we wanted to add more predictor variables to the model measured at various levels, cross-tabulation would not be useful.

The logistic technique constrains probabilities from ranging outside the fixed limits of 0.0 and 1.0 by taking the natural log of the odds of an event formed by the ratio of the probabilities for and against an outcome. Remember, odds refers to the probability of an event occurring (P) versus the probability of it not occurring (Q, or $1 - P$). The natural log (e) is an irrational number (like π, "pi") approximately equal to 2.71828. Don't be intimidated by "$\log_e .4286$" in the example below. All you have to do on your calculator is press the second function button and then the button marked "e^x," "E lin" "Log e," or "$_{\text{LN}}$," depending on the calculator, after you have obtained the quotient of P/Q. We take a simple example where the probability (P) = 0.30:

$$\text{Logit} = \log_e \frac{P}{Q} = \log_e \frac{.30}{.70} = \log_e .4286 = .847 \tag{13.1}$$

The logit for a probability of imprisonment of 0.30 is -0.847. The logit for someone with a probability of imprisonment of 0.70 (the complement of 0.30) is positive 0.847. Each probability value has the same absolute logit value as its complement (0.90 has the same as 0.10, 0.75 has the same as 0.25, and so forth). Probabilities of less than 0.50 yield negative logits, and probabilities greater than 0.50 yield positive logits; a probability of exactly 0.50 has a logit of 0. As illustrated in Figure 13.1, these calculations yield an elongated S-shaped probability curve that looks like the standard normal curve cut in half. Both from the shape of the curve and from the math involved, you can readily see that a one-unit increase in X does not have a constant effect on Y as it does in OLS regression. When the probabilities are very high or very low, a one-unit increase has minimal impact. As you note from the curve, the independent variable has its greatest impact when the probabilities are around 0.5 (where the slope is steepest).

Let us see what the bivariate logit regression values are for our sentence type/crime seriousness example in Table 13.1.

INTERPRETATION: PROBABILITIES AND ODDS

We take the bottom half of the printout beginning with the B value for CRSER (0.6965) first. Beta is not as readily interpretable in logistic regression as it is in OLS regression. This value tells us that a one-unit increase in crime seriousness results in an increase of the *log odds* of going to prison by 0.6965, not a very useful intuitive interpretation as it stands. Before we can give you a more readily understandable interpretation it is necessary to go through some calculations. Let us see how we use this value to calculate probabilities and odds. The formula for calculating a predicted probability in logistic regression is given as

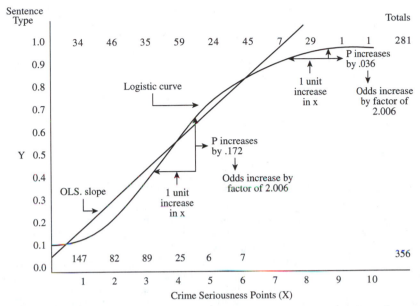

FIGURE 13.1. Illustration of Logit and OLS regression with a dichotomous dependent variable (sentence type) and continuous independent variable (crime seriousness). Numbers within the graph represent the number of cases at each level of X (e.g., there are 147 + 34 = 181 cases with 1 crime seriousness point).

$$P' = \frac{_e a + bX}{1 + _e a + bX} \tag{13.2}$$

TABLE 13.1 Bivariate Logistic Regression of Crime Seriousness on Sentence Type

Initial − 2 Log Likelihood 874.218 (constant only in the model)
  − 2 Log Likelihood 686.934 (with crime seriousness included)
  Model Chi-Square 187.284   df = 1   Sig 0.00000

CLASSIFICATION TABLE FOR SENT

		PREDICTED		
		PROBATION	PRISON	
OBSERVED		0	1	
Probation	0	318	38	89.33%
Prison	1	115	166	59.07%
		Overall		75.98%

VARIABLE	B	S.E.	WALD	df	SIG.	exp(B)
CRSER	0.6965	0.0630	122.185	1	0.00001	2.006
Constant	−2.2836	0.1999	130.523	1		

where P' = the predicted probability
      a = the Y intercept
      e = the base of natural logarithms ($\sim$2.71828).

The probability of prison for a person with 4 crime seriousness points is calculated below:

$$P' = \frac{_e a + bX}{1 + _e a + bX} = \frac{_e -2.2836 + .6965(4)}{1 + _e -2.2836 + .6965(4)}$$

Step 1. Substitute the numbers into the formula:

$$P' = \frac{_e .5024}{1 + _e .5024} = \frac{1.653}{2.653} = .623$$

Step 2. Multiply ($0.6965 \times 4 = 2.786$) and add ($-2.2836 + 2.2836 = 0.5024$). Exponentiate $_e$-0.5024 = 1.653 and divide = 0.623.

An offender with 4 crime seriousness points has a probability of 0.623 of imprisonment, and conversely, a 0.377 probability of non–prison (probation). The ratio of these two probabilities ($0.623/0.377 = 1.65$ rounded) is the odds of imprisonment. Calculating the probability of an offender with 5 crime seriousness points going to prison (see Table 13.2, where all probabilities from 1 to 10 points have been calculated for you) we find that he has a 0.768 probability, and a 0.232 probability of not going to prison. The ratio of these two probabilities is ($0.768/0.232 = 3.31$ rounded). The increase in the odds of going to prison of someone with 5 points over someone with 4 points is simply the larger odds divided by the smaller odds ($3.31/1.65 = 2.006$). If you take any of the odds in Table 13.2 and divide it by the odds immediately above it you will (with tolerance for an awful lot of rounding) arrive at 2.006, which is the antilog of beta ($_e 0.6965 = 2.006$). You can now see how, although the increase in the *probability* of Y depends on the specific value of X, the *odds* increase by a constant amount. Thus, an increase of 1 crime seriousness point doubles the odds of being sentenced to prison regardless of how much it increases the probability.

Note from Table 13.2 that the probability changes are greatest from 2 to 3 (0.162) and from 3 to 4 (0.172) crime seriousness points, with very little change noted at the upper values. However, regardless of how much or how little the probabilities change, the odds still increase by a factor equal to the antilog of beta (2.006) per unit increase in X.

TABLE 13.2 Predicted Probabilities, Change in Probability, and Odds of Imprisonment by Crime Seriousness Points

CRIME SERIOUSNESS POINTS	P_{prison} ($_e a + bx / _e a + bx$)	Q ($1 - p$)	P CHANGE ($p_2 - p_1$)	ODDS (p/q)	ODDS RATIO (Odds$_2$/Odds$_1$)
1	0.170	0.830	—	0.20	2.006
2	0.290	0.710	0.120	0.41	2.006
3	0.452	0.548	0.162	0.82	2.006
4	0.623	0.377	0.172	1.65	2.006
5	0.768	0.232	0.144	3.31	2.006
6	0.870	0.130	0.102	6.69	2.006
7	0.930	0.070	0.060	13.28	2.006
8	0.964	0.036	0.034	26.79	2.006
9	0.982	0.018	0.018	54.54	2.006
10	0.991	0.009	0.009	110.11	2.006

The next number in Table 13.1 is the standard error used for placing confidence intervals around b, followed by the **Wald statistic.** The Wald statistic is a test of statistical significance testing the null hypothesis that $b = 0.0$ in the population. Wald has a chi-square distribution and can be interpreted the same way. Some statistical packages report t as the test of significance, which is simply the square root of Wald with one degree of freedom. Finally we see $\exp(B)$, which is the antilog of B, and is the constant amount of change in the dependent variable in odds per unit increase in the dependent variable. We may conclude from these results that crime seriousness has a strong impact on sentence type.

ASSESSING THE MODEL FIT

In OLS regression the R-squared statistic and F value allow us to assess how "good" the model is. As you may suspect, assessing the fit with logistic regression is a little more complicated. The first value we see in Table 13.1 is the initial **−2 log likelihood** (−2 LL) value of 874.218. This value assesses how "likely" the observed results are given the parameter estimates. Because the likelihood is a probability, and thus a decimal number less than one, −2 times the natural logarithm of the likelihood is used. The first −2 LL value is the likelihood with only the constant included in the model. To determine how well the independent variable predicts the dependent variable, −2 LL is computed again with the independent variable added to the model. We see that this value is 686.934. Subtracting −2 LL with the independent variable in the model from the initial −2 LL, we get $874.218 − 686.934 = 187.284$, which is the value given as the **model chi-square.** This value represents the improvement in predicting values of the dependent variable knowing values of the independent variable over making the same predictions not knowing them (think of it in PRE terms). As we see, the improvement is highly significant.

We can also assess the model fit using the classification table. The table tells us that 318 of the 356 (89.33%) who actually received probation were correctly classified, as were 166 of the 281 (59.07%) who were sent to prison, yielding an overall percentage of 75.9% who were correctly classified. We have mispredicted $115 + 38 = 153$ cases, or if you like, we have made 153 errors. Without knowing the independent variable the number of errors we would have made would be N − modal category (think back to our discussion of lambda). Our sample N is 637 and the modal category is 356, so we would make 281 (44.1%) errors. Proportional reduction in error is $e_1 − e_2/e_1 = 281 − 153/281 = 0.455$.

Now that you have a basic understanding of logit regression you are ready for a discussion of multiple logistic regression in the next section.

MULTIPLE LOGISTIC REGRESSION

We now extend our discussion of logistic regression to the multivariate case by adding prior record and race to the model. A preliminary chi square showed that whites (45%) and blacks (43%) had almost identical probabilities of being imprisoned. Computer results indicating the combined effects of crime seriousness, prior record, and race (0 = white, 1 = black) on the probability of imprisonment are given in Table 13.3. Note that the initial −2 LL value is exactly the same as it is in Table 13.1, because it is the −2 LL with only the constant in the model. With the three predictor variables included in the model the −2 LL value is 539.168. The improvement of 335.05 ($874.218 − 539.168 = 335.05$) is

TABLE 13.3 Logistic Regression: The Effects of Crime Seriousness, Prior Record, and Race on Sentence Type

Initial −2 Log Likelihood 874.218 (constant only in the model)
  −2 Log Likelihood 539.168 (all independents in the model)
   Model Chi-Square 335.050   df = 3   Sig. 0.00000

CLASSIFICATION TABLE FOR SENT

		PREDICTED		
		PROBATION	PRISON	
OBSERVED		0	1	
Probation	0	316	40	88.76%
Prison	1	77	204	72.60%
		Overall		81.63%

VARIABLE	b	S.E.	WALD	df	SIG.	R	exp(b)
RACE	−.84792	0.229	13.672	1	0.0002	−.1155	0.4283
PRREC	0.30576	0.031	95.671	1	0.0000	0.3273	1.3577
CRSER	0.75392	0.074	101.458	1	0.0000	0.3373	2.1253
Constant	−3.2053	0.272	138.796	1	0.0000		

the model chi-square value and is analogous to the *F* test in OLS regression multivariate models. The classification table shows that overall 81.63% of the cases were correctly predicted by the model. Thus, the addition of race and prior record to the model containing only crime seriousness improved the percentage correctly predicted by 5.65% (81.63 − 75.98 = 5.65).

Examining the predictor variables we observe a *B* value for race of −0.8479. This means as we move from white (0) to black (1) there is a 0.8479 *decrease* in the log odds of imprisonment. The exp (*B*) value of 0.4283 means that a black defendant, on average, is 2.33 times less likely to be imprisoned than a white defendant when crime seriousness and prior record are controlled. As we have said before, the interpretation of the odds ratio is easier in terms of whole numbers than in terms of decimals. If we changed the log odds value into a positive value (+0.8479) and took the antilog, we would obtain 2.33 (or you could simply divide 1 by 0.4283 = 2.33). Because we changed the sign, we must change the interpretation to read: After controlling for crime seriousness and prior record, on average, white defendants are 2.33 times more likely than black defendants to be imprisoned in this jurisdiction.

Turning to the legally relevant variables, we note that a per unit increase in prior record results in a 0.3058 increase in the log odds, or a 1.3577 increase in the odds ratio, of imprisonment. Similarly, a per unit increase in crime seriousness results in a 0.7539 increase in the log odds, and a 2.1253 increase in the odds ratio. We remind you again that in logistic regression it is the odds ratios that increase by a constant amount, not the probabilities, which have to be calculated for each unique value. The Wald statistics for all three variables are highly significant.

The *R*s in the model are partial correlations assessing the effect of each variable given the presence of the others in the model. *R* is calculated using formula (13.3):

$$R = \frac{\text{Wald} - 2(\text{df})}{-2 \, \text{LL}_{\text{Con}}}$$

(13.3)

where
$$\text{Wald} = \text{the Wald statistic for the variable}$$
$$2(\text{df}) = 2 \text{ times the degrees of freedom for the variable}$$
$$-2\,\text{LL}_{\text{Con}} = \text{the } -2\,\text{LL of the model containing only the constant.}$$

The R for race is thus

$$R = \sqrt{\frac{13.672 - 2}{874.218}} = \sqrt{.01335} = -.1155$$

Since the final step is taking the square root, the result will always be positive. Thus we must apply the sign of the corresponding logit regression coefficient to it.

We can now use the information to determine the probability of an offender being sent to prison given his race, his crime seriousness score, and his prior record. We do so by substituting the parameter estimates and values for each of the variables into the extension of the logistic equation:

$$P' = \frac{{}_e a + b_1 X + b_2 X + b_3 X}{1 + {}_e a + b_1 X + b_2 X + b_3 X}$$

where
$$b_1 X = \text{race coefficient multiplied by the given race value } (0 = \text{white, } 1 = \text{black})$$
$$b_2 X = \text{crime seriousness coefficient multiplied by a given crime seriousness value}$$
$$b_3 X = \text{prior record coefficient multiplied by a given prior record value.}$$

Suppose that we wished to assess the probability of a white offender going to prison if he has 2 crime seriousness points and 4 prior record points. We perform the following calculations:

$$P = \frac{{}_e{-3.2053 + (-.84792)(0) + .75392(2) + .30576(4)}}{1 + [{}_e{-3.2053 + (-.84792)(0) + .75392(2) + .30576(4)}]}$$

$$= \frac{{}_e{-3.2053 + 0 + 1.50784 + 1.22304}}{1 + ({}_e{-3.2053 + 0 + 1.50784 + 1.22304})}$$

$$= \frac{{}_e{-0.47442}}{1 + [{}_e{-0.4742}]} = \frac{.662}{1.662} = .3835$$

Thus a white offender would have a 0.3835 probability of being sent to prison. Let us calculate the probability of a black offender with the same scores being imprisoned:

$$P = \frac{{}_e{-3.2053 + (-.84792)(1) + .75392(2) + .30576(4)}}{1 + [{}_e{-3.2053 + (-.84792)(1) + .75392(2) + .30576(4)}]}$$

$$= \frac{{}_e{-3.2053 + (-.84792) + 1.50784 + 1.22304}}{1 + ({}_e{-3.2053 + (-.84792) + 1.50784 + 1.22304})}$$

$$= \frac{{}_e{-1.32234}}{1 + [{}_e{-1.32234}]} = \frac{.2665}{1.2665} = .2104$$

A black offender with 2 crime seriousness and 4 prior record points thus has a 0.2104 probability of being imprisoned, which is 0.173 less than a white offender. This is only true at the level of 2 crime seriousness and 4 prior record points; other levels will produce other differences in probabilities.

TABLE 13.4   Odds Ratios

RACE	P_{prison} $(_e a + bx/1 + _e a + bx)$	Q $(1 - p)$	P CHANGE $(p_2 - p_1)$	ODDS (p/q)	ODDS RATIO $(Odds_2/Odds_1)$
White offender	0.3835	0.6165	—	0.6221	
Non–white offender	0.2104	0.7896	0.173	0.2665	0.4283

Let us put the results of these two calculations in a table (Table 13.4) to show that a one-unit increase in race results in a decrease in the odds ratio (0.2665/0266/0.6221) of 04283. Again, you could reverse P/Q to get a more intuitively interpretable result (0.6221/0.2665 = 2.33) as long as you also reverse the interpretation. Remember, the odds ratio represents a constant difference in the odds of incarceration for white and black offenders regardless of how large or how small the difference in the probability is. It is also important to remember that it is the antilog (exp$B$) of the regression coefficient (B) that is interpreted as a constant change in the dependent variable (an increase or decrease in the odds ratio) per unit change in X given the presence of other predictors in the equation.

SUMMARY

Logistic regression is an excellent technique for assessing the impact of a number of independent variables measured at different levels on a categorical dependent variable. Logit constrains the probabilities of an either/or outcome from ranging beyond their inherent limitations of 0.0 and 1.0. Logit regression allows the researcher to make predictions about outcomes in terms of probabilities and odds. Probabilities do not change consistently with each unit change in the independent variable, but the odds ratio, which is the antilog of the logistic regression coefficient, does. The impact of the independent variable is tested for significance using the Wald statistic, which is interpreted exactly like the chi-square test. The fit of the model is assessed by the model chi-square, which is obtained by subtracting the -2 LL value obtained with the independent variable in the model from the -2 LL value obtained without the independent variable in the model (the logic is similar to a PRE assessment).

Multiple logistic regression is used when we have a dichotomous or polychotomous dependent variable. The main point to remember is that it is the antilog (exp$B$) of the regression coefficient (B) that is interpreted as a constant change in the dependent variable (an increase or decrease in the odds) per unit change in X given the presence of other predictors in the equation.

PRACTICE APPLICATION: LOGISTIC REGRESSION

After viewing the correlation and regression results on self-esteem and acceptance of homosexuals from the practice application in Chapter 12, the instructor then decided to see if a person's social distance score predicts his or her attitude regarding the legitimizing of homosexual marriages, scored 0 for "no" and 1 for "yes" to the question: Should homosexual marriages be legalized in the United States?

	B	S.E.	WALD	df	SIG.	EXP(*B*)
Social distance	1.0873	0.550	3.908	1	0.0483	2.966
Constant	−6.3508	3.819	2.765	1	0.0963	

Compute the probability and odds for a person scoring 4, 5, and 6 on the social distance scale and show that each one-unit increase in social distance results in an approximate threefold increase in the odds of favoring the legalization of homosexual marriage.

The probability of a person with 4 social distance points favoring legalization is:

$$P' = \frac{_e a + bX}{1 + _e a + bX} = \frac{_e -6.3508 + 1.0873(4)}{1 + _e -6.3508 + 1.0873(4)}$$

$$= \frac{_e -2.0016}{1 + _e -2.0016} = \frac{.1357}{1.1357} = .1195$$

Do the calculations for 5 and 6 social distance points and place them in a table.

SOCIAL DISTANCE POINTS	P_{favor} $(a + _e bx/a + _e bx)$	*Q* $(1 - p)$	P CHANGE $(p_2 - p_1)$	ODDS (p/q)	ODDS RATIO $(Odds_2/Odds_1)$
4	0.119	0.880		0.135	2.966
5	0.286	0.714	0.167	0.400	2.966
6	0.543	0.457	0.257	1.188	2.966

The initial −2 LL was 13.46; with social distance in the model it is 7.65. Is the model a good fit? Yes, 13.46 − 7.65 = 5.81. This value is the model chi-square with 1 df. This value exceeds 3.841; we can therefore conclude that the model is a good fit.

PROBLEM

1. The table below summarizes the logistic regression analysis predicting likelihood of post-traumatic stress disorder from severity of damages due to severe flooding. Severity of damages was coded from 0 to 5 with 0 representing no significant damage or inconvenience, 1 represented damage to property, 2 represented damage to home and property, 3 was damage to home and property as well as loss of employment due to flooding, 4 represented damage to property and significant injury to self or family, and 5 indicated death of a friend of family member.

Initial -2 Log Likelihood 69.315 (constant only)
    -2 Log Likelihood 57.871 (flood severity included)
        Model Chi-Square 11.444   df $= 1$ $p = 0.0007$

CLASSIFICATION TABLE
PREDICTED PTSD

		NO	YES	
Observed	No	15	10	60%
PTSD	Yes	6	19	76%
			Overall	68%

VARIABLE	B	S.E.	WALD	df	SIG.	EXP(B)
SEVERITY	0.7960	0.2739	8.4447	1	0.0037	2.2167
Constant	-2.0297	0.7803	6.7661	1	0.0093	

a) What is the prediction equation?
b) Calculate the log odds ratios by completing the following table:

X	P $_e(a + bX)/1 + _e(a + bX)$	Q $1 - p$	P CHANGE $(p_2 - p_1)$	ODDS p/q	ODDS RATIO (Odds$_2$/Odds$_1$)
0					
1					
2					
3					
4					
5					

c) Where do the most significant changes occur?
d) Test the null hypothesis that $b = 0$.
e) What conclusions can you draw from these findings?

APPENDIX A

STATISTICAL TABLES

TABLE 1   **Areas of the Normal Curve**

STANDARD DEVIATION UNITS	0.	0.01	0.02	0.03	0.04	0.05	0.06	0.07	0.08	0.09	STANDARD DEVIATION UNITS
0.0	.0000	.0040	.0080	.0120	.0160	.0199	.0239	.0279	.0319	.0359	0.0
0.1	.0398	.0438	.0478	.0517	.0557	.0596	.0636	.0675	.0714	.0753	0.1
0.2	.0793	.0832	.0871	.0910	.0948	.0987	.1026	.1064	.1103	.1141	0.2
0.3	.1179	.1217	.1255	.1293	.1331	.1368	.1406	.1443	.1480	.1517	0.3
0.4	.1554	.1591	.1628	.1664	.1700	.1736	.1772	.1808	.1844	.1879	0.4
0.5	.1915	.1950	.1985	.2019	.2054	.2088	.2123	.2157	.2190	.2224	0.5
0.6	.2257	.2291	.2324	.2357	.2389	.2422	.2454	.2486	.2517	.2549	0.6
0.7	.2580	.2611	.2642	.2673	.2704	.2734	.2764	.2794	.2823	.2852	0.7
0.8	.2881	.2910	.2939	.2967	.2995	.3023	.3051	.3078	.3106	.3133	0.8
0.9	.3159	.3186	.3212	.3238	.3264	.3289	.3315	.3340	.3365	.3389	0.9
1.0	.3413	.3438	.3461	.3485	.3508	.3531	.3554	.3577	.3599	.3621	1.0
1.1	.3643	.3665	.3686	.3708	.3729	.3749	.3770	.3790	.3810	.3830	1.1
1.2	.3849	.3869	.3888	.3907	.3925	.3944	.3962	.3980	.3997	.4015	1.2
1.3	.4032	.4049	.4066	.4082	.4099	.4115	.4131	.4147	.4162	.4177	1.3
1.4	.4192	.4207	.4222	.4236	.4251	.4265	.4279	.4292	.4306	.4319	1.4
1.5	.4332	.4345	.4357	.4370	.4382	.4394	.4406	.4418	.4429	.4441	1.5
1.6	.4452	.4463	.4474	.4484	.4495	.4505	.4515	.4525	.4535	.4545	1.6
1.7	.4554	.4564	.4573	.4582	.4591	.4599	.4608	.4616	.4625	.4633	1.7
1.8	.4641	.4649	.4656	.4664	.4671	.4678	.4686	.4693	.4699	.4706	1.8
1.9	.4713	.4719	.4726	.4732	.4738	.4744	.4750	.4756	.4761	.4767	1.9
2.0	.4772	.4778	.4783	.4788	.4793	.4798	.4803	.4808	.4812	.4817	2.0
2.1	.4821	.4826	.4830	.4834	.4838	.4842	.4846	.4850	.4854	.4857	2.1
2.2	.4861	.4864	.4868	.4871	.4875	.4878	.4881	.4884	.4887	.4890	2.2
2.3	.4893	.4896	.4898	.4901	.4904	.4906	.4909	.4911	.4913	.4916	2.3
2.4	.4918	.4920	.4922	.4925	.4927	.4929	.4931	.4932	.4934	.4936	2.4
2.5	.4938	.4940	.4941	.4943	.4945	.4946	.4948	.4949	.4951	.4952	2.5
2.6	.4953	.4955	.4956	.4957	.4959	.4960	.4961	.4962	.4963	.4964	2.6
2.7	.4965	.4966	.4967	.4968	.4969	.4970	.4971	.4972	.4973	.4974	2.7
2.8	.4974	.4975	.4976	.4977	.4977	.4978	.4979	.4979	.4980	.4981	2.8
2.9	.4981	.4982	.4982	.4983	.4984	.4984	.4985	.4985	.4986	.4986	2.9
3.0	.4987	.4987	.4987	.4988	.4988	.4989	.4989	.4989	.4990	.4990	3.0
3.1	.4990	.4991	.4991	.4991	.4992	.4992	.4992	.4992	.4993	.4993	3.1
3.2	.4993	.4993	.4994	.4994	.4994	.4994	.4994	.4995	.4995	.4995	3.2
3.3	.4995	.4995	.4995	.4996	.4996	.4996	.4996	.4996	.4996	.4997	3.3
3.4	.4997	.4997	.4997	.4997	.4997	.4997	.4997	.4997	.4997	.4998	3.4
3.5	.499767										
3.6	.499841										
3.7	.499892										
3.8	.499928										
3.9	.499952										
4.0	.499968										
4.1	.499979										
4.2	.499987										
4.3	.499991										
4.4	.499995										
4.5	.499997										
4.6	.499998										
4.7	.499999										
4.8	.499999										
4.9	.500000										

$$\text{Argument} = \frac{Y - \mu_Y}{\sigma}$$

TABLE 2   Critical Values of Student's *t*-Distribution

ν \ α	0.9	0.5	0.4	0.2	0.1	0.05	0.02	0.01	0.001	α \ ν
1	.158	1.000	1.376	3.078	6.314	12.706	31.821	63.657	636.619	1
2	.142	.816	1.061	1.886	2.920	4.303	6.965	9.925	31.598	2
3	.137	.765	.978	1.638	2.353	3.182	4.541	5.841	12.924	3
4	.134	.741	.941	1.533	2.132	2.776	3.747	4.604	8.610	4
5	.132	.727	.920	1.476	2.015	2.571	3.365	4.032	6.869	5
6	.131	.718	.906	1.440	1.943	2.447	3.143	3.707	5.959	6
7	.130	.711	.896	1.415	1.895	2.365	2.998	3.499	5.408	7
8	.130	.706	.889	1.397	1.860	2.306	2.896	3.355	5.041	8
9	.129	.703	.883	1.383	1.833	2.262	2.821	3.250	4.781	9
10	.129	.700	.879	1.372	1.812	2.228	2.764	3.169	4.587	10
11	.129	.697	.876	1.363	1.796	2.201	2.718	3.106	4.437	11
12	.128	.695	.873	1.356	1.782	2.179	2.681	3.055	4.318	12
13	.128	.694	.870	1.350	1.771	2.160	2.650	3.012	4.221	13
14	.128	.692	.868	1.345	1.761	2.145	2.624	2.977	4.140	14
15	.128	.691	.866	1.341	1.753	2.131	2.602	2.947	4.073	15
16	.128	.690	.865	1.337	1.746	2.120	2.583	2.921	4.015	16
17	.128	.689	.863	1.333	1.740	2.110	2.567	2.898	3.965	17
18	.127	.688	.862	1.330	1.734	2.101	2.552	2.878	3.922	18
19	.127	.688	.861	1.328	1.729	2.093	2.539	2.861	3.883	19
20	.127	.687	.860	1.325	1.725	2.086	2.528	2.845	3.850	20
21	.127	.686	.859	1.323	1.721	2.080	2.518	2.831	3.819	21
22	.127	.686	.858	1.321	1.717	2.074	2.508	2.819	3.792	22
23	.127	.685	.858	1.319	1.714	2.069	2.500	2.807	3.767	23
24	.127	.685	.857	1.318	1.711	2.064	2.492	2.797	3.745	24
25	.127	.684	.856	1.316	1.708	2.060	2.485	2.787	3.725	25
26	.127	.684	.856	1.315	1.706	2.056	2.479	2.779	3.707	26
27	.127	.684	.855	1.314	1.703	2.052	2.473	2.771	3.690	27
28	.127	.683	.855	1.313	1.701	2.048	2.467	2.763	3.674	28
29	.127	.683	.854	1.311	1.699	2.045	2.462	2.756	3.659	29
30	.127	.683	.854	1.310	1.697	2.042	2.457	2.750	3.646	30
40	.126	.681	.851	1.303	1.684	2.021	2.423	2.704	3.551	40
60	.126	.679	.848	1.296	1.671	2.000	2.390	2.660	3.460	60
120	.126	.677	.845	1.289	1.658	1.980	2.358	2.617	3.373	120
∞	.126	.674	.842	1.282	1.645	1.960	2.326	2.576	3.291	∞

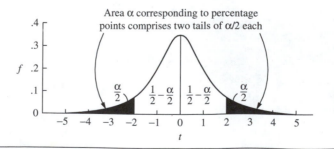

Area α corresponding to percentage points comprises two tails of $\alpha/2$ each

TABLE 3 Random Numbers

74	18	32	90	50	9	43	34	72	34
21	10	70	18	14	52	35	61	6	88
14	71	6	3	36	99	78	85	75	48
61	47	53	60	59	7	91	66	16	42
28	76	13	75	38	18	10	15	2	92
26	9	14	2	32	3	48	13	30	72
9	10	44	67	50	10	9	45	51	34
21	68	13	26	16	45	75	82	45	99
48	42	27	87	54	11	51	30	10	69
85	38	2	63	66	76	82	67	18	59
83	15	73	6	78	25	82	41	24	82
52	53	94	23	62	93	90	83	96	63
17	15	83	83	1	79	45	82	6	23
81	56	37	17	77	98	78	93	56	11
17	8	6	70	21	44	24	8	6	15
4	62	95	67	74	21	73	17	5	20
72	53	96	53	27	33	43	97	66	50
34	61	14	40	41	19	78	77	97	2
62	32	2	98	90	57	70	19	52	35
67	75	28	37	94	8	14	15	57	25

TABLE 4   0.1 Per Cent Points of the *F*-Distribution

If $F = \dfrac{X_1}{\nu_1} \Big/ \dfrac{X_2}{\nu_2}$, where X_1 and X_2 are independent random variables distributed as χ^2 with ν_1 and ν_2 degrees of freedom respectively, then the probabilities that $F \geqslant F(P)$ and that $F \leqslant F'(P)$ are both equal to $P/100$. Linear interpolation in ν_1 or ν_2 will generally be sufficiently accurate except when either $\nu_1 > 12$ or $\nu_2 > 40$, when harmonic interpolation should be used.

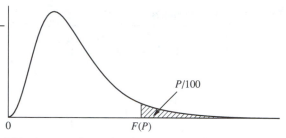

(This shape applies only when $\nu_1 \geqslant 3$. When $\nu_1 < 3$ the mode is at the origin.)

$\nu_1 =$		1	2	3	4	5	6	7	8	10	12	24	∞
$\nu_2 =$	1*	4053	5000	5404	5625	5764	5859	5929	5981	6056	6107	6235	6366
	2	998.5	999.0	999.2	999.2	999.3	999.3	999.4	999.4	999.4	999.4	999.5	999.5
	3	167.0	148.5	141.1	137.1	134.6	132.8	131.6	130.6	129.2	128.3	125.9	123.5
	4	74.14	61.25	56.18	53.44	51.71	50.53	49.66	49.00	48.05	47.41	45.77	44.05
	5	47.18	37.12	33.20	31.09	29.75	28.83	28.16	27.65	26.92	26.42	25.13	23.79
	6	35.51	27.00	23.70	21.92	20.80	20.03	19.46	19.03	18.41	17.99	16.90	15.75
	7	29.25	21.69	18.77	17.20	16.21	15.52	15.02	14.63	14.08	13.71	12.73	11.70
	8	25.41	18.49	15.83	14.39	13.48	12.86	12.40	12.05	11.54	11.19	10.30	9.334
	9	22.86	16.39	13.90	12.56	11.71	11.13	10.70	10.37	9.894	9.570	8.724	7.813
	10	21.04	14.91	12.55	11.28	10.48	9.926	9.517	9.204	8.754	8.445	7.638	6.762
	11	19.69	13.81	11.56	10.35	9.578	9.047	8.655	8.355	7.922	7.626	6.847	5.998
	12	18.64	12.97	10.80	9.633	8.892	8.379	8.001	7.710	7.292	7.005	6.249	5.420
	13	17.82	12.31	10.21	9.073	8.354	7.856	7.489	7.206	6.799	6.519	5.781	4.967
	14	17.14	11.78	9.729	8.622	7.922	7.436	7.077	6.802	6.404	6.130	5.407	4.604
	15	16.59	11.34	9.335	8.253	7.567	7.092	6.741	6.471	6.081	5.812	5.101	4.307
	16	16.12	10.97	9.006	7.944	7.272	6.805	6.460	6.195	5.812	5.547	4.846	4.059
	17	15.72	10.66	8.727	7.683	7.022	6.562	6.223	5.962	5.584	5.324	4.631	3.850
	18	15.38	10.39	8.487	7.459	6.808	6.355	6.021	5.763	5.390	5.132	4.447	3.670
	19	15.08	10.16	8.280	7.265	6.622	6.175	5.845	5.590	5.222	4.967	4.288	3.514
	20	14.82	9.953	8.098	7.096	6.461	6.019	5.692	5.440	5.075	4.823	4.149	3.378
	21	14.59	9.772	7.938	6.947	6.318	5.881	5.557	5.308	4.946	4.696	4.027	3.257
	22	14.38	9.612	7.796	6.814	6.191	5.758	5.438	5.190	4.832	4.583	3.919	3.151
	23	14.20	9.469	7.669	6.696	6.078	5.649	5.331	5.085	4.730	4.483	3.822	3.055
	24	14.03	9.339	7.554	6.589	5.977	5.550	5.235	4.991	4.638	4.393	3.735	2.969
	25	13.88	9.223	7.451	6.493	5.885	5.462	5.148	4.906	4.555	4.312	3.657	2.890
	26	13.74	9.116	7.357	6.406	5.802	5.381	5.070	4.829	4.480	4.238	3.586	2.819
	27	13.61	9.019	7.272	6.326	5.726	5.308	4.998	4.759	4.412	4.171	3.521	2.754
	28	13.50	8.931	7.193	6.253	5.656	5.241	4.933	4.695	4.349	4.109	3.462	2.695
	29	13.39	8.849	7.121	6.186	5.593	5.179	4.873	4.636	4.292	4.053	3.407	2.640
	30	13.29	8.773	7.054	6.125	5.534	5.122	4.817	4.581	4.239	4.001	3.357	2.589
	32	13.12	8.639	6.936	6.014	5.429	5.021	4.719	4.485	4.145	3.908	3.268	2.498
	34	12.97	8.522	6.833	5.919	5.339	4.934	4.633	4.401	4.063	3.828	3.191	2.419
	36	12.83	8.420	6.744	5.836	5.260	4.857	4.559	4.328	3.992	3.758	3.123	2.349
	38	12.71	8.331	6.665	5.763	5.190	4.790	4.494	4.264	3.930	3.697	3.064	2.288
	40	12.61	8.251	6.595	5.698	5.128	4.731	4.436	4.207	3.874	3.642	3.011	2.233
	60	11.97	7.768	6.171	5.307	4.757	4.372	4.086	3.865	3.541	3.315	2.694	1.890
	120	11.38	7.321	5.781	4.947	4.416	4.044	3.767	3.552	3.237	3.016	2.402	1.543
	∞	10.83	6.908	5.422	4.617	4.103	3.743	3.475	3.266	2.959	2.742	2.132	1.000

*Entries in the row $\nu_2 < 13$ must be multiplied by 100.

TABLE 4   1 Per Cent Points of the *F*-Distribution

If $F = \dfrac{X_1}{\nu_1}\Big/\dfrac{X_2}{\nu_2}$, where X_1 and X_2 are independent random variables distributed as χ^2 with ν_1 and ν_2 degrees of freedom respectively, then the probabilities that $F \geq F(P)$ and that $F \leq F'(P)$ are both equal to $P/100$. Linear interpolation in ν_1 or ν_2 will generally be sufficiently accurate except when either $\nu_1 > 12$ or $\nu_2 > 40$, when harmonic interpolation should be used.

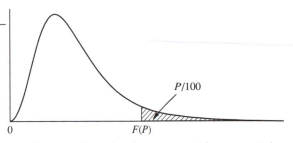

(This shape applies only when $\nu_1 \geq 3$. When $\nu_1 < 3$ the mode is at the origin.)

$\nu_1 =$		1	2	3	4	5	6	7	8	10	12	24	∞
$\nu_2 =$	1	4052	4999	5403	5625	5764	5859	5928	5981	6056	6106	6235	6366
	2	98.50	99.00	99.17	99.25	99.30	99.33	99.36	99.37	99.40	99.42	99.46	99.50
	3	34.12	30.82	29.46	28.71	28.24	27.91	27.67	27.49	27.23	27.05	26.60	26.13
	4	21.20	18.00	16.69	15.98	15.52	15.21	14.98	14.80	14.55	14.37	13.93	13.46
	5	16.26	13.27	12.06	11.39	10.97	10.67	10.46	10.29	10.05	9.888	9.466	9.020
	6	13.75	10.92	9.780	9.148	8.746	8.466	8.260	8.102	7.874	7.718	7.313	6.880
	7	12.25	9.547	8.451	7.847	7.460	7.191	6.993	6.840	6.620	6.469	6.074	5.650
	8	11.26	8.649	7.591	7.006	6.632	6.371	6.178	6.029	5.814	5.667	5.279	4.859
	9	10.56	8.022	6.992	6.422	6.057	5.802	5.613	5.467	5.257	5.111	4.729	4.311
	10	10.04	7.559	6.552	5.994	5.636	5.386	5.200	5.057	4.849	4.706	4.327	3.909
	11	9.646	7.206	6.217	5.668	5.316	5.069	4.886	4.744	4.539	4.397	4.021	3.602
	12	9.330	6.927	5.953	5.412	5.064	4.821	4.640	4.499	4.296	4.155	3.780	3.361
	13	9.074	6.701	5.739	5.205	4.862	4.620	4.441	4.302	4.100	3.960	3.587	3.165
	14	8.862	6.515	5.564	5.035	4.695	4.456	4.278	4.140	3.939	3.800	3.427	3.004
	15	8.683	6.359	5.417	4.893	4.556	4.318	4.142	4.004	3.805	3.666	3.294	2.868
	16	8.531	6.226	5.292	4.773	4.437	4.202	4.026	3.890	3.691	3.553	3.181	2.753
	17	8.400	6.112	5.185	4.669	4.336	4.102	3.927	3.791	3.593	3.455	3.084	2.653
	18	8.285	6.013	5.092	4.579	4.248	4.015	3.841	3.705	3.508	3.371	2.999	2.566
	19	8.185	5.926	5.010	4.500	4.171	3.939	3.765	3.631	3.434	3.297	2.925	2.489
	20	8.096	5.849	4.938	4.431	4.103	3.871	3.699	3.564	3.368	3.231	2.859	2.421
	21	8.017	5.780	4.874	4.369	4.042	3.812	3.640	3.506	3.310	3.173	2.801	2.360
	22	7.945	5.719	4.817	4.313	3.988	3.758	3.587	3.453	3.258	3.121	2.749	2.305
	23	7.881	5.664	4.765	4.264	3.939	3.710	3.539	3.406	3.211	3.074	2.702	2.256
	24	7.823	5.614	4.718	4.218	3.895	3.667	3.496	3.363	3.168	3.032	2.659	2.211
	25	7.770	5.568	4.675	4.177	3.855	3.627	3.457	3.324	3.129	2.993	2.620	2.169
	26	7.721	5.526	4.637	4.140	3.818	3.591	3.421	3.288	3.094	2.958	2.585	2.131
	27	7.677	5.488	4.601	4.106	3.785	3.558	3.388	3.256	3.062	2.926	2.552	2.097
	28	7.636	5.453	4.568	4.074	3.754	3.528	3.358	3.226	3.032	2.896	2.522	2.064
	29	7.598	5.420	4.538	4.045	3.725	3.499	3.330	3.198	3.005	2.868	2.495	2.034
	30	7.562	5.390	4.510	4.018	3.699	3.473	3.304	3.173	2.979	2.843	2.469	2.006
	32	7.499	5.336	4.459	3.969	3.652	3.427	3.258	3.127	2.934	2.798	2.423	1.956
	34	7.444	5.289	4.416	3.927	3.611	3.386	3.218	3.087	2.894	2.758	2.383	1.911
	36	7.396	5.248	4.377	3.890	3.574	3.351	3.183	3.052	2.859	2.723	2.347	1.872
	38	7.353	5.211	4.343	3.858	3.542	3.319	3.152	3.021	2.828	2.692	2.316	1.837
	40	7.314	5.179	4.313	3.828	3.514	3.291	3.124	2.993	2.801	2.665	2.288	1.805
	60	7.077	4.977	4.126	3.649	3.339	3.119	2.953	2.823	2.632	2.496	2.115	1.601
	120	6.851	4.787	3.949	3.480	3.174	2.956	2.792	2.663	2.472	2.336	1.950	1.381
	∞	6.635	4.605	3.782	3.319	3.017	2.802	2.639	2.511	2.321	2.185	1.791	1.000

TABLE 4   5 Per Cent Points of the F-Distribution

If $F = \dfrac{X_1}{\nu_1} \bigg/ \dfrac{X_2}{\nu_2}$, where X_1 and X_2 are independent random variables distributed as χ^2 with ν_1 and ν_2 degrees of freedom respectively, then the probabilities that $F \geqslant F(P)$ and that $F \leqslant F'(P)$ are both equal to $P/100$. Linear interpolation in ν_1 or ν_2 will generally be sufficiently accurate except when either $\nu_1 > 12$ or $\nu_2 > 40$, when harmonic interpolation should be used.

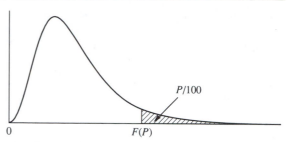

(This shape applies only when $\nu_1 \geqslant 3$. When $\nu_1 < 3$ the mode is at the origin.)

$\nu_1 =$	1	2	3	4	5	6	7	8	10	12	24	∞
$\nu_2 = $ 1	161.4	199.5	215.7	224.6	230.2	234.0	236.8	238.9	241.9	243.9	249.1	254.3
2	18.51	19.00	19.16	19.25	19.30	19.33	19.35	19.37	19.40	19.41	19.45	19.50
3	10.13	9.552	9.277	9.117	9.013	8.941	8.887	8.845	8.786	8.745	8.639	8.526
4	7.709	6.944	6.591	6.388	6.256	6.163	6.094	6.041	5.964	5.912	5.774	5.628
5	6.608	5.786	5.409	5.192	5.050	4.950	4.876	4.818	4.735	4.678	4.527	4.365
6	5.987	5.143	4.757	4.534	4.387	4.284	4.207	4.147	4.060	4.000	3.841	3.669
7	5.591	4.737	4.347	4.120	3.972	3.866	3.787	3.726	3.637	3.575	3.410	3.230
8	5.318	4.459	4.066	3.838	3.687	3.581	3.500	3.438	3.347	3.284	3.115	2.928
9	5.117	4.256	3.863	3.633	3.482	3.374	3.293	3.230	3.137	3.073	2.900	2.707
10	4.965	4.103	3.708	3.478	3.326	3.217	3.135	3.072	2.978	2.913	2.737	2.538
11	4.844	3.982	3.587	3.357	3.204	3.095	3.012	2.948	2.854	2.788	2.609	2.404
12	4.747	3.885	3.490	3.259	3.106	2.996	2.913	2.849	2.753	2.687	2.505	2.296
13	4.667	3.806	3.411	3.179	3.025	2.915	2.832	2.767	2.671	2.604	2.420	2.206
14	4.600	3.739	3.344	3.112	2.958	2.848	2.764	2.699	2.602	2.534	2.349	2.131
15	4.543	3.682	3.287	3.056	2.901	2.790	2.707	2.641	2.544	2.475	2.288	2.066
16	4.494	3.634	3.239	3.007	2.852	2.741	2.657	2.591	2.494	2.425	2.235	2.010
17	4.451	3.592	3.197	2.965	2.810	2.699	2.614	2.548	2.450	2.381	2.190	1.960
18	4.414	3.555	3.160	2.928	2.773	2.661	2.577	2.510	2.412	2.342	2.150	1.917
19	4.381	3.522	3.127	2.895	2.740	2.628	2.544	2.477	2.378	2.308	2.114	1.878
20	4.351	3.493	3.098	2.866	2.711	2.599	2.514	2.447	2.348	2.278	2.082	1.843
21	4.325	3.467	3.072	2.840	2.685	2.573	2.488	2.420	2.321	2.250	2.054	1.812
22	4.301	3.443	3.049	2.817	2.661	2.549	2.464	2.397	2.297	2.226	2.028	1.783
23	4.279	3.422	3.028	2.796	2.640	2.528	2.442	2.375	2.275	2.204	2.005	1.757
24	4.260	3.403	3.009	2.776	2.621	2.508	2.423	2.355	2.255	2.183	1.984	1.733
25	4.242	3.385	2.991	2.759	2.603	2.490	2.405	2.337	2.236	2.165	1.964	1.711
26	4.225	3.369	2.975	2.743	2.587	2.474	2.388	2.321	2.220	2.148	1.946	1.691
27	4.210	3.354	2.960	2.728	2.572	2.459	2.373	2.305	2.204	2.132	1.930	1.672
28	4.196	3.340	2.947	2.714	2.558	2.445	2.359	2.291	2.190	2.118	1.915	1.654
29	4.183	3.328	2.934	2.701	2.545	2.432	2.346	2.278	2.177	2.104	1.901	1.638
30	4.171	3.316	2.922	2.690	2.534	2.421	2.334	2.266	2.165	2.092	1.887	1.622
32	4.149	3.295	2.901	2.668	2.512	2.399	2.313	2.244	2.142	2.070	1.864	1.594
34	4.130	3.276	2.883	2.650	2.494	2.380	2.294	2.225	2.123	2.050	1.843	1.569
36	4.113	3.259	2.866	2.634	2.477	2.364	2.277	2.209	2.106	2.033	1.824	1.547
38	4.098	3.245	2.852	2.619	2.463	2.349	2.262	2.194	2.091	2.017	1.808	1.527
40	4.085	3.232	2.839	2.606	2.449	2.336	2.249	2.180	2.077	2.003	1.793	1.509
60	4.001	3.150	2.758	2.525	2.368	2.254	2.167	2.097	1.993	1.917	1.700	1.389
120	3.920	3.072	2.680	2.447	2.290	2.175	2.087	2.016	1.910	1.834	1.608	1.254
∞	3.841	2.996	2.605	2.372	2.214	2.099	2.010	1.938	1.831	1.752	1.517	1.000

TABLE 5   **Critical Values of the Chi-Square Distribution**

ν \ α	.995	.975	.9	.5	.1	.05	.025	.01	.005	.001	α / ν
1	0.000	0.000	0.016	0.455	2.706	3.841	5.024	6.635	7.879	10.828	1
2	0.010	0.051	0.211	1.386	4.605	5.991	7.378	9.210	10.597	13.816	2
3	0.072	0.216	0.584	2.366	6.251	7.815	9.348	11.345	12.838	16.266	3
4	0.207	0.484	1.064	3.357	7.779	9.488	11.143	13.277	14.860	18.467	4
5	0.412	0.831	1.610	4.351	9.236	11.070	12.832	15.086	16.750	20.515	5
6	0.676	1.237	2.204	5.348	10.645	12.592	14.449	16.812	18.548	22.458	6
7	0.989	1.690	2.833	6.346	12.017	14.067	16.013	18.475	20.278	24.322	7
8	1.344	2.180	3.490	7.344	13.362	15.507	17.535	20.090	21.955	26.124	8
9	1.735	2.700	4.168	8.343	14.684	16.919	19.023	21.666	23.589	27.877	9
10	2.156	3.247	4.865	9.342	15.987	18.307	20.483	23.209	25.188	29.588	10
11	2.603	3.816	5.578	10.341	17.275	19.675	21.920	24.725	26.757	31.264	11
12	3.074	4.404	6.304	11.340	18.549	21.026	23.337	26.217	28.300	32.910	12
13	3.565	5.009	7.042	12.340	19.812	22.362	24.736	27.688	29.819	34.528	13
14	4.075	5.629	7.790	13.339	21.064	23.685	26.119	29.141	31.319	36.123	14
15	4.601	6.262	8.547	14.339	22.307	24.996	27.488	30.578	32.801	37.697	15
16	5.142	6.908	9.312	15.338	23.542	26.296	28.845	32.000	34.267	39.252	16
17.	5.697	7.564	10.085	16.338	24.769	27.587	30.191	33.409	35.718	40.790	17
18	6.265	8.231	10.865	17.338	25.989	28.869	31.526	34.805	37.156	42.312	18
19	6.844	8.907	11.651	18.338	27.204	30.144	32.852	36.191	38.582	43.820	19
20	7.434	9.591	12.443	19.337	28.412	31.410	34.170	37.566	39.997	45.315	20
21	8.034	10.283	13.240	20.337	29.615	32.670	35.479	38.932	41.401	46.797	21
22	8.643	10.982	14.042	21.337	30.813	33.924	36.781	40.289	42.796	48.268	22
23	9.260	11.688	14.848	22.337	32.007	35.172	38.076	41.638	44.181	49.728	23
24	9.886	12.401	15.659	23.337	33.196	36.415	39.364	42.980	45.558	51.179	24
25	10.520	13.120	16.473	24.337	34.382	37.652	40.646	44.314	46.928	52.620	25
26	11.160	13.844	17.292	25.336	35.563	38.885	41.923	45.642	48.290	54.052	26
27	11.808	14.573	18.114	26.336	36.741	40.113	43.194	46.963	49.645	55.476	27
28	12.461	15.308	18.939	27.336	37.916	41.337	44.461	48.278	50.993	56.892	28
29	13.121	16.047	19.768	28.336	39.088	42.557	45.722	49.588	52.336	58.301	29
30	13.787	16.791	20.599	29.336	40.256	43.773	46.979	50.892	53.672	59.703	30
31	14.458	17.539	21.434	30.336	41.422	44.985	48.232	52.191	55.003	61.098	31
32	15.134	18.291	22.271	31.336	42.585	46.194	49.480	53.486	56.329	62.487	32
33	15.815	19.047	23.110	32.336	43.745	47.400	50.725	54.776	57.649	63.870	33
34	16.501	19.806	23.952	33.336	44.903	48.602	51.966	56.061	58.964	65.247	34
35	17.192	20.569	24.797	34.336	46.059	49.802	53.203	57.342	60.275	66.619	35
36	17.887	21.336	25.643	35.336	47.212	50.998	54.437	58.619	61.582	67.985	36
37	18.586	22.106	26.492	36.335	48.363	52.192	55.668	59.892	62.884	69.346	37
38	19.289	22.878	27.343	37.335	49.513	53.384	56.896	61.162	64.182	70.703	38
39	19.996	23.654	28.196	38.335	50.660	54.572	58.120	62.428	65.476	72.055	39
40	20.707	24.433	29.051	39.335	51.805	55.758	59.342	63.691	66.766	73.402	40
41	21.421	25.215	29.907	40.335	52.949	56.942	60.561	64.950	68.053	74.745	41
42	22.138	25.999	30.765	41.335	54.090	58.124	61.777	66.206	69.336	76.084	42
43	22.859	26.785	31.625	42.335	55.230	59.304	62.990	67.459	70.616	77.419	43
44	23.584	27.575	32.487	43.335	56.369	60.481	64.202	68.710	71.893	78.750	44
45	24.311	28.366	33.350	44.335	57.505	61.656	65.410	69.957	73.166	80.077	45
46	25.042	29.160	34.215	45.335	58.641	62.830	66.617	71.201	74.437	81.400	46
47	25.775	29.956	35.081	46.335	59.774	64.001	67.821	72.443	75.704	82.720	47
48	26.511	30.755	35.949	47.335	60.907	65.171	69.023	73.683	76.969	84.037	48
49	27.249	31.555	36.818	48.335	62.038	66.339	70.222	74.919	78.231	85.351	49
50	27.991	32.357	37.689	49.335	63.167	67.505	71.420	76.154	79.490	86.661	50

TABLE 5   Critical Values of the Chi-square Distribution (*Continued*)

ν	α .995	.975	.9	.5	.1	.05	.025	.01	.005	.001	α	ν
51	28.735	33.162	38.560	50.335	64.295	68.669	72.616	77.386	80.747	87.968		51
52	29.481	33.968	39.433	51.335	65.422	69.832	73.810	78.616	82.001	89.272		52
53	30.230	34.776	40.308	52.335	66.548	70.993	75.002	79.843	83.253	90.573		53
54	30.981	35.586	41.183	53.335	67.673	72.153	76.192	81.069	84.502	91.872		54
55	31.735	36.398	42.060	54.335	68.796	73.311	77.380	82.292	85.749	93.168		55
56	32.490	37.212	42.937	55.335	69.918	74.468	78.567	83.513	86.994	94.460		56
57	33.248	38.027	43.816	56.335	71.040	75.624	79.752	84.733	88.237	95.751		57
58	34.008	38.844	44.696	57.335	72.160	76.778	80.936	85.950	89.477	97.039		58
59	34.770	39.662	45.577	58.335	73.279	77.931	82.117	87.166	90.715	98.324		59
60	35.534	40.482	46.459	59.335	74.397	79.082	83.298	88.379	91.952	99.607		60
61	36.300	41.303	47.342	60.335	75.514	80.232	84.476	89.591	93.186	100.888		61
62	37.068	42.126	48.226	61.335	76.630	81.381	85.654	90.802	94.419	102.166		62
63	37.838	42.950	49.111	62.335	77.745	82.529	86.830	92.010	95.649	103.442		63
64	38.610	43.776	49.996	63.335	78.860	83.675	88.004	93.217	96.878	104.716		64
65	39.383	44.603	50.883	64.335	79.973	84.821	89.177	94.422	98.105	105.988		65
66	40.158	45.431	51.770	65.335	81.085	85.965	90.349	95.626	99.331	107.258		66
67	40.935	46.261	52.659	66.335	82.197	87.108	91.519	96.828	100.55	108.526		67
68	41.713	47.092	53.548	67.334	83.308	88.250	92.689	98.028	101.78	109.791		68
69	42.494	47.924	54.438	68.334	84.418	89.391	93.856	99.228	103.00	111.055		69
70	43.275	48.758	55.329	69.334	85.527	90.531	95.023	100.43	104.21	112.317		70
71	44.058	49.592	56.221	70.334	86.635	91.670	96.189	101.62	105.43	113.577		71
72	44.843	50.428	57.113	71.334	87.743	92.808	97.353	102.82	106.65	114.835		72
73	45.629	51.265	58.006	72.334	88.850	93.945	98.516	104.01	107.86	116.092		73
74	46.417	52.103	58.900	73.334	89.956	95.081	99.678	105.20	109.07	117.346		74
75	47.206	52.942	59.795	74.334	91.061	96.217	100.84	106.39	110.29	118.599		75
76	47.997	53.782	60.690	75.334	92.166	97.351	102.00	107.58	111.50	119.850		76
77	48.788	54.623	61.586	76.334	93.270	98.484	103.16	108.77	112.70	121.100		77
78	49.582	55.466	62.483	77.334	94.373	99.617	104.32	109.96	113.91	122.348		78
79	50.376	56.309	63.380	78.334	95.476	100.75	105.47	111.14	115.12	123.594		79
80	51.172	57.153	64.278	79.334	96.578	101.88	106.63	112.33	116.32	124.839		80
81	51.969	57.998	65.176	80.334	97.680	103.01	107.78	113.51	117.52	126.082		81
82	52.767	58.845	66.076	81.334	98.780	104.14	108.94	114.69	118.73	127.324		82
83	53.567	59.692	66.976	82.334	99.880	105.27	110.09	115.88	119.93	128.565		83
84	54.368	60.540	67.876	83.334	100.98	106.39	111.24	117.06	121.13	129.804		84
85	55.170	61.389	68.777	84.334	102.08	107.52	112.39	118.24	122.32	131.041		85
86	55.973	62.239	69.679	85.334	103.18	108.65	113.54	119.41	123.52	132.277		86
87	56.777	63.089	70.581	86.334	104.28	109.77	114.69	120.59	124.72	133.512		87
88	57.582	63.941	71.484	87.334	105.37	110.90	115.84	121.77	125.91	134.745		88
89	58.389	64.793	72.387	88.334	106.47	112.02	116.99	122.94	127.11	135.978		89
90	59.196	65.647	73.291	89.334	107.56	113.15	118.14	124.12	128.30	137.208		90
91	60.005	66.501	74.196	90.334	108.66	114.27	119.28	125.29	129.49	138.438		91
92	60.815	67.356	75.101	91.334	109.76	115.39	120.43	126.46	130.68	139.666		92
93	61.625	68.211	76.006	92.334	110.85	116.51	121.57	127.63	131.87	140.893		93
94	62.437	69.068	76.912	93.334	111.94	117.63	122.72	128.80	133.06	142.119		94
95	63.250	69.925	77.818	94.334	113.04	118.75	123.86	129.97	134.25	143.344		95
96	64.063	70.783	78.725	95.334	114.13	119.87	125.00	131.14	135.43	144.567		96
97	64.878	71.642	79.633	96.334	115.22	120.99	126.14	132.31	136.62	145.789		97
98	65.694	72.501	80.541	97.334	116.32	122.11	127.28	133.48	137.80	147.010		98
99	66.510	73.361	81.449	98.334	117.41	123.23	128.42	134.64	138.99	148.230		99
100	67.328	74.222	82.358	99.334	118.50	124.34	129.56	135.81	140.17	149.449		100

ANSWERS TO ODD NUMBERED PROBLEMS

CHAPTER 1

1. a) Descriptive—describes the phenomenon under investigation Inferential—techniques that enable one to generalize from a sample to a population.
   b) Reliability—the consistency with which repeated measures produce the same results across time and across observers. Validity—how well the measures derived from the operation reflect the concept.
   c) Statistics—describe elements of a sample. Parameters—describe elements of a population.
   d) Sample—a subset of a group. Population—all elements of a group.
3. a) inferential
   b) descriptive
   c) inferential
   d) inferential
   e) descriptive
11. The *population* would be the 122,000 residents in the county. Since it would be extremely difficult to get the actual number of pets in every household, we would draw a *sample*, a subset of the population. The value we are interested in is the average number of pets for the entire population that is a population *parameter*. Since we can't use the entire population and are using the sample, we will measure the number of pets in the sample, specifying a *descriptive statistic*. By means of *inferential statistics*, we would infer the value of the population parameter on the basis of the sample statistic.

CHAPTER 2

1.

SCORE	FREQUENCY	PERCENT	CUMULATIVE PERCENT
20	3	30.0	30.0
19	1	10.0	40.0
18	2	20.0	60.0
17	2	20.0	80.0
16	1	10.0	90.0
15	1	10.0	100.0
Total	10	100.0	

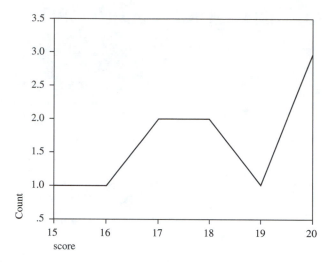

3.

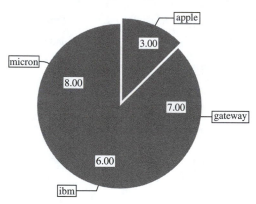

5.   a)

INTERVAL WIDTH = 5			
INTERVAL	FREQUENCY	PERCENT	CUMULATIVE PERCENT
95–99	2	6.7	6.7
90–94	3	10.0	16.7
85–89	5	16.7	33.3
80–84	1	3.3	36.7
75–79	7	23.3	60.0
70–74	5	16.7	76.7
65–69	0	0	76.7
60–64	3	10.0	86.7
55–59	1	3.3	90.0
50–54	0	0	90.0
45–49	2	6.7	96.7
40–44	1	3.3	100.0
Total	30	100.0	

b)

INTERVAL	INTERVAL WIDTH = 10 FREQUENCY	PERCENT	CUMULATIVE PERCENT
90–99	5	16.7	16.7
80–89	6	20.0	36.7
70–79	12	40.0	76.7
60–69	3	10.0	86.7
50–59	1	3.3	90.0
40–49	3	10.0	100.0
Total	30	100.0	

c)

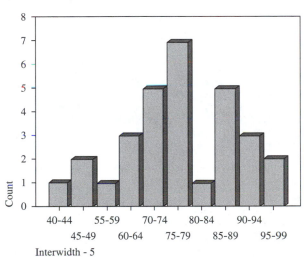

Interwidth - 5

d)

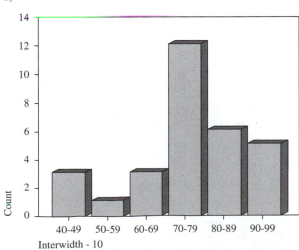

Interwidth - 10

e) More accurate representation of data with smaller interval sizes.

CHAPTER 3

1. mean = 4.125, mode = 3, median = 3
3. a) positive skew
   b) negative skew
   c) normal
5. median = $63.00, negative skew. A few low utility bills, but 50% of the bills were $63.00 or greater.
7. a)

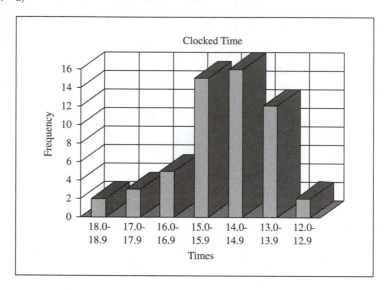

   b) 14.79
   c) 14.87
   d) no
9. a) mean = 26.19, median = 25.59
   b) Q_1 = 19.89, Q_3 = 33.61
   c) Q = 13.72
   d) s = 11.38
11. a) 57.77
    b) 60
    c) s^2 = 171.88; s = 13.11
    d) 48
13. a) mean = 34.65; median = 35.33; standard deviation = 4.50
    b) Q = 5.85
15. IQV_1 = .8694; IQV_2 = 1.00; Class two has the greater variation in majors.
17. Team A
    Team C
    IQV_A = 0.9995; IQV_B = 0.3795; IQV_C = 0.9960

CHAPTER 4

1. a) 0.4772   e) 0.4991
   b) 0.3413   f) 0.4985
   c) 0.4941   g) 0.1915
   d) 0.1293   h) 0.3749

3. a) 0.0495   e) 0.1587
    b) 0.3085   f) 0.0250
    c) 0.0015   g) 0.0250
    d) 0.1251   h) 0.2266
5. a) 0.9010   e) 0.1374
    b) 0.6171   f) 0.1093
    c) 0.9500   g) 0.0109
    d) 0.5468   h) 0.2313
7. a) $z = +0.20$
    b) $z = -1.00$
    c) $z = -2.00$
    d) $z = +2.00$
    e) $z = +2.30$
    f) $z = +0.50$
    g) $z = -3.00$
    h) $z = -1.50$
9. a) 33.4
    b) 91.45
    c) 6.68%
    d) 24.17%
    e) 312.35
11. a) 0.019
    b) 0.0015
    c) 0.039
    d) 0.31
    e) 0.00038
    f) 0.0045
13. a) 190   e) 210
    b) 18,564   f) 230,300
    c) 111,930   g) 3
    d) 1   h) 1,820
15.

# HEADS	$_NC_R$	$(P^R)(Q^{N-R})$	PROBABILITY
0	1	0.015625	0.015625
1	6	0.015625	0.09375
2	15	0.015625	0.234375
3	20	0.015625	0.3125
4	15	0.015625	0.234375
5	6	0.015625	0.09375
6	1	0.015625	0.015625

17. a) $\mu_b = 131.5$, $\sigma_b = 9.93$
    b) $\mu_b = 7.2$, $\sigma_b = 1.70$
    c) $\mu_b = 45$, $\sigma_b = 6.54$
    d) $\mu_b = 240$, $\sigma_b = 7.75$

CHAPTER 5

3. a) Select numbers at random between 1 and 39,360. Find the names that correspond to the numbers selected.
    b) 39,360/200 = 196.8. Select a random number between 1 and 197. Identify the name corresponding to that random start. Select every 197th name starting with the first name selected.
    c) Cluster sampling would require dividing the population into similar, meaningful groups. With a directory, one could cluster names by letters of the alphabet, then randomly select 3 or 4

letters. Then select all names beginning with the selected letter. Advantages—it would be easier to select the sample. Disadvantages—it could bias the sample toward family groups or ethnic groups which share the same name.

5. a) Cluster sampling to select the prison, systematic random sampling to select the inmate.
   b) If all prisons are similar, then this sampling model will work well. If the prison populations are distinctly different, a stratified random sample may be preferred.

7. a)

SAMPLE	MEAN
3,3	3
3,5	4
3,7	5
3,9	6
3,11	7
5,3	4
5,5	5
5,7	6
5,9	7
5,11	8
7,3	5
7,5	6
7,7	7
7,9	8
7,11	9
9,3	6
9,5	7
9,7	8
9,9	9
9,11	10
11,3	7
11,5	8
11,7	9
11,9	10
11,11	11

b)

MEAN	FREQUENCY
3	1
4	2
5	3
6	4
7	5
8	4
9	3
10	2
11	1

c) $\mu = 7; \sigma = 2.83$
d) $\mu_{\bar{x}} = 7; \sigma_{\bar{x}} = 2.00$
e) $\mu = \mu_{\bar{x}}; \sigma_{\bar{x}} = \sigma/\sqrt{N} = 2.8284/\sqrt{2}$

9. a) $45.7 \leq \mu \leq 54.3$
   b) $64.05 \leq \mu \leq 65.95$

c) $11.22 \leq \mu \leq 12.78$
d) $243.77 \leq \mu \leq 256.22$
e) $111.15 \leq \mu \leq 138.85$

11. a) False
     b) True
     c) True
     d) False
     e) True

13. The most variance would occur if the population is split half and half on a variable, with the proportions p and q each equal to 0.50. The maximum variance is equal to $pq = (.5)(.5) = 0.25$.

15. a) $\pi = 0.54$
     b) $.51 \leq \pi \leq 0.57$

17. n = 384

CHAPTER 6

1. a) 0.0359
    b) 0.0718
    c) 0.9641

3. a) True
    b) False
    c) True
    d) True

5. By controlling the alpha level

7. a) Retain H_0 Retain H_0 Reject H_0
    b) Reject H_0 Reject H_0 Retain H_0
    c) Reject H_0 Retain H_0 Retain H_0

9. $t = -1.57$, df = 29, p > 0.05; Retain H_0

11. $z = -2.00$, Reject H_0

13. $t = 1.90$, df = 83, $p < 0.05$; Reject H_0

15. a) $t = -4.22$, df = 9, $p < 0.01$
     b) $4.00 \leq D \leq 10.04$
     c) Any pre and post test utilizing one sample

CHAPTER 7

1. a) Between
    b) $SS_B = 1,664.133$; $SS_W = 51.60$; $SS_J = 1,713.733$
    c) $H_0 : \mu_1 = \mu_2 = \mu_3$; $[F = 193.504, df = 2, 12, p < 0.001]$
    d) $\eta^2 = 0.970$
    e)

	MEAN DIFF	SIG
High school—College Advanced degree	−13 −25.80	0.000 0.000
College High school Advanced degree	13 −12.80	0.000 0.000
Advanced High school degree College	25.80 12.80	0.000 0.000

f)

SOURCE OF VARIANCE	SS	df	MEAN SQUARE	f	SIG	η^2
Between groups	1664.133	2	832.067	193.504	0.000	0.970
Within groups	51.600	12	4.300			
Total	1715.733	14				

3.   a) $SS_B = 70.950$; $SS_W = 90.78$; $SS_J = 161.733$
     b) $H_0 : \mu_1 = \mu_2 = \mu_3$; $[F = 4.689, df = 2, 12, p < 0.05]$
     c) $\eta^2 = 0.439$
     d)

		MEAN DIFF.	SIG.
Cancer	Leo	3.65	0.184
	Sag.	5.42	0.032
Leo	Cancer	−3.65	0.184
	Sag.	1.77	0.584
Sagittarius	Cancer	−5.42	0.032
	Leo	−1.77	0.584

e)

SOURCE OF VARIANCE	SS	df	MEAN SQUARE	f	SIG.	η^2
Between groups	70.950	2	35.475	4.689	0.031	0.439
Within groups	90.783	12	7.565			
Total	161.733	14				

CHAPTER 8

1.   Expected Frequencies

	A	B	C	D
4+	5.54	7.47	8.58	9.41
2-3	7.5	10.13	11.63	12.75
0-1	6.96	9.40	10.79	11.84

$x^2 = 31.83$, df = 6, $p < 0.001$

3. $x^2 = 3,876$, df = 2, NS
5. $x^2 = 60.19$, df = 6, $p < 0.001$; C = 37
7. $x^2 = 6.84$, df = 1, $p < 0.01$; $\phi = 0.07$
9. $H = 12.86$, df = 3, $p < 0.005$

CHAPTER 9

1. $\lambda = 0.186$
3. 2: $\lambda = 0.27$; 7: $\lambda = 0.26$
5. a) $\gamma = 0.387$, p $<$ 0.05
   b) d = 0.259, p $<$ 0.01
   c) tau-b = 0.227, p $<$ 0.05
   d) $V = 0.252$, p $<$ 0.05
7. $r_s = 0.881$, p $<$ 0.001

CHAPTER 10

1. $\gamma = 0.661$; college graduate $\gamma = 0.355$
   non-college graduate $\gamma = 0.915$
   $\gamma_p = 0.571$
3. a) $\gamma = 0.684$
   b) $d = 0.394$
   c) $[x^2 = 31.038, df = 1, p < 0.001]$; $V = 0.394$

CHAPTER 11

1. a)

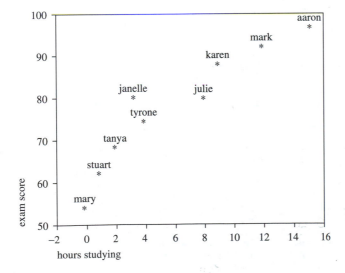

b) b = 2.54
c) a = 62.36
d) $Y' = 62.36 + 2.54(X)$
e) $Y' = 75.06$

f)

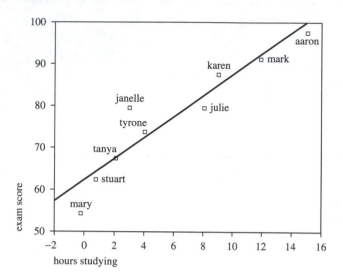

g) $S_{y \cdot x} = 5.11$

h) $Y' = 82.68; 72.66 \le Y' \le 92.70$

i) $[r = 0.935; t = 7.43, \text{df} = 8, p < 0.001]$

3. Total sum of squares $= 1292.1$, residual sum of squares $= 772.2$
Therefore: $\frac{1292.1 - 772.2}{1292.1} = 0.402$ (same as problem 2, part j).

5. a) positive relationship
   b) 0.805
   c) 58.33
   d) 123
   e) 15.75
   f) 70.4 years plus or minus 15 years
   g) $r = 0.508$, $t = 1.865$, not significant

CHAPTER 12

1. a) The zero-order correlations indicate that (1) social class is positively related to number of books read ($r = 0.488$, r squared $= 0.238$), and gender is negatively related to number of books read ($r = -0.20$, r squared $= 0.04$). Higher class persons read more books than lower class persons, and females read more books than males.
   b) $r_{xy \cdot v} = 0.472$
   c) The multiple correlation coefficient of 0.504 indicates that social class and gender jointly account for 25.4% of the variance in number of books read in a year.
   d) The unstandardized partial slope for social class is 0.261, indicating that for every unit increase in social class 0.261 more books are read. The unstandardized partial slope for gender is -1.072, indicating that for every unit increase in gender (moving from female to male) about one less book is read.

3. a) Correlation attendance/coffee sales $= 0.713$
   b) Correlation temperature/coffee sales $= -0.433$
   c) Correlation attendance/temperature $= -0.066$
   d) $r_{xy \cdot v} = 0.713$
   e) Multiple correlation coefficient $= 0.810$, r squared $= 0.657$. Temperature accounts for an additional 16.3% of the variance in coffee sales over that accounted for by attendance alone (49.4%).

5. a) Multiple r = 0.935, a = −34.98, b education = 3.11, b_{IQ} = 0.212
    b) $40,210
    c) $24,590

CHAPTER 13

1. a) $P' = \dfrac{_ea + bX}{1 + _ea + bX}$

    b)

FLOODING SEVERITY	P_{Ptsd} $(_ea + bx/_ea + bx)$	Q $(1 - p)$	P CHANGE $(p_2 - p_1)$	ODDS (p/q)	ODDS RATIO $(Odds_2/Odds_1)$
0	0.116	0.884	—	0.131	2.2167
1	0.225	0.775	0.109	0.290	2.2167
2	0.392	0.608	0.167	0.644	2.2167
3	0.589	0.411	0.197	01.433	2.2167
4	0.760	0.240	0.171	3.166	2.2167
5	0.875	0.125	0.115	7.000	2.2167

    c) From 2 to 3 flooding severity points
    d) Wald = 8.4447, p = .0037. Reject the null that $b = 0$.
    e) As the severity of flood damage increases so does the likelihood of acquiring PTSD.

GLOSSARY

Abscissa. The horizontal axis of a graph; the x axis.

Adjusted R squared. The R^2 value in a regression equation adjusted for sample size and for the number of independent variables in the equation.

Alpha level. The proportion of area on the normal curve that included the critical region. Conventionally set at .05, .01, or .001. Also called a *significance level.*

Alternative or research hypothesis. A formal statement declaring that the sample value of an attribute is significantly different from the population value or that the value of sample 1 is significantly different from the value of sample 2.

Analysis of variance (ANOVA). A statistical technique used for assessing significance of difference between three or more means by using the ratio of within-group variance to between-group variance.

Antecedent variable. A variable that precedes both the dependent and independent variable in time.

Association. The degree to which two variables are associated, related, or connected (see measures of association).

Bar chart. A graphic display for nominal and ordinal data or grouped interval or ratio data. Bars represent qualitatively different categories and are constructed to a height corresponding to the proportion of observations in the category.

Between-group sum of squares. Sum of squares based on the deviation of group means from the grand mean. When divided by *df*, it is the between-group variance estimate.

Census. A complete tabulation of a characteristic of interest for all elements of a population.

Central limit theorem. A principle asserting that a sampling distribution will approach a normal distribution as N gets large even if the population being sampled is not normally distributed.

Chi-square distribution. A positively skewed probability distribution, the shape of which is determined by degrees of freedom.

Chi-square goodness-of-fit test. A nonparametric test used to determine if an observed set of frequencies fits the theoretically expected frequencies.

Chi-square test of independence. A nonparametric test used to determine if the distribution of one variable in a table is independent of the distribution of another by comparing the observed frequencies with the frequencies expected under conditions of chance.

Coefficient of alienation. The proportion of variance in the dependent variable not accounted for by the independent variable.

Coefficient of determination. The Pearson correlation squared. A value that expresses the proportion of the variance in the dependent variable that is accounted for by the independent variable.

Conditional distribution. The distribution of one variable in a table under fixed values of a second variable.

Conditional odds. The odds of being in a given category of the dependent variable given placement in a given category of the independent variable.

Confidence interval. A range of values constructed around a point estimate of a population parameter.

Consistent estimate.   An estimate that is consistent with its parameter. The larger the random sample the greater the consistency of estimate and parameter.

Contingency coefficient.   A chi-square-based measure of association for tables bigger than 2×2. C does not have a PRE interpretation.

Continuous variable.   A variable that can potentially take on any value.

Correlation   Statistical techniques that are used to assess how strong the link between two variables is, or to assess the accuracy of a prediction.

Correlation coefficient (Pearson's r).   A measure that estimates the strength and direction of linear association between two variables. Pearson's r ranges from -1.0 to 1.0.

Covariance.   The covariance of two sets of scores from their respective means.

Cramer's V.   A chi-square-based measure of association for tables bigger than 2×2.

Critical region.   The area under the sampling distribution that contains unlikely outcomes.

Critical value.   The minimum value of a calculated statistic such as z, t, F, and chi-square needed to reject the null hypothesis and conclude that the sample results are not likely to be the result of chance.

Cumulative frequency (CF).   The cumulative frequency is the frequency obtained by adding the number of observations in each category to the score values preceding it.

Data.   Information about some domain of interest expressed numerically (singular, *datum*).

Degrees of freedom.   The number of values in a sample that are free to vary in the calculation of a statistic.

Dependent variable.   A variable assumed to be influenced or predicted by other variables (independent variables). Also sometimes called a criterion variable.

Descriptive statistics.   Statistics that describe a data set in simple and direct ways.

Discrete variable.   A variable that takes on only a finite number of values according to a classification scheme.

Dummy variables.   Variables created for inclusion in a regression equation from a categorical variable. K-1 variables are created and coded I in the presence of an attribute and O in its absence.

Efficient estimate.   An estimate of a population parameter in which the distribution of a statistic is clustered around the parameter being estimated. The most efficient estimator of all possible estimators has the smallest sampling variance.

Eta squared.   The ratio of the between-group sum of squares and the total sum of squares. The proportion of variance in the dependent variable explained by the independent variable.

Explained sum of squares.   Sum of squares explained by all independent variables in a model plus interaction.

Explanation.   An elaboration outcome in which an initial relationship between two variables is explained away by an antecedent variable.

F distribution.   A family of theoretical probability distribution of the ratio of two independent sample variances used for assessing statistical significance. Each F distribution is defined by its between and within degrees of freedom.

First-order partial relationship.   A relationship between two variables examined within fixed categories of one control variable.

Frequency distribution.   A distribution of observations indicating the number of times each score or value occurs.

Gamma.   A measure of association between two variables with ordered categories.

Heterogeneity of variance. A condition that exists when the variances of the two sub-samples are not equal.

Histogram. A graphic display of interval- or ratio-level data consisting of contiguous lines of a height corresponding to the number of observations in the interval.

Homogeneity of variance. The assumption that the variances of two subsamples being tested are equal.

Independent variable. A variable assumed to influence or predict another variable (the *dependent variable*).

Index of qualitative variation. A measure of variation suitable for qualitative data (nominal and interval data).

Inferential statistics. Statistical techniques whereby inferences about populations are based on information derived from samples.

Interaction. An effect that occurs when the relationship between two variables is significantly different across categories of a third variable. Similar to specification in tabular analysis.

Interpretation. An elaboration outcome in which an initial relationship disappears when a third variable is controlled for. The third variable helps us to interpret how the independent variable affects the dependent variable.

Interquartile range. A measure of variation in an ordered distribution identifying the middle 50% of the scores.

Interval estimate. An estimate of a population parameter within a specified range of values.

Interval level. A measurement level of a continuous, quantitative variable that has equal unit intervals but no real zero point.

Intervening variable. A variable that mediates, or intervenes between, the independent and dependent variable that helps us to understand the relationship between the two.

Kruskal-Wallis one-way ANOVA. An ordinal-level, nonparametric test of significance for three or more samples of rank-ordered data.

Kurtosis. The degree of curvedness or peakedness of a distribution.

Lambda. A nominal-level measure of association.

Leptokurtic. A curve that has the characteristic of thinness or peakedness. *X*-positive kurtosis.

Line graph. A graphic display of some quantitative variable indicating change over some time period.

Logistic regression. A regressionlike technique for analyzing the effects of a set of independent variables on a qualitative, dichotomous dependent variable.

Main effects. The sum of squares explained by an independent variable. Sometimes called model effects.

Marginals. The summations of column and row frequencies in a contingency table.

Mean. The arithmetic average of a distribution of data.

Mean square (MS). A sum of squares divided by its degrees of freedom to yield a variance estimate.

Measurement. The assignment of numbers to observations according to a set of rules.

Measurement errors. Errors due to the lack of complete reliability in the instruments used to measure variables.

Measures of central tendency. Measures that locate the various ways in which the data cluster at the center of a distribution (mean, mode, median).

Measures of dispersion. Measures that describe the amount of scatter or spread of a distribution of data about their mean (sum of squares, variance, standard deviation.)

Median. The point in a distribution of data below and above which half of the scores are located.

Mesokurtic. A curve that has the characteristic of normality; neither peaked or flattened. X-zero kurtosis.

Midpoint. The point of a class interval that is halfway between the interval's real lower and real upper limits.

Mode. The most common score in a distribution of data or the largest category of a variable.

Multiple correlation coefficient. A coefficient estimating the combined effect of two or more independent (or predictor) variables on a dependent (or criterion) variable.

Multiple regression. A statistical technique estimating the combined effect of several independent variables on a continuous dependent variable. Also a technique for estimating the unique effect of single variables on the dependent variable given the presence of the other variables in the model.

Multivariate analysis. The simultaneous analysis of more than two variables.

Necessary and sufficient cause. A cause or condition that must be present for the effect to occur and that can cause the event all by itself.

Necessary cause. A cause or condition that must be present for the effect to occur.

Negative association. An association or relationship in which high values on one variable are associated with low values on another.

Nominal level. A measurement level for discrete, qualitative variables whose categories do not bear any relationship of magnitude to one another. We can only name and classify nominal variables.

Normal curve. A symmetrical bell-shaped curve based on a theoretical distribution of an infinite number of probability observations.

Normal curve table. A table supplying the area under the normal curve between a z score and the mean (see Appendix A).

Null hypothesis. A formal statement declaring that the sample value is equal to the population value or that the value of sample 1 is equal to the value of sample 2. A statement of *no difference.*

Odds. The probability of an event occurring (P) divided by the probability of the event not occurring (Q, where $Q = 1 - P$).

Odds ratio. The ratio of two conditional odds.

One-tailed test or directional hypothesis. A hypothesis test used when a researcher has theoretical reasons for believing that any departure from the null hypothesis will occur in one tail of the distribution.

Operational definition. The definition of a concept in terms of the operations used to measure it.

Ordinal level. A measurement level of a discrete, qualitative variable whose categories do bear a relationship of magnitude to one another but do not have the property of equal intervals.

Ordinary least squares. A method used to determine the regression equation by minimizing the sum of squares (minimizing the error) around the regression line.

Ordinate. The vertical axis of a graph.

Parameters. Measurable characteristics of a population that are not known but can be estimated by statistics.

Parametric statistics. A set of statistical techniques used under the assumptions that the populations from which samples are drawn are normally distributed and have a known standard deviation.

Partial correlation. The association between two variables, controlling for the effects of one or more other variables.

Partial gamma.   An index of the strength of association between two variables, controlling for the effects of other variables.

Percentage.   The number of observations in a particular category divided by the number of observations in all categories; the quotient is then multiplied by 100.

Phi.   A chi-square based measure of association for 2×2 tables.

Pie chart.   A graphic display of categorical data in which a circle (the pie) is divided into segments proportional to the percentage of cases in each category.

Platykurtic.   A curve that has the characteristic of flatness.

Point estimate.   An estimate of a population parameter at a specific single value.

Polygon.   A graphic display of a distribution of observations in which adjacent class intervals marked by their midpoints are connected by a straight line.

Population.   The totality of cases, subjects, events, or individuals who share some common characteristic.

Probability.   A mathematical tool for making predictions based on either a priori knowledge (classical probability) or previous observations (empirical probability). Probability is a ratio of events or outcomes to the total possible events or outcomes.

Proportion.   The number of observations in a particular category divided by the number of observations in all categories.

Proportional reduction in error (PRE).   An interpretational feature of some measures of association. It is the reduction in errors that are made in predicting the dependent variable with knowledge of the independent variable over making predictions without knowledge of the independent variable.

Range.   The difference between the highest and lowest scores in a distribution of data.

Rate.   The actual number of occurrences of some phenomenon divided by possible occurrences of that phenomenon over a defined period of time.

Ratio.   The number of observations in one category divided by the number of observations in some other category.

Ratio level.   A measurement level of a continuous, quantitative variable that has equal unit intervals and a true zero point.

Real lower and upper limits.   Those points of a particular number that fall one-half unit below and above their apparent limits.

Regression.   Statistical techniques involving the prediction of one variable from another.

Regression line.   The line describing the best linear fit between two interval or ratio variables.

Regression slope.   A measure of the average amount of change in the dependent variable predicted per unit change in the independent variable. Also known as *beta*.

Replication.   An elaboration outcome in which controlling for another variable does not change the nature of the original bivariate relationship.

Robustness.   The ability of a statistical test to withstand violations of its assumptions without seriously damaging the interpretation.

Sample.   A subset of a population.

Sampling distribution of means.   A theoretical probability distribution of all possible unique sample means of size N drawn from a population.

Sampling error.   The difference between the value of a sample statistic and the value of its corresponding population parameter.

Sampling frame.   A technical term for the actual list of the sampling units from which the sample will be drawn. The sampling frame should ideally correspond to the target population but rarely does.

Scattergram.   A graphic representation showing the joint distribution of two interval or ratio variables.

Scheffé test.   A multiple comparison test of pairs of group means that complements an ANOVA test to determine which means differ from which other means.

Second-order partial relationship.   A relationship between two variables, controlling for two additional variables.

Simple random sampling.   A method of selecting cases from a population in which every case has an equal probability of being selected.

Size.   The magnitude of the size of a class interval obtained by subtracting its real lower limit of its interval from its real upper limit.

Skewness.   A measure of asymmetry in a distribution curve in which the preponderance of scores are on one side of the mean or the other.

Somer's *d*.   An ordinal-level measure of association that is computed either symmetrically or asymmetrically according to which variable is considered dependent.

Spearman's rank order correlation (rho).   A measure of linear association for rank ordered data.

Specification.   An elaboration outcome in which the researcher specifies under what condition(s) of the control variable the original relationship remains true.

Specification errors.   Errors made in specifying the nature of a statistical model: (1) omitting theoretically relevant variables, (2) including irrelevant variables, and (3) specifying a linear model when the data are curvilinear.

Spuriousness.   An elaboration outcome in which the bivariate relationship is shown to be false, being explained away or interpreted by the control variable. The correlation itself is not false; what is false is the interpretation of the relationship as a causal one.

Standard deviation.   The square root of the variance. A measure of dispersion reflecting how well the mean of a variable represents the central tendency of a population or sample.

Standard error.   The standard deviation of a sampling distribution.

Standard error of *r*.   A measure used to place confidence intervals around *r;* the standard deviation of a theoretical distribution of *r*s.

Standard error of the difference.   The standard deviation of the sampling distribution of differences between means.

Standard error of the estimate.   A measure of the variability around the regression line.

Standard normal curve.   A theoretical normal curve that has been standardized to a mean of zero and a standard deviation of 1.

Standardized partial regression slope.   An index of the amount of change in the dependent variable per unit change in an independent variable, controlling for one or more other independent variables where all variables have been standardized.

Statistics.   Measurable characteristics of a sample used to infer population characteristics. Also, a set of mathematical techniques for collecting, analyzing, interpreting, and presenting quantitative data.

Stratified random sampling.   A method of sampling by which cases are selected from sublists of the population either proportionately or disproportionately.

Sufficient cause.   A cause or condition that is sufficient in itself to produce an effect.

Sum of squares.   Sum of the squared deviations of scores around the mean. A measure of dispersion.

Suppressor variable.   A control variable that hides or "masks" the true nature of an association between two variables.

***t* distribution.**   A distribution used for significance testing with interval and ratio data when sample sizes are small. It is a family of distributions defined by the number of degrees of freedom. Popularly used for large samples also because it becomes identical to the *z* distribution when $df > 120$.

t **test.**   Used to test a hypothesis about a mean and about the difference between two means. The *t* test formulas differ according to whether variances of the two sub-samples are equal or not.

Tau-b.   An ordinal-level measure of association.

Total sum of squares.   The sum of the squared deviations from the grand mean. Divided by *df*(N − 1); it is a total variance estimate.

Two-tailed test or nondirectional hypothesis.   A hypothesis test used when the research hypothesis is concerned with outcomes in both tails of the distribution.

Two-way ANOVA.   Analysis of variance between two or more categories of the dependent variable within categories of two independent variables.

Type I (or alpha) error.   An error that occurs when the null hypothesis is rejected when it should have been retained; that is, a significant difference is claimed when there is none.

Type II (or beta) error.   An error that occurs when we retain the null hypothesis when it should have been rejected; there is a significant difference but we fail to claim it.

Unbiased estimate.   An estimate of the population parameter whose expected value equals the parameter being estimated.

Univariate analysis.   The analysis of a single variable in the form of frequencies, rates, percentages, etc.

Unstandardized partial regression slope.   An index of the amount of change in a dependent variable per unit change in an independent variable, controlling for one or more other unstandardized variables.

Variable.   Any trait, characteristic, or attribute that can change (vary) from observation to observation.

Variance.   Sum of squares divided by N − 1. A measure of dispersion.

Within-group sum of squares.   The sum of the squared deviations of each score in a subgroup from the subgroup mean.

***Y*-intercept.**   The point at which the regression line (slope) crosses the *y*-axis. The *y*-axis (a) is the value of *y* where *x* equals zero.

Yule's *Q*.   A PRE measure of association for 2 × 2 tables.

z **score.**   A raw score that has been standardized by subtracting the distribution mean from it and dividing by the standard deviation.

INDEX